Language, Cognition, and Biblical Exegesis

Scientific Studies of Religion: Inquiry and Explanation

Series editors: Luther H. Martin, Donald Wiebe, William W. McCorkle Jr.,
D. Jason Slone and Radek Kundt

Scientific Studies of Religion: Inquiry and Explanation publishes cutting-edge research in the new and growing field of scientific studies in religion. Its aim is to publish empirical, experimental, historical, and ethnographic research on religious thought, behaviour, and institutional structures. The series works with a broad notion of scientific that includes innovative work on understanding religion(s), both past and present. With an emphasis on the cognitive science of religion, the series includes complementary approaches to the study of religion, such as psychology and computer modelling of religious data. Titles seek to provide explanatory accounts for the religious behaviors under review, both past and present.

The Attraction of Religion, edited by D. Jason Slone and James A. Van Slyke
The Cognitive Science of Religion, edited by D. Jason Slone and William W. McCorkle Jr.
Contemporary Evolutionary Theories of Culture and the Study of Religion, Radek Kundt
Death Anxiety and Religious Belief, Jonathan Jong and Jamin Halberstadt
The Mind of Mithraists, Luther H. Martin
New Patterns for Comparative Religion, William E. Paden
Philosophical Foundations of the Cognitive Science of Religion, Robert N. McCauley with E. Thomas Lawson
Religion Explained?, edited by Luther H. Martin and Donald Wiebe
Religion in Science Fiction, Steven Hrotic
Religious Evolution and the Axial Age, Stephen K. Sanderson
The Roman Mithras Cult, Olympia Panagiotidou with Roger Beck

Language, Cognition, and Biblical Exegesis

Interpreting Minds

Edited by
Ronit Nikolsky, István Czachesz,
Frederick S. Tappenden, and Tamás Biró

BLOOMSBURY ACADEMIC
LONDON • NEW YORK • OXFORD • NEW DELHI • SYDNEY

BLOOMSBURY ACADEMIC
Bloomsbury Publishing Plc
50 Bedford Square, London, WC1B 3DP, UK

BLOOMSBURY, BLOOMSBURY ACADEMIC and the Diana logo
are trademarks of Bloomsbury Publishing Plc

First published in Great Britain 2019
Paperback edition published 2021

Copyright © Ronit Nikolsky, István Czachesz, Frederick S. Tappenden,
Tamás Biró and Contributors, 2019

Ronit Nikolsky, István Czachesz, Frederick S. Tappenden and Tamás Biró
have asserted their right under the Copyright, Designs and Patents Act,
1988, to be identified as Editors of this work.

All rights reserved. No part of this publication may be reproduced or transmitted
in any form or by any means, electronic or mechanical, including photocopying,
recording, or any information storage or retrieval system, without prior
permission in writing from the publishers.

Bloomsbury Publishing Plc does not have any control over, or responsibility for,
any third-party websites referred to or in this book. All internet addresses given
in this book were correct at the time of going to press. The author and publisher
regret any inconvenience caused if addresses have changed or sites have ceased
to exist, but can accept no responsibility for any such changes.

A catalogue record for this book is available from the British Library.

A catalog record for this book is available from the Library of Congress.

ISBN: HB: 978-1-3500-7810-9
       PB: 978-1-3502-2540-4
       ePDF: 978-1-3500-7811-6
       eBook: 978-1-3500-7812-3

Series: Scientific Studies of Religion: Inquiry and Explanation

Typeset by Integra Software Services Pvt. Ltd.

To find out more about our authors and books visit www.bloomsbury.com
and sign up for our newsletters.

Contents

Notes on Contributors	vi
Preface	ix
Introduction: Cognition, Evolution, and Biblical Exegesis *István Czachesz*	1
1 Cognitive Science and Biblical Interpretation *István Czachesz and Gerd Theissen*	13
2 Emotional Fear in Pentateuchal Legal Collections *Thomas Kazen*	40
3 Liquid Life: Blood, Life, and Conceptual Metaphors in the Hebrew Bible and the Ancient Near East *Anne Katrine de Hemmer Gudme*	63
4 "To Love"(אהב) in the Bible: A Cognitive-Evolutionary Approach *Ronit Nikolsky*	70
5 "The Glory of the Lord Has Risen upon You": Some Observations on the "Glory"-Language of Isa. 56–66 Based on a Cognitive Semantic Approach *Marilyn E. Burton*	88
6 The Influence of Categorization on Translation Meaning *Shelley Ashdown*	99
7 Imaging Resurrection: Toward an Image Schematic Understanding of Resurrection Beliefs in Second Temple Judaism *Frederick S. Tappenden*	112
8 Liturgical Linguistics: Toward the Syntax of Communicating with the Superhuman Agent in Judaism *Tamás Biró*	129
9 Forgiveness of the Sinless: A Classic Contradiction in 1 Jn in the Light of Contemporary Forgiveness Research *Rikard Roitto*	149
10 Christian Beginnings and Cultural Evolution *István Czachesz*	162
Notes	179
Bibliography	203
Index of Ancient Sources	229
Index of Modern Authors	241
General Index	245

Contributors

Shelley G. Ashdown is Department Head of the College of International Studies at the Graduate Institute of Applied Linguistics (Dallas, Texas). Her research is a broad mix of biblical Hebrew, cognitive anthropology, African traditional religion and worldview. She is the author of numerous articles, including "Cognitive Semantic Approach to Redeemer (Gō'ēl) in Deutero-Isaiah" (*Acta Theologica*, 2015), "Tribal Religions from the Heart: Hebrew *Lēb* and Torobo *Oltau*" (*Journal for the Study of Religions and Ideologies*, 2013), and "An East African Hermeneutic of Luke 11.5–10" (*e-Theologos*, 2012).

Tamás Biró is Senior Research Fellow at the Department for Assyriology and Hebrew at ELTE Eötvös Loránd University, as well as Associate Professor and Vice-Rector of the Jewish Theological Seminary—University of Jewish Studies, Budapest, Hungary. He obtained his PhD at the University of Groningen, working on computational phonology. His research focuses on formal and cognitive approaches to language and religion, as well as on various aspects of Jewish culture and tradition.

Marilyn Burton gained her PhD from the University of Edinburgh in 2014. She is the author of *The Semantics of Glory: A Cognitive, Corpus-Based Approach to Hebrew Word Meaning* (2017); her main research focus is the interaction between contemporary linguistics, particularly cognitive methodology, and biblical exegesis.

István Czachesz is Professor of Biblical Studies at the University of Tromsø in Norway. His research concentrates on the New Testament, Early Christian literature, and the Cognitive Science of Religion. He is co-chair of the "Mind, Society and Religion: Cognitive Science Approaches to the Biblical World" program unit of the Society of Biblical Literature, co-editor of the *Studies on Early Christian Apocrypha* series, and book review editor of the *Journal for the Cognitive Science of Religion*. His most recent books include *Cognitive Science and the New Testament: A New Approach to Early Christian Research* (2017), *The Grotesque Body in Early Christian Discourse* (2012), and *Mind, Morality and Magic: Cognitive Science Approaches in Biblical Studies* (2013, co-edited with Risto Uro).

Anne Katrine de Hemmer Gudme is Associate Professor of Hebrew Bible Studies at the University of Copenhagen in Denmark. Her research focuses on religious ritual in the Hebrew Bible, such as vows, sacrifices, and gifts to the gods, and on ritualized social practices, such as hospitality, gift-giving, and meals. She is co-chair of the "Anthropology and the Bible" research unit with the European Association of Biblical Studies and committee-member of the Society of Biblical Literature's program unit, "Mind,

Society and Religion: Cognitive Science Approaches to the Biblical World". She is co-editor of the book *Magic and Divination in the Biblical World* (2013, co-edited with Helen Jacobus and Phillippe Guillaume) and author of *Before the God in This Place for Good Remembrance* (2013) as well as a number of articles on religion and ritual in the Hebrew Bible and cognate literature.

Thomas Kazen is Professor of Biblical Studies at Stockholm School of Theology (University College, Stockholm). His research interests include the historical Jesus, purity, ritual and cult, law and halakah, emotions, sex, and hierarchy, and he takes an interest in biopsychological and socio-cognitive approaches. He has published *Jesus and Purity Halakhah: Was Jesus Indifferent to Impurity?* (2002/2010), *Issues of Impurity in Early Judaism* (2010), *Emotions in Biblical Law: A Cognitive Science Approach* (2011), *Scripture, Interpretation, or Authority? Motives and Arguments in Jesus' Halakic Conflicts* (2013), and *Smuts, Skam, Status: Perspektiv på samkönad sexualitet i Bibeln och antiken* (2018, in Swedish).

Ronit Nikolsky is Senior Lecturer at the chair of Culture and Cognition in the Faculty of Humanities in the University of Groningen, The Netherlands. She completed her doctoral thesis on Early Christian Monasticism at the Hebrew University in the Department of Comparative Religion. She is co-editor of *Rabbinic Traditions between Palestine and Babylonia* (Brill, 2014), and a co-chair of the research unit "Evolution and the Biblical World" in the European Association of Biblical Studies. Her area of expertise is Rabbinic Literature, especially the *Midrash Tanchuma*. She works on Rabbinic Literature with a cognitive approach, focusing on emotions and is an author of numerous articles using this approach.

Rikard Roitto is University Lecturer of Biblical Studies, New Testament, at Stockholm School of Theology. In his research, he integrates historical-critical methods with social, psychological, and cognitive sciences to understand early Christian texts and communities. His research interests include social identity, norms, rituals of penance and forgiveness, conflict resolution, and baptism in early Christianity. He has written several articles on ritual practices of reproof, repentance, penance, intercession for forgiveness, and reintegration of deviant group members in early Christianity.

Frederick S. Tappenden is Principal and Dean, and Professor of Theology, at St. Stephen's College at the University of Alberta. His research focuses on the integration of the cognitive and social sciences in the study of ancient Christian and Jewish writings, particularly the texts and traditions associated with the apostle Paul. Dr. Tappenden's first monograph, *Resurrection in Paul: Cognition, Metaphor, and Transformation* (SBL 2016), was awarded a 2017 Manfred Lautenschläger Award from the University of Heidelberg. He co-chairs (with Catherine Playoust) the "Religious Experience in Antiquity" program unit of the Society of Biblical Literature, and serves on the steering committee of the "Mind, Society, and Religion in the Biblical World" program unit. He is also an editor for the Database of Religious History (based at the Cultural Evolution of Religion Research Consortium, University of British Columbia).

Gerd Theissen is Professor Emeritus of New Testament at the University of Heidelberg, Germany. He did his habilitation on early Christian miracle stories (1972), and has worked as an assistant at the University of Göttingen, the University of Bonn, University of Copenhagen, and as a secondary school teacher. His main research interests lie in the sociology, psychology, and theory of early Christianity, the Historical Jesus, and Theory of the early Christian religion and theology of the New Testament. He is the author of *The Religion of the Earliest Churches* (1999) and *The Shadow of the Galilean* (1987), co-author of *The Historical Jesus: A Comprehensive Guide* (1988) and co-editor of *The Social Setting of Jesus and the Gospels* (2001). In 2002, he was awarded the Burkitt Medal by the British Academy. It was granted to him "in recognition of special service to Biblical Studies," as being one of the pioneers in using sociological methods for the study of the New Testament.

Preface

This volume examines the many ways that the cognitive sciences reorient and challenge our understanding of language and textual interpretation within the context of biblical studies, and the study of early Christianity and early Judaism.

In the past two decades, insights from the study of the human mind (drawing on diverse disciplines, such as cognitive science, cognitive neuroscience, neuroimaging, and experimental psychology) have increasingly received attention in several areas of cultural studies and the humanities. In the study of religion, the cognitive science of religion (CSR) emerged as a movement embracing such methods. This wave of innovation also reached biblical studies.

The emerging discipline of the CSR has particularly focused on religious beliefs and rituals from a cognitive perspective, but there has been less research undertaken on religious texts and narratives in this paradigm. This volume addresses this lacuna.

The papers presented in this collection represent the outputs of two international scholarly meetings: the one is the "First International Workshop on the Cognitive Study of Religious Texts," held at the University of Groningen in March 2010, organized by the Centre for Religion and Cognition and supported by the Groningen Research School for the Study of Culture (ICOG), The Groningen University Fund (GUF) and the department of Languages and Cultures of the Middle East (TCMO); and papers from the "Mind, Society, and Tradition" program unit of the 2011 international meeting of the Society of Biblical Literature (ISBL) which took place in London, England. Both scholarly meetings shared the related emphases on cognitive approaches to language and textual interpretation within the CSR as well as the application of this approach to biblical studies.

The aim of the Groningen workshop was to initiate a research program that studies the mental processes behind the creation and use of religious texts, both oral and written. The organizers sought to develop a new method, provisionally termed "cognitive philology," which combines awareness of cognitive processes with proficiency in working with religious texts. This new approach, therefore, employs insights from recent results in various branches of cognitive science, including the cognitive science of religion, as well as in the fields of religious studies, cultural studies, cultural evolution, philology, and literary theory.

Extending from the Groningen workshop, the 2011 ISBL meeting probed topics of language, cognition, and linguistic theory as they relate to broader issues of textual interpretation and the CSR. The papers from this meeting employ a range of approaches—cognitive linguistics, generative linguistics, ritual theory, and cognitive grammar.

The resulting volume covers a good selection of passages and topics to demonstrate the fruitfulness of cognitive methods in biblical interpretation. We are putting in front of the reader a volume which brings together various methods in the cognitive sciences, linguistics, philology, biblical studies, and religious studies, in a theoretical and textual balance. By this we hope that the volume will contribute to the cognitive approach to the study of the Bible and ancient religion generally, and will prove useful both for the scholarly endeavor and in the classroom.

We would like to thank the editors of the series Scientific Studies of Religion: Inquiry and Explanation for their interest in the project, Lucy Carroll for her support throughout the editorial process, and Ana-Elena Moldovan for her efficient help with compiling the indices.

Ronit Nikolsky
István Czachesz
Frederick S. Tappenden
Tamás Biró

March 2019

Introduction: Cognition, Evolution, and Biblical Exegesis

István Czachesz

While cognitive science approaches to religion have, to date, focused largely on religious beliefs and rituals, they paid little attention to religious texts and the interpretive practices of religious communities. Within biblical studies, since the mid-2000s, there have been several monographs and edited volumes that have sought to examine biblical texts from a broadly cognitive perspective, including a number of applications of cognitive linguistics. Our aim in this volume is to draw on the existing strengths of both research traditions and explore many of the ways that insights from the cognitive sciences can impact and expand the interpretation of sacred texts. To this end, biblical exegesis stands as our primary nexus point.

What does the word "cognitive" mean at all? The noun "cognition" and the corresponding adjective "cognitive" have been used in divergent meanings in both academic language and everyday parlance. For some, cognition implies rational thought processes. Antonio Damasio in his *Descartes' Error* argued against this restrictive view of cognition (Damasio 1994). Although cognitive scientists rarely if ever equated cognition with rationality, Damasio's book was significant because it highlighted the importance of the role of emotions in human thinking, decision-making, and moral reasoning. In a less restrictive sense, cognition means everything that the mind is doing, including emotions, conscious, and subconscious thoughts. The mind, conversely, can be defined as the entity that thinks and feels. A criticism often leveled at this broader understanding of cognition is that it still reinforces mind–body dualism. Indeed, how does the mind relate to brain and body? Without discussing these complex problems in detail, we can note that in the philosophy of mind cognition has been usually understood as a function of the brain.[1] Simple examples of cognitive tasks, however, demonstrate that the sensory organs and the entire body can be performing cognition in concert with the brain. For example, when we walk in a straight line toward an object we keep the image of the object in the center of our visual field, rather than calculating its position in the surrounding space and comparing it with our own position, which would be the method corresponding to a more traditional view of cognition. When tackling some problems, considering the body and even other actors and objects as parts of a single cognitive system is a meaningful approach, which can be summarized under the umbrella term of "situated cognition"; whereas concentrating on information processing in the brain is more rewarding when thinking about other problems.

Cognitive science approaches to the study of biblical literature started to take shape in the mid-2000s, drawing inspiration from a variety of academic disciplines, such as cognitive science, the cognitive science of religion, computational linguistics, cognitive linguistics, evolutionary theory, and the neuroscientific study of religious experiences. The Hebrew Bible and the New Testament, which constitute the traditional *foci* of biblical studies, are collections of texts that were created and transmitted in the context of religious practices during extended periods of human history. While the religious and historical contexts of biblical literature already featured prominently in these previous studies, the exegetical aspects of the texts have received less attention, with the main exception of applications of conceptual blending theory (see below). In contrast, in this volume, the main emphasis falls on the texts themselves, while not losing sight of the religious, cultural, and historical contexts. Without the need for a comprehensive presentation of previous research in this introduction, it will suffice to mention a couple of representative studies.[2] In 2003, two programmatic articles by Luther H. Martin and István Czachesz outlined plans for the cognitive study of biblical literature, focusing on memory systems, the ritual context of the transmission of ideas, and general theories and models of the cognitive science of religion (Czachesz 2003; Martin 2003). In 2007, drawing on the tradition of cognitive linguistics, Vernon Robbins outlined a program of connecting conceptual metaphor theory with socio-rhetorical analysis (Robbins 2007). In the following years, three collected volumes of essays explored a variety of topics in biblical literature, ranging from Jewish ritual systems and the Qumran sect to early Christian god concepts, rituals, magic, and morality (Luomanen et al. 2007; Czachesz and Biró 2011; Czachesz and Uro 2013). Several monographs and an edited volume provided applications of cognitive linguistics (especially the models of conceptual metaphor and blending theory) to the study of biblical literature (Howe 2006; Lundhaug 2010; Stovell 2012; Thaden 2012; Houston 2014; Howe and Green 2014; Lancaster Patterson 2015; Robinson 2016; Tappenden 2016; Burton 2017). The neuroscientific study of religious experiences inspired research on Paul's and Jesus's subjective experience, respectively (Shantz 2009; Czachesz 2013b). Thomas Kazen examined the role of emotions in the legal passages of the Pentateuch (Kazen 2011). In recent years, monographic treatments of Jewish religion and early Christianity have been published (Levy 2012; Uro 2016; Czachesz 2017a; Theißen et al. 2017). Meanwhile, cognitive approaches to other ancient Mediterranean religions have been developed, including classical Greek religion (Eidinow 2011; Larson 2016), ancient mystery cults (Bowden 2010), the cult of Mithras (Beck 2006; Martin 2015; Panagiotidou and Beck 2017), and the Isis-Sarapis cult (Pachis 2010).

Carrying forward the work accomplished by those pioneering studies, and other contributions that we cannot discuss at this point, this volume has a distinct textual and exegetical focus. What does an "exegetical focus" mean? Biblical scholars study texts for different reasons, these texts include both canonical and extra-canonical Jewish, Christian, and other ancient sources. One reason is that the central role of texts and their interpretation characterizes both Judaism and Christianity (especially within

Protestantism), the religious traditions that provided the foundations of modern biblical scholarship (together with a number of other important influences). Various critical methods of working with texts have emerged from these contexts; conversely, scholarship in biblical studies absorbed a variety of literary, linguistic, historical, social scientific, and other theories and methods. A second reason is that texts are considered to be sources of knowledge about important theological and ethical matters in several religious traditions, a phenomenon that will be addressed in some contributions to this volume. Religious texts can be used in many ways in both religious and academic settings, and it has to be noted that the critical tools of biblical studies (such as inquiring about the authorship, historical setting, motivation of writing, compositional techniques, and original audience of a text) are not necessarily employed in other contexts.[3] A third reason is that scholars, both religious and nonreligious, read biblical and other texts simply because these are their most important sources of information about ancient Judaism and Christianity. Despite the undeniable importance of archaeology, we rely on texts as our main sources for most aspects of ancient civilizations and religions. In a broad sense, any of the above-mentioned uses of texts can be called "exegetical," without restricting the meaning of the term to textual interpretation in Christian theological (and homiletical) settings. The exegetical focus of the present volume implies the critical, academic reading of the text in the above-mentioned contexts, while employing a distinctly cognitive perspective.

The multidisciplinary research project of cognitive science provides the theoretical and methodological background of the exegetical studies presented in this volume. What is cognitive science? Cognitive science is the study of the mind, with the participation of several academic disciplines, including psychology, anthropology, linguistics, philosophy, evolutionary theory, and other fields. The so-called cognitive turn in psychology started in the 1950s and one of the early impulses for the study of mental structures came from emerging computer science (Bechtel 2001; Eysenck and Keane 2005). On the basis of the kinds of internal operations that computers could perform on the data stored in memory, scholars started to theorize the structure and functioning of the human mind. Starting with the 1970s, neuroimaging technology has increasingly allowed researchers to observe brain activity. Studies performed with the help of such tools allowed scientists to make inferences about the contribution of various parts of the brain to cognitive functions. These studies contributed to knowledge about the brain gained by other means, such as from the study of patients with brain lesions (damage to the brain caused by illness or trauma).

The astounding versatility and efficiency of the human mind begs explanation. One of the influential theories addressing this problem is the theory of the modularity of mind. Jerry Fodor suggested that the mind includes a number of modules that deal with different kinds of information (Fodor 1983). The modules are loosely related to the senses and are domain-specific, that is, they deal with some aspect of the world and process only information that is relevant to that aspect. According to Fodor, there are also central systems in the mind, which operate in a domain-general way, enabling us to integrate information related to different aspects of the environment. A different theory of modularity has been put forward by evolutionary psychologists. Evolutionary psychology studies the human mind from the perspective of evolution, theorizing about the kinds of minds that helped the survival of our ancestors (see below). John Tooby and Leda Cosmides, together with a number of other scholars, reasoned that evolution created specialized cognitive systems in the human mind that coped with specific cognitive tasks in the environment of our ancestors (Cosmides and Tooby 1987, 277–306; Cosmides and Tooby 1994; Tooby and Cosmides 2000). This version of modularity is called *massive modularity*, or the "Swiss army knife" model of the brain. While specialized cognitive modules are useful for dealing with specific tasks efficiently, they make it very difficult to learn new things, innovate, or develop a unified sense of self and consciousness that humans have. Steven Mithen addressed this problem by suggesting a three-phase evolution of the mind: a general-intelligence mind capable of learning and decision-making; a mind of specialized intelligences (a simpler version of the Swiss army knife model) that deal with different domains efficiently; and a mind with flow of knowledge and ideas (cognitive fluidity) between domains (Mithen 1996).

The earliest cognitive theories of religion were proposed by Stewart Guthrie and E. Thomas Lawson during the 1970s, followed by an expansion of the field in the 1990s. Guthrie suggested that religion is rooted in an anthropomorphic interpretation of the environment (Guthrie 1993, 2013). Lawson, together with Robert N. McCauley, asked how the human mind represents rituals and what this implies for the structure of rituals (Lawson and McCauley 1990; McCauley and Lawson 2002). They answered these questions by putting forward the ritual form theory. According to Lawson and McCauley, the human mind represents actions in terms of an agent acting on a patient with the help of an instrument. For example, John (agent) hits (action) the ball (patient) with a bat (instrument). However, unlike ordinary actions, in a ritual, one of these components is connected to a superhuman agent (god). For example, in baptism, a priest (connected to God by ordination) baptizes an infant (or adult in certain denominations) with the help of water. This is an example of a special-agent ritual because the agent of the action (the priest) is connected more directly to a superhuman agent than either the infant or the water. According to Lawson and McCauley, special-agent rituals have long-lasting effects and are performed only once with the same participants (i.e., a priest performs many baptisms, but only one baptism on any single infant). Special-agent rituals generate intense emotions and people invest considerable time and resources into performing them.

Meanwhile, Pascal Boyer drew on his anthropological fieldwork to formulate the theory of minimal counterintuitiveness as a core feature of religious concepts (Boyer 1994a, 2001). To explain why religious ideas appear in a limited set of varieties that are found in virtually every human society, Boyer argued that religious concepts are rooted in cross-culturally consistent ontological categories. The human mind makes use of such categories because they allow us to deal with our environment quickly and efficiently: once we know that the thing we see is an animal, we will expect it to move on its own, seek food, and have offspring like itself, but we will not expect it to talk, for example. Concepts that violate the expectations we attach to these ontological categories are more memorable than ordinary concepts or concepts that are only strange but not in a way that violates our related ontological expectations. Specifically, minimally counterintuitive agents with access to socially strategic information in people's minds are at the center of religion (including gods, spirits, demons, and ancestors). Boyer's theory has been one of the most influential among cognitive theories of religion.

Another anthropologist, Harvey Whitehouse, offered a cognitive account of religious transmission in the theory of the divergent modes of religiosity or Modes Theory (Whitehouse 1995, 2000, 2004). According to Whitehouse, some religious groups operate in the imagistic mode, performing intense rituals that generate personal but theologically inconsistent memories. With reference to memory studies, Whitehouse classified these memories as episodic memories (memories of concrete events of one's life). In contrast, groups in the doctrinal mode perform rituals that repeatedly transmit information with low emotional intensity. Such information is stored as semantic memories, that is, in the form of lexical information and facts without direct connection to a concrete time and place in the individual's life. Whitehouse also suggested that groups operating in the imagistic mode are small scale and exclusive, whereas groups operating in the doctrinal mode are large scale, uniform, and efficiently missionizing.

The cognitive science of religion had grown into a diverse field by the 2000s, with seminal new contributions on rituals (Boyer and Liénard 2006; Liénard and Boyer 2006), god beliefs (Barrett 2004; Pyysiäinen 2009; Bering 2011), cooperation (Bulbulia and Sosis 2011; Norenzayan 2013), religious experience (Taves 2009; McNamara 2009), embodied cognition (Geertz 2010; see below), and magic (Pyysiäinen 2004; Czachesz 2007d; Sørensen 2007). Experimental work has been underway, putting various cognitive theories to the empirical test (Sørensen and Nielbo 2014). More recently, experimental techniques have been brought to fieldwork on religion (Xygalatas 2013), with the reasoning that reproducing religious phenomena in the lab always causes distortions and actual religious behavior can be best observed in its original setting. Computer models and computational tools in general have also gained currency in the cognitive study of religion. Some models tested basic assumptions and provided heuristic insights about theoretical and historical problems (Bainbridge 2006). Other ambitious projects have been launched with the goal of modeling large-scale historical developments based on actual data from past and present societies (Chalupa 2015; Slingerland and Sullivan 2017).[4]

At the same time that the cognitive science of religion was emerging, new discussions about the nature of the human mind started within cognitive science itself about the proper boundaries of the mind. Merlin Donald created the concept of *exogram* to denote external traces that carry information outside the brain (Donald 1991, 314–19). Exograms have been attested in all human cultures, and recently even in Neanderthals (Hoffmann et al. 2018), including body markings, grave decorations, notations, paintings, and writing systems. According to Andy Clark and David Chalmers, humans and their thinking tools form coupled systems so that it is justified to speak of an *extended mind* in many cases (Clark and Chalmers 1998). Edwin Hutchins described how navigating a ship involves complex interactions between crew members as well as between people and instruments (Hutchins 1995). Hutchins called this type of cognitive performance *distributed cognition*, suggesting that cognition does not take place in any individual part of the system (consisting of the ship and its crew in the above example) but emerges from the interaction of the parts.

Proponents of the theory of *embodied cognition*, in turn, suggested that we think with our bodies as much as with our brains. Theories of embodied cognition come in different flavors. Scholars defending embodied views of cognition often contrast their approach with computational models of the mind. A computational model implies that the mind carries out operations on symbols that are stored in memory, much like a modern computer functions. The main activity of an embodied mind, in contrast, consists of connecting perception with action. As we move through the environment, we perceive new opportunities for action; actions, in turn, lead to new perceptions, creating what is called the *perception-action loop* (Varela et al. 1991). Another issue in embodied cognition is the nature of *mental representations*. In a broad sense, a mental representation means something in the mind that stands for something external. In classical cognitive science, mental representations are symbolic and abstract: for example, the same representation "table" is used to mean different kinds of table (Mandik 2001). These representations are also *amodal* in that the same representation can be employed when "table" is written or spoken about. In embodied cognition, either the entire existence of mental representations or at least their symbolic and amodal character is denied (Wilson and Foglia 2011). For example, Larry Barsalou developed a model of perceptual symbols, emphasizing that concepts retain the modes of perception (Barsalou 1999, 577, 2008). Thus, the mental representation of an apple is not an abstract symbol with attributes of color, shape, smell, and taste attached to it. Rather, the representation of an apple consists of a combination of the color, shape, smell, and taste that we perceive. Barsalou also suggested ways to build representations of more complex concepts and beliefs based on the combination of perceptual symbols (Barsalou 2003, 1177–87; Barsalou and Katja Wiemer-Hastings 2005; Barsalou et al. 2003, 84).

Although embodied theories offer intriguing new perspectives on various aspects of cognition, they do not make other approaches obsolete. As the philosopher of mind Andy Clark noted, human cognition could be revolutionary precisely because it uses a new kind of cognitive machinery that understands the world in conceptual terms (Clark 2001, 135–38). Extended, distributed, and embodied theories often imply different possibilities of choosing the boundaries of a cognitive system. Thus, it could be meaningful to study the mind in the context of the brain for some purpose and consider perceptual information (including messages to and from parts of the body) as external inputs and outputs. At the other end of the spectrum, a group of humans and objects (and artifacts) can be studied as a single system if this yields new insights.

George Lakoff and Mark Johnson pioneered an influential embodied approach to language, also known as *cognitive linguistics* (Lakoff and Johnson 1999, 2003). They argued that abstract thought is inherently dependent on bodily experience. We learn basic concepts from direct physical experience (by virtue of having an embodied mind) and build all other concepts by metaphorical extensions of basic concepts. Gilles Fauconnier and Mark Turner described a more formal model of embodied cognition, suggesting that metaphors arise as the mind creates mappings across mental spaces (Fauconnier and Turner 2002). Their conceptual metaphor theory provides an account of how all learning and thinking consist of blends of metaphors based on simple bodily experiences. These blends are then themselves blended together into an increasingly rich structure that makes up our mental functioning in modern society. Finally, Zoltán Kövecses presented one of the most advanced versions of conceptual metaphor theory, extending the theory to consider cross-cultural differences in cognitive processes and linguistic expressions (Kövecses 2005).

Cognitive approaches to religion in general, and to biblical studies in particular, have also been informed by new developments in evolutionary theory. As we have seen, evolutionary psychology inspired pioneering scholarship in the study of religion (including the work of Guthrie and Boyer). When Charles Darwin formulated his theory of evolution, his main interest was the history of biological species. Darwin did not know how traits are inherited and was unaware of the existence of genes. In the neo-Darwinian theory of evolution, in contrast, genes are the protagonists (Mayr 2001). Population genetics is the cornerstone of modern evolutionary science: population genetics studies how genes are inherited and how their relative frequencies change in populations (Stearns and Hoekstra 2005, 70–98; Okasha 2015). The properties of an organism matter because the genes that shaped them will be passed on to the organism's offspring and result in the development of traits that are similar to the parents' traits. If a heritable trait increases the chances of the organism to leave offspring (which means, in evolutionary terminology, an increase in reproductive fitness) it is likely that the genes responsible for the respective traits will occur in ever greater numbers in subsequent generations. This is the essence of the theory of natural selection. From this brief presentation of the concept of evolution it should have become clear that various ideas that are often associated with evolution in popular imagination, such as struggle, optimization, or the interpretation of fitness as strength, are not central interests of modern evolutionary theory.

Considering a cultural phenomenon such as religion in the context of human evolution raises the important question of how evolution and culture are connected. Theories of evolution and culture come in at least three different forms. First, evolutionary psychology emphasizes that the human mind has been shaped by more or less consistent environmental conditions for tens of thousands of years, before humans started to live in large societies, invented agriculture, and spread out to previously unknown habitats. These conditions (associated with humans inhabiting African savannahs in the Pleistocene period, which is dated between 2.5 million and 12,000 years ago), provided evolutionary pressures that shaped the human mind in fairly consistent ways before *Homo sapiens* started to migrate out of Africa (traditionally dated to around 100,000 years ago, but potentially pushed back in time by recent archaeological findings). Some of the implications of evolutionary psychology include the hypothesis of specialized systems of the brain that deal efficiently with salient problems, such as predation, mating, contagion, and various aspects of social life. The massive modularity hypothesis, outlined above, is an example of evolutionary psychological theories that also influenced the cognitive study of religion. Evolved mental systems, on this account, constrain human culture, which can only take forms that are enabled by the existing mental structures. As a result, even though cultural forms are very diverse, this diversity is neither random nor limitless. For example, languages, despite their great diversity, use a limited variety of sounds and phonetic combinations that our minds, speech organs, and senses are able to produce and process.

The second kind of possible connection between evolution and culture is so-called gene-culture coevolution. Cultural practices, if they persist over a sufficiently long period of time, will constitute evolutionary pressures, just as other environmental factors do. Well-documented genetic adaptations to culture include the shape of the human larynx (assumedly an adaptation to language) and the ability to digest milk in adults, at least in many populations (Jablonka and Lamb 2005, 286–317). According to the theory of *cognitive ratcheting*, proposed by Michael Tomasello, small changes in the mind lead to small changes in the artifacts, which, in turn, initiate further changes in the mind (Tomasello 1999; cf. Tomasello et al. 1993). It is possible, however, that the notable cases of genetic adaptation to cultural pressures (such as language and dairy farming) constitute exceptions rather than the rule: it has been argued that the spread of beneficial mutations usually takes longer than the relatively short history of dairy farming (Gibbons 2010). In special circumstances, however, genetic mutations can spread faster than normal. Artificial selection leads to rapid evolution in animals and plants. It has been argued that cultural practices (such as endogamy) or historical circumstances (such as isolation) can also result in faster than usual genetic changes in human populations.[5]

Finally, it has been suggested that evolutionary theory (and especially the model of natural selection) can be applied to the study of cultural transmission. It is obvious that humans pass on not only genes but also cultural items (such as ideas, stories, and artifacts) to their offspring. Biologist Richard Dawkins proposed already in the 1970s that culture is passed on in the form of so-called *memes* (Dawkins 2006). According to Dawkins, memes are small units of culture that can be inherited independently of each other. Examples of memes are "tunes, ideas, catchphrases, clothes fashions, ways of making pots or of building arches" (Dawkins 2006, 192). The concept of the meme has been criticized on different accounts (Kundt 2011). First, it is not straightforward to isolate memes from other memes: for example, is Buddhism a meme? Second, what is the building material of a meme? Third, the mechanisms of copying memes are not well known: specifically, it seems that they are copied with less fidelity than genes.

Addressing the latter problem, Dan Sperber argued that pieces of culture are not copied with high enough fidelity so that something like natural selection could act on them; the stability of cultural traits is due to psychological biases rather than to the faithfulness of copying (Sperber 1996, 2000). According to Sperber, among the range of possible forms a cultural bit can take there are optimal forms dictated by psychological factors, which he calls *attractor positions*. For example, people will copy the idea of a ghost with low fidelity (missing or distorting details and adding new ones), but the idea will remain relatively stable across generations because the idea of a ghost is constrained by innate psychological structures (cf. Boyer 2001, 155–60).

It has been suggested that although Sperberian attraction influences culture, it does not exclude other processes of transmission, such as natural selection. In other words, psychological biases form constraints that limit the range of possible forms of culture that can survive in the long run; however, there is still possibility for variation and selection within those limits (McElreath and Henrich 2007; Czachesz 2017a, 42–48).

For example, although concepts of ghosts are fundamentally shaped by evolved, cross-culturally consistent psychological mechanisms, particular representations of ghosts, tales about ghosts, or practices related to ghosts and spirits can take different forms so that cultural evolutionary processes can shape them. When Sperber and Boyer talk about "epidemiology" they actually mean convergence in cultural transmission. Our brains can produce a variety of ideas but eventually the ideas held by different individuals will be fairly similar—not because of social conformity but as a result of they having similar minds. It is remarkable, however, that convergence is a known phenomenon of biological evolution, too. For example, eyes and wings evolved several times, not because species inherited or learned these traits from each other but because they live in similar environments. This does not mean, however, that the respective species cannot have very different structures in other respects. The fact that environmental constraints lead to similar solutions does not mean that selection cannot take place and produce a variety of solutions within the given constraints. Instead of focusing too much on the problem of attraction *versus* selection, we can speak about the "viral" qualities of cultural bits in the sense that they are transmitted irrespective of their benefits for the organism.

Overview of the present volume

The contributions to this volume put the theoretical insights discussed in this introduction into action, exploring how, complemented by other theories and methods, they can be made fruitful for biblical exegesis. Following a programmatic chapter on cognitive interpretation, seven chapters focus on the Hebrew Bible, the ancient Near East, and aspects of Jewish tradition, in an approximately chronological order. The remaining contributions to the volume turn to the writings of the New Testament, including the broader contexts of Late Antiquity and Early Christianity.

In a programmatic study, István Czachesz and Gerd Theißen revisit five areas of biblical exegesis from the perspective of cognitive science. First, the relation between text and cognition is considered, asking about the ways texts influence our cognition and the roles that texts play in religious practice. Second, cognitive factors in the diachronic analysis of texts are explored, such as the causes of stability and change in texts while they are being transmitted. Third, the authors discuss cognitive factors in the synchronic analysis of texts, concentrating on differences between types and forms of texts in terms of cognitive categories. Fourth, the chapter focuses on cognitive factors at play in reception history, attempting to explain the long-term success of some texts. Fifth, cognitive factors in the meta-textual reception of texts are examined, especially in the ascription of sacredness and "canonical" status.

Thomas Kazen in his contribution writes about the role of fear in legal texts in the Pentateuch. Fear of foreigners is conspicuous in laws regulating relationships with other peoples. The fear of divine punishment is frequently employed as a deterrent in motivating obedience. Fear of demonic or supernatural powers is implicit in certain rituals, not least in some that effect purification or atonement. The chapter pulls together discussions of different types of fear belonging to diverse contexts, asking about the role of fear in various law codes and exploring how fear counteracts or interacts with other emotions, such as empathy and disgust. The analysis is connected to recent discussions about the interrelationship, dating, and social contexts of different law codes.

Anne Katrine de Hemmer Gudme draws on conceptual metaphor theory to examine the conceptualization of blood and life in the Hebrew Bible and the ancient Near East. In the Hebrew Bible, blood is described as life itself. It has often been argued that the Hebrew Bible's understanding of blood as life sets it apart from its neighboring cultures, but in fact similar views of the relationship between blood and life can be found in both Greek and Mesopotamian texts. De Hemmer Gudme proposes that employing the conceptual metaphor of the human body as a container sheds new light on this ancient Near Eastern notion.

Ronit Nikolsky's study is based on Merlin Donald's theory of the three stages of human cognitive evolution—the mimetic, mythic, and theoretic cognitive strategies. It shows how the three concepts help understand and describe the use of the verb "to love" (אהב) in the Bible, by categorizing the biblical texts as products of the three cognitions: poetry as mimetic (Song of Songs), narratives as mythic, and legal text as theoretic. This categorization helps to understand how the meaning of the verb develops from the meaning that is closer to the biology than to the imaginary symbolic one, by the process of blending. Ignoring this development and these categories skews the understanding of the verb, and leads to false inferences from the legal to the narrative, while ignoring the data from the Song of Songs altogether.

Marilyn Burton in her contribution turns to Trito-Isaiah, considering the methodological consequences of applying a cognitive semantic perspective to ancient languages. Burton emphasizes the capacity of such a method to produce a detailed and objective picture of a semantic domain, thus providing the semantic background against which anomalies in the usage of the domain's language may be best observed. The second part of the chapter exemplifies the exegetical potential of such an analysis through the examination of the "glory"-language of Trito-Isaiah. Based on the results of her prior full-length study of the semantic domain of כבוד, Burton examines how the distinctive use of "glory"-language in Isaiah 56–66 serves to highlight the eschatological character of these chapters, and reveals new insights into the thought-world of its author.

Shelley Ashdown explores the influence of categorization on translation meaning. Contemporary cognitive science, Ashdown suggests, offers new insights on how categories function in cognition, and, in particular, how categories governing knowledge and the sociocultural context impact translation understanding. The primary aim of this chapter is to present a functional approach to categorization and the consequences for translation. Ashdown explores how both cultural exegesis and biblical exegesis are necessary to identify salient categories of meaning specific to a target audience of a translation. In a case study, she discusses what color categories of the Akan people of West Africa mean for the translation of Zech. 1:8 and 6:1–8.

Frederick Tappenden's chapter employs conceptual metaphor theory to study resurrection in Second Temple Judaism. While notions of resurrection pervade many sectors of second temple Jewish thought, the exact nature of what constitutes and enables resurrection to be identified is disputed among modern scholars. Seeking to offer an integrative explanation for such variety, this chapter employs theories of embodied cognition in examining a selection of pre-70 CE Jewish texts. The analysis reveals a web of interconnected metaphors premised upon both verticality and path image schemata. While these metaphors evince varying degrees of specificity and complexity, it is demonstrated that a recurrent series of conceptual structures undergird the various resurrection descriptions represented in the period literature.

Tamás Biró outlines a syntax of communicating with the superhuman agents in Judaism. This contribution draws on the postulate of the cognitive science of religion that religious phenomena utilize mental structures that evolved for everyday purposes. Biró argues that, from a cognitive perspective, prayer is a form of communication, adding a culturally postulated superhuman agent as an addressee. After reviewing how late structuralist and early generative syntax analyzed the constituents of a sentence, the chapter employs a corresponding methodology to understand the composition of Jewish liturgy. Finally, adopting the approach of Lawson and McCauley (see above), Biró proposes a three-stage path turning the mental representation originally corresponding to a helping action into the central element of prayers.

Rikard Roitto in his chapter writes about forgiveness in the First Epistle of John. Forgiveness in 1 John is an enigma, which has produced countless scholarly suggestions. This chapter evaluates a selected number of scholarly perspectives on the problem in the light of contemporary research on forgiveness, including insights from related fields in the behavioral sciences. Roitto suggests a novel interpretation, emphasizing that 1 John aims to form the identity and the practical communal life of the community, and the discourse on forgiveness is an aspect of this ambition. He concludes that although the statements may be considered self-contradictory from an emic theological perspective, they promote a balance of social practices that helped the Johannine community to prevail.

In the last chapter of the volume, István Czachesz examines the spread of Early Christianity from the perspective of cultural evolution. Czachesz identifies the structure of social networks as the most important factor, which, in turn, influenced the generation of memorable ideas and the use of religious elements as symbolic identity markers. In Early Christianity, weak social ties enabled large-scale cooperation across geographically and sociologically distant groups and individuals. As a consequence, the social composition and structure of the movement favored the emergence of innovative theological ideas. Some of these ideas functioned as powerful symbolic identity markers, which further enhanced solidarity in cooperative associations of varying sizes between groups. Finally, both memorable ideas and social identity markers found their way in great numbers into literary compositions.

Taken together, the contributions demonstrate how cognitive approaches shed new light on a range of exegetical topics and problems in both Hebrew Bible and New Testament studies, including new perspectives on the historical and cultural contexts of biblical literature, Jewish liturgical tradition, Bible translation, and the expansion of Early Christianity.

Acknowledgments

I would like to thank Frederick S. Tappenden for his helpful suggestions, especially on recent publications using conceptual metaphor and blending theory in biblical interpretation.

1

Cognitive Science and Biblical Interpretation

István Czachesz and Gerd Theissen

There are two kinds of exegetes: first, the ones who study words for the sake of matters; second, the ones who study matters for the sake of words (Jacob Grimm). They who study words for the sake of matters ask what the text can reveal about the history or the religious universe that it represents. They who study matters for the sake of words wish to use our knowledge of the history and religion of the Bible to interpret concrete texts. Biblical scholars have so far made use of cognitive approaches to religion in order to enhance our understanding of early Jewish and early Christian religion (Czachesz 2017b). These studies proceeded from concrete texts to ask questions about cognitive structures behind concepts, rituals, and moral behavior that the text mentions or that can be identified in the background of the text. It is also possible, however, to reverse the process, and ask whether our enriched knowledge about religion allows for a better understanding of the texts by shedding new light on words and their history, supporting philological and text-critical analysis, and providing new understandings of the process of transmission, as well as of the forms and functions of texts. In what follows we want to put forward a few considerations with regard to these new opportunities. We will concentrate on five domains, in particular:

1. Cognitive factors at the *production* of the text. What is the relation between texts and cognition? Are texts changing expressions of cognitive patterns, which remain more or less unchanged, while being realized in always new forms? How do texts influence our cognition? What kind of role do texts play in religious practice?
2. Cognitive factors at the *diachronic transmission* of texts. How can we account for stability and change in texts as they are transmitted? Texts are subject to evolutionary processes in different ways. Do they change so that they become accommodated to the structure of the human mind? Which tendencies of change can we observe in this process?
3. Cognitive factors at the *synchronic analysis* of texts. Can we understand differences between types, forms, and genres of texts in terms of cognitive categories? For example, metaphorical texts have a different relation to their referents than non-metaphorical texts.

4. Cognitive factors at the *reception* of the text. How can we explain the long-term success of some texts? Are some texts more successful than others because they are better adapted to human cognitive structures?
5. Cognitive factors at the *meta-textual classification* of texts, especially at the ascription of sacredness and "canonical" status. How do some texts become canonical? Which pre-scientific theories have the greatest chance to validate the sacred status of texts successfully and promote their acceptance?

It is important to note that whereas we suggest that our five topics offer a heuristic map for understanding the complex problem of the genesis and use of religious literature, we do not ignore overlaps or interactions among these areas. For example, the impact of the text on the reader or listener is an important factor during the formative period of the text as well as in its later history of reception, and in both phases changes can be introduced to the text as a result. However, the text can be changed to different degrees in different periods and contexts, allowing for adaptations to cognitive constraints at some point (when optimization processes are dominant), while making such changes is more difficult in other contexts and periods (when reception receives the main focus). This further directs attention to the connection between reception history and canonization, inasmuch as the canonical (or sacred) status of a text strictly limits the conditions under which it can be used or changed.

What do we mean by the "adaptation" of religious texts? Humans inherit genes, behaviors, ideas, and artifacts from their forebearers, all of which are influenced by evolution (Jablonka and Lamb 2005; Stone et al. 2006; Jablonka and Lamb 2007, 353–65). Since genetic evolution is slow, we can assume that most of the mental structures that evolved in our hominid and human ancestors, because they have helped their survival, are with us and largely determine the setup of the human mind. Naturally, we also share these structures with people living in biblical times. There are also interactions between different types of evolution. Our anatomy and physiology arguably determine the ways we can evolve in any dimension. For example, we cannot acquire just any language: we must use sounds that we can articulate and hear. It is also important that the tools and ideas we have influence our genetic evolution (Deacon 1997; Richerson and Boyd 2004). For example, evolution adapted our larynx to the use of language and the skills of our ancestors evolved further by using tools. In terms of evolution, we are both similar to and different from the people who lived in the first century Mediterranean world. Most important, similarities include maturationally natural features, which develop in children in fairly constant ways in a wide range of environmental and cultural circumstances and are therefore cross-culturally recurrent (McCauley 2000, 2011), such as the distinction we make between living and non-living things and other aspects of cross-culturally shared ontological categories (see below). Furthermore, social learning relies on such evolved abilities (e.g., speech), and the information that we learn is also fundamentally shaped by such abilities (e.g., vision, memory, ontological distinctions). Finally, differences between people living in the first-century Mediterranean and ourselves are due mostly to evolution that has taken place in other domains than in our genes.

Our suggestions proceed from the following general thesis: texts are subject to selective processes in cultural transmission and will be shaped in ways that correspond to human cognitive capacities. Texts need to be able to raise attention, be understood, be stored in cultural memory in the long run, and remain accessible for retrieval from cultural memory. The better some text fulfills these criteria, the more successful it will be in cultural transmission. Although textual transmission can be influenced by historical accidents (such as the loss of a huge number of books at the burning of the Royal Library of ancient Alexandria in 48 BC), the impact of cognitive factors will become increasingly important if we examine processes on sufficiently large timescales. Among all ancient documents that have been transmitted and read in the history of Western civilization, biblical literature inevitably belongs to the most widely known and used group of texts.

In a sense, the aim of every interpretation is to find out what happens in the authors' and readers' cognition as they write or read texts, respectively. The promise of a cognitive approach lies in its potential to explain such cognitive processes with reference to general models. Cognitive models are rooted in various research traditions. Modern linguistics postulates the existence of universal mental structures, which we do not acquire by learning languages (including our mother tongue), but which are maturationally natural and help us learning and understanding natural languages. Artificial intelligence research deals with cognitive processes that can be implemented as computer programs (although artificial intelligence does not have to be psychologically realistic). Evolutionary psychology and evolutionary anthropology look for adaptive patterns of thought, perception, processing, and emotion, which are trans-culturally widespread and about which we can theoretically presuppose that all people have had them in any part of the world at any time in history. Neuroimaging makes processes in our brains visible and correlates them with our behavior and experience. Psychology, since its cognitive turn, looks for internal, mental processes in humans. Before the cognitive turn, such processes were deemed to be inaccessible, and their study was not considered viable or important. A cognitive approach also provides insights about cultural variables, and therefore its application to the interpretation of texts with varied historical backgrounds is a promising perspective. It is imperative, beyond doubt, to mobilize the wealth of knowledge about cognitive processes for the interpretation of concrete, culturally shaped texts. Cognitive approaches to texts share the principal insight that describing, classifying, and analyzing physically tangible texts is not yet sufficient to understand them. We also have to come to grips with the cognitive models that govern their production and reception.

Consequently, cognitive processes are equally relevant for the interpretation of religious texts, whether we select the author, the reader, or the text itself as the focus of our interpretation. To delineate our methodology, we would like to introduce the concept of the *cognigram*. Evolutionary anthropologist Miriam N. Haidle (2009; 2014) introduced cognigrams to offer graphical representations of cognitive processes that underlie the production of an artifact, such as a spear. When we adopt the term to cognitive exegesis, we are looking for cognigrams that represent processes in the minds of people as they write and read texts. Without understanding such invisible cognitive processes governing text production and reception, we would be unable to understand a text, even if our visual and auditory systems could process it. Cognigrams rely on two kinds of cognitive processes. Maturationally natural cognition, which we already introduced above, develops in fairly constant ways in children in a wide range of environmental and cultural circumstances and is therefore cross-culturally recurrent. It is important to note that maturational naturalness does not simply arise from genetic inheritance but from genetic information that is activated by environmental factors during child development. Other cognitive processes that come "naturally" to us involve practiced naturalness (McCauley 2011), which is based on goal-directed learning. Riding a bicycle, for example, might come quite naturally to some of us, but it is acquired by specific practice rather than spontaneous learning. The interpretation of (religious) texts involves both types of abilities. On the one hand, linguistic communication and many cognitive structures, including religious ones, are maturationally natural; on the other hand, aesthetic judgment, scientific thinking, and many theological concepts involve practiced naturalness.[1]

The cognitive interpretation of religious texts explores connections between human cognition and religious documents in a two-way process. On the one hand, there is a deductive process, in which the results of cognitive science and evolutionary studies are used to interpret religious texts (biblical literature in our case). When using the results of cognitive and evolutionary science, we assume that people in antiquity shared basic cognitive structures with us, and therefore the models of cognitive science are relevant for the study of humans who lived two thousand years ago. On the other hand, ancient texts carry imprints of the cognition of human beings who lived in a different cultural environment than ours. In an inductive process, we can look for the reflection of people's cognigrams in the artifacts they left behind, and try to use such cues to draw the cognitive profile (cognigram) of the creators and users of the texts. We can expect this profile to be partly similar to ours, but also different in some ways. Although the time that separates us from people living in antiquity is short if measured on an evolutionary timescale, culture is capable of changing in such a period of time—demonstrated, for example, by the cultural consequences of the industrial revolution. Time to time we have to ask whether the imprints of ancient minds on the texts should be interpreted in terms of pan-human cognitive factors shared by ancient people and us, or whether they reflect cultural differences. Ancient texts are therefore precious artifacts, similar to the primitive tools that paleoanthropologists use to understand the human mind of our prehistoric ancestors. In this way, the cognitive study of (ancient) religious texts can contribute to a better understanding of human cognitive processes, including both its pan-human nature and cultural manifestations.

To carry the analogy further, texts are not only products of cognition; they are also tools we think with. Religious texts have been used in rituals, provided tools for manipulating reality in magical practices, or for organizing human societies; they have been the sources of philosophical reflection and legislation. They have been instrumental in changing the course of European history in the Reformation, and in reflecting on historical traumas. Religious texts have affordances; that is, they lend themselves to particular cognitive and cultural uses.

Texts production and cognition: The place and significance of texts in religion from a cognitive perspective

From the cognitive point of view, texts are external memory stores. In religions, beliefs are stored and transmitted in two different forms: as memories (technically speaking, connection patterns of neural networks) in the brains of human beings, and as information recorded in texts as well as in other artifacts. To give examples of the latter, sacred objects, sanctuaries, ritual vestments, churchyards, and the configuration of physical space record and transmit information about the belief system and mythology of a religion. That is why we can read archaeological data as if we were reading texts and apply hermeneutical methods to them similar to the ones that we use to decipher ancient written sources. Texts are special kinds of religious artifacts, which store information using the medium of language. Artifacts, including texts, interact with beliefs stored in people's minds. That artifacts are important in religion needs no particular explanation among biblical scholars. Taking one step further, we can easily see that texts and other artifacts are not mere recordings of people's beliefs but constitutive parts of religious systems (Czachesz 2013a). Reformation, for example, was largely driven by interpretations of biblical literature. Protestant theology, in general, defines itself as an ongoing exegetical enterprise and regards the Bible as an active agent rather than a passive container of data. Gerhard Ebeling and Karlfried Froehlich championed the hypothesis that the history of the Church is the history of biblical interpretation (Ebeling 1947; Froehlich 1978). In evangelical churches,[2] the Bible has deep influence on almost every single event on believers' everyday lives, which has been examined from a cognitive perspective (Malley 2004). We can also think of examples from outside of the realm of Protestantism. The relics of the saints, the shroud of Turin, the Torah, or the temple of Jerusalem do not simply record and convey information from the past, but clearly play a constitutive role in the respective religious systems.

Artifacts and human memory are not entirely symmetrical parts of religious systems: human minds perform cognitive tasks that artifacts cannot. It is the reader who reads the text, and not the other way around. The point is, however, that religions (especially the ones under consideration in this volume) are unthinkable without a constant interaction between their beliefs and texts (as well as other artifacts). On a general level, human language (and material culture) has shaped the human mind as much as humans shaped their environments, in a process known as "cognitive ratcheting"(Tomasello 2009 [1999]; cf. Tomasello, Kruger, and Ratner 1993): small changes in the mind lead to small changes in the artifacts, which, in turn, initiate further changes in the mind. As our previous examples demonstrate, such mutual influence is clearly visible in many religious traditions, which often recognize it and reflect on it very explicitly.

The oldest form of representing texts is the oral medium. In a sense, oral literature is nothing else than the acoustic representation of mental representations, which makes it difficult to speak of such literary works as "artifacts" that would autonomously exist in the same way as, for example, axes and arrows exist. But an understanding of oral literature as the mere externalization of a pre-existing mental content is equally problematic. Orality studies and psychological studies of orality have demonstrated that oral literature is not something that exists in a readymade form in the heads of singers. In his *Memory in Oral Traditions*, David C. Rubin analyzed different types of oral literature and concluded that when people recall texts, they rely on features such as the organization of meaning, imagery, and sound patterns, the latter including rhyme, alliteration, and assonance, as well as rhythm and music (Rubin 1995, 10). The process of producing a text relies on its sequential organization: "Oral traditions, like all oral language, are sequential. One word follows another as the physical effects of the first word are lost. As the song advances, each word uttered changes the situation for the singer, providing new cues for recall and limiting choices" (Rubin 1995, 175). Oral texts are thus best understood as artifacts that are created during every performance on the spot. Every instance of oral literature is an artifact that exists only momentarily. This is not unique to oral literature: academic lectures read from notes and improvised jazz also share the short-lived nature of oral artifacts. The momentary, sequential, and improvised nature of these artifacts does not mean, however, that their actual appearance would be entirely random. Cognitive schemata, such as narrative scripts, provide blueprints for all examples of improvised artifacts. The examination of these cognitive factors and the process of the oral performance provide interesting new research perspectives for biblical scholars, who regularly deal with texts created in the oral medium.

It is widely recognized that the oral medium played a significant role in the formation of early Christian literature, to which we will return below. It would be a mistake, however, to regard early Christianity as a purely oral culture, or to limit the examination of cognitive factors to oral texts alone (cf. Kelber 2008; Czachesz 2009a). The nature of ancient literacy was such that memory played a significant role in all aspects of it. Ancients habitually read aloud, had texts read to them by slaves, or listened to public readings (Starr 1987; Johnson 2000). Owning books had the significant function of signaling social and intellectual status, and most reading was social activity: typically, books were read and discussed in bookstores or at dinners and symposia held in private homes. When listening to a text and subsequently discussing it with a group of peers, people encountered literature as an oral/aural rather than visual event (Rawson 1985; Johnson 2000, 612–15). Authoring texts also involved memory to a great extent. The use of written sources was constrained in several ways. First, books were written continuously, without punctuation or word division (*scriptio continua*), thus providing no visual aids that would help the eye in finding particular passages. Second, the scroll format was less than optimal for jumping across different parts of a book to find a passage or compare different passages. Third, ancients did not use desks on which they could have laid out scrolls (or later codices), which would have enabled them to use multiple sources critically (in a modern sense) when writing a new text (Downing 1992, 2000, 174–98; Houston 2014, 197–204). Again, relying on memory or having slaves to read out sources aloud (which again involved the use of memory) could provide solutions to overcome such difficulties. For the study of biblical literature it is therefore imperative to understand cognitive factors that underlie the memorization and retrieval of texts for the purpose of retelling, discussing, or authoring literature.

In addition to rethinking the relationship between beliefs and texts, a cognitive approach to biblical literature also has the potential of shedding new light on the connection between texts and rituals. On the one hand, texts reflect on rituals, giving us clues about ritual practices as well as the views that ancient people held about their own rituals, such as Paul's discussion of the Corinthians' ritual meal in 1 Corinthians 11. Cognitive theorizing about how people think of rituals offers new perspectives on the interpretation of these passages (e.g., Uro 2016, 128–53; Czachesz 2017a, 88–121). On the other hand, rituals provide contexts, in which texts are transmitted. This is obviously the case in oral transmission, but also literate artifacts (prominently, the Bible itself) appear in various ritual contexts and their religious use and transmission would be unthinkable without such contexts. Cognitive work on the effect of rituals on memorization is a promising perspective for studying these processes (Whitehouse 2004; Czachesz 2010c; Uro 2016, 154–77; Czachesz 2018a).

Cognitive factors at the diachronic transmission of texts: How texts change in oral and literate transmission

Texts are passed on from one generation to the other similarly to genes or behavioral patterns. They are part of what Eva Jablonka and Marion Lamb called the symbolic inheritance system (Jablonka and Lamb 2005, 193–231; Jablonka and Lamb 2007). The diachronic analysis of texts covers the history of transmission of a text before its recording in writing, the history of its transmission as it is being copied as a literary artifact, and its subsequent uses as a written source. We can identify four tendencies in the process of textual transmission:

(a) The tendency of increasing coherence. Coherence increases in a text by solving contradictions, connecting unconnected parts, and changing details that do not square with accepted patterns so that they would fit into them smoothly. Obtrusive elements are mitigated and interpretations are added to details that are difficult to understand. In terms of cognitive theory, this process can be understood as the assimilation of information to the cognitive schemata (see below) of the author and first readers of the text, which include both pan-human cognitive structures and culturally transmitted patterns of thought. This tendency should result in a continuous optimization of texts so that they become ever more polished and homogeneous units, where the mutual relations between the elements of the text and between the meanings of the elements display an ever-increasing coherence. Using the concept of A. J. Greimas, we could speak of an increasing isotopy of the text (Greimas 1983, 69–101).[3] However, texts do not always seem to comply with these expectations. In long units of transmitted texts we can find motifs that do not make sense, and puzzling utterances that we cannot crack by the usual means of interpretation. This suggests that we have to look for additional tendencies in the transmission of texts.

(b) The tendency of maintaining relevance. As a text migrates through geographical space and historical time, culturally shaped and transmitted cognitive schemata in the minds of readers will sometimes differ from the cognitive schemata that influenced the formation of a text at a previous point of its history. In his pioneering experiments, Frederic Bartlett studied how a text originating from a foreign culture was recalled and observed the tendency that readers remember and transmit texts in ways that make them correspond to their own expectations. Bartlett coined the term schema (plural schemata) to denote the packages of expectations that underlie this process (Bartlett 1932).[4] He demonstrated that information that does not correspond to cognitive schemata will be either forgotten or assimilated. Texts are thus being constantly updated so that they remain relevant in ever-changing circumstances. This process can result in discrepancies within the original text, the tendency to maintain the relevance of the text in the present working against the tendency to increase coherence and isotopy. That is, whereas such changes and additions will assimilate the text to the cognitive schemata of the contemporary reader, they will often create incoherence within the text itself. Thus, we can observe a tendency to increase the relevance of the text, which is connected to a decrease of the coherence of the text. This can be observed especially in redactional layers in transmitted texts. Redactors often introduce new interpretations that depart from previous layers, resulting in tensions between the new layer and the very tradition that the redactor attempts to amend and make relevant.

(c) The tendency of conservation. Often texts are transmitted for their own sake, including "blind motifs," which nobody understands exactly anymore, but which are nevertheless attractive, precisely because no one understands them. We can thus observe a conservation of motifs. Once they have emerged, texts gain a certain inertia, which they preserve also in face of the tendencies of increasing coherence and relevance. Texts can display a surprising stubbornness: variants that once get included in a text can persist with surprising stability.

(d) The tendency of accumulating counterintuitive elements. According to recent empirical studies, in some circumstances, motifs and concepts that do not fit into our cognitive schemata can be remembered better than information that confirms to cognitive schemata perfectly (Barrett and Nyhof 2001; Boyer and Ramble 2001; Upal et al. 2007; see below). Information that violates maturationally natural ontological categories has received particularly much attention in the cognitive science of religion, but information that violates culturally acquired schemata seems to be memorable, as well (Steenstra 2005; Porubanova et al. 2013). How non-schematic information is transmitted and remembered depends on many factors, of which we mention only two at this point: (1) violations of cognitive schemata cannot be too excessive and (2) a text can contain only a limited amount of violations.

One of the objectives of cognitive exegesis is to explain under which circumstances each of the four tendencies will shape a text during transmission. First, we expect that texts will develop internal coherence, driven by the influence of authors' and readers' innate (maturationally natural) and culturally acquired cognitive schemata. Second, we also expect that texts develop features that make them fit into the cognitive schemata of their readership at any point of transmission. We can call these two processes (increase of coherence, on the one hand, and actualization, on the other) *assimilative* processes, because they shape texts in ways that make them increasingly correspond to authors' and readers' cognitive schemata. There is an obvious tension between the two assimilative tendencies: the cognitive schemata of readers can be different from those of the first authors and readers, which is why actualization takes place in first instance. Actualization will therefore decrease the internal coherence of the text, unless the text is so thoroughly rewritten that it actually becomes a new text with a newly achieved internal coherence. For example, thorough revisions or adaptations of literary works, remakes of classical movies, or popular adaptations of classical music approach or achieve such a goal. The tendencies of conservation and the introduction of counterintuitive elements, in contrast, will shape texts in ways that make them fit into readers' cognitive schemata less. We can therefore call these tendencies *dissimilative* processes.

The question arises as to how different elements introduced by the above-mentioned four tendencies can be connected and preserved in one and the same text. Some observations about the reception of texts will be helpful in this respect. First, texts can be read as meaningful units even if they are actually not completely coherent and homogeneous. Reading seems to follow the principles of Gestalt psychology. As we read, we complement lacking elements and correct obtrusive motifs. In other words, not only the production, but also the reading of texts includes assimilation, by which we can experience less than optimally composed texts as meaningful. For this reason, every text can tolerate smaller tensions and obtrusions, which create exceptional opportunities for interpreters to reconstruct the history behind the final form of the text. Second, we can observe another mechanism in reception, which is in many ways the counterpart of the previously mentioned tendency. During reception, readers not only "repair" texts, assimilating them to their expectations, but often they focus on discrepancies and oddities consciously or subconsciously, which can increase the chance of the text to achieve an impact. For example, the story of Abraham binding Isaac (Gen. 22) is such a breathtaking narrative exactly because it violates moral intuitions by suggesting that a father would kill his son. This mechanism is similar to the fourth tendency of textual transmission discussed above. However, whereas during the process of transmission counterintuitive elements can be added or omitted, during reception this is not an option: at this phase, the text will either succeed or fade into oblivion as whole. We will soon return to this problem at the discussion of canonization.

Oral transmission and form criticism

Whereas orality studies have influenced the study of biblical texts since the beginnings of modern biblical scholarship,[5] cognitive science provides new ways to understand the dynamics of oral transmission and yields new insights about particular textual problems (e.g., Czachesz 2010a). Much of the work conducted in the cognitive science of religion bears immediate relevance to the study of oral transmission. The transmission of narratives has been a classical area of memory studies since the pioneering experiments of Frederic Bartlett, which we briefly mentioned above. In some of Bartlett's experiments, subjects were presented with written stories, which they had to recall after different intervals. In another experimental setup, called serial reproduction, the text resulting from a subject's recall became the text that another participant had to memorize. Cognitive studies on the transmission of religious concepts followed Bartlett's basic experimental design, and also corrected its various shortcomings. Variables included the types of texts (from folktales to mere lists), the interval of recall (from a few minutes to several weeks and even months), and the cultural groups involved in the experiments (from the United States to Gabon and Nepal). These experiments imitate the circumstances of oral transmission insofar as the text has to be reproduced from memory, often following longer time intervals, but also differ from them, because the text is initially encountered as a visual, rather than aural, artifact.

In general, the experiments confirmed the existence of cross-culturally consistent cognitive effects in the transmission of ideas. We have already referred to the finding that the violation of cognitive schemata can increase the chances of a textual element to be remembered (Tendency 4). The theory of minimal counterintuitiveness, formulated by Pascal Boyer, accounts for the memory effect of the violation of cross-cultural ontological expectations. Counterintuitive concepts violate expectations attached to cross-culturally attested ontological categories, such as HUMAN, ANIMAL, PLANT, ARTIFACT, and (natural) OBJECT (Keil 1979, 48; Atran 1989; Boyer 1994b). If such violations are kept to a minimum, the respective ideas will be remembered better in the long run. However, if violations are multiplied, the concept will have less chance to be retained in memory. As a consequence, minimally counterintuitive concepts are transmitted at higher rates than either ordinary or maximally counterintuitive items (Barrett and Nyhof 2001; Norenzayan and Atran 2004; Gonce 2006; Slone et al. 2007). Bizarre (or paradoxical) items, which do not violate ontological expectations, will be often changed so that they actually become counterintuitive. Ideas that violate culturally transmitted schemata also seem to be benefitted in transmission to some degree (Steenstra 2005; Porubanova et al. 2013). However, the exact circumstances and conditions of this effect are yet to be explored. Some empirical studies examined the transmission of stories that violated narrative scripts (cf. Boyer and Ramble 2001, 538–39). Such a violation of narrative elements occurs, for example, in many parables (see below) and in the story of Christ as a self-debasing divine figure (Phil. 2:5–8). Yet another important domain is the use of emotionally laden motifs in narratives, which have been shown to increase memorability for the emotional elements as well as for all details of the narrative (Laney et al. 2004).

A cognitive approach can also be used to re-think a much-debated axiom of form criticism. On the one hand, form critics postulate the initial existence of simple oral genres, which are varied and become ever more diverse in transmission. It was hoped that by reconstructing the original generic structures one can eventually find the original form of the tradition. On the other hand, the opposite of this postulate is equally plausible: in the beginning, complex forms with a less solid structure could exist, which later became adapted to the widely known textual forms (Haacker 1981). Shall we postulate the "pure form" as the starting point of the transmission process, or rather as its result? Probably neither of these alternatives is correct. We suggest that the structure of a literary form is actually a cognitive schema, which is used to generate new exemplars of a genre repeatedly, the schema itself remaining hidden in the competent human mind behind the texts, never externalized in a pure form. A "cognitive form criticism" or a "cognitively elaborated form criticism" reconstructs hidden competences behind the accessible performance of texts, that is, cognitive entities that are documented in their textual realizations.[6] Forms and genres are thus cognigrams that are used to produce and process texts.

Literate transmission (source criticism and redaction criticism)

Whether texts are shaped by the same tendencies in oral and literate transmission is a question under intense debate. Is there a fundamental discontinuity between the two types of transmission? (Ong 1982; Kelber 1983). Or are differences perhaps mitigated by the influence of secondary orality? (Uro 1998; Uro 2003; Ong and Hartley 2012, 11, 133–34). Public readings of written texts bring the texts back to the oral medium and exert additional influence on oral literature. In Section "Text production and cognition: The place and significance of texts in religion from a cognitive perspective," we argued that memory played an important role in all aspects of ancient literacy. In addition to the case of secondary orality, memory was a crucial factor at the citation of sources, in intellectual discussions, and in the very process of composition (Eve 2016; Czachesz 2017a, 83–87). Consequently, cognitive research on the recall of stories and ideas is directly relevant to the study of literate transmission.

Cognitive studies may prove to be helpful in clearing up some questions in source criticism. Against skeptical voices, which deny that we could observe general tendencies in the transmission of oral and literary texts (Sanders 1969), it could enable us to find such rules. Cognitive experiments with stories give support to the hypothesis that miraculous elements are accumulated in the transmission. We can see that paradoxical motifs without counterintuitive traits are transformed into counterintuitive ones. For example, we can expect that a story about a man who recovers from coma will be transformed into an instance of resurrection from death. However, a look at biblical traditions also reveals that such a tendency is not absolute. For example, the author of the Gospel of Matthew often minimized the miraculous elements in the miracle stories that he took from tradition.[7] It would be an especially remarkable finding if we could prove that there is a general tendency toward the accumulation of counterintuitive elements in the transmission.

Cognitively oriented redaction criticism is interested in much more than only the introduction of abbreviations, extensions, and modifications to texts. Such an approach asks about the models that the redactor followed in his or her work. Using the terminology introduced above, we are looking for the cognigrams in the redactor's mind that determined his or her use of the sources. These cognigrams also influenced texts that were written later with the intention of complementing or replacing the original work, examples of which could be found in both canonical and apocryphal literature.

Whereas in oral transmission stories are at the mercy of memory effects, which, in the long run, level out and neutralize the individual biases of the transmitting agents, in literate transmission the cognigrams of a single individual can be more decisive. The cognigrams that lead the gospel authors' hands incorporated a number of generic, stylistic, and linguistic elements, information derived from (Hellenistic) Jewish tradition, cognitive schemata gained from Graeco-Roman culture and education, and social conventions. We have previously mentioned the puzzle of why Matthew downplayed the miraculous elements in the presentation of Jesus's mission. Possibly this bias against counterintuitive details derives from cognitive schemata shaped by ancient elite culture. It has been shown that packages of information containing many intuitive and a few counterintuitive details will be remembered the best in the long run (Norenzayan and Atran 2004). In the oral phase of transmission, counterintuitive features will accumulate until they reach an optimal level in the narrative. In literate transmission, however, cognitive schemata deriving from the author's education and social background that have been incorporated into the author's cognigram can leave their imprint on the text more effectively. Literate transmission, for example, enables the accumulation of heavily counterintuitive scientific knowledge (McCauley 2011). We can thus explain deviations in the Gospel of Matthew from the expected tendency toward counterintuitive details by hypothesizing that the author's cognigram included a bias, influenced by elite literate culture, to suppress miraculous elements (Eve 2002). When we speak about a bias against too many miracles as a schematic constraint, we consciously emphasize the cognitive nature of the process. It was not the author's intention to achieve a particular goal, or his calculated rhetorical maneuvers, or his theological vision that resulted in the observed features of the text. The author's cognigram might or might not be accessible to the author's conscious reflection. It might or might not be brought into direct connection with his or her immediate social environment, socioeconomic status, or personal life. Such factors are certainly in the background and a reconstruction of them remains a valid objective. The reconstruction of the cognigrams, however, does not depend on the explicit identification of such historical circumstances, but solely on the identification of the cognitive schemata that contributed to the cognigram, which, in turn, left its imprint on the literary artifact.

Another important cluster of schemata in the cognigrams of the gospel authors was related to the figure of Jesus. Such schemata depended on the kinds of cultural, educational, and personal factors that we already considered in the previous paragraph. However, as already mentioned, there is no need to connect the cognigram or its elements directly to particular religious groups, movements, or socioeconomic conditions in the first instance. Such considerations are valid and interesting but they follow as a second step of the reconstruction of the historical background. Let us now consider how the cognitive schemata about Jesus's figure influenced the redaction of the four gospels and how, through these writings, they influenced authors who continued or complemented each of the canonical gospels.

(a) The cognigram that lead the hand of the author of the Gospel of Mark included a schema about Jesus as a mysterious divine figure, or "Son of God," who lets himself be known gradually. The truly counterintuitive nature of his figure will be fully revealed first when he is crucified and resurrected. The original text of the Gospel of Mark ends, however, exactly where the puzzle would be resolved (Mk 16:8). The women flee from the empty tomb and say nothing to anyone. The secret remains unrevealed. It can be argued that the so-called longer ending (16:9–20) was added to the narrative because it emphasizes the minimally counterintuitive (ghost-like) nature of the risen Jesus, and thereby forms a cognitively more appealing, more memorable account of the resurrection (Czachesz 2007b, c). This lack of a truly counterintuitive character of the resurrected Jesus could provide motivation for the authors of the other gospels to further elaborate the story.

(b) The cognigram of author of the Gospel of Luke included schemata about Jesus as a powerful agent. The author's goal was first of all to provide a narrative of the deeds of his protagonist. Jesus's words are also understood as part of his actions. The sequential organization of the narrative is foremost among the cognitive schemata governing the production of this text. The Book of Acts was written as a sequel to the Lucan gospel and offers a picture of Jesus as being present in the lives of his followers after his resurrection.[8] A cognitive analysis of the character of Jesus in Acts offers a promising perspective for understanding the connection between the respective christologies of the two books as cognitive schemata about Jesus. In these schemata, narrative scripts played a significant role: that is, the cognigrams of the authors already contained narrative structures, rather than using narratives as mere vehicles to express preexisting, static Christological images (cf. Czachesz 1995).

(c) In the cognigram behind the Gospel of Matthew, the schema of Jesus as a teacher is dominant. Arguably, the author also regards himself as a teacher. He tends to organize his material in a systematic way: for example, Jesus's teachings are arranged into five great speeches, which are carefully structured and laid out in a meaningful order. From the sayings that are included in these speeches we can reconstruct a picture of the resurrected Jesus who is present in the world until the end of times. In the history of reception, the Teaching of the Twelve Apostles (Didache) has been viewed consistently as a sequel to the Gospel of Matthew. This text also consists of a systematic composition of sayings and teachings.

(d) In the cognigram of the author of the Gospel of John, there is a dominant schema of Jesus as a figure sent from heaven. He is sent to the people to deliver a new commandment, that is, the commandment of altruistic love. The disciples are expected to persist in such a love ("abide in my love," Jn 15:9) and build a new community. The Paraclete (also translated as "Helper" or "Advocate") will remind them of all things that Jesus taught them, so that their joy may be complete. In this case, the sequel to the gospel is an epistle, the central motif of which is the definition of God as Love: "God is love, and those who abide in love abide in God, and God abides in them" (1 Jn 4:16). The letter was clearly written so that the joy of the community "may be complete" (1 Jn 1:4).

We can note that the exact mechanisms that create the common schemata in the respective cognigrams behind the writings and their sequels can change from time to time. In the case of the Gospel of Mark, both the long ending of the gospel and the other (synoptic) gospels were influenced by the cognigram's imprint on the actual text. In the case of the Gospel of Luke, either the cognigram of the same author (complemented by new schemata) shaped the sequel or the cognigram of the author of Acts was heavily influenced by the knowledge of the gospel text (and possibly by personal relationship). In the case of Matthew and Didache, the cognigrams might or might not have influenced each other. In this case, it is also possible that the readers' cognigrams played an important role in connecting the two writings, which helped readers identify common traits in the two texts directly. Finally, scholarly hypotheses about the connection of the Johannine epistles to the Fourth Gospel leave various possibilities for explaining the similarities between the respective cognigrams behind the two texts, ranging from common authorship to a shared community behind the text or later attempts to validate the gospel in a changing context.

Textual history and textual criticism

Textual criticism studies the extant manuscripts of a text, comparing variant readings and attempting to reconstruct the developmental lines that resulted in the current forms, including attempts to recover or at least approach the author's original text. For textual critics it makes a difference whether a certain variant resulted from unconscious errors or intentional changes. The use of cognitive criteria is especially promising in cases of unconscious errors, where the result is another meaningful text. In such cases chances are great that the mistake remains undiscovered and gets transmitted in the long run. The following short list of typical changes in manuscripts is intended to give a general impression of the nature of the problem.

(a) The confusion of sounds due to hearing errors (e.g., by scribes who copied texts after dictation) was especially common when it came to sound patterns involved in so-called iotacism. In Koine Greek, all of the following letters or combinations of letters were pronounced as a long iota: η, ι, υ, as well as ει, οι, υι. As a consequence, long and short vowels became confused, which could affect the spelling of other syllables, as well. For example, such a confusion of vowel length occurred probably in Romans 5:1, where the indicative form εἰρήνην ἔχομεν ("we have peace") became a subjunctive (which expresses wish or command in the first person): εἰρήνην ἔχωμεν ("let us have peace").

(b) Confusing letters by visual errors is another frequent source of change in the texts. Confusions occurred especially frequently within the following groups of letters: (i) C E Θ O, (ii) Γ Π Τ, (iii) λλ Μ, (iv) Δ Λ. For example, in 2 Peter 2:13, the word ΑΓΑΠΑΙΣ (the dative case of "agape feasts" or "love feasts") became ΑΠΑΤΑΙΣ (the same case for "dissipations").

(c) Homoioteleuton is the copying error when one or more words are omitted because two groups of words are ending the same way. For example, the verse Luke 12:9 is missing in some manuscripts because both the previous and the following verses end with the expression τῶν ἀγγέλων τοῦ θεοῦ ("the angels of god").

Given that we can relatively clearly identify a group of such standard errors in the Greek manuscript tradition (and a similar set can be compiled for other languages, as well), a great part of text-critical processes can be reduced to computational problems.

On the one hand, such a formalized presentation of the issue would make it possible to use computer simulations for modeling evolutionary tendencies in the manuscript tradition. Insights from such models could be used, in turn, to refine the heuristic strategies of textual criticism. On the other hand, researching cognitive processes behind errors could provide better insights about the whole process of manuscript production. A similar approach can be applied to many of the intentional changes in the manuscripts, such as the standardization of grammar or the assimilation of similar passages across the gospels to each other. Finally, we can study the cognigrams that motivated the smaller or larger adjustments of the text to make it comply with certain theological convictions. This is in fact a late occurrence of an assimilative tendency, adapting the text to readers' cognitive schemata, which were different from the cognitive schemata of the author and the earliest readers.

Cognitive factors at the synchronic analysis of texts: The example of forms and genres

All synchronic approaches to the text take its present form, without considering its historical development and different layers, and examine its coherence and structure, linguistic and discursive properties, pragmatic qualities, and the place of smaller units in the whole composition. Linguistic approaches, rhetorical criticism, composition criticism, narrative criticism, and reader-response criticism are among the frequently used methods in the synchronic analysis of biblical literature.[9] How a cognitive perspective can enhance our knowledge of the text in these areas can be exemplified by the case of the search for coherence. In a text, coherence is created by words with overlapping semantic fields (such as explained by the theory of isotopy)[10] and by syntactic connections. Such analysis, however, seldom yields very surprising new knowledge; it mostly confirms what a reader with sufficient literate education would intuitively discover in the text anyway. Forms and genres are also cognitive tools that serve to create coherence.[11] They can be understood as generalized packages of expectations that govern both the production and the consumption of texts. They reduce misunderstandings, because in the frame of a certain genre there are standard expectations leading and constraining the understanding of the text.

From the perspective of the cognitive approach, genres and forms can be isolated by considering different cognitive schemata including (i) categories and (ii) scripts. (i) Cognitive categories are conceptual cuts that we make in the world when we process information. Some of them are maturationally natural (and therefore cross-culturally recurrent), whereas others are culturally determined. (ii) Narrative scripts, in turn, are organizations of elementary episodes that help us understand events in the world. According to Roger C. Schank and Robert P. Abelson, frequently encountered episodes are organized into mental templates called "scripts" (Schank and Abelson 1977, 1995). Scripts are evoked when relevant information is encountered, and make it clear what is going to happen in a given situation and what the actions of various participants indicate. Arguably, not only first-hand experience but also information gained from social learning can be organized into scripts. Therefore, narrative genres and forms can be understood as mental scripts, that is, cognitive schemata consisting of elementary actions. Using script theory, it is possible to interpret, for example, "passion narrative," "miracle story," and "gospel" as cognitive scripts and understand how they function in texts (Czachesz 2003, 2007a, 2010a). In addition to categories and scripts, knowledge about other aspects of cognitive processing can be also used to study genres and forms. For example, the organization of lists and maxims appears to follow constraints set by the limitations of working memory (Czachesz 2003). This bears relevance, among others, to the study of genealogies, different lists of the apostles, the beatitudes, woes, and other lists of sayings, or various chain-like patterns in Revelation (horsemen, seals, trumpets, etc.).

Among the many perspectives that a cognitive approach opens up for synchronic exegesis, we will consider insights about the violation of cross-culturally recurrent and culturally shaped schemata in interpreting literary forms. We have introduced the notion of maturationally natural ontological expectations and their violation in Section "Text production and cognition: The place and significance of texts in religion from a cognitive perspective." Based on this body of research, we can distinguish three types of ideas with regard to their relation to schematic expectations. (i) Counterintuitive ideas include violations of maturationally natural (and therefore cross-culturally attested or "universal") ontological categories; (ii) paradoxical ideas (also called "bizarre" concepts in cognitive research) contain violations of everyday experience, but these irregularities only concern cultural and individual experience and do not violate cross-cultural expectations about basic ontological categories; (iii) intuitive ideas comply with schematic expectations in all respects. We will use the example of the parables and miracle stories to exemplify the possibilities of using this simple typology.

Parables

The genres that involve metaphorical language provide plenty of opportunities for cognitive analysis. Metaphors always connect two basic elements: a source domain and a target domain (Lakoff 1993).[12] For example, in the metaphor "Life is a journey," the source domain is the domain of "journey" (evoked by the word "journey" in the sentence) and the target domain is "life" (evoked by the word "life"). The metaphor invites us to project various elements of the source domain of journey onto the target domain of life. Metaphors are also characterized by an element of surprise. Let us consider the following sentence: "The moon swims through the valley of the river Neckar." In terms of syntactic rules, the moon can be connected with any verb. However, the connection with the verb "to swim" is one that violates expectations attached to the meaning of the verb in language users' everyday expectations. On this account, a metaphor is a concept set against a context that is "counter-determined" (Weinrich 1967). The connection of different domains and the element of surprise are important aspects of metaphors, both of which are intimately tied up with the transmission and use of mental schemata: in the context of cognitive schemata we can understand better how metaphors function.

We can approach classical categories of metaphorical language in biblical literature with the help of the three types of ideas described above. Parables connect a source domain known from everyday life with a target domain that is situated in transcendent reality. Their subject matter is God or the relation between humans and God. Using cross-culturally attested ontological categories, we can define the sphere of immanent reality. As we have seen, our cross-culturally shared ontology comprises humans, animals, plants, artifacts, and natural objects. Concepts that squarely fit into these ontological categories (i.e., they fulfill expectations related to these ontological categories) describe our experience of the immanent world. All remaining concepts necessarily contain violations of our maturationally natural ontological expectations. Among such concepts we find the ones that describe the realm of the divine, including God (or gods), angels, spirits, devils, and demons. Parables in biblical literature thus connect source domains with immanent, non-counterintuitive characteristics with target domains of transcendent, counterintuitive characteristics. In the parables, biblical literature uses knowledge about the immanent to convey messages about the realm of the divine.[13]

(a) This general idea does not hold for so-called example stories. In this case, both the source domain and the target domain remain within the realm of intuitive ontology. The listener is expected to behave similarly as (or, in some cases, differently than) the characters of the narrative do: as the good Samaritan (Lk 10:25–37) and the repentant tax collector (Lk 18:9–14), but not as the fool rich (who thinks his riches will save his soul; Lk 12:13–21). Yet within these stories we can find paradoxical elements: for example, it is the foreigner, the Samaritan, who helps the victim of the robbers, and not the priest or the Levite.

(b) The actual parables, in turn, bridge the two realms. The source domain itself contains unlikely stories with "extravagant" (P. Ricoeur) elements, which belong to the paradoxical ideas in our cognitive typology. These include the unrealistically high debt of the unforgiving servant (Mt 18:21–35), the equal wage of the workers who have worked for different lengths of time (Mt 20:1–16), etc. Such paradoxical elements also serve as indicators that point to the realm of the transcendent that is in the target domain.

(c) Allegories can be also clearly distinguished in our typology. In this case, the source domain contains counterintuitive elements, as well. For example, animals speak or have many heads. One may notice that even though these images are counterintuitive, they do not refer to transcendent realities as our thesis would predict (see above). It can be noted that the counterintuitive traits remain fairly limited in these instances. For example, breaking off the branches of the oil tree and grafting them again (Rm 11:11–24) is paradoxical but not counterintuitive; attributing speech to the tree is, however, counterintuitive, because we do not expect plants to use language.

(d) In the similitudes, in contrast, the source domain contains neither counterintuitive nor paradoxical elements. It is usual that crops grow without the intervention of the farmer (Mk 4:26–29) or that mustard grows higher than many other plants (Mk 4:30–32). Paradoxical elements with a signaling function might occur in the source domain: for example, in the parable of the sower (Mk 4:1–20), an unrealistic quantity of seed is sown to rocky and barren soil, perhaps referring to God's generosity (cf. Mt 5:45). Similitudes imply counterintuitive elements in their target domain, that is, the realm of the divine.

In contemporary biblical studies one can observe a tendency to abandon the division of parables into subcategories, introduced by classical form criticism, because they seem to be difficult to define (Zimmermann 2007).[14] A cognitive analysis of forms can prove itself helpful in finding new meaning in the classical taxonomy.

Miracle stories

By definition, miracle stories always contain paradoxical or counterintuitive elements, which violate maturationally natural or other expectations. Miracle stories fall into different categories in this respect.

(a) In the case of *therapies*, the basic process confirms both universal and culture-specific expectations. For example, healing with saliva (e.g., Mk 7:33) is an intuitive technique, which is also effective in terms of biological mechanisms: saliva contains healing substances (Oudhoff et al. 2008). What about healing by touch? The transference of various negative and positive properties by touch seems to be an intuitive notion (Uro 2013a). In various experiments, for example, subjects disliked the idea of wearing a thoroughly cleaned sweater that was worn for one hour by someone who experienced misfortune (e.g., had a leg amputated) or had a moral taint (e.g., was a convicted murderer) (Nemeroff and Rozin 1994, 2000). When it comes to positive effects of touch, every parent knows that touch relieves pain. Indeed, touch seems to be an effective pain reducer in straightforward biological terms (Anonymous 2010; Kammers et al. 2010). As far as the use of touch and other intuitive processes in miracle stories is concerned, however, two remarks have to be added. First, many therapies in biblical literature change intuitive healing processes (which might or might not comply with modern scientific theory) into paradoxical events by adding extraordinary difficulties (Theißen 1998): for example, the blind man in John 9 has been blind since birth. Counterintuitive traits can be introduced, as well: for example, the centurion's slave is healed from a distance (Lk 7:1–10). Second, counterintuitive elements are often being introduced at the level of reflection, that is, to interpret both intuitive and paradoxical healings, such as by attributing the healing to divine intervention, or explaining the sickness by divine punishment or demonic influence (Czachesz 2007d, 2010b).

(b) *Exorcisms* respond to demonic possession, where the actions and words of the possessed individual are seen to be controlled by a demon. In concrete terms, the "I" of the person is replaced by the "I" of the demon: for example, when Jesus asks the possessed person a question, it is the demon that answers (e.g., Mk 1:23–26; 5:1–13). Demons are ambiguous entities in terms of mental representation. On the one hand, there are cross-culturally attested intuitions about the continuation of psychological functions after death, suggesting that some kind of belief in spirits is not unequivocally counterintuitive as such (Bering 2002, 2006, 2011). On the other hand, the idea of a demon that migrates from one living thing to another

(Mk 5:11–13), lends superhuman strengths to the possessed person (Mk 5:3–5), recognizes a divine agent whom people do not recognize (Mk 1:24), or foretells the future (Acts 16:16) is certainly counterintuitive. Whereas the exorcist does not necessarily possess counterintuitive qualities (Paul casts out the demon in the last example above), the involvement of counterintuitive agents is assumed. The apostles cast out demons invoking the name of Jesus. According to Matthew 12:22–32, Jesus's exorcisms also presuppose the involvement of counterintuitive qualities: Jesus must be in connection with some counterintuitive agency, either being "Son of David" himself, or invoking "Belzebul, the ruler of the demons." In the case of therapies the attribution of healing to counterintuitive agency seems to be optional, while it seems obligatory in the case of exorcisms, where the exorcist always has to conquer powerful superhuman agents.

We can note that many pre-modern cultures also know "adorcisms", meaning the "domestication of spirits" or "cult of spirits" instead of their expulsion (Heusch 1962; Lewis 2005, ix–xxiv). Therapies in biblical literature often appear as processes of restoring the patient's strength or spirit (Mk 5:12; Acts 21:10), suggesting a relation to the concept of adorcism. Yet the texts do not connect this aspect of the therapies with the transfer of spiritual entities explicitly. Probably the closest parallel to adorcism in (early) Christianity is the communication of the Holy Spirit, especially if we consider it in the context of prophetic and charismatic groups of Christianity. As far as exorcism is concerned, it removes harmful spiritual presence and restores the boundaries of human existence.

(c) The so-called *nature miracles* always include counterintuitive elements. They violate the intuitive order of reality in order to produce positive, life-saving results. For example, the miracle worker walks on water (Mk 6:45–53), bread is multiplied without baking (Mk 6:35–44), water is transformed into wine (Jn 2:6–10), and decomposing dead bodies come back to life (Jn 11:38–44). Whereas no one would doubt that these events are extraordinary or surprising, it might be helpful to consider briefly how they include violations of universal ontological expectations, which makes them counterintuitive in a technical sense. In some of our examples, it is easy to see why this is the case. We do not expect natural objects or artifacts (such as bread) to multiply spontaneously, which is a capability that we only attribute to living things. At other times, some more detailed analysis is needed to find out whether a miracle contains a counterintuitive element. Whereas changing water into wine is a miraculous event by both modern and ancient standards, one could argue that Jesus's miracle in Cana does not necessarily violate ontological expectations: liquids sometimes change into other liquids by human intervention or otherwise. A closer look, however, reveals that water and wine belong to different ontological categories: the former is a natural substance, whereas the latter is an artifact. Although fermentation occurs in nature, producing wine (in this case, excellent wine) is impossible without human intervention. Furthermore, we do not expect natural objects to transform into artifacts without human intervention: artifacts are made by humans. Let us note that in our analysis it is not the practical problem of producing wine from water (as opposed to other materials) that makes the miracle counterintuitive. Agricultural know-how, in general, is too recent on an evolutionary timescale to be part of our maturationally natural ontology. Thus an idea that contradicts such knowledge (e.g., using an unusual raw material) would be paradoxical but not counterintuitive. The counterintuitiveness of the story results from an artifact emerging without human intervention, which contradicts the very definition of an artifact. Walking on water also needs further elaboration, because walking on natural objects in general does not violate our innate ontology. The counterintuitive nature of the miracle probably involves particular expectations about liquids in folk-physics, that is, maturationally natural expectations about the physical world (Atran 1989, 1990; Barrett 2008). The problem invites a more fine-graded analysis of intuitive ontology, which we cannot undertake at this place (cf. Keil 1979; Kelly and Keil 1985).

By their surprising and counterintuitive character, these narratives prompt the reader to construct explanations that involve counterintuitive agency. In some cases, this is very straightforward: walking on water is made possible by the counterintuitive qualities of the agent who violates folk-physics. In other cases, however, explanations could be formulated in other ways as well, such as attributing counterintuitive qualities to the bread or wine in the miracle. For a number of reasons, however, counterintuitive agents are much more powerful concepts than counterintuitive versions of concepts in other ontological categories (Boyer 2001, 155–231; Pyysiäinen, 2009). Most important, counterintuitive agents matter more than other counterintuitive concepts because they have minds, are capable of social interaction, and make moral judgments. Looking for counterintuitive agents behind miraculous events is thus how the human mind naturally reacts to such events. In this way, miracles direct the reader's attention to the realm of the transcendent. Whereas the counterintuitive quality of the miracles is constant cross-culturally, the particular transcendent reality that readers postulate behind the miraculous event is culture-specific. The miracles initiate symbolic elaboration, whereby readers connect various aspects of the narrative with culturally postulated qualities of the divine and with other culturally transmitted elements of religious thought and practice. For example, the multiplication of bread in its Johannine version (Jn 6) is connected with the interpretation of the Eucharist; in the story of Jesus's resurrection of Lazarus (Jn 11), the resurrection miracle is connected with the idea of being resurrected in the present life.

Cognitive factors at the reception of the text: The reception history of biblical texts and biblical concepts

In this domain, the main question is why some texts achieve influence while others do not. We are using the notion of selective processes that act on bits of culture (such as ideas, behaviors, artifacts, texts) in the process of transmission. As István Czachesz argued previously, a cognitive approach helps us understand how mainstream Christology emerged in the competition of a number of alternative visions in the first and second centuries (Czachesz 2007b, c). On this account, the mainstream view succeeded not because it was the oldest or because it was supported by the powerful elites, but because it was optimally adapted to the structure of the human mind. If we look at different representations of Jesus's resurrection (or of the resurrected Jesus) in our sources, we can see that they violate innate ontological expectations to different degrees. Empirical results of memory research (cf. Section "Oral transmission and form-criticism") demonstrated that ideas violating intuitive ontological expectations minimally, as well as packages of ideas that contain an optimal ratio of intuitive and counterintuitive elements, have the greatest chance to be remembered in the long run, and therefore they enjoy an advantage in cultural transmission. According to the memorability hypothesis (or optimal transmission hypothesis), ebionite Christological alternatives are too little counterintuitive, whereas docetic Christologies are too much counterintuitive.

The view that Jesus was not resurrected (in body) accommodates his figure to the ontological expectations about human beings. However wise, heroic, pure, and exceptional such a Jesus might have been, such an account was disadvantaged in the chain of memorizations and recalls and its effect on cultural memory remained limited. In the Acts of John, which exemplifies the docetic alternative, Jesus is on the Mount of Olives, talking with John, at the same time that he is being crucified on Golgotha. Being at two places at the same time obviously violates intuitive ontology. But the Jesus on the Mount of Olives does other things that violate ontological expectations, as well: he radiates light, becomes invisible while speaking to John, and finally ascends to heaven. Besides being at two places simultaneously, his two "exemplars" have two different minds as well: the one in the cave does not feel the sufferings of the one on Golgotha. Some docetic accounts divided Jesus into three or even four different elements. Such a Christology is excessively counterintuitive and has therefore limited chance to be remembered. The mainstream idea can be exemplified by Paul's account in 1 Corinthians 15:3–8 (reporting previous tradition) and the passion and resurrection narratives of the four canonical gospels. In these accounts, Jesus dies a violent death, which is not different from the violent deaths of many other humans at his time. Three days after his death, however, he is resurrected by God and seen by several eyewitnesses. Like other ghosts and spirits, Jesus receives an ambiguous physical substance after his resurrection. The gospel narratives make more of his counterintuitive physical properties when he suddenly appears before his disciples in a house with closed doors, or disappears from them in the middle of a conversation (e.g., Lk 24:31; Jn 20:19, 26). These episodes violate expectations about the physical properties of human beings, but leave intact most other intuitive expectations: as a result, they offer a cognitively optimal view that has the greatest chance to impact cultural memory.

Proceeding from Czachesz's hypothesis of early Christian transmission (Czachesz 2003, 2007e), Gerd Theißen treated the problem of "Jesus and Paul" from a cognitive perspective, to explain how Paul, the "missionary to the gentiles," succeeded with his particular Christological vision (Theißen 2007). The success of this Christological view relies on the attractive nature of counterintuitive ideas. Paul put the "foolishness of the cross" (1 Cor. 1–2) into the focus of his message consciously and connected it with the tradition of the gospels. Such a Christology became particularly persuasive, because it surrounded a counterintuitive message with an aura of plausibility. Much of Jesus's parables and wisdom teaching are directly plausible and intuitive. The theology of the cross in Paul's teaching, however, gave this tradition a provocative edge, which made it noticeable in the field of competing ancient religions. By combining the Pauline kerygma of Christ with the synoptic tradition of Jesus, Christianity received optimal chances of transmission and expansion.

Cognitive factors at the meta-textual classification of texts: The canonization of texts and canon theories

The status of the texts in the biblical canon as sacred texts provided them with an exceptionally great chance to be preserved and to exert influence on human culture. In order to achieve such a status, the texts went through a process of sacralization and canonization. Some writings could already contain "pre-canonical" elements, which claimed to communicate divine revelation or were originally composed for ritual purposes. Other texts, however, could have a completely secular background, such as the Song of Songs. Paul's epistles communicate high claims to authority and present ideas in ways that aspire for a canonical status. Such canonical claims, however, remained yet to be acknowledged and extended to the text as a whole. Most important, the canonical claims of the texts themselves had to be supported by a metatextual theory, so that the texts become accepted and used by various communities as authoritative and sacred. The process of canonization was determined by two interacting factors: first, the differential use and circulation of texts, depending on the internal claims and qualities of the texts themselves as well as on external circumstances, such as social networking and circulation; second, the theoretical scaffolding that made the sacred and canonical nature of some texts explicit. Finally, once texts receive a canonical status in a religious system, the durability of the system as a whole warrants their long-term stability.

Cognitive theory allows for a new understanding of the selective process that leads to the acceptance of particular texts as canonical. We have already mentioned relevant factors at the discussion of the history of reception (Section "Cognitive factors at the consumption of the text: The reception history of biblical texts and biblical concepts"), where we attempted to understand why some texts exert a deeper influence on cultural memory. (1) The memorability hypothesis about the selective advantage of counterintuitive ideas can be extended to the composition of larger textual units. An optimal level of counterintuitiveness applies not only to individual concepts (such as the image of the resurrected Jesus), but also to complex assemblies of ideas (such as the whole complex of the concepts and images in a text). If a text contains some counterintuitive elements embedded in a larger set of intuitive elements, it is likely to have a greater impact on the reader, to be better remembered, and ultimately to achieve greater popularity and to have a greater chance to be recognized as canonical. (2) The circulation of texts and the effect of circulation on canonization are other important factors. For example, the epistles of Paul circulated widely due to the apostle's extensive and complex social networks (Czachesz 2011a). The texts were read and copied by many people in a huge geographical area. This is very likely to have catalyzed the early canonization of these writings. (3) Finally, the ritual use of religious texts influences their canonization in different ways: if a text can be more easily adopted for ritual practice or incorporates traditional passages from the very beginning, its repeated use in a ritual context creates strong and possibly emotionally laden memories and increases its chances to be considered as sacred.

Canonical criticism and holistic approaches[15]

The approach that Brevard S. Childs (1979) developed is based on two axioms: first, the final form of the text has a privileged position in interpretation, and it has to be considered before any of the previous forms; second, the text has to be interpreted in the context of the whole canon. The real meaning of a text is thus not the meaning of the hypothetically recovered original tradition, but its meaning in the context of the final form of the text. This approach can be seen as a consistently realized form of redaction criticism, which is applied not only to the changes in a text (additions, omissions, modifications), but also to any tradition incorporated by the author—since ultimately it was the author's decision to include any source. In such a way, canonical criticism can be added as a final step to the previous methodological steps of historical criticism to examine the text as a whole. Any passage has to be interpreted thus in the context of the final, canonical version of the writing. By this move, the composition of biblical writings has become a major theme of biblical interpretation, and the terms "composition criticism" and "history of composition" have been in use for decades (e.g., Haenchen 1968, 24; Rendtorff 1983). In composition criticism, the synchronic perspective is privileged above the diachronic one. And here comes the final step: all texts have to be interpreted in their canonical context. The canon is not a loose collection of independent writings, but a meaningful composition: every text has to be understood in this whole.

The problem arises, however, that none of the authors of the individual writings had such a higher compositional level in mind. Are exegetes presupposing here coherence and order that no one ever intended? There are two possible answers to the question. (i) First, one can argue that the work of the author transcends the author's intention. A hermeneutical approach that presupposes the superiority of the work above its author could validate the canonical reading of the final form of the text, also in cases where connections arose by pure chance. For example, in the expressions "the heavens torn apart" (Mk 1:10) and "the curtain of the temple was torn in two" (Mk 15:38), the Gospel of Mark uses the same verb, σχίζειν. Probably the author of the text did not intend such a correspondence at all. It is only the reader who postulates a connection between the two instances of "tearing." The reader's intention complements the intentions that governed the author's final redaction of the text. In this way, the postmodern hermeneutics of the inspired reader can support canonical interpretation. (ii) The second possibility is a pre-modern approach that ascribes a second author to the whole text: that is, God directed the hand of the author, through God's Spirit, to create a meaningful work. B. Childs's theory proceeds from such a principle. The full canon is an intended whole, which has been created by God's influence on the authors of the biblical texts. Since the full canon encompasses both the Hebrew Bible and the New Testament, it can be used as the basis of a biblical theology of the whole Bible. The context of the full canon includes the New Testament from the very start: that is, the books of the Hebrew Bible were written as parts of the whole canon in first instance.

Many scholars, who otherwise accept the canonical approach to the Hebrew Bible and the New Testament separately, refuse to take such a step, since that would mean that the Christian reading of the Hebrew Bible is the only possible reading (Rendtorff 1994).

Canonical criticism and canonical process interpretation proceed from the assumption that the meaning of the text emerges at the end of the process of canonization or during the process itself. Theoretically speaking, it is possible to reckon with goal-oriented processes in human history. Human intention is forward-looking. Humans have an ability to represent the future mentally, make plans, and coordinate their efforts to move toward distant goals in time. But intention alone is not sufficient to explain the emergence of a meaningful product, the creation of which took many centuries and involved a variety of geographical locations and historical situations. Is it possible to maintain a sense of "teleological" orientation without recourse to supernatural guidance? A cognitive approach can give an answer to this question that falls in line with the logic of hermeneutical theory: successful ideas are ones that correspond to the capacities of the human mind. The powers of canonization, which guided the formation of the texts for such a long period, are in fact nothing else but constraints of human cognition.

The canonical approach, which gives preference to the final form of writings, and even to collections of writings, occupies an ambiguous position in the typology of exegetical methods. It belongs to the family of diachronic methods, insofar as it presupposes a history that provides the context for interpreting the final form of the text. However, it also belongs to the group of synchronic approaches, because it asks about the form and structure of the text as we have it. It can be also called a functionalist approach, because it is interested in the ways the text functions in a real-life context. Furthermore, as it develops theories of canon, it also deals with meta-textual theories. In any case, the examination of theories of canon is a fruitful area of application of cognitive approaches.

Literary criticism tackled many similar problems throughout the twentieth century.[16] The focus first shifted from the author's intention to the text, labeling the traditional axiom of tying the meaning of the text to the author's intention as "intentional fallacy." A number of text-centered approaches dealt with the literary work as a given whole, taking a synchronic perspective. Finally, attention shifted to the reader, who plays an active role in the creation of meaning. These developments have influenced biblical hermeneutics and have been drawn on by many exegetes (e.g., Frye 1982; McKnight 1985; Oeming 2006). A cognitive approach offers important tools for carrying on this critical tradition, and taking it to a new level, indeed, because it utilizes knowledge about cognitive structures that are shared by the ancient authors, their original readership, and the modern reader. Meanwhile, cognitive science is able to deal with culture-specific cognitive patterns, as well, explaining how cultural differences arise from cross-culturally shared cognitive elements.

Theories of canon

Literary canons (similarly to cultural and artistic canons) contain a set of artifacts (literary works, in our case), which are recognized by a cultural community as significant in at least two ways. First, being canonical in an aesthetic sense, literary classics are models for the creation of new texts. They are to be imitated. Second, literary and cultural canons represent or discuss important values and themes of a community. For example, literary works that are regarded as classics often deal (explicitly or implicitly) with questions of national identity, the interpretation of major historical events, humanistic and religious values, social institutions, family models, gender roles, to name only a few. Texts in a literary canon are often interpreted by literary critics, historians, social scientists, philosophers, artists, and other professionals, and provide a shared system of reference for public discussion and intellectual exchange.

Religious canons, such as the biblical canons of Judaism and Christianity, are similar to nonreligious literary canons in some ways, but different in other respects. Religious canons, similarly to other literary canons, are recognized as important texts by a community and represent or discuss basic values and themes of the community. They are also interpreted by professionals and provide a shared system of symbols and references. Texts in a religious canon, however, are unique and authoritative in ways that we cannot find in literary canons. They constitute a closed system, which can be interpreted, but cannot be changed or extended as a result of new cultural developments. In this respect they are different from legal canons, which are both interpreted and systematically extended.[17]

We can provide the following definition of a religious canon: "A canon includes normative texts that can be used to reconstruct the symbol system of a religion time to time and make it habitable for a religious community by interpreting the texts of the canon" (Theißen 2008, 341–44, esp. 41). For a religious community, canonical texts provide the normative foundation of its myths, cult, and ethos. They are not meant to be imitated or emulated, but to be interpreted. One can identify four criteria of the canonical status of biblical writings.

1. Canonical writings express a claim to normativity by their reference to the transcendent. This reference can be established, for example, by a teaching of inspiration. In every religion, there are many more texts with a claim to canonical status than texts that are officially canonical. This makes it necessary to look for further criteria.
2. We can add the cultic use of a text as a second criterion. A canon is a list of texts that are being read in service.[18] These writings can testify of divine revelation, but they are not necessarily regarded as divine revelations.
3. The third criterion of canonical status arose when the authority of the entity, of which the text testified, was transferred to the testifying writing itself. Canonical texts count as final and closed as far as the extent of the text is concerned. This has been expressed by so-called canon formulas since the writing of the Book of Deuteronomy: nobody can add anything to the text or take away anything from it.[19]
4. The definitiveness of the text also holds for the selection of texts. Canonical texts belong to a collection of writings, which is closed—at least ideally. Already the Second Epistle of Peter presupposes a collection of Paul's letters (2 Pet. 3:16). At the end of the second century, Irenaeus regards the canon of the four gospels

to be final (Irenaeus, Against Heresies 3.11.8). The idea of a final selection is not necessarily in contradiction with the actual debates about the selection that continued much longer. The idea of the canon was in fact necessary so that such a debate could take place.

How can the cognitive approach contribute to the research of these issues? We propose that the theory of ritual competence facilitates a better understanding of the process of canonization (Lawson and McCauley 1990; McCauley and Lawson 2002, 8–26). First, E.Th. Lawson and R.N. McCauley argue that every believer has the competence to judge whether a given action is a religious ritual or not. Second, they suggest that the human mind represents rituals just as it represents any other ordinary action, parsing the action into three components: agent, action, and patient. That is, the agent does something to the patient (by means of an instrument). Third, in religious rituals one of the elements is connected to a divine being (or culturally postulated superhuman agents, in Lawson and McCauley's terminology). If the divine is most closely associated with the agent of the ritual (such as the priest in baptism), the changes that the ritual causes will be final (or "superpermanent"), and such special agent rituals cannot be normally repeated with the same participants. Special patient and special instrument rituals (in which the divine is connected to either the instrument or patient of the rituals more closely than to the agent of the ritual) have less permanent effects and are therefore repeatable. The act of communication through a text is also an action that can be understood in similar terms: the author attempts to influence the reader, using the text as an instrument. The text will be regarded as sacred if one of the three participants (author, text, or reader) has a connection with the divine. In this framework, we can adapt ritual form theory to understand the logic of different theories of the sacredness of texts. First, the text will be expected to have the greatest impact on the reader if the author is connected to God more directly than either the text or the reader is connected to God. In this case, a divine author will be presupposed behind the human author, who authorizes and inspires him or her. The idea of inspiration can be extended to the subject of the writing (*inspiratio rerum*) or to the actual words written (*inspiratio verborum*). Second, there are contemporary theories of the "inspired reader," who is responsible for elevating the text to a sacred status (cf. Körtner 1994). Finally, there are various theories that establish a semantic connection between the content of the text and the realm of the transcendent.

It might appear paradoxical that (in terms of our analysis) the idea of a superpermanent effect of the text on the reader is supported by theories that connect the author of the text directly with God. In this case, the text and the reader can be inspired, as well. In contrast, theories of sacred texts that proceed from the idea of the inspired reader (i.e., they presuppose that the reader is the participant of the reading process that is most closely connected to God) establish a less permanent effect of the text on the reader. If the subjective experience of the reader becomes the only criterion of the authority of the canon, however, the idea of a canon will erode in the long run, because such subjective experience is very selective and occurs at the reading of only some parts of the texts spontaneously. The theory of an inspired author, in turn, leads to the assumption that trivial or difficult passages must also have a meaning, and will provide motivation for finding meaning in face of every difficulty.

This takes us back to our initial suggestion: using knowledge about the cognitive aspects of religion can help us to a deeper understanding of biblical literature. Our quick survey of possible research areas and avenues hopefully convinced the reader that such an approach indeed has the potential of growing into a fruitful paradigm in biblical interpretation. Taken together, the cognitive approach is not a new method besides existing methods; it rather provides already well-established methods of biblical exegesis with a new depth, adding to them a cognitive dimension. Drawing on cognitive research about mental schemata, memory processes, emotions, agency, ontological templates, language competence, and other aspects of the human mind provides us with the necessary tools that we can use to explore and map out this exciting territory.

2

Emotional Fear in Pentateuchal Legal Collections

Thomas Kazen

Introduction

This chapter is part of a larger project on the role of emotions in Pentateuchal legal collections, which I completed in 2011. The results are published in *Emotions in Biblical Law: A Cognitive Science Approach* (Kazen 2011).[1] The book deals with four emotions: disgust, empathy, fear, and a sense of justice, but in this chapter I will focus on fear. Fear of foreigners is conspicuous in laws regulating relationships with other peoples. Fear of divine punishment is frequently employed as a deterrent in motivating obedience. Fear of demonic or supernatural powers is implicit in certain rituals, not least in some that effect purification or atonement. It should be pointed out that this is not a study of the semantics of fear (יראה, פחד, *yir'a, pahad*, etc.), but of the emotional role that fear seems to play within and behind the texts that are discussed.

Examining the role of fear in various legal collections, I note how fear both counteracts and interacts with other emotions, particularly empathy and disgust. I also relate my analysis to recent discussions about the interrelationship, dating, and social contexts of various Pentateuchal legal collections.

Background

Cognitive science is a wide umbrella, housing a number of quite diverse fields. My own interest lies in aspects associated with the evolution and development of mind, rationality and morality, in particular, emotions that influence human behavior and behavior norms such as moral and/or ritual actions, and instructions. Since such emotions are both biologically evolved and culturally shaped, I think that insights from evolutionary biology, ethology and neuroscience, as well as from developmental psychology, can be used as heuristic tools for interpreting ancient texts dealing with moral and ritual issues. My presuppositions include the criticisms against the Cartesian paradigm that have been voiced by neuroscientists like Antonio Damasio, as well as by linguists and philosophers such as George Lakoff and Mark Johnson, all of whom point to the deficiency of a traditional Western view of the role of reason, and favor a concept of an embodied mind (Damasio 1994, 248; Lakoff and Johnson 1999, 16–44, 235–66). Damasio's examples from neuroscientific research have often been quoted—and criticized—in scholarly literature (Damasio 1994; cf. Damasio 1999, 2003),[2] reminding us that "mind derives from the entire organism" (Damasio 1994, 225) and that bodily emotions are intimately involved in human processes of reasoning and moral judgment (Damasio 1994, 245–52; cf. Kekes 1992, 444).

The long story of the dichotomy between reason (good) and passions (bad) in Western thought, going back to Plato and Aristotle, cannot be told here. There were nuances and acknowledgments of a basic relationship between cognition and emotion (cf. Knuuttila 1998), but in general we have inherited a more or less dichotomous anthropology that is still very influential: it serves reason best to remain detached from human passions. Immanuel Kant concluded that reason, unlike other organs of the body, has no natural function to preserve the human organism—for this purpose instincts would be more precise—but must rather be understood as intent on producing human morality. From an evolutionary point of view, Kant was wrong. David Hume came closer to the truth, claiming that reason should be subordinate to the passions; it ought to serve and obey the emotions (Teehan 2003, 53). If we, as John Teehan suggests, "can forgive the rhetorical excess of Hume's statement" (Teehan 2003, 53), it is shown to be quite in accord with an evolutionary paradigm. Nothing prevents us from explaining the evolution of uniquely human cognitive capacities by their adaptive value.

The philosophical dichotomy has spilled over into other and newer fields too. Lawrence Kohlberg, who builds on Piaget (cf. Piaget 1948) for his influential stage theory of moral reasoning, understands morality to develop from an idea of conventional obligations into a genuine understanding of moral obligations, through objective evaluation of right and wrong in a rational process (Kohlberg 1971; Kohlberg et al. 1983). Others have suggested that emotions play a much larger role for moral evaluation than usually recognized. Jonathan Haidt, in an argument based on experiments, suggests a "social intuitionist model," meaning that moral judgments are often triggered instantly by intuition, and then only subsequently rationalized (Haidt 2001, 814–34; Haidt 2003). Moral reasoning is as much a result of moral judgment as a cause of it. Haidt claims that "for affectively charged events … an intuitionist model may be more plausible than a rationalist model" (Haidt 2001, 817). Judgment would then be caused by quick moral intuitions and then followed by a slower rationalizing argument, if necessary.

Although biologically based on human emotional capacity, and thus innate, moral intuitions are shaped by culture during "developmentally timed periods of high neural plasticity, as though the brain 'expected' certain types of experience to be present at a certain time to guide its final wiring" (Haidt 2001, 827; cf. Moll 2005). Culture in qualified sense actually affects the biological default setting of the developing brain during a period of several years of human childhood and early adolescence.[3]

Moral emotions

The definition of a moral emotion is tricky. Emotions that are often deemed moral include awe, elevation, fear, guilt, contempt, anger, and disgust (Looy 2004, 222–23), but all sorts of emotions can have a bearing on moral issues. Haidt attempts a definition based on Gewirth's understanding of morality, which specifies the material conditions of a moral issue; hence his definition of moral emotions: "*Emotions that are linked to the interests or welfare either of society as a whole or at least of persons other than the judge or agent*" (Haidt 2003, 853. Haidt's italics).

Based on such a definition, Haidt finds two prototypical components of moral emotions and suggests that moral emotionhood is a matter of degree. Emotions that are triggered by disinterested elicitors and emotions that motivate some kind of prosocial action are considered more moral than others. The result is that anger, elevation, guilt, and compassion (or sympathy/empathy) score high, while fear, pride, sadness, and happiness score low. Gratitude, contempt, disgust, shame, and embarrassment are placed in between (Haidt 2003, 853–54).

Haidt admits that his typology is fairly speculative. In addition, another definition of morality might produce a different understanding of moral emotions. Many other alternatives are possible and each emotion has several subtypes (Haidt 2003, 854).

Haidt's categorization of emotions in families might be of more immediate interest. Contempt, anger, and disgust are all *other-condemning* emotions that are sometimes thought of as immoral. However, anger is often a response to injustice, either toward oneself or toward others. Disgust can be taken to protect human integrity and contempt is often seen as a blend of the two. Together they might be understood as guardians of the moral order. A second family of *self-conscious* emotions consists of shame, embarrassment, guilt, and pride. These put constraints on people's individual behavior in a social context. Shame and embarrassment clearly take various forms in different societies, depending on the degree of separation between moral norms and social conventions, and in some cultures hierarchical structures are heavily involved. Pride is a possible opposite of shame.[4] Feelings of guilt are triggered not only by consciousness of having caused harm or injustice per se, but particularly by the threat one's actions have caused to human relationships. These emotions make people conform to the moral order and abide by moral rules. The *other-suffering* family is the third, embracing distress at another's distress, and empathy/sympathy.[5] Empathic feelings are triggered by the perception of others' suffering and induce prosocial action or altruistic behavior. A fourth family consists of *other-praising* emotions, such as gratitude, awe, and elevation. In contrast to the previous emotions, these are responses to good deeds and have not been subject to much empirical research (Haidt 2003, 855–64).

Fear

A serious objection to this family schema is that it assumes an underlying view of morality as focused on action tendencies, i.e., as motivation to act rather than action itself; this understanding is questionable, as is the bracketing of self-interested emotions. Hence there is little room for fear in Haidt's version of the schema, although he does acknowledge its role in law-abiding or norm-respecting behavior (Haidt 2003, 864). In that respect, fear exhibits a relationship to the self-conscious emotions of shame, embarrassment, and guilt. In fact, a clear delimitation between self-interested and self-conscious emotions might be difficult to uphold. Furthermore, a number of moral and/

or ritual behaviors can be understood as resulting from a complicated interaction or tension between self-interested and disinterested emotions, self-conscious and other-condemning emotions, or between low and high action tendency emotions.

Fear is in fact generally considered as one of the primary emotions associated with morality,[6] and manifests itself as a sudden response to direct stimuli. It is often treated together with anxiety, but differs from the latter by being post stimulus rather than anticipatory. It has several aspects: as a subjective experience it is associated with somatic and autonomic responses and relates to coping behavior, especially avoidance and escape (Öhman 2000, 574).

Like anger, pain, and feelings of hunger, fear has evolved to protect the physical organism from damage and death. Most situations in which fear is experienced can be classified into four broad categories: *interpersonal situations, death and injury as well as illness, animals,* and *agoraphobic fears* (Öhman 2000, 575, referring to Arrindell et al. 1991). All four types represent situations during the history of evolution in which fear as a protective reaction kept living organisms away from potentially dangerous contexts: hostile strangers or enemies, damaging or lethal actions, predators and poisonous or large animals, and open places, lacking security, with nowhere to seek refuge quickly.

Although human fear is biologically based, it is shaped by evolution in such a way that we fear "situations that threatened the survival of our ancestors" (Öhman 2000, 576). This means that on the one hand it evolved because it was functional, on the other hand it may not always represent the most efficient response to a threatening situation, although, as several scholars have pointed out, it is not the response itself that is the problem, but the fact that it is triggered in the wrong context or has too low a threshold (Öhman 2000, 577). Since during the course of evolution, fast discovery of threat has had high survival value, fear has evolved as a more or less automatic response to stimuli, which bypasses traditional pathways in the brain, with the result that "affect precedes inference" (Zajonc 1980; cf. Öhman 2000, 578). Much research has been performed on how fear is elicited by stimuli outside the subject's awareness.

Fear of foreigners

Ethnocentrism and xenophobia

Fear of outsiders is very reasonable from the perspective of evolutionary biology. Xenophobia is found in a number of social species, from insects through birds and rodents, to monkeys and apes (references in McEvoy 2002, 45–46). Human children experience fear of strangers from the age of three months (McEvoy 2002, 46). Ethnocentrism can be understood as a "sentimental structure," the result of cultural elaboration and individual rationalization of basic evolutionary emotions, which has developed because it has some adaptive value (McEvoy 2002, 40).[7] Ethnocentric tendencies must be understood as context-sensitive. The experienced availability of resources, as well as cognitive recognition of the limits of group membership, governs to a significant degree the balance between selfish and altruistic behaviors in a population (cf. Dunbar 1987; McEvoy 2002; de Waal 1996, 212–14; de Waal 2006, 161–65).[8]

Ethnocentrism and xenophobia may serve to protect the integrity of the group, by reserving resources for the in-group and guarding against foreigners taking advantage of the reciprocal altruism practiced within the group while not contributing. Another effect is to block the likewise innate human propensity for empathy, which otherwise would inhibit aggression, thus making it easier to exercise violence against out-groups (Bandura 1999). Such out-group hostility is mitigated, however, not only by empathy, but also by a contradictory attraction to some aspects or characteristics of outsiders, that has been explained as an adaptive evolutionary trait, necessary for the gene flow and for counteracting inbreeding (Fishbein 2002).

One partial explanation for the development of hostility toward out-groups is disease-avoidance; hostility toward an out-group would have been adaptive since pathogens were avoided. Furthermore, out-group members would not act according to in-group practices that might have evolved to protect members from local pathogens (Faulkner et al. 2004; Navarrete and Fessler 2006). Navarrete and Fessler suggest that "disease-avoidance mechanisms may have given rise to the association between norm violations and feelings of disgust" (Navarrete and Fessler 2006, 280).

This could provide a partial explanation to certain ideas of impurity, although it is not to be confused with popular hygienic explanations for the purity laws in general. While singular food avoidances and negative attitudes to certain irregular conditions of the body could have developed from collective experience, all attempts to explain dietary laws or purity rules at large from considerations of preventive hygiene have failed (cf. Houston 1993, 69–70). Disease-avoidance might, however, explain certain links between hostile attitudes toward strangers and the association of strangers with disgusting practices.

Underprivileged foreigners in the Covenant Code

Rules dealing with in-group/out-group relationships and the treatment of foreigners often show signs of being shaped by emotional fear. This is sometimes reinforced by emotional disgust, but in other contexts mitigated by empathy. The latter is often the case in the so-called Covenant Code in the book of Exodus (Exod. 21–3). Here, immigrants (גרים) are mostly envisaged as an at least partially integrated out-group, belonging to the poorer segment of society. There is a difference between such foreigners and Israelites, but empathy is a more prominent factor in these laws than fear.

A clear difference between Israelites and foreign peoples can be found in the rules for manumission of slaves (Exod. 21:2–11). Israelite female slaves may not be sold to a foreign people (לעם נכרי), at least not after having served an Israelite master and (presumably) had sexual relations with him. This does not apply to foreign slaves; the law is said to concern Israelite slaves specifically (21:2).

In other respects, however, immigrants are embraced by the same empathic treatment as other underprivileged groups (22:20–6 [English Translation 21–7]). An immigrant (גר, *ger*) must not be oppressed, just as widows and orphans may not be maltreated. A difference is suggested when it comes to loans: money may not be lent for interest to anyone belonging to "my people, who is poor/needy, among you" (את עמי את העני עמך, v. 24 [ET 25]): this might imply that money may be lent at interest to foreigners. The rule in vv. 25–6 (ET 26–7) about not taking the cloak of a neighbor (רֵעַ, reaʿ) as a pledge overnight, should be understood to concern the immigrant too; the גֵּר (ger) is probably included in the concept of "neighbor."

The prohibition of oppressing immigrants is motivated by the experience of having been foreigners in Egypt (v. 20, ET 21). In the narrative world of the text, an emotional match, based on own first-hand experience, is visualized. For the actual recipients of the Covenant Code, a cognitive type of empathy, based on human capacity for perspective-taking, seems more appropriate at first. The appeal to a shared inherited experience has the effect, however, of adding an affective component to the concern for resident foreigners and from a historical point of view, the complicated political situation and tribal demography of ancient Israel should have ensured that a number of people actually had first-hand experience of minority situations. The scope and meaning of the term גֵּר (ger) compared to other terms for immigrants and foreigners is much contested (see Sparks 1998, 239–45; Nihan 2011; and the brief discussion in Kazen 2011, 116–17), but it could at times be used for landless or displaced Israelites, forced to migrate because of starvation or loss of land. This means that the appeal to Egypt, while basically on a cognitive level, might also indicate shared experiences of migration, hunger, and poverty, since it is structured as to trigger a multilayered empathy.

The command against oppressing an immigrant returns (23:9), and this time the appeal to shared experience is enhanced: "You yourselves have experienced the immigrant's life/existence" (ואתם ידעתם את נפש הגר). The seventh year rest is motivated by the poor gaining access to the crops (23:10–11) and the sabbath day rest is, in distinction to the Decalogue, motivated by concern for working animals, slaves, and the immigrant (23:12).

The inclusion of the immigrant or resident foreigner in the laws concerning underprivileged groups reveals something about the social situation in which this text was shaped and suggests a historical context in which strangers rarely attained prominence in society. Not that all immigrants were necessarily poor, but the "typical" immigrant was considered as such (cf. Nihan 2011).

This fits with a pre-exilic date of the Covenant Code. Most scholars regard this section as a fairly independent block of ancient materials.[9] The individual laws may be rooted in customary law, i.e., they originate from oral and local legal tradition that was administered on the family or village level, functioned in a "self-executing" manner (Jackson 2006, 29–35; cf. Jackson 1989, 197–98), and gained its authority from being regarded as cultural conventions.[10] The collection as such, however, is related to the Code of Hammurabi (Wright, David 2003, 2009). Such legal collections seem not to have been created as new legislations, but were literary works incorporating older materials (Viberg 1992, 16–17).[11] Close correspondences between the Covenant Code and Hammurabi's law suggest direct dependence, as has convincingly been demonstrated by Wright (Wright 2003; Levinson 2004, 288–97).[12] Although Van Seters thinks that this points to the Babylonian exile as the most plausible period of origin, Levinson has demonstrated the lack of hard evidence for such a position. During the period of Neo-Assyrian hegemony, Hammurabi's law attracted increased interest and by far the highest number of extant copies after the period of its composition comes from this time (Wright, D. 2003, 67–71; Levinson 2004, 293–97). A number of scholars thus agree on a late eighth or seventh century BCE dating (Stackert 2007, 17). This makes the suggestion quite plausible that the גרים (*gerim*) of the Covenant Code at least include northern refugees during a period of Assyrian intervention and after the fall of Samaria.[13] At this period, we would expect a number of displaced and landless immigrants, who constituted a vulnerable group in society.

So far we have discussed immigrants (גרים, *gerim*), in the sense of displaced Israelites or foreigners that are at least partially incorporated in one's own society. A different attitude with regard to "real" out-group becomes visible at the end of the Covenant Code. The section in Exod. 23:20–33 is usually regarded as a somewhat later addition, directed outwards rather than inwards (Kratz 2000, 142). Here, foreign peoples are named (Amorites, Hittites, Perizzites, Canaanites, Hivites, and Jebusites) and understood as threatening enemies that the Lord will wipe out (והכחדתיו, v. 23). As we might expect, the problem is their idolatry; the Israelites should not worship or serve their gods, nor copy their lifestyle; hence they must not enter into any covenant with them, since this would lead the people to sin against the Lord and serve other gods (v. 24, 32–33). The focus is, however, not on the Israelites engaging in genocide; the text is rather to be understood as a command to break down and shatter the idolatrous monuments of the foreign peoples (v. 24). God will send fear and cause confusion that will drive the enemies away (v. 27), and although he will give their enemies "in their hand," it is God who will drive them away (v. 31).

While the text contains threats (the angel of the Lord will not forgive disobedience, v. 21; if you serve foreign gods you will be trapped, v. 33) and promises (if you serve the Lord, he will bless bread and water, keep diseases away, and give you long life, vv. 25–6), it does not explicitly appeal to fear in the sense of xenophobia, but rather to fear at the prospect of divine punishment, something that will be discussed further in the next section. The references to diseases as well as blessed bread and water are, however, conspicuous. These may be read as implicit indications of ethnocentric attitudes, reflecting an adaptive safeguarding of insufficient resources, fear of disease, and avoidance of foreign practices; all these block to some degree the empathy that is extended to immigrants and prevent it from encompassing foreign peoples at large, so allowing aggression. While such mechanisms are partly visible in the Covenant Code, they become more pronounced in other legal collections.

Fear as constraint in Deuteronomy

The core of Deuteronomy (parts of Deut. 12–26) is usually taken to be modeled on the Covenant Code, revising and updating it in conformity with current practice (Levinson 1997; Kratz 2000, 114–33; Levinson 2004).[14] Van Seter's attempt to reverse this order has met with little approval, and must be considered as most unlikely (Van Seters 2003; Levinson 2004; Norin 2006; Wright 2009, 22–23). The context of Deuteronomy is that of cult centralization, something not presupposed in earlier legislation, and even explicitly contradicted by the altar law of Exod. 20:24–6.[15] This new historical context necessitates a revision and a rewriting of a number of laws. By retrojecting present concerns into the past, Deuteronomy transforms previous tradition (Levinson 1997, 150).[16]

Questions of origin, composition, and dating of Deuteronomic law have received no consensus answers. Most scholars have assumed several strata and a long period of development. Reinhard Kratz suggests two possible dates for an *Ur-Deuteronomium*: after the downfall of Samaria, or after the downfall of Judah, considering the latter alternative to be more plausible. This would amount to an early exilic dating of an *Ur-Deuteronomium* (Kratz 2000, 132 "But not a great deal depends on this"). The traditional view, however, associates a Deuteronomic core with social and religious changes during Hezekiah and Josiah, culminating in attempts at cult centralization under the Josianic rule (Levinson 1997, 21–22, 49–50). Although acknowledging that the connection between the discovery of the Torah scroll, covenant renewal, and centralization in 2 Kgs 22–23 is the work of the Deuteronomist, Levinson nevertheless defends the traditional view that dates a Deuteronomic core to the time of Josiah, i.e., late seventh century (Levinson 1997, 9–10).[17] The idea that a Deuteronomic core should be dated to the late pre-exilic period, i.e., during the latter half of the seventh century BCE, is shared by many scholars (Otto 2002, 5–19; 2007, 126–36; Wright 2009, 97, 323, 356–57). It was, of course, further expanded and revised through the exile and into the Second Temple period.

The introduction to the main body of Deuteronomic law focuses on cult centralization. While the Covenant Code concludes with a warning against foreign peoples and an injunction to destroy and annihilate foreign cults, Deuteronomy utilizes this tradition to enforce the idea of one singular place for worship and sacrifice (Deut. 12:2–27). The Israelites have now become the agents of driving foreign peoples away (12:2). In spite of this, however, ethnocentric and xenophobic implications are not exploited in the introduction; cult centralization is the prime concern at this point. The framework of Deuteronomy is, however, different. It is focused on the conquest in which God delivers enemies into the Israelites' hand, while they carry out the actual conquest (Deut. 2:24, 31; 3:2, 18, 20; 7:2, etc.), which is understood as the uprooting and extinction of competing peoples. This is closely associated with the threat of idolatry that these peoples represent, and exhibits emotional fear, at times coupled with disgust.

Covenant Code material on immigrants or integrated foreigners (גרים, *gerim*), together with the other customary underprivileged groups, widows and orphans, are first echoed in Deut. 10:17–19. This text belongs to what Kratz calls the internal and more paraenetic framework, consisting of chapters 5–11 and 27–30 (Kratz 2000, 114–33). The section in question (10:12–11:30) elaborates on the *shema* (6:4–9), referring to divine love as the cause of election. In this context, God is characterized as the god of gods, a terrible hero, and the guarantor of justice for the orphan and widow, loving the immigrant (גר, *ger*), giving him food and clothing. Here God is given the role of, and replaces, Hammurabi, who set up his stela "to provide justice for the homeless girl and widow."[18] At the same time God is portrayed as himself fulfilling the requirements of the covenant, giving further emphasis to the subsequent command: "And you shall love the immigrant, because you were immigrants in the land of Egypt" (10:19). The motivation is repeated from the Covenant Code and has by now become a standard *topos*, (כי גרים הייתם בארץ מצרים).[19] The reference to divine love, however, is conspicuous, since this love has just been proclaimed as the reason for the election of Israel, and thus, implicitly, for redemption from Egypt (10:15). The same love is now directed toward the immigrant and the people are challenged to likewise love the immigrant, remembering that their own redemption and election depend on that type of love. There is thus a strong emotionally charged type of empathy appealed to, which inhibits an expected group egoism and counteracts xenophobia.

The core of this material could, just as the Covenant Code, be related to intra-Israelite displacement and loss of land, followed by poverty and starvation, which would fit a seventh-century pre-exilic date. An exilic *Sitz-im-Leben* for this text seems less likely; it does not fit with a picture of a limited number of vulnerable immigrants living among the Israelites. A post-exilic context is likely for the final form of the text, which ties it to the exodus narrative, Egypt becoming a metonym for Babylon.

The category of underprivileged immigrants returns several times in the main body of Deuteronomic law, together with orphans and widows. In 14:29 and 26:12–13 they are added to the Levites, who as a result of cult centralization risked marginalization: they should be allowed the remains from fields, olive trees, and vines and they are supposed to receive the third year tithe (Kratz 2000, 121). All four are included with family and slaves in the now-centralized celebration of the Feast of Weeks (16:11–12) as well as the Feast of Booths (16:14) in Jerusalem. References to the immigrant, orphan, and widow, echoing the Covenant Code, are especially frequent in Deut. 24:17–22.[20] The prohibition to oppress a day-laborer and the poor explicitly applies to brothers and immigrants equally (24:14). This exemplifies a type of altruism, extending empathic behavior outside tribal or ethnic borders.

However, when it comes to foreign peoples or real out-groups, Deuteronomy exhibits a more severe attitude than the Covenant Code, both in the body of Deuteronomic law (Deut. 12–30) and in the framework. Deut. 7:1–3 contains strict rules for interaction with foreign peoples. Covenants, contracts, or inter-marriage with neighboring nations are strictly prohibited; these peoples should simply be annihilated (7:2).[21] As already indicated, these instructions are part of a narrative context, preparing the people for conquest, and are associated with the risk of apostasy and a fear of idolatry. In this context, fear of what is foreign is reinforced by disgust, expressed by the word "abominable" (תועבה, *to'eva*). Idols are abominated by God and should be abominated by Israelites, lest they be annihilated too (7:25–26). The term תועבה (*to'evah*) elsewhere expresses bodily disgust. It is used in many instances for denouncing objectionable practices, i.e., "abominable" acts, whether we prefer to categorize them as ritual or moral (cf. Preuß 1995). In Deuteronomy it usually refers to idolatry,[22] but also to defective sacrifice, invalid offerers, false weights, and remarriage with a remarried divorcee. In 14:3 it is used to characterize all categories of unclean food, as an equivalent to another term for disgust, שקץ (*sheqets*), used by P in Lev. 11.[23] תועבה (*to'evah*) is thus a term for a primary physical and emotional reaction of disgust, often being used secondarily for what was understood as repulsive behavior (cf. Milgrom 2000a, 1569),[24] and frequently associated with the practice of foreign peoples. Deuteronomic law explicitly states that such abominable practices are reasons for God driving away foreign peoples in favor of Israel (18:12).

In the composite war laws of chapter 20 we find clear tensions between vv. 10–14, which allow the taking of spoils, including women and children, and vv. 15–18, which allow nothing but total annihilation of neighboring peoples. The latter is motivated by the risk of Israel imitating their foreign abominations (תועבתם, *to'avotam*). The subsequent notice regarding the captive woman contains no such conditions (Deut. 21:10–14). These verses likely belong to different layers, one correcting or complementing the other. Although not explicitly spelled out, a fear of apostasy, reinforced by disgust, can be understood behind these ethnocentric sentiments expressed in Deuteronomy.[25]

While the role of fear in the ethnocentric sentiments expressed in the Deuteronomic core is seldom spelled out, it may be inferred in particular from the framework, where fear of foreign peoples is mentioned explicitly in a number of instances (1:21, 29; 3:2, 22; 7:18–19; 20:1, 3, 8; 31:6, 8). All of these belong to contexts in which the people are told not to be afraid of their enemies in battle. On the one hand, fear is not portrayed as the *cause* of an aggressive type of xenophobia on the part of the Israelites. On the other hand, fear seems to be utilized here in a somewhat paradoxical way; although the injunction is *not* to be afraid, the effect of these instructions may be to evoke enough fear of foreign peoples to block empathy and think in terms of ethnic cleansing. Israel is consistently portrayed as risking assimilation, and this is something that the Deuteronomic framework vehemently resists. One of the methods is fear, and interestingly enough, this fear is not only caused by foreign peoples, but is as much associated with the threat of divine punishment, which will receive our attention in the section "Fear of divine punishment."

Fear (sometimes together with disgust) is thus utilized, particularly in the framework, to outline the limits of the in-group, and indirectly to restrict empathic tendencies and attraction to out-groups. The purpose or, at least, the effect of this is to protect group integrity, since empathy and attraction might otherwise lead to assimilation. In the central part of Deuteronomy, we also find traces of disease-avoidance and disgust at foreign practices, but this is alongside evidence for various types of empathic reactions toward immigrants, building on the underlying Covenant Code.

Further developments in the Holiness Code

Although the Holiness Code (Lev. 17–26) was previously considered to be the oldest core of Leviticus,[26] there is an increasing tendency today to regard it as later than the preceding sacrificial and purity laws (Lev. 1–16), and even to consider a Holiness School (H) as responsible for redacting at least Leviticus and possibly other parts of the Pentateuch as well (Milgrom 1991, 3–63, 2000a, 1319–67; 2000b, 2440–46; Knohl 1995, 199–224).[27] In any case it is reasonable to regard the Holiness Code as later than the Deuteronomic law (Cholewiński 1976; cf. Grünwaldt 1999; Otto 1994, 2; 1999, 284; Nihan 2004, 82–98; Kratz 2000, 110–11; Levine 2003, 11, 18). While Deuteronomy had access to certain shared traditions that also lie behind some of the food laws in Leviticus,[28] the Holiness Code shows signs of awareness of both the Covenant Code and Deuteronomic law.[29] It presupposes Deuteronomic cult centralization and changes induced by this development (Lev. 17; 23).[30] This suggests a post-exilic date for the Holiness Code.[31]

Lev. 19 focuses on holiness. Here we find instructions concerning harvesting: it should not be carried out too thoroughly since leftovers must be reserved for the poor and the immigrant (גר, *ger*; Lev. 19:9–10; repeated in 23:22). The elements, although not the particular conclusion, are present in the Covenant Code (Exod. 22:10–11) and the explicit commandment in Deuteronomic law (Deut. 24:19–22). In the Holiness Code it is followed by injunctions not to withhold the wages of a worker overnight (19:13), not to curse a deaf person or to trip a blind person (19:14),[32] to be fair in judgment and not to take revenge (19:15–18). These injunctions are part of a list, including rules on sacrifice, the mating of animals, certain sexual transgressions, first fruit laws, meat with blood, cutting of hair and beard, prostitution, divination, and fair weights and measures. Most of these rules are concluded by the statement: "I am the Lord."

The injunction not to oppress the immigrant returns toward the end of this section (19:33–34), and goes together with the standard motivation: "You were immigrants in Egypt." Just as in Deuteronomy, the command is to love the immigrant; unlike Deuteronomy the command is to love the immigrant "as yourself," something that a little earlier was stated about the neighbor (19:18). The presupposition is that a resident foreigner should be treated just like a native (19:34). This emphasis on equal treatment is particular to the Holiness Code and goes together with a repeated claim that various holiness laws are valid for, and supposed to be followed by immigrants to the same extent as by native Israelites.[33] In Deuteronomic law, on the other hand, immigrants are not generally expected to conform to Israelite holiness.[34]

Christophe Nihan suggests that a change in the legal status of the immigrant in H, as compared to earlier legal texts (Covenant Code and the Deuteronomic law), goes together with a change in social and economic status (Nihan 2011).[35] While immigrants are still supposed to be dependent, according to those passages that reflect earlier legal collections,[36] in H they are actually envisaged as capable of becoming rich, lending money, and even owning Israelite slaves (Lev. 27:47–54), something only paralleled in Neh. 5 (Nihan 2011). Although immigrants are supposed to comply with a number of laws that previously concerned Israelites only (certain food laws and sacrificial laws),[37] and avoid those sins that pollute the land (Lev. 18:24–30), Nihan however suggests that they are never required to follow commands to achieve holiness (Nihan 2011).[38] This is supposed to relate to God's separation of the Israelites as holy in order for them to own land (Lev. 20:22–30), something an immigrant could never do, even if he became rich.

I hesitate at this last conclusion, because the sins to be avoided and the motivation (the land will vomit out its inhabitants) for Israelite holiness in Lev. 20 are too similar to the sins and the motivation in Lev. 18, where both Israelites and immigrants are addressed. The requirements are basically the same, except for the requirement to separate between clean and unclean animals, which is what causes the subsequent language of separation and holiness.

A sharp difference in the Holiness Code is found between immigrants (גרים, *gerim*) and foreign peoples (גוים, *goyim*), between integrated outsiders and "real" out-group. Those who do not follow the holiness laws, whether natives or immigrants, are killed or "cut out" (כרת),[39] because behavior that goes against the Holiness Code is associated with the former inhabitants who were expelled from the land because of their practices (Lev. 18:24–30; 20:22–26; 26:14–39). These peoples were "vomited out" because of their "abominations."

The terminology for expressing disgust is similar to that of Deuteronomy. The term תועבה, (to'evah), while absent in P, is frequently used in the Holiness Code, expressing disgust for a number of actions; it is used for same-sex male penetration (Lev. 18:22; 20:13), and as a blanket term for summarizing all the incest and sexual rules of Lev. 18, including bans on sex with animals and with women during menstruation (Lev. 18:26, 27, 29, 30).[40] The forbidden behaviors in Lev. 18 are expressly associated with the practices of the Egyptians and in particular of the Canaanites (v. 3) that made the land unclean (v. 27) and caused it to spit or vomit (קיא) out its inhabitants (v. 28). The imagery is repeated in Lev. 20:22, at the end of the corresponding list of sexual laws, where not only the land, but also God, is said to have felt disgust (this time not *to'evah* but *quts*, cf. שקץ in chapter 11) at the repulsive behavior of the former inhabitants (v. 23). This obviously refers to the preceding list of sexual sins, but is associated with the distinction between clean and unclean animals in the conclusion (vv. 24–5) and the motivation (20:26) is that the people should be holy as God is holy (cf. 11:44).

Just as in Deuteronomy, the role of fear is seldom spelled out explicitly in the Holiness Code, but here, too, disgust interacts with fear. The intersection of disgust and fear is well known; both emotions are adaptive, and have a functional value in protecting an organism against perceived threats. Both are innate but culturally conditioned in similar manners. Perceived threats of bodily harm or of being rejected, i.e., threats to bodily and social integrity, cause people to avoid unknown others, and to experience fear and/or disgust (Woody and Teachman 2000).

The strong language of disgust that we find in the Holiness Code can be interpreted as partly based on fear of foreign practices, i.e., xenophobia. At the same time, some of these practices do not seem to be unknown, in which case the language of disgust has the function of scaring people into obedience by associating certain behaviors with foreigners.

It seems that the Holiness Code has not just further developed an empathic attitude toward immigrants from the Covenant Code and the Deuteronomic core, but expects a higher degree of integration and appeals to shared experience and divine concern. At the same time the Holiness Code has integrated the harsh attitudes toward foreign peoples found in the Deuteronomic framework. Disgust at foreign behavior is extended to a number of practices and utilized for convincing Israelites of the need to protect group integrity at all costs, implicitly suggesting xenophobic and ethnocentric propensities. Neither affective nor cognitive empathy can mitigate divine and human condemnation of foreign behaviors; in this way empathy is efficiently constrained by strong associations of otherness and feelings of revulsion, and thus restricted to complying immigrants, who are expected to follow Israelite norms to a greater extent than previously.

An analysis of the emotions displayed in the Holiness Code thus strengthens the idea of a post-exilic context, in which the Israelite society contains a larger proportion of non-Israelites than before, some of whom were wealthy. Experiences of hardships and exile have resulted in an attitude to resident non-Israelites that displays an experiential type of empathy with a strong affective component. Love for one's neighbor and the immigrant is seen as a part of holiness law to the same extent as ritual and sexual instructions. This is dependent, however, on the integrated outgroup adapting to social and religious norms, thus becoming increasingly assimilated. Fear is not expressed toward this group as such, but the requirements that immigrants should comply in most respects with Israelite holiness law suggest a fear that they might otherwise pollute both sanctuary and community and put the people at risk. Fear is also expressed of foreign peoples and of foreign practices, as well as of being once more exiled from the land, although mainly through the use of disgust language.

The provenance of the Holiness Code is thus likely to be understood as the emerging and somewhat limited Jewish Temple state under the early Persian rule, in which Israelites were striving for a high degree of Torah faithfulness and *gerim* sometimes had an unquestionable position in society. Non-Israelites seem to have become increasingly accepted, both by necessity and because of Israelite experience of the exile, but on the condition that they adapt to Israelite practice. Otherwise they would constitute a serious threat to Israelite identity, religion, and culture, similar to those surrounding foreign nations, whose powers were feared and whose practices were abhorred.

Fear of divine punishment

As already mentioned, fear of the unknown or other is frequently balanced by attraction, in a paradoxical way. While such attraction may be understood as adaptive, having evolved because it counteracts inbreeding (cf. Fishbein 2002), and hence functional on one level, it can clearly be understood as causing problems for the integrity, cohesion, and group identity of a people. The need to control such attraction is displayed by the law about the captive woman (Deut. 21:10-14) and the problems involved are further illustrated by narratives about Israelite men taking foreign women.[41] While such women could become fully integrated more easily than male immigrants, they were still considered a threat to Israelite religion and faithful obedience to the law, which must somehow be dealt with. Threats of divine punishment are thus utilized to strengthen the impact of various laws. Fear of God is employed both explicitly and implicitly as a deterrent in order to enforce obedience. Interestingly enough, this intimidating technique is used for reinforcing not only fear of foreigners, but also empathy toward them.

Scaring people to empathy

Fear as deterrent characterizes the theophany that concludes the Ten Commandments (Exod. 20:18-20). In the Covenant Code itself this can be exemplified particularly in the apodictic laws, although one could argue that the death penalty in general has a deterring function and relies on fear of a divine command. Similarly, the threat to "consecrate to destruction" (חרם, *haram*) for worshiping other gods (Exod. 22:19 [ET 20]) refers at least in the present literary context back to the threat of divine punishment following the First Commandment (Exod. 20:5). Fear of God is implicitly suggested in the casuistic laws on keeping others' property (Exod.

22:6-14 [ET 7-15]). A declaratory oath is involved, a self-curse, which relies on divine punishment as the inevitable consequence of false swearing. Fear clearly has a deterrent function here, although not explicitly spelled out (Westbrook and Wells 2009, 46-47).

References to fear of God are more explicit in the apodictic laws. According to Exod. 22:21-3 (ET 22-4), God's wrath will come upon those who maltreat immigrants, widows, and orphans. The talion principle applies, so that disobedience to this humanitarian law will result in a similar fate; the perpetrator will be killed by God. Empathy is thus motivated by fear of divine punishment. This also applies to the following rule about lending and taking pledges (Exod. 22:24-6 [ET 25-7]). If the poor man's cloak is not returned before night he will call on the compassionate God who will listen. Here the threat is less explicit, but the juxtaposition of the two laws and the repetition of the statement that God will listen, implies the same punishment. One could argue that these threats are in effect an appeal to the recipients' experience of war and loss of family, seeking an affective response to the imagined fate of one's own family and, in extension, to the fate of those who are presently struck by such unfortunate circumstances. In the latter case God's care for the underprivileged is motivated by him being merciful (חנון, *hanun*). God is thus portrayed as capable of an affective and/or cognitive type of empathy that challenges the recipients of the command. However, such appeals are apparently not considered sufficient, since fear of divine punishment is adduced to effect obedience.

In the concluding supplement to the Covenant Code (Exod. 23:20-33), fear of divine punishment is a more or less explicit motivation for obeying the messenger or angel of the Lord (Exod. 23:20-1). As already mentioned above, God will annihilate the six foreign peoples mentioned (Amorites, Hittites, Perizzites, Canaanites, Hivites, and Jebusites) by sending fear and confusion (Exod. 23:27). While the Israelites are envisaged as the instruments for this (vv. 24, 31), the emphasis lies on divine intervention. While the prohibition against entering into covenants with these peoples is motivated by the risk of idolatry (Exod. 23:32-3), the Israelites are not, however, scared into obedience as in subsequent legal collections. Although this section is (Proto-)Deuteronomistic in character, it does not yet display the techniques of deterrence that can be found in Deuteronomy.

Deterrent techniques in Deuteronomy

As already mentioned, fear of foreign peoples and the threat of idolatry that they represent play a prominent role in Deuteronomy. The conclusion to the Covenant Code corresponds to Deut. 7, which was discussed in the previous section. Deut. 7:1 mentions the same six nations that should be "consecrated to destruction," adding one: the Girgashites. The emphasis here is on avoiding intermarriage and destroying cult places and idols, rather than on annihilation. We have also discussed the ambiguous war laws (Deut. 20), with their conflicting views on the taking of booty, followed by the law of the captive woman, which contains no conditions (Deut. 21:10-14), as probably belonging to different redactional layers.

In Deuteronomy, fear of divine punishment for disobedience is clearly expressed. Sometimes it is also stated that God will cause fear among his enemies (Deut. 2:25; cf.

7:23).⁴² This is not conspicuous, however, in the humanitarian laws that correspond to those in the Covenant Code, where fear of divine punishment is not a major motivation. In Deut. 10:12–11:1, for example, fear of God (יראה את יהוה) is "fear" in the sense of religious attachment and service rather than fear of punishment: "Yahweh, your god, you shall fear him and serve him and adhere to him and swear in his name" (Deut. 10:20). Humanitarian behavior is motivated by empathy and love (10:19), rather than by fear of punishment. This applies to the list of humanitarian laws in Deut. 24:6–22 as well. The motivation for returning the poor man's cloak before sundown is divine blessing and righteous status (Deut. 24:13). Even the one threat in the case of paying the day-laborer the same day, is relatively mild, or at least indirect: (v 15) "you will incur (the guilt of) sin" (והיה בך חטא).

The Deuteronomic framework, however, expressly utilizes fear of divine punishment to deter Israel from associating with foreign peoples. We have already seen that this fear is often associated with emotional disgust and used for outlining the limits of group belonging, in order to protect group integrity. Fear of divine punishment seems to be part of this strategy, too. God will revenge apostasy (7:10), the Israelites are warned against being caught in the trap of idolatry (7:16, 25). Participation in such disgusting activities will result in the Israelites themselves being "consecrated to destruction" and annihilated (7:26; 8:19–20). Prophets, idolaters, and cities that advocate idolatry must be promptly annihilated (Deut. 13).

The use of fear of divine punishment as a deterrent to make people comply with the law is most accentuated in the curses (Deut. 28:15–68).⁴³ This is a vehement crescendo leading up to the exile, containing all thinkable and unthinkable atrocities and horrors that could possibly fall upon the people in case they would not obey the law. The list gives numerous examples of fear of death and disease as well as of animal fear and of interpersonal fear. The latter category is mostly focused on war, siege, occupation, and captivity by enemies, which means that fear of divine punishment actually reinforces fear of foreigners. In this way, any attraction to the unknown or other is countered by all possible means.

I am the Lord: A demand for holiness

The Holiness Code's focus on Israelite holiness is motivated by an understanding of Yahweh's holy presence as a potential life-threatening danger to the people. This is the case already in the sacrificial laws and purity laws (Lev. 10:1–3; 15:31; 16:2), but spelled out and developed in the Holiness Code.

The laws in Lev. 17–27 are so frequently interspersed with the comment "I am Yahweh" that a full list is unnecessary. In a sense, this statement carries with it an implicit threat: God is holy and requires holiness. Disobedience against the Holiness Code puts not only the perpetrator but also the people at large at severe risk.

Occasionally this is spelled out in full. In Lev. 18:24–30 the laws on sexual relationships are concluded with an explanation: they cause uncleanness to the land, and this is the reason why the land vomited out its former inhabitants. This is followed by a warning: this could happen to the Israelites as well. Fear of divine punishment thus becomes a motivation for adhering to these "moral" purity laws. Similarly, the *karet* punishment is stated for inappropriate handling of the *shelamim* sacrifice (Lev.

19:5–8), for sacrifices to Molok (20:1–6), and for a priest who approaches sacrificial gifts in a state of impurity (22:1–3). But even the frequent repetition of "I am Yahweh" within the humanitarian laws of Lev. 19 implies a divine threat against those who do not follow these rules, even if this is not explicitly stated.

Just like Deuteronomy, the Holiness Code uses threats of divine punishment as a deterrent measure, for scaring people into obedience. This is most obvious in Lev. 26, which is related to Deut. 28, but carries particular traits of the Holiness Code. The context is one of promise and threat associated with the keeping of the Holiness Code. Obedience will cause God never to loathe the people (v. 11), but if the people loathe God's commands (v. 15), God will loathe them (v. 30). If they are exiled, however, although the land will have to be compensated for its sabbaths by lying waste, God will not loathe the people and break the covenant, although they have loathed God's commands (vv. 43, 44). The promises and threats seem to refer to the laws of worship, sabbaths, and land in Lev. 23–5. The idea of God feeling disgust is previously found in Lev. 20:23, and the imagery of the land vomiting out the people because of its disgusting practices is found in Lev. 18:24–30 and 20:22–6, but there is nothing about the sexual sins of Lev. 18–20 in Lev. 26. Moreover, a different term for disgust is used,[44] and it is not the land that loathes the people, but God. The land is not portrayed as actively vomiting the people out, but passively as being laid waste by God (vv. 32–5). The *topos* of exile is the same as in Lev. 18:25–8 and 20:22–4, but the imagery is quite different and there are good reasons for assigning this section of the Holiness Code to a late stage.[45]

Like Deut. 28, the warnings of Lev. 26 do not refer to any specific sins, but to disobedience of God's commands in general. The list of fearful punishment relates especially to the latter part of the Holiness Code, i.e., its laws of worship, sabbaths, and land (Lev. 23–5), since those are the issues alluded to, while the sexual sins from the earlier chapters are not. The list of threats in the Holiness Code, however, is not as vehement as that of Deuteronomy and although frightening, it does not repeatedly emphasize fear as the result of these punishments. While Deuteronomy's list ends in exile, the Holiness Code suggests conversion and return, explaining the necessity of the exile through the land's need of restitution, because of the sabbaths that were not kept. Although enemies are mentioned in Lev. 26, their role is downplayed, by God's speaking in the first person; God is envisaged here as the direct agent of most punishing acts and there is no emphasis on foreign peoples as enemies to be feared. The impression is that this has already happened and that a strong reminder should be sufficient for the recipients to fear God enough to keep the holiness laws, which are necessary for continued restoration. Lev. 26 does not really seem to count on people's fear of foreigners for upholding ethnocentrism. The text does threaten with divine punishment, but is not as aggressive as the corresponding passage in Deuteronomy.

Dangerous demons and purification rites

In the Holiness Code, we have noted that divine holiness was considered dangerous, and that this necessitated adherence to particular holiness laws. Just as in the case of fear of punishment, a fear of dangerous holiness can be utilized as deterrent for enforcing legal obedience. There is a difference, however, between this type of fear of the divine and compliance because of threats of divine punishment. Punishment is more like a ruler's display of power to enforce his will, while the dangers associated with divine holiness are immediate and irrational, dependent on the supernatural and uncontrollable nature of divine beings.

This characteristic is something that divine beings share with lesser divinities and demonic powers. Their holiness, impurity, or influence is experienced as threatening in similar ways and they are feared not because they have instituted particular rules or laws, but because of their presence or essence, which may threaten human lives and thus needs to be handled appropriately. Fear of demonic powers can thus be seen to lie behind a number of behaviors that the modern mind would classify as ritual. We should, however, again remind ourselves that the ancients, just like a number of present-day non-Western cultures, would not have made a clear distinction between moral and ritual actions (cf. Kazen 2008; 2011, 20–31).

Fear of the demonic world

Fear of the supernatural, divine beings or demons, was a natural part of life in the ancient world. Such fear carries traits of all four analytical categories previously mentioned. Death, injury, or illness was often ascribed to invisible causes, such as the influence of personal spirits or demons, regardless of whether visible causes were available in addition. *Fears of death and disease* are thus blended with *interpersonal fear*. Fear of demons is also akin to *animal fear*, since demons are envisaged as nonhuman, or "post-human" beings, and often take on animal traits. Like some of the real or imagined animals threatening human beings, demons are often associated with *open places*, deserts, waters, and foreign areas, which are unsafe and in which it is difficult to seek refuge quickly or to protect oneself.

Vestiges of demon belief and demonic fear can be seen in a number of purification rites, in spite of more or less successful attempts to integrate them within a priestly sacrificial system. Following the lead of Yehezkel Kaufmann, many of these rites can be read as originally intent on exorcising demonic powers, and "retained magical features, so deeply rooted as to defy extirpation" (Kaufmann 1960, 102). Others, such as Baruch Levine and Jacob Milgrom, have subscribed to this general view, although they all differ as to the extent to which priestly theology managed to refashion or abolish earlier magical and demonic ideas. We will not enter that discussion here, nor the one about evolutionary interpretations of religion in general. Suffice it to point out those purification rites that are particularly suggestive of an underlying fear of demonic activity.

Sending demons back to where they belong

The most conspicuous rites may be those at the beginning of the purification from skin disease, and after the repair of a "leprous" house (Lev. 14:1–7, 14–18, 25–9, 49–53). After inspection, purification begins with a bird rite. At the end of the purification period subsequent to the healing of skin disease, blood and oil from the ʾasham (אשם) offering are smeared on the right ear, thumb, and big toe of the healed person.

This smearing has obvious similarities with Zoroastrian practices for chasing away the corpse demoness, as described in *Vendidād*, although the latter rites include the treatment of many more parts of the body (*Vendidād* 8.40–71. Cf. Kazen 2015).

In the bird rite at the beginning of purification from skin disease, or after the repair of a "leprous" house, two "live," probably wild, birds are used (Milgrom 1991, 833–34), together with cedar wood, red wool, and hyssop. One bird is slaughtered over a bowl with water, after which the other is dipped in it, together with the wood, wool, and hyssop. The healed person is sprinkled and the live bird is released in the open fields. The rite is generally interpreted as transferring the disease or demonic influence to the live bird, which takes it away, never to return again (Wright 1987a, 77–78. For Namburbi rituals to purify houses, see Maul 1994, 97–100). In Mesopotamian religion, impurity is often seen as the result of demonic activity and a number of rituals aim at exorcising the demons, sending them back to their origin. These may be the river, the open uninhabited country, or the underworld (Maul 1994, 248–61). Similarly, the Hittites thought of open areas and the underworld, together with mountain areas and foreign lands, as disposing places for impurities, although evils were generally thought of in more impersonal terms (Maul 1994, 261–71).

The use of red wool in purification or disposal rites is also found in Mesopotamian transfer rituals, for example in a *Shurpu* ritual, in which the patient is sprinkled, although the wool itself is burnt (Shurpu i 9–23 [the red wool is mentioned in lines 14 and 21], in Reiner 1958, 11), in a *Malli* thread manipulation ritual (Malli i 37–40, in Wright 1987a, 41–42), or in a number of transfer rites. In a Mesopotamian healing ritual, red wool is tied to the foot of a frog that is explicitly said to return the evil to its steppe. Red wool is also used in an amulet from ancient Uruk (Text no. 248, Vs. 4, in Weiher 1998, 58, 60; cf. Scurlock 2002, 215) and in a Neo-Assyrian goat ritual (Scurlock 2002, 211–12). The release of birds is mentioned in Mesopotamian and Hittite texts, both as carriers of evil in various rites, and in prayers and incantations (Maul 1994, 90–91, 93; cf. all the "bird-*namburbis*," 229–69). Numerous examples are provided by Wright and Milgrom (Wright 1987a, 80–83; Milgrom 1991 834). Birds occur frequently in Hittite and Hurrian sacrificial rites in association with chthonic deities.[46] Milgrom suggests that birds are chosen in the priestly ritual not because they are favored by chthonic deities, but only because they transport the evil away (Milgrom 1991, 834). The use of two birds in Ugaritic texts, as a typical sacrifice for the *'Inasu-'Ilima*, the "mankind of the gods" or divinized dead, is conspicuous, however, although in these texts both birds are sacrificed.[47]

The bird rite in Lev. 14 is probably the surviving apotropaic rite that retains most original traits, since it is not incorporated into the sacrificial system, and is not forced in under the *hattat* (חטאת) umbrella—perhaps because the wild birds crucial to the rite were no sacrificial animals (cf. Milgrom 1991, 833). While the priest has been made to effect the sprinkling and release, he only seems to supervise the ritual arrangements and the slaughtering. Milgrom suggests that the rite "was retained not because Israel's priests wanted it but probably because the people at large demanded it, practiced it, and would not have tolerated its deletion" (Milgrom 1991, 838).

A similar function to ward off demonic evil is likely for the origin of the scapegoat ritual (Lev. 16). Space allows only a most cursory discussion. The ritual is barely integrated into the sacrificial system but goats are at least sacrificial animals, although the goat for Azazel is not a sacrifice, but rather a vehicle. The identification of Azazel with a desert demon (e.g., de Vaux 1964, 86–87; Levine 1974, 79–82; Kaufmann 1960, 114–15; Milgrom 1991, 1020–21) has been questioned; express identification is said to be late and the sending away has even been interpreted as a liberation.[48] In view of the use of animals as vehicles for sending away evil elsewhere in ancient Near East (ANE) texts, however, this must be deemed very unlikely (Maul 1994, 90–91). The Day of Atonement ritual looks very much like the conflation of two rites, and Milgrom's suggestion that at one stage the cleansing of the sanctuary was accomplished by a pair of goats through a rite closely resembling the bird rite is plausible (Milgrom 1991, 1044). Milgrom also suggests that originally this was no calendrical rite but an emergency rite, as most similar ANE rituals.[49]

Exorcistic purgation of temples by animal carcasses is known from the ANE; the most well-known concerns the Babylonian *Akitu* or New Year festival. Wright has collected numerous Hittite and Mesopotamian parallel rituals with purification motives (Wright 1987a, 31–74). Often an animal or a person is sent away, adorned or accompanied by gifts of appeasement. Evil is thus returned to its origin: the open country or steppe, foreign lands, or the underworld. In a ritual from the *Shurpu* series, impure material is disposed of in the wilderness, where desert deities are active.[50] The association of wilderness or open, uninhabited country with the underworld is common in Mesopotamian texts (Milgrom 1991, 1072). Nevertheless, Wright stresses the differences between the biblical rite and Hittite or Mesopotamian parallels: the scapegoat is just a transporter, not a substitute, and Azazel is not an angry deity in need of appeasement (Wright 1987a, 49–50, 53–54, 72–74). This is true, of course, for the priestly adaptation of the rite that is described in Leviticus. As for its origin, however, Wright admits that it may have carried just those traits in which the biblical rite now differs from ANE parallels due to priestly alterations (Wright 1987a, 73–74).

Demonic threat and revenge

The red heifer, burned to obtain ashes for the purification water (Num. 19) is another apotropaic rite, most probably originating as exorcist magic to ward off demonic threat. The rabbinic awareness of, and uneasiness about, the rite's apparent exorcist character is displayed by the oft-quoted saying of Yohanan ben Zakkai, in response to a gentile question, in which he explains the red heifer rite by comparing it to exorcism (*Pesiq. Rab Kah.* 4:7). While Yohanan subsequently gives a theological explanation to his disciples, the tradition is evidence for the fact that the exorcist nature of the rite was generally acknowledged, although not necessarily accepted.

The slaughtering, burning, and collecting of ashes are all done by laymen. As in the bird rite, the priest's role is mainly to supervise the event, except for an initial gesture, sprinkling some blood toward the sanctuary, and throwing the cedar wood, red wool, and hyssop into the fire. The same ingredients are used as in the bird rite. The rite is incorporated into the sacrificial system to the extent that is possible without loss of its crucial characteristics; it is explicitly identified as a *hattat* (חטאת) sacrifice (Num. 19:9, 17), but almost as an afterthought, justifying its purificatory effect. Like a *hattat*, it purifies the recipients. Unlike the *hattat*, however, the sprinkling is mainly on people, as in the bird rite. The initial gesture toward the sanctuary seems more like a forced adaptation (cf. Milgrom 1981). The sprinkling of ashes seems to have been carried out by minors, at least toward the end of the Second Temple period, which further attests to its origin outside of the priestly system (*mPar.* 3:2–4; *Barn.* 8:1).[51]

Yet another rite with apotropaic traits is the breaking of a heifer's neck in the case of an unsolved murder (Deut. 21:1–9). The explicit purpose of this rite is to erase the collective bloodguilt that otherwise would apply, in view of the fact that no murderer can be found and the blood of the victim thus cannot be avenged.[52] The rite has been subject to numerous interpretations, many of which are speculative, with little grounding in the text.[53] Its basic character as an elimination ritual, focused on the bloodguilt that adheres to the land, seems nevertheless obvious.[54] Interestingly, the rite is said to effect *kipper*, atonement, which may lead to an association with the *hattat* sacrifice, although the present rite is wholly outside of the priestly sacrificial sphere. The agents of every specified action are the elders (and judges) of the nearest town. The priests pop up in v. 5, like puppets with no active function whatsoever, although in theory they are ascribed the authority to decide in disputes and assaults. In actual fact they seem to do nothing; their purported role is fulfilled by the elders and judges. It is very difficult to avoid the conclusion that their sudden appearance is due to a redactional insertion at a late stage in the textual formation, turning the focus from the ancient rite to the similarly appended prayer for forgiveness (vv. 8 [or 8a], 9) (cf. Milgrom 1981, 478; Tigay 1996, 475; Otto 1999, 265–68. For a different view, see Willis 2001, 149–58).

The focus on bloodguilt and revenge fits with the Deuteronomic law about cities of refuge (Deut. 19:1–13). In cases of inadvertent murder, no danger seems to threaten the perpetrator as long as he stays within a city of refuge. In some unexplained manner, the existence of cities of refuge seems to eliminate bloodguilt (19:10). According to the parallel passage in Num. 35:9–34, the killer may even return without danger after the death of the high priest. A danger does, however, threaten the people, if the murder is not avenged in the case of premeditated murder, or, when the murderer is unknown, unless the heifer rite is carried out. While it is *not explicitly* stated in Deut. 21, collective bloodguilt seems to be associated with some kind of impurity of the land, the *'adamah* on which the corpse has been found. According to Deut. 19:13, some misfortune implicitly results from the negligence of blood revenge. And according to Num. 35:33–4, the land (*'erets*) must be neither profaned, nor made impure by the shedding of blood, and the land can only have atonement (*kuppar*) for shed blood by the blood of the murderer. This is clearly purity language related to the concept of the holiness of the land that is prominent in the Holiness Code, and associates unavenged bloodguilt and thus the heifer rite with corpse impurity.[55] The contamination of the ground by corpses is, however, conspicuous in Zoroastrian religion, where the corpse is thought of as being entered by the corpse demoness at death, and in certain circumstances subsequent purification of the ground was deemed necessary (Choksy 2005, 11, 16–19).[56] Although this applies to corpses in general and not particularly to unavenged murder, Persian burial practices seem to have been intent on protecting the earth from impurity, by the use of either burial towers or stone tombs (Choksy 2005, 17).[57] Victims of murder that were left on the ground would, however, contaminate the earth with demonic influence.

Milgrom suggests that "corpse contamination evoked an obsessive, irrational fear in individuals" (Milgrom 1991, 275). This is corroborated by the fact that Herod had problems settling people in Tiberias because it was built over a burial ground. The isolation and the cry of the person with a skin disease ("impure, impure"), to protect others from unintended contact, also suggests an underlying fear (Lev. 13:45–6). The obviously apotropaic vestiges of the above-mentioned rites suggest a fear of demonic influence or activity, unless this is warded off by appropriate means; the bird rite and the burning of the red heifer have exorcist traits, and the scapegoat is clearly a transfer rite, too. Rites in cases of corpse impurity or murder are necessary in order to avoid misfortune or death. While in the Holiness Code the punishments for defiling the sanctuary or the land—death, *karet* (כרת), or expulsion—always come from God, these rites suggest a widespread fear of other lesser powers, inhabiting the underworld, wastelands, or open places to which various impurities and evils are returned. The basic emotion of fear in all its aspect can thus be understood as one underlying component of ideas of impurity and rites of purification.

Conclusions

In spite of scoring low in some schemas of moral emotions, fear certainly plays an important role in human behavior, including those actions that we would usually designate "moral." Although basically a self-interested emotion, fear has a self-conscious side, which sometimes allows it to play an important role in motivating adherence to various legal precepts. Fear can in fact be utilized both for reinforcing empathic attitudes and for counteracting them. Fear of that which is unknown or foreign often goes together with disgust and the two emotions interact and blend. Both fear and disgust have an evolutionary adaptive value, protecting the organism against perceived threats of bodily harm or of being rejected, i.e., these emotions respond to threats against bodily or social integrity.

In this chapter we have looked particularly at fear of foreigners, fear of divine punishment, and fear of demonic influence. In the Covenant Code, fear of divine punishment actually motivates prosocial action—it reinforces empathic attitudes—and although we may find traces of disease-avoidance, there is no explicit expression of xenophobic fear. In the Holiness Code fear similarly motivates compliance with holiness laws. Although fear functions as a deterrent in both cases, the Holiness Code expresses fear of divine essence rather than retaliatory action. The danger is constituted by the numinous power of divine holiness, which necessitates a closer integration of non-Israelite immigrants. At the same time, xenophobic attitudes are implicitly expressed although partly masked behind strong disgust language. People are scared into obedience through the association of unacceptable moral and ritual behaviors with foreigners and expulsion from the land.

The situation in Deuteronomy is slightly different. In the Deuteronomic core, we find traces of disease-avoidance and disgust at foreign practices, but in particular evidence for various types of empathic reactions toward immigrants, building on the underlying Covenant Code. Fear is not, however, appealed to for obedience to particular rules. Although the Israelites are seen as the agents of the driving away of foreign peoples, this is not exploited for ethnocentric or xenophobic purposes to any great extent. In the Deuteronomic framework, however, the primary role of fear seems to be deterrence against foreign peoples and their idolatrous practices. The focus is on idolatry and the threat of divine punishment for disobedience, not against particular commandments, but in general. This comes to a climax in the curses, the function of which clearly is to enforce obedience by scaring the people with every possible threat. Although that which is supposed to be feared is divine punishment, what in effect threaten the Israelites are foreign practices and hence foreign peoples. Fear of God is thus exploited to strengthen ethnocentric attitudes and to evoke xenophobia.

The fear of demonic influence or harm, displayed in some purification rites in the purity laws of Leviticus, as well as in certain apotropaic rites in Numbers and Deuteronomy, is more akin to the fear of divine holiness that we find in the Holiness Code. These are rituals that seem to lie at the intersection of the priestly cult with popular religion. Fear of becoming, and especially remaining impure is bolstered by divine threats, but under the surface demonic influence is detectable. The rites discussed contain a number of traits that are plausibly associated with demons and their habitats, with parallels available in other ANE texts.

Fear of demonic influence can be understood to involve all four generally acknowledged types: interpersonal fear, fear of death, disease and injury, fear of animals, and fear of open places—as demons often take animal form and are often associated with desert places. Fear of divine punishment naturally involves the first two, but fear of foreigners, at least fear of foreign lands (as in exile), might be understood to involve the fourth category in addition, if what we call agoraphobic fear is taken in a broad sense as fear of unknown places, or locations that lack safety and protection.

We have talked consistently of fear, although fear is sometimes distinguished from anxiety as being post-stimulus rather than anticipatory. The distinction is difficult to uphold, however, since reasonable (or even unreasonable) anticipations function as stimuli. In most of the cases discussed above, fear concerns anticipated events and motivates their prevention. Since human belief systems are based on experience and worldview, we might question whether it is justified to uphold a sharp distinction between anxiety and fear.

Our observations concerning the role of fear in different Pentateuchal collections and layers may be related to the tricky discussion of the date and provenance of various material. A pre-exilic date for the Covenant Code seems reasonable. Fear of divine punishment is utilized for motivating adherence to humanitarian rules, and the empathy appealed to displays no immediate experience of exile or strong foreign influence. There is no explicit xenophobic fear expressed, and it is unlikely that such a text would be shaped in a context where Israelites are about to be occupied or live among foreigners. Immigrants seem to be a marginal group with regard to number as well as to socioeconomic status. The concluding supplement at the end of Exod. 23, however, is different, referring to the annihilation of neighboring peoples. Although there are Deuteronomistic traits, Deuteronomy's deterrent techniques are largely absent in this section.

In Deuteronomy the difference between the role of fear in core passages and in the framework is evident. While the Israelites are the agents of driving away neighboring peoples in the core, this is not exploited for ethnocentric or xenophobic purposes. The framework, however, as well as some of the material that is often regarded as supplements (Kratz 2000, 133), combines "love" for immigrants with strong xenophobic tendencies. Laws concerning immigrants are developed in a direction that suggests an emotionally charged experiential type of empathy, which would counteract an otherwise strong xenophobic tendency. Immigrants are still, however, understood as dependent and in limited number. This does not fit an exilic context. Fear and disgust are combined against the idolatrous practices of foreigners, and fear of divine punishment for assimilation is expressed to the extreme, especially in the curses of Deut. 28, where the consequences of exile are not only suggested but also described. The need to strengthen group integrity seems acute. This suggests a post-exilic, rather than a pre-exilic context. Deuteronomy's growth and development is a long complex process, and one should perhaps be content with the suggestion that the role of fear and interacting emotions does not preclude a pre-exilic Deuteronomic core, while suggesting a post-exilic context for much of the framework.

The Holiness Code presupposes greater integration between Israelites and immigrants, and has further developed empathic attitudes from the Covenant Code and the Deuteronomic core, appealing to shared experiences and divine concern. At the same time, Deuteronomy's harsh attitudes toward foreign peoples and their idolatry are also taken up. An implicit xenophobia is displayed, which no empathy can mitigate. The context, however, is one of divine holiness, which threatens the community, unless it conforms to various holiness laws. This also applies to resident immigrants, some of whom have attained a higher status than immigrants previously used to do. There is no explicit fear expressed against this group as such, but there is a fear that they might pollute community and sanctuary, and thus put the people at risk. A strong fear is displayed that the lack of holiness might lead to (a new) exile, although the explicit references are to the expulsion of former inhabitants. All this suggests a post-exilic date, more precisely during the early Persian period, at a time when the Second Temple was being established and the people were equated with the Jerusalem temple community. The supplement in Lev. 26 is probably a little later, from a time when this community has become more established. In this chapter fear is employed to scare people into more general obedience, although the threats are not half as vehement as the Deuteronomic curses on which it depends. God has become the sole agent of the prospective punishments and the text does not really appeal to xenophobic propensities to obtain group cohesion.

The apotropaic rites that express fear of demonic activities are difficult to date or contextualize. On the one hand they retain archaic traits and are likely to represent popular practices. On the other hand many of them give the impression of being squeezed into an emerging cultic system without fitting too well into the systemic constructions and categories that are attempted. Although the practices and some of the textual material are probably much older, most of these traditions are likely to have received their present shape and place within the Pentateuch at a fairly late stage of redaction, during the Persian period.

3

Liquid Life: Blood, Life, and Conceptual Metaphors in the Hebrew Bible and the Ancient Near East

Anne Katrine de Hemmer Gudme

In the following I shall suggest the category of conceptual metaphors as a lens through which to view the well-known notion in the Hebrew Bible that life resides in the blood, or rather that the blood *is* life. I shall turn first to the linking of blood and life in the Hebrew Bible and other ancient texts and then to conceptual metaphors.[1]

Life and Blood

In the Hebrew Bible and in ancient Greek and Mesopotamian texts blood is described as life itself. The blood is life and it animates the body in a way analogous to a battery that energizes a mechanical toy.

The key biblical passage is found in Gen. 9; the waters of the great flood have subsided and Yahweh is addressing Noah, setting down a new set of rules for the world now that the earth and its inhabitants have been given a fresh start. Yahweh blesses Noah and his descendants and commands them to be fertile and to fill the earth. Delivering every beast and bird and fish into their hand, he also permits humans to give up their strictly vegetarian diet and to become carnivores. This extended menu is immediately followed by a restriction in verse 4: "But flesh with its life (בנפשו), with its blood (דמו), you shall not eat."

Several commentators have noted how the blood in Gen. 9 is not a mere symbol of life—it *is* life (Vervenne 1993, 453; Gilders 2004, 18). The blood contains its own power and energy. Consider the blood of the murdered Abel that screams indignantly to Yahweh from the ground that has swallowed it (Gen. 4:10–11). Blood is life and life is not an acceptable part of the human diet, which is why it is separated from the flesh before it is eaten. This is emphasized in Deut. 12 in a passage that permits the consumption of meat in a profane context so that the butchering of an animal can take place even if it is not dedicated as a sacrifice in the sanctuary: "Only be certain not to eat the blood, for the blood is the life (כי הדם הוא הנפש), and you shall not eat the life with the flesh. You shall not eat it, you shall pour it out on the ground like water (כמים)" (vv. 23–4, cf. v. 16).

If the meat is slaughtered and offered as a sacrifice in the sanctuary, as for instance with the *shelamim* or well-being offering, the blood is not to be poured out "like water" but rather dashed around the sides of the altar: "And Aaron's sons the priests shall dash (וזרקו) the blood on the altar all around (סביב)" (Lev. 3:2, cf. vv. 8 and 13). Here it seems appropriate to address two common misunderstandings regarding the role of the blood in the Hebrew Bible. One is that it is forbidden to eat the blood, that is the life, because it belongs to Yahweh; the other is that the Hebrew Bible, with its particular focus on the significance of the blood, distinguishes itself significantly from its neighboring cultures in Mesopotamia and Greece. In what remains of this section I address both in turn.

"All fat is Yahweh's"

It is a common assumption that the prohibition against the consumption of blood in the Hebrew Bible is due to the circumstance that the blood, and with it the life, belongs to Yahweh (Milgrom 1991, 215–16). This understanding, however, is based on an erroneous reading of what is actually written about the blood in the prescriptions for the *shelamim* in Lev. 3.

The *shelamim* distinguishes itself by being the only type of sacrifice in the Hebrew Bible where the main part of the sacrificial animal's flesh is assigned to the donor and his family (Jensen 1998, 179–90). The fat (חלב) of the animal and the kidneys (הכלית) are to be burnt on the altar for Yahweh (Lev. 3:3–5.9–11.14–16). The fat is called "the food of the fire offering" (לחם אשה) and "a pleasing odor for Yahweh" (ריח ניחח, Eberhart 2011, 24–29). As mentioned above, however, the blood is to be dashed (זרקו) "on the altar all around" (סביב). In 3:16–17 the prescriptions regarding the *shelamim* are concluded in the following way: "All fat is Yahweh's (ליהוה כל־חלב). It is a perpetual statute for your generations in all your dwellings: you shall not eat any fat or any blood." Neither blood nor fat is allowed for consumption, but it is only the fat that is specifically identified as belonging to Yahweh (Jensen 2000, 273). The fat is converted into smoke on the altar and as such it ascends to Yahweh, but the blood is dashed on the sides of the altar and from there it presumably seeps into the ground (Jensen 2000, 276; Eberhart 2002, 30).[2] Thus the handling of the blood in connection with the *shelamim* is not significantly different from the handling of the blood in connection with profane slaughter, where the blood is poured out on the ground "like water." In both cases, the consumption of blood is prohibited and therefore the blood is disposed of.

In the Hebrew Bible, then, though the consumption of blood is forbidden because blood is understood to be life, no explanation is given as to why such consumption of life is not allowed. The common explanation that all life, like all fat, belongs to Yahweh does not in fact appear in the text (Gilders 2004, 18–19).[3]

Hans Jørgen Lundager Jensen has suggested that the blood and the life are to return to the earth, because the earth in the Hebrew Bible is the source of life. It is the earth that sprouts (תדשא) plants and trees on Yahweh's command (Gen. 1:11). The earth is not an independent being with a creative force that stands in opposition to Yahweh's, but it is capable of bringing forth (תוצא) the green plants in Gen. 1:12 and in that it becomes the source of life (Jensen 2000, 272, 276–77). Here we may find an answer to why life may not be eaten together with the flesh. According to Deut. 22:6–7, if one finds a bird's nest they are not to take the mother but only the nestlings and the eggs. The reason for the prohibition given in 22:7 is "that it may go well with you and that you may prolong days," but the rationale appears to be that the proper conduct is to eat from the earth's larder, but never to exhaust the source of life (Jensen 2000, 276–77). Extending this logic to Lev. 3, the nestlings and the eggs relate to the mother as the flesh relates to the blood: that is, the products and riches of earth or life relate to the earth or life itself. Just as man at the end of his life must return to the ground from which he was taken (Gen. 3:19), the blood, which is the life, must return to its source, the earth.

The Greeks and the Mesopotamians

It is often argued that the identification of blood with life in the Hebrew Bible is one of the features that distinguishes so-called ancient Israelite religion from the religions of its neighboring cultures (McCarthy 1969, 166–76; Milgrom 1991, 706; Vervenne 1993, 458–60; Biale 2007, 10).[4] The neighbors, such as Greece and Mesopotamia, were not in the least interested in blood, and if they were, blood had connections with the sinister deities of the underworld and was therefore identified with death rather than life (Vervenne 1993, 459).[5]

The link between blood and the chthonic particularly rests on a well-known passage from the *Odyssey*, where Odysseus journeys to the nether world to question the deceased seer Tiresias (Book XI). Odysseus follows the advice of Circe, and begins by digging a pit in which he pours libations of honey and milk, wine and water, and a sprinkling of barley meal. Finally he slaughters a black sheep and a black ram and their blood is poured into the pit. The spirits of the dead crowd around the pit, drawn by the fresh blood, and Odysseus has to keep them at bay with his sword to prevent them from drinking because he wants Tiresias to have the first sip. It is clear that the dead crave the blood and when they drink it, it seems to transform them; Tiresias is unable to foretell anything for Odysseus until he has tasted the blood (XI, 95–96) and Odysseus' own mother, Anticlea, does not seem to recognize her son until she has been allowed to drink (XI, 152–54). These narratives suggest that, even in Greek tradition, the dead hunger for the life that they are lacking and that the life, the blood, when given to them, returns to them some of their former strength and identity.[6] Like the Hebrew Bible, this passage seems to identify blood with life.

An identification of blood with life may also be behind the *Iliad*'s graphic description of the death of Hyperenor: "Thereafter Atreus' son smote with a thrust in the flank Hyperenor, shepherd of the host, and the bronze let forth the bowels, as it clove through, and his soul (ψυχή) sped hastening through the stricken wound, and darkness enfolded his eyes" (Book XIV, 516–19).[7] According to Jan Bremmer, *psychê* in Homeric literature has no psychological connection and it does not refer to a unitary soul. These aspects are later developments in the concept of *psychê* in Greek thought (Bremmer 2010, 11–29). In Homer, *psychê* rather denotes a kind of life-force: "*Psychê* is the basis for life and without it life is no longer possible" (Bremmer 2010, 12). Therefore, it seems reasonable to read the description of Hyperenor's death as an example of a Greek text that identifies blood with life as the life-force, *psychê*, leaves Hyperenor's body through his mortal wound.[8]

If we turn to Mesopotamia two texts in particular spring to mind: *Atrahasis*, the story of the hero, who survived the flood, and the epic poem *Enuma Elish*, which tells the story of how Marduk became the king of the gods.

In *Atrahasis*, the mother goddess Mami, who is also known as Nintu and Ninhursag, creates humanity with the help of the wise god Ea/Enki. The birth goddesses are also present. Humanity is created from a mixture of clay and the blood of the god Geshtu-e, who has been killed: "Nintu shall mix clay with his flesh and blood. Then a god and a man will be mixed together in clay" (Tablet I, iv, Dalley 1991, 15). In *Atrahasis*, the purpose of humanity is to "bear the load of the gods."

In *Enuma Elish* there is a very similar account of the creation of humanity: Marduk also decides to create humans so that they can work instead of the gods:

> Let me put blood together, and make bones too. Let me set up primeval man: Man shall be his name. Let me create a primeval man. The work of the gods shall be imposed (on him), and so they shall be at leisure. (Tablet VI, 5–8; Dalley 1991, 260–61)

The task falls on Marduk's father, Ea, who forms humanity from the blood of the deity, Qingu, who has been condemned to death and executed (Tablet VI, 33–35).

Whereas in Gen. 2:7 man is created by forming the dust from the ground and adding "the breath of life" (נשמת חיים), in *Atrahasis* humanity is created from blood and clay, and in *Enuma Elish* humanity is created simply from blood. In *Atrahasis*, the blood functions as a parallel to the breath of life in Gen. 2:7.[9] It is the substance that animates the flesh. In *Enuma Elish*, the blood constitutes the basis for both the body of the new creature and the life *inside* it (cf. Lambert 1993, 194).

Conceptual metaphors

The examples mentioned above are not an attempt to offer an exhaustive analysis of ancient Greek and Mesopotamian attitudes to blood, but they should be sufficient to illustrate that in Greece and Mesopotamia blood was not exclusively associated with death. Blood was rather perceived in accordance with the view found in the Hebrew Bible, namely as identical with or possessing life.[10]

Blood is the life of the flesh and if it is poured out, the flesh becomes inanimate. This identification of blood with life can of course be due to the empirical observation that when the blood leaves the body, so does life. This was how the Danish philologist Johannes Pedersen saw it: "Life is very closely connected with this red fluid which runs through the body; if it runs out, life itself runs out" (Pedersen 1926, 1.172). There is an additional way, however, to view the identification of blood with life and this is where the theory of conceptual metaphors becomes relevant.[11]

Conceptual metaphor theory originates in the field of cognitive linguistics. It rests on the assumption that metaphorical expressions are not merely the results of culturally established conventions of language and thought, but that they are actually rooted in deeply embedded and unconscious conceptual structures in the human brain.[12] Most complex conceptual metaphors are based on the so-called primary or primitive metaphors (Gibbs et al. 2004, 1197). Primary metaphors often occur cross-culturally and they are closely related to the concrete physical human experience of being a body in time and space (Slingerland 2004, 15–17). One example of a primary metaphor is the conception that MORE IS UP.[13] The understanding of MORE (increase) as UP (verticality) rests on a number of common everyday bodily experiences, such as orientating oneself vertically in space and an experience of quantity. If you add more liquid to a container or if you add stuff to a pile, the level goes up. In this way, our bodily experiences create a physical and tangible basis for our understanding of a concept like quantity. This leads to expressions such as "the prices have gone up" and "turn the volume down," where price and volume are quantified in terms of height (Johnson 1987, xv; Lakoff and Johnson 1999, 51).

Another example is the conception that PURPOSES ARE DESTINATIONS. Here the metaphor is based on an experience of going to a place to achieve something, such as walking to the coffee maker to get a cup of coffee; the achievement of a goal is linked with the experience of *getting there*, thus leading to expressions such as "he'll finish the job, but he's not quite there yet" (Lakoff and Johnson 1999, 52–53).

One bodily experience that is particularly helpful in understanding the identification of blood with life is our intimate awareness of our bodies as three-dimensional containers (Johnson 1987, 21). This awareness forms the basis for a metaphor such as ANGER IS HEATED LIQUID IN A CONTAINER. This metaphor leads to English expressions such as "let off steam," "blow your stack," and "make my blood boil." In the Hebrew Bible, there is a similar metaphor in use when an angry person is described as one whose nose becomes hot (ויחר־אף, for example of Jacob in Gen. 30:2 and of Yahweh in Exod. 4:14). These examples all point to notions of anger being conceptualized as a boiling liquid that bubbles and explodes and boils over. The metaphor is also rooted in an experience of the human body as a container filled with fluids such as blood, urine, and sweat, which can be heated if one is under pressure or exerts oneself physically (Gibbs et al. 2004, 1195–96). The expressions noted here can of course be explained with reference to the empirical experience of seeing a liquid come to the boil in a pot, but it is just as reasonable to assume that they are based on an experience of the body as a container filled with fluids (Gibbs et al. 2004, 1195).

The identification of blood with life in the Hebrew Bible, Mesopotamia, and Greece can be similarly based on a common empirical experience that life leaves the body simultaneously with the blood, but it may also be based on a conceptual or primary metaphor that stems from a universal physical experience that life is flowing in its container, the body. This is how we arrive at the concept of blood, liquid life, which can be poured into animals and people and which can again be poured out at death and return to the earth from where it can continue to act and yell and accuse if it sees fit.

The interesting thing about conceptual and primary metaphors is that, though in many ways they can be seen as universal and based on common human physical experiences, they are often expressed in different ways in different cultures (cf. Slingerland 2008a, 185–218). This means that one should not be too surprised that in the Hebrew Bible a dietary taboo was developed on the basis of the identification of blood with life, whereas in Greece and Mesopotamia no such dietary rule was present. Equally, one cannot conclude from the absence of a dietary restriction on the consumption of blood that the ancient Greeks and Mesopotamians were indifferent to blood or that they did not identify it with life (cf. Stowers 1998, 189–91; contra Vervenne 1993, 459–60). As we have seen there is nothing in the Greek and Mesopotamian sources to indicate indifference to blood.

It is also worth noting that conceptual metaphors are not exclusive. In the Hebrew Bible there is an unambiguous perception that blood is life. At the same time there is an equally unambiguous perception that breath is life, as in Gen. 2:7 where Yahweh forms man and breathes "the breath of life" (נשמת חיים) into his nostrils.[14] Just as the clay is mixed with blood in *Atrahasis* to bring it to life, so the dust is mixed with the breath of life as the animating ingredient in Gen. 2. Thus in the Hebrew Bible there are two different perceptions of where and what the animating ingredient is, but these two perceptions are not at odds with one another. Conceptual metaphors are not used to exclusively describe what the world is like. They do not eliminate ambiguity (Slingerland 2008a, 185). They enable humans to describe and understand feelings and concepts on the basis of a common physical experience.

The fat is life?

In fact, there may be a third perception in the Hebrew Bible of what the animating ingredient is, namely, the fat (חלב) that belongs to Yahweh. In his sweeping study, *Muelos: A Stone Age Superstition about Sexuality*, Weston La Barre traces the belief that life is the marrow (μυελός) and that it resides in the human body inside the bones, in the brain, and in semen.[15] This belief has, according to La Barre, led to as diverse phenomena as head hunting, pederasty, and the persistent conviction that masturbation causes mental illness (La Barre 1984). It may be that, although not explicitly stated in the Hebrew Bible, the reservation of the fat for Yahweh parallels the prohibition on the consumption of the blood; the blood must not be consumed because it is life and should return to its source, namely the earth, and the fat must not be eaten, because it is life and should return to its source, presumably Yahweh.

The restriction in the Hebrew Bible on the fat and kidneys of the sacrificial animal resembles the Greek sacrifice (θυσία) where the fat and bones are reserved for the gods (Jensen 1998, 279–81). According to the poet Hesiod, Prometheus tricked Zeus into choosing the inferior and inedible part of the sacrifice so that the juicy meat would be allotted to humans (see Vernant 1989, 21–86). La Barre suggests, however, that there was a certain sense of logic to the outcome of the story:

> Actually, nothing is more logical than that spirits should be served spirit-food. The gods are not being cheated, but are getting the stuff of life. The sacrifice to them of fat and bones therefore keeps immortal gods immortal. (La Barre 1984, 85)

So perhaps in the Hebrew Bible *fat is life* just as *blood is life*; both are *life* that originates from different sources and therefore must be handled differently at the time of death.[16]

Liquid life

To sum up, the notion in the Hebrew Bible and in Greek and Mesopotamian texts that the blood is the life of the body can be viewed as an example of a conceptual metaphor, "the body is a container filled with fluids." This understanding of blood as life is cross-cultural and it is deeply embedded in human cognition because it is rooted in the physical experience of the body as a container filled with fluids that can pulsate and bleed. The blood that flows red and warm is liquid life. It animates the body and brings humans to life, and when life ends the dead body, the container, must be drained so that the blood can return to the earth from whence it came.

4

"To Love"(אהב) in the Bible: A Cognitive-Evolutionary Approach

Ronit Nikolsky

Introduction

This chapter examines the use of the root *'-h-b* (אהב, to love) in the Hebrew Bible from a cognitive-evolutionary approach. It will show that the word "love" is used in three different meanings, which comply with three cognitive strategies described by Merlin Donald in his study on the evolution of human cognition, and will follow how the root translates from one strategy to the other.

The chapter will therefore demonstrate that ignoring the variety of cognitive strategies renders the research un-attentive to the text. It also shows that the meaning of emotional words in their biblical usage may be quite different from the one in our culture, so the modern meaning of the emotions should not be assumed to have existed in the biblical text; our current understanding of the word includes additional cultural narratives and conventions which the word has acquired throughout the years since the biblical text was formed. Further, this research validates the theory of Constructed Emotions, as developed by Lisa Feldman Barrett, which claims that there are no "basic emotions," but that every culture categorizes certain concepts as emotional and others as not (Feldman Barrett 2017). Feldman Barrett's theory also claims that "concepts" are not a result of language, but are the reason for it: neurons that fire as a team on a regular basis form a "cognitive concept," and such a concept may be assigned a word in a certain culture, and thus become more stable in the brain (Feldman Barrett 2017), but the focus of the article is on the biblical usage of the word.

I will first briefly describe Donald's evolutionary-cognitive strategies, then outline cases where the root "to love" is used in the Bible, and lastly discuss my approach in comparison with other studies of "love" in the Bible (viz., Ackerman 2002, 437–58; Wolde 2008, 1–24; Brenner 1997; Kazen 2011; Mirguet 2016, 224–65).

> An early version of this article was presented as a lecture in the workshop Cultural Evolution of Religion in 2017 in Helsinki, which was organized by the project "Ritual and the Emergence of Early Christian Religion" (REECR), in the University of Helsinki headed by Risto Uro, and co-organized by the project "Changes in Sacred Texts and Traditions" (CSTT), in the University of Helsinki, headed by Prof. Jutta Jokiranta.

I will not relate to the prophetic literature or wisdom literature, both for the limited scope available for this chapter as well as the unique use of the verb in these literatures, which merits a separate study.

Donald's theory: Three cognitive strategies for creating culture

Donald's describes in his book *Origins of the Modern Mind*[1] three[2] major cognitive transformations leading from the non-symbolic cognitions of animals to the fully symbolic representations of humans. These are three new uniquely human systems of memory representation that find their expression in three stages of human culture.

The first transformation from primate cognition was into *mimetic cognition*. The mimetic strategy is based on the human cognitive property of voluntary retrieval of memory, and it enabled a supramodal (i.e., cross-sensory systems), motor-modeling of the memory. The second, into *mythic cognition*, developed a specialized mimetic subsystem, the phonological apparatus (which in itself is devoid of meaning), into verbal capacity by inventing lexicality (where a meaning is attached to the phoneme). The third transition, into *theoretic cognition*, introduced external memory storage and retrieval system, and a new working memory architecture (Donald 1993, 739).

"The structural arrangement of these uniquely human representational systems is hierarchical" says Donald, with the skills of each stage serving as a necessary but not sufficient condition for the next (Donald 1991).[3]

Mimetic cognition

The first transition, into mimetic cognition, entailed the motor skill of humans to use the whole body as an intentional representational and communication device, and they used it for translating event perceptions into action. Mimetically reenacted sequences require a highly abstract modeling process, involving input from various senses and producing action in a variety of bodily systems (Donald 1991, 162–200, 1993, 740–43). Donald talks about the human reaction to rhythm as exemplifying mimetic cognition, as well as other examples:

Rhythm is an excellent example for mimetic skill, in which an abstract perceptual event (such as a temporal pattern of sound) is "modeled" by the motor system. Humans seem unable to resist rhythm ... to imitate, rehearse and modify the rhythmic sounds ... to virtually any skeletomuscular system in the body, ultimately creating the cultural product of dance; other mimetic culture products are "complex games, extended competition, pedagogy through directed imitation ... a subtler and more complex array of facial and vocal expressions, and public action-metaphor such as intentional group display of aggression, solidarity, joy, fear and sorrow" (Donald 1993, 740–741).

Mimetic representation is still essential to those who work with the body, like actors, athletes, or traditional constructional skills such as arts and crafts.

But the inherent fuzziness and ambiguity of mimetic representation resulted in it reaching a level of complexity where a method of disambiguating about the mimetic messages would be an adaptive benefit. This new level was the Mythic Cognition, which serves as a communication device of greater speed and power.

Mythic cognition

As the first step into mythic cognition, Donald talks about lexical invention, namely, the assignment of a unique sign to a specific meaning. Phonology is a specialized mimetic subsystem, which had developed as a primary manner of expressing the lexical invention (Donald 1991, 201–68, 1993, 743–44).

Language with its lexical, syntactic, and morphological features became the default tool for mythic cognition despite the great respiratory dangers associated with a descended larynx. This, according to Donald, points to the great survival value of phonology to archaic humans. As for the cultural product of mythic cognition, Donald says:

> The natural product of language is narrative thought … language, like mimesis, evolved primarily as a method of modeling reality. Dunbar has argued that the normal social use of language is storytelling about other people—gossip—and he has produced observational data to prove this. But day-to-day storytelling in a shared oral culture eventually produces collective, standardized narrative version of reality, particularly of past events; and these become what we call the dominant "myths" of a society. (Donald 1993, 745)[4]

The development of Mythic Cognition did not eliminate the expression of the mimetic one: "mimetic skill continued (and continues) to serve its traditional social purposes perfectly well: it still provides the cognitive foundation for institutions like dance, athletics, craft, ritual, and theater" (Donald 1993, 744).

Theoretic cognition

The transition into the third cultural-cognitive stage involves technological rather than biological developments, as Donald describes it:

> Since the upper paleolithic humans have gradually developed three new representational devices. The first was *visuosymbolic invention* … writing systems. The second was *external memory*. The third was the emergence of very large, externally nested cultural products called *theories*. (Donald 1991, 273; 1993, 745)

At the crux of the theoretic cognition is the externalization of memory. The development of external mediums for the storage of symbolic content allows humans to circumvent the limitations of biological working memory. This change also entails a new architecture of the human brain, one which is focused on information retrieval and not retention (Donald 1991, 269–360; 1993, 744–48).

With the development and increase of external symbolic storage, a society is no longer dependent on personal distribution of knowledge, since any individual, after proper training, can access the symbolically coded information. They gather information from the external storage just as they used to scan the natural environment, only now the processing will occur on two levels: the first is the items displayed in the external memory, which are treated natural objects and events, and second is when these items are processed as symbolic representations. Literacy, which was developed in the mythic cognition stage, is a prerequisite for encoding and decoding the external memory.

Donald's stages as analytic concepts[5]

The three cognitive strategies come each with a set of behaviors and a range of cultural artifacts which stem from it; typical to evolution, the one does not disappear with the emergence of the next, and thus humans are free to activate each of the strategies with all its accompanying behaviors and artifacts at will. And indeed, we can recognize the core strategy being activated in accordance with the circumstances: In a dance party, for example, certain manners of dressing or movements are possible, but the same behavior is unaccepted in other circumstances, where verbal communication is expected as the core behavior. Similarly, the core of verbal behavior, which is focused on people and their incentive to act is expected in certain circumstances, such as intimacy with a family member, a close friend, or a psychologist. A different form of verbal interaction is expected in a workplace or official institutions, where the content of the communication should always take into account externally decided categories (being a student, a secretary, or a professor) and the hierarchies attached to them regardless of individual biography or the interpersonal sentiments. In the former, the presentation of the self has a strong component of mythic cognition, and the latter— theoretic cognition. In mythic cognition, the scope of emotions expressed is wider, and engagement with personal experience is central, while in theoretic cognition the focus is on the official ideology or legal system, and issues of wealth, social markers such as status, titles, or official identity take the fore. People are cued by the circumstances to choose a total strategy for their behavior, which is very often culturally regulated.[6]

The sharp distinction between the three cognitive strategies is mainly an academic construction; in the reality all strategies exist to some extent in modern human behaviors and cultures at all times, and each strategy is tainted by the others. In fact, the border between the categories is not strict, and they can be seen as a continuum, where the later stages of one cognitive strategy are already the early stages of the next. One therefore finds cultural artifacts that belong to one strategy in the overall sense, but have markers of other strategies. Yet the core character of the artifact may still be recognized in many cases.

An important aspect to keep in mind is that the cultural capital of the society— namely, all the material and non-material cultural artifact used in all three strategies— are basically the same. The most obvious example is language: a person can use English in both mythic and theoretic cognition, and while some of the vocabulary might change, much of it still remains the same. The same holds true to mimetic cognition, in a pre-linguistic stage, the sounds and rhythms produced in a mimetic context by an individual socialized into an English-speaking culture would be the same as those of their narrative language in the case of mythic cognition.

This combination of similar cultural capital and different cognitive strategies is at the crux of this study, since when studying the use of the verb "to love" in the Hebrew Bible, I study what the same verb—i.e., the same cultural artifact—means in the different cognitive strategies, starting from the mimetic and moving to the mythic and theoretic. The change in the meaning of "to love" from one strategy to the next is done by various cultural cognitive processes, such as a type of blending, by which qualities of the artifact are expressed in one way in the mimetic strategy and then are merged into or transform to qualities typical to the mythic strategy.[7]

The example of language brings us closer to the present study. The Hebrew Bible as we know it today is a written text, and in this respect, it represents theoretic cognition (being an imprinting of memory on external storage). But beyond this obvious trait, we can see the various cognitive strategies active behind the various texts of the Bible, and to some extent, and without being very restrictive about it, these strategies agree with a distinction between literary forms or genres. Genres that rely heavily on the auditory and other sensory aspects of language, such as poetry or songs, exhibit more aspects of mimetic cognition than genres which develop a long storyline absorbed in causal explanations and rich in subplots, such as narrative texts. The latter exhibits more of the traits of mythic cognition. As of theoretic cognition, we find it represented in texts which are close to what we today call theories, the content of which is general truths which do not refer to any case in a particular time. Such are legal texts which portray generic or idealistic modes of behavior or give general juridical instructions.[8] These rules are expected to be deductively applied to particular real-life cases, if such occur, but are not in themselves describing such cases.

I would like to stress that in this chapter, I use the concepts "mimetic," "mythic," and "theoretic" only in the Donaldian manner, which is different from the commonsensical usage, or even from the usual academic use of these concepts.

The use of the verb "to love" (אהב) in the Bible

I have chosen to study the verb "to love" as part of my research on emotions from a cultural-cognitive perspective. In my previous work, in order to learn about emotions, I focus on a protagonist's incentive for action within narratives and other types of texts. In this chapter I take a similar approach. I will be looking at what are the actions that take place in the syntactic and the storied environment of the root "to love" (אהב); that is, I am interested in the actions of the agent (usually either a person or God in the biblical context) in connection with the verb "to love." As we shall see, the action depends on the cognitive strategy in which the organism finds itself: mimetic, mythic, or theoretic.

Exploring the use of the root "to love" in biblical texts does not imply that the Bible understood "love" as an "emotion" as we think of emotions nowadays, or even in the

Greek notions of *pathos*; earlier studies have already shown the contrary, as will be discussed below. I will therefore not study a variety of other verbs or biblical words which seem to agree with the modern understanding of "to love," but I will look into the use to one particular root, אהב, and follow its use in the biblical texts. As we will see, these uses represent the different cognitive strategies outlined by Donald.

I will not be working on the prophetic literature, both because the tasks would be too big for one article, and also because of the secondary nature of the verb in this literature: in prophetic literature, the verb is often used metaphorically or parabolically to illustrate the behavior of the nation or the relationship with god, and this secondary nature merits a separate study. Instead, my focus will rest upon texts that are associated with the three cognitive strategies described above, namely poetry for mimetic cognition, narratives for mythic, and legal texts for theoretic cognition, and see how the verb "to love" is used in them.

The Song of Songs: Love in mimetic cognition

The mimetic nature of the Song of Songs

The biblical book Song of Songs is a collection of songs (Zakovitch 1992, 3) describing the erotic attraction between a young woman and a young man; these songs were possibly performed in wedding celebrations. They are telling, mostly in the first person (the protagonists telling what they feel) or second person (when one protagonist speaks to the other) about the beauty of the loved one, and about efforts to reach intimacy. There are also dialogues of the protagonists with secondary characters, such as the "guards of the city" or "the daughters of Jerusalem." The texts do not culminate in a continuous drama or plot, but remain a fragmentary collection.

As poetic techniques, the Song of Songs uses repetitions, rhythmic sentences, rhymes, alliterations, parallelisms of all sorts, and others techniques (Zakovitch 1992, 24). All these are typical for poetry in general, and for ancient Hebrew poetry in particular, and are considered as memory anchors for the performer as well as activating the mimetic memory of the listener (van Es 2012, 69–91). These mimetic aspects make the audience involved with the visuo-audial aspect of the song, prior to being involved with the meaning of the words or the fragmentary narratives.

The fact that the Song of Songs is of the more basic cognition, i.e. mimetic, does not mean that the text itself is from an early period. In fact, is seems to be, at least in its present form, from a later strata of the Bible, i.e., from the Hellenistic period.[9] What is "early" or rather "mimetic" about it are its characteristics as a cultural product, that is, its nature as mimetic cognitive artifact. Thus, studying the meaning of the verb "to love" in the Song of Songs exemplifies its use in a mimetic context.

The text and its analysis

> By night on my bed I sought him whom my soul (נפשי, *naphshi*) loves (שאהבה, *sheʼahavah*); I sought him, but I found him not.

Let me rise[10] and go about the city, in the streets and in the broad ways, I wanted to seek him whom my soul loves. I sought him, but I found him not.

The watchmen that go about the city found me: "Did you see him, whom my soul loves?"

Scarce had I passed from them, when I found him whom my soul loves. I held him, and would not let him go, until I had brought him into my mother's house, and into the chamber of her who had conceived me. (Song 3:1–4)

In this song, we hear a first person teller saying that she could not sleep in her bed at night because she missed the one her soul loved;[11] she therefore got up and walked around the city in search of him, and when she found the loved one, she held him and brought him to her room in her mother's house.

The context is erotic; love is the obsessive sexual attraction to a particular individual, who comes to occupy the woman's imagination (i.e., memory) even when he is not around (i.e., at night when she is trying to sleep). The teller is motivated to leave her bed at night in search of physical proximity with the loved one. When he is found, he is taken back to the "chamber," i.e., keeping the physical proximity with the loved one, and strongly suggesting sexuality.

Conceptualizing love in mimetic cognition

Enumerating the characteristics of love in the Song of Songs will serve as typifying love in the context of mimetic cognition, and these characteristics will be concepts which will be the point of comparison with the findings of the mythic and theoretic forms of cognition. Here are the characteristics:

- **The verb "to love" in the Song of Songs denote the sexual-erotic semiotic context**: We saw that love belongs to the erotic-sexual semiotic sphere; it is something that is happening to the soul (נפש, *nephesh*). In the Song of Songs, it is happening to a woman, while the man protagonist in the book uses other verbs to describe their attraction, such as: לבבתני, *libavtini* (4:9, translated as "ravished my heart"); הרהיבוני, *hirhivuni* (6:5, translated as "they have overcome me").
- **The verb "to love" in the Song of Songs is used to denote engagement with a particular individual (particularity)**: As the woman was searching for one particular individual, not looking for any man, love can be said to be directed toward a particular person; the woman does not just pick any man she encounters, but the sexual attraction is to a particular one; this point would be different in theoretic cognition.
- **The verb "to love" in the Song of Songs denotes coercion**: There is no talk of choice or control of love in the Song of Songs; it is something that happens to the person without the possibility of resistance. This again would be changed in the context of theoretic cognition.
- **The verb "to love" in the Song of Songs drives the person to act (incentivizing action)**: Love drives the organism into action; not any action, but one aiming at physical closeness with the loved one.

- **The action caused by the verb "to love" in the Song of Songs is irregular (irregularity of the action):** The discourse in Song 3.1–4 suggests that being in bed at night is the normal course of events, but getting up and roaming the city is not; still, this is what the teller is driven to do. This action is of high investment of energy, i.e., acting beyond that which is expected in the circumstances, and can be typified as "obsession." The irregularity of the action is noticed by other members of the social group.

I would also add that there is no talk about marriage or wedding in the text, even though the historical context could have been that. Further, there is no negative attitude toward the erotic love, nor any hint for "immorality." What we currently experience as negative, immoral, or "secular" attitude toward erotic love in our cultures is a result of institutional control of sexuality, which regulates parental investment or birth rights; such control existed, no doubt, in biblical times as well, but alongside of the inhibition of sexuality, a society has to make sure that sexuality and procreation exist, to avoid population decline, and encourage population increase. The Song of Songs presents the promotion of sexuality. Albeit not immoral, what is acknowledged in the Song of Songs is the high investment of energy in love, which renders the organism acting irregularly, or even "sick" ("I am love-sick," Song 2:5). What we do not find in the text which expresses the mimetic cognition is conceptualizing a biographical self, with a name, a personal biography, and a goal in life, characteristics which are typical to mythic cognition.

Other occurrences of אהב in the Song of Songs support the characteristics above: It is acted by females in 1:3–4; it is considered a sickness (2:5) and therefore, irregular. It is as strong as death (8:6) thus no wonder it moves the whole organism to act (1:7). Being focused on a particular object (2:3), and being obsessive, i.e., not allowing other things to disturb while it happens (2:7).

When moving to study love in narrative texts, we find that the meaning is transformed.

Love stories: Mythic cognition

Mythic cognition and narratives

Perceiving reality as a story is a cognitive strategy. This strategy focuses on explaining human action (or that of other personified beings) in terms of a will to act and the result of the action; the product of this strategy is the storying of human actions as a series of circumstances and choices.

Through the various cognitive processes, such as personification, recursion, metaphorizing, and others,[12] humans apply the categories from the biological family on the general society, the country, or other imagined communities; this results in the large impersonal social units to be as engaging for the individual as the real people from the immediate small group of familiar individuals, and the stories of these large units become as meaningful as stories about real known people. Language has developed as the most prominent tool for expressing stories, first orally, then in writing. As individuals, the "storied people" of narrative artifacts become a model of behavior; as metaphorized entities (such as THE NATION IS A PERSON) they explain the social values as well as the history of the group.

Narrative texts are abundant in the Bible, and among them, many have storylines which are motivated at least partially by the verb "to love." A non-comprehensive list of stories where the root אהב is used initiating the main actions of the plot includes the story of Isaac loving Rebekah (Gen. 24:67), Isaac loving Esau and Rebekah loving Jacob (Gen. 27), Jacob loving Rachel (Gen. 29), Shechem loving Dinah (Gen. 34), Jacob loving Joseph more than his other sons (Gen. 37–44), Samson being blamed by his wives for not loving them (Jud. 14–16), Elkanah loving his barren wife Hannah (1 Sam. 1), Saul loving David (1 Sam. 16), Jonathan loving David (1 Sam. 18, 20, 2 Sam. 1), Michal loving David (1 Sam. 18), and Amnon loving Tamar (2 Sam. 13).

The text and its analysis

The text to be studied here is the love story of Elkanah and Hannah (1 Sam. 1:1-10). The story is about the man Elkanah who had two wives, Hannah and Peninnah. With the latter he had children, but the former was barren. Elkanah used to go every year to worship and to sacrifice to the Lord in the temple in Shiloh. The story goes on (verse 4 onward):

> And it came to pass one day, when Elkanah sacrificed, that he gave to Peninnah his wife and to all her sons and her daughters portions, but unto Hannah he gave a double portion, **because he loved Hannah** (כי את חנה אהב, *ki 'et Hannah 'ahev*). But the Lord had closed her womb. And her rival vexed her sore, to make her fret, because the Lord had closed her womb.
>
> And as he did so year by year, when she went up to the house of the Lord, so she vexed her; therefore she wept, and would not eat.
>
> And Elkanah her husband said to her: "Hannah, why do you weep, and why do you not eat, and why does your heart grieve? here, I am better to you than ten sons!"

Elkanah's words seem not to have influenced Hannah, and she prayed to God for a son, and got him in the end. This son was Samuel, who later became an important prophet during a critical time in Israelite history.

In the context of the yearly sacrifice in Shiloh, Elkanah gives a double portion of the meat to the barren Hannah because he loves her. This raises Peninnah's anger against Hannah, and she hurts her. Hannah is disturbed and weeps. The husband tries to appease the barren wife, saying that he is better for her than children, but she is not appeased, and prays to God to have a son. The story ends with the barren wife getting the child she has longed for, Samuel, who will be the one to anoint the future first king of the children of Israel.

To compare with the findings about love (אהב) in the Song of Songs, we see that love in this story is not equated with sexual activity, certainly not exclusively, since Elkanah apparently has had sexual relations with his fertile wife, while he is still not described as loving her.

With regard to incentive to act and the nature of the act: Elkanah's love motivates him to prefer Hannah to Peninnah and give her more than her portion[13] of the sacrificial meal. This action is perceived as injust, and thus "irregular," and is noticed by Peninnah who then works to irritate Hannah. Elkanah's love is the ultimate reason behind the important historical event of the birth of Samuel and thus, what appeared as an "irregular" behavior of the mimetic cognitive level has becomes an irregular action which results in "social unrest."

Checking these findings against other love stories in the Hebrew Bible, we find similar traits in many of them: love leads to irregular or socially imbalanced behavior which eventually influences the course of personal life, or of history. Here are some of the major narratives where we find this formula (in all cases the root אהב is used):

Isaac loving Rebekah (Gen. 24:67): This love helped Isaac get over his mourning for his mother, thus away from the expected sorrow and into a new state of mind.

Isaac loving Esau and Rebekah loving Jacob (Gen. 27): Isaac's love is apparently the expected behavior (father's love of the first born), Rebekah's love changes the course of history by making the younger son receive the blessing of the father. While the plot fits well with the boys' previous agreement (the selling of the first-born rights by Esau), the outcome is still the result of love causing Rebekah to trick Isaac into blessing the wrong child.

Jacob loving Rachel (Gen. 29): Love ignores the proper order of marrying out the daughters, and motivates Jacob to work for his father in law more than he planned.

Shechem loving Dinah (Gen. 34): This love indeed follows the social rules, but it is improper, since it works against God's instruction not to intermarry. Consequently this love brought disaster upon the lover and his ethnic group.

Jacob loving Joseph more than his other sons (Gen. 37–44): This love motivated the older brothers to mistreat Joseph. It all ended well only because it was apparently part of God's plan and agreed with Joseph's dreams, but in terms of human behavior, the improper love of Jacob brought about Joseph's hybris and the brothers' jealousy.

Samson. Samson was blamed twice by his wives for not loving them (Jud. 14:16, 16:15), because he failed to treat them as preferred individuals, that is, to entrust them with information which could, and eventually did, harm him: in the first case, the solution to a riddle, and in the second, about his own physical weakness. Samson is said to have loved only the second woman, Delilah, (Jud. 16:4) but did not voluntarily make her into a preferred person in terms of trust (Jud. 16:7, 13). Samson's love is therefore of mimetic nature, and in this respect, the usage of the verb is close to its usage in the Song of Songs.[14] It is the women in the story who claim that Samson does not love them, referring to mythic love, i.e., that he is not engaging with them in a conversation, or benefits them outside the sexual context.

David. The verb "to love" (אהב) is never applied to David. But before becoming a king, he himself was loved by a few people, all of whom from the house of the king Saul. The first being Saul himself (1 Sam. 16:21), then by Jonathan, Saul's son (1 Sam. 18:1, 3, 20:17, 2 Sam. 1:23, 26), and by Michal, Saul's daughter (1 Sam. 18:28). Further, David is said to have been loved by all of Saul's slaves (1 Sam. 18:22), or, at least this is how things are presented to David himself and all the people of Judea and Israel (1 Sam. 18:16). While the discourse of the Davidic narratives is of particular individuals and their relationships, the status of these people, as the reigning king and the future king, makes these relationships point to the political sphere. The loves in David's stories seem to accompany, if not to explain, the transition from the reigning of the house of Saul to the house of David, the latter being hegemonic in the biblical narrative overall. Therefore, beyond telling the interpersonal story, the narrative has a *pars pro toto* meaning of asserting the validity of David's dynasty rather than Saul's. This process, of turning from personal into political, is quite common in the ancient Near East as well as in our current cultures,[15] and for our purpose, these two points (the personal and the political) mark the transition from the mythic cognition (the personal) into the theoretic one (the political).

King Solomon. Solomon is said to have loved two things: in the beginning of his life he loved God (1 Kgs. 3:3) even though he still worshipped foreign gods, and toward the end of his life it is said that he loved foreign women (1 Kgs. 11:1, 2). Both these love actions had consequences for Solomon's life and for the history of the Judeo-Israelite society. I will discuss loving God in the section on theoretic cognition. With regard to the foreign women, they are said to have turned his heart toward worshipping foreign gods, and consequently the Judeo-Israelite kingdom was divided by God. While on the surface, it seems that the story is similar to previous mythic cognition stories about love which, by its nature of being irregular or counterintuitive, changes the course of history, there is something imminently different in Solomon's story. Solomon is said to love a *category* of women, not any unique person.[16] This contradicts the concept of "particularity" which we have seen in the mimetic cognition, and which is also present in the cases of mythic cognition which we have seen so far: Elkanah loved Hannah, he did not love a category, such as "a wife," since he had another wife whom he did not love; so were the cases with Isaac, Rebekah, and Jacob who each loved one son and not the other(s). This categorization turns the woman more into a concept than a concrete person, and is therefore more a "universal entity," which is typical to theoretic cognition, and not "a particular person" which, in my understanding, is typical to the mythic cognition.

The stories discussed earlier, about the patriarchs and Elkanah, affect the listener by getting them involved with the life of another human being. If a lesson was to be learned, such as the disaster that follows from mixing with the nations (Dina), or why the younger child continues the family line (Isaac, Jacob), it is learned by way of induction from the individual to the whole group, including the listener.

Conceptualization of love in mythic context

In the mythic cognitive strategy, love, while not opposed to being sexual, also extends to other aspects of life. Love is an incentive for irregular interpersonal action; it takes the form of the loving person preferring the loved one and benefiting him or her more than is socially accepted. The unruly preference is recognized by the environment, and causes social imbalance. The loving couple may be a man and a woman, but other relationships are also indicated by the verb "to love," such as parents and children. All this is part of the biography of individuals who are named and known and have a life-story in the biblical narrative. This was not the case in mimetic love which, while directed toward a particular individual, was fragmentary and lacked the acquaintance with the biography of the people involved.

The important development is that in mythic cognition love begins to signify things other than its mimetic sexual meaning. We can place this development on a continuum of love-motivated stories, which start with love still being primarily sexual, close to the mimetic form, through stories which are about personal preference of another person, but this preference explains the historical situation of the ethnic situation (the stories of the patriarchs), to narratives where the love story is but a thin framing which is used to indicate or argue the benefit of some rules or regulations. The thinness of the frame and the personal story is lost in favor of categories of people (i.e., "foreign women" loved by Solomon).

To compare the function of love in the mythic cognitive strategy with the five points I have conceptualized about mimetic one:

- **Sexual context**: This is not exclusive in mythic cognition; the sexual nature and the physical proximity change into caring and preferring the loved-ones by giving them gifts or special attention.
- **Particularity**: As a rule, this seems to be the case in mythic cognition just like in the mimetic one. But in the case of king Solomon there is a development into loving a whole category (foreign women), and thus complying more with being a "rule" and not a personal story.
- **Coercion**: This seems to still be the case in mythic cognition as it was in the mimetic: love is a force that compels a person to act, it appears spontaneously, not leaving the person with a choice whether to love or not; this will change in the theoretic cognition.
- **Incentivizing action**: As in mimetic cognition, also in the mythic, love incents action: the person who loves is driven to act upon it.
- **Abnormality of the action**: Similar in mythic and mimetic cognitions.

Theoretic cognition: Love in legal text

Theoretic cognition deals with universal truths and the principles that are behind worldly phenomena. It therefore does not focus on the unique and the personal, as mythic cognition, nor does it rely on sensory input as mimetic cognition, but rather on conceptualized logic such as mathematical rules. It is thus impersonal, and its rationality is not focused on the human, as mythic cognition.

One cultural artifact of theoretic cognition is societal laws that ensure what came to be conceptualized as "justice." This concept entails universality of proper behavior, and the accountability of the social group, and the regime, for enforcing the proper behavior.

In the ancient Mediterranean, the law was imposed by a ruler who received his authority from the gods, the ultimate rulers of the world. Since the Bible's overall narrative sees God as the ultimate ruler, He is the source of the ultimate justice and of all rules. These rules are spelled out in the legal texts. For the sake of looking into theoretic cognition, I will look into these legal texts in the Bible.[17]

As a general observation, there are twenty-nine verses where the verb "to love" appears in texts of legal nature. Of these, six are cases where God loves,[18] and in all the others, people are the subject or the implied subject of the verb "to love."[19] Of these latter twenty-three cases, there are seven cases where people are said to love other people, and in the rest, two-third of the cases, people are said to love God. I will look at each of these categories separately.

God as the loving person[20]

The cases where God loves are of a narrative nature, and are not commanding, instructing or expounding rules to be followed. The texts where God loves are adjacent to legal texts and are framing them.

One unique case (Deut. 10:18) tells that God loves the foreigner (*ger*). This love is instructive for the Israelites, who are then commanded to love the *ger* as well. Out of love, God gives the foreigner clothes and food. Thus this love follows the pattern familiar from the mythic cognitive strategies: it is a non-erotic love, in which the one who love prefers the loved one beyond what is expected, such as giving them clothes (like Jacob to Joseph) and food (like Elkanah to Hannah). What makes this case close to the theoretic cognition (on the continuum from mythic to theoretic) is that God loves a category of people, the *ger*, and not a particular individual.

All other five cases of God loving speak of God's love toward the people of Israel. The simplest case (Deut. 23:6) tells that God loves the people and this is why he turned Balaam's curse of the Israelites into a blessing. This is again following the familiar structure of the lover benefiting the loved one. More elaborated are cases (Deut. 4:37; 10:15) where God has loved the forefathers, and therefore benefits the offspring (by preferring them over other people, and bringing them out of Egypt).

Again, this falls for the most part under the familiar pattern: he who loves benefits the one loved. But the cases where God loves people on account of the forefathers suggest an innovation: benefiting the loved one is not a spontaneous result of the acquaintance of the two parties, it has a reason, which is not in the lover and the loved, but a promise made in the past. The level of spontaneity is, therefore, reduced.

Even lesser spontaneity is suggested in Deut. 7:12–13: the text says that if the people adhere to God's laws, God will love them, as he has promised to the forefathers. As a consequence of this love, God will benefit the people by making them fruitful with offspring and agricultural products. Love and its benefits are therefore a part of a "deal": love is gained in exchange for adhering to God's laws.

To sum up, narratives about the love of God show a transition from the mythic love to one which is less spontaneous (as will be the case in the more legalistic texts) and less personal (as we have seen happening already to King Solomon, who loved the category "foreign women").

Love between people in legal texts

Four different objects of love are mentioned in legal text, in cases where people love other people: one's master (Exod. 21:5; Deut. 15:16), one's wife (Deut. 21:15–16), the foreigner (*ger*; Lev. 19:34; Deut. 10:10), and the fellow Israelite (Lev. 19:18). Of these, the first two cases follow characteristics of mythic love, except the aspect of particularity, as the genre does not talk about particular people: a slave loving his master more than his freedom, and a husband loving one wife more than the other. Love in these cases is spontaneous and goes against the socially expected, these are, then, transitional cases: they have some characteristics of mythic love, but they are being generalized and turned into a rule, not a unique case, and in this respect they are theoretical. In the case of the slave, love results in physical proximity of the lover (slave) to the loved (master/family), as we have seen in the mimetic strategy in the Song of Songs; in the case of the husband, loving one wife more than the other, the lover (husband) wants to benefit the loved (one wife) more than expected, as was the case in mythic cognition, only here, the law is resisting this inclination, indicating that he may not do so.

The next two cases, of people loving the foreigner and the fellow Israelite, we also find an innovation of theoretic cognitive nature: a command to love. However, the other aspect, benefiting the loved one, is still there. The command to love will be the common usage in the next category.

The command to love

The command to love is the most prevailing use of the verb "to love" in legal texts, and in most cases (except those mentioned above) the object of love is God; an example is: "This commandment which I command you to do, to love the Lord your God" (Deut. 11:22).[21]

More has been written about love in legal texts than other loves in the Bible. Mostly in the context of ancient Near Eastern parallels, emphasizing the hierarchical aspects of the verb. But this strict hierarchical aspect is an innovation of the theoretic cognitive strategy; in the previous strategies, it was the disregard to hierarchy and correctness that was characteristic of the usage, and the fact that love went against social norms. Love brought about a turn in history, precisely because it went against the expectation.

Three things changed in love when used in texts which represent a theoretic cognitive strategy in its core: first, that love has a reason, second, it is done intentionally, and third, love is beneficial for the lover (e.g., when the people love God they get a fertile land) and not to the loved one, as was in the mythic cognition. These characteristics stand in contrast to previous cognitive strategies where love was spontaneous and unintentional, sometime to the level of harming the lover (like Jacob who had to work seven more years for Laban), and it moved the lover to endow the loved with benefits.

Conceptualizing the usage of the verb "to love" in theoretic cognition in comparison with its usage in the mimetic and mythic cognitions render the following:

- **Sexual context**: This was the major focus in mimetic cognition, one of the options in mythic one, and hardly ever the focus in theoretic cognition.

- **Particularity**: Particularity goes against the idea of theoretic cognition, since this cognition focuses on inducing universal concepts and categories. Therefore it is hardly found in legal texts, and when they are (such as God loving the forefathers), God is the one loving, and the texts are not legal texts per se, but are framing them. This notion continues its beginnings at the end of the continuum of mythic cognition, where the protagonists stood for more than their own particular person, such as David standing for his whole dynasty and Solomon loving a category of women.
- **Irregularity of the action**: Being a rule that has to be followed, theoretic love hardly leaves room for love to be abnormal or irregular. What might be "left over" from the abnormality is found in the framing narratives (God loves the Israelites more than other nations), and as the demand for preference of God over all other gods.
- **Coercion**: This is perhaps the most innovative aspect of theoretic cognition: love is not coercive, but is dependent on the will of the lover; only in this manner, can a command to love (God) be issued.
- **Incentivizing action**: This aspect of love is greatly transformed in texts of theoretic cognition. The one who performs the action in legal text is God, when he is making the land and the people fertile. But God is not the one who loves in legal texts, he is the one loved. This is a complete role reversal from what we saw in the other forms of cognitions.[22]
- **Hierarchical relation**: This was much emphasized by previous scholars (Ackerman 2002; Wolde 2008, 16–17), but is in fact typical mainly of theoretic cognition, resulting from the artifact being of a generalized nature, and of God commanding it. One may argue that also in mythic cognition one finds hierarchies of the persons involved (husband loving wife, parent loving offspring), but these hierarchies are stricter and more emphatic in the theoretic cases, where one is commanded to love.

Discussion

Many studies have been devoted to the verb or the concept "love" in the Bible. The intention of this study was to show the advantages of taking a cognitive evolutionary approach, particularly the stages of cognitive evolution suggested by Merlin Donald in *Origins of the Modern Mind*. Assigning various biblical texts to these stages was based on the type of cognitive strategy behind the text, which in general overlap with literary genres, and not on textual sources of the Bible. This categorization yielded results which have otherwise not been apparent, and even resulted in a somewhat skewed understanding of the meaning of אהב ("to love").

I chose to follow one verb, "to love" (אהב), not assuming a semantics of romantic love, with all its modern associations, or any other emotion or feeling, but instead, to analyze its usage according to the action associated with it. By this, the current study differs from the work of Kazen (2011, 6, 37–41), who looked at how the modern notion of "empathy" is used as an argumentation in legal texts in the Bible; so he was not restricting himself to a particular verb, but searched for the modern notion. Similarly, Mirguet (2016, 455), in her study, was not focusing on a particular verb when she studied the response to the pain of others in the biblical text (intentionally not verbalizing this action in any modern emotional term). In another aspect, Mirguet's and my study are similar in that they both look for the action, a "cluster of actions" as formulated by Mirguet, or as "incentive to act" as I phrased it, to understand the meaning of biblical emotions.

The study began with the Song of Songs; this book exhibits many aspects of mimetic cognition, being of poetic nature with a possible performative function as well as being devoid of a firm narrative (as in mythic artifacts) or universal categorization (as in theoretic ones). Mimetic artifacts are not common in the biblical corpus, given that this cognitive strategy is preverbal and thus not easily represented in verbal artifacts such as the Bible. Love in this context is in nexus to sexuality, albeit it is happening in the "soul" (*nephesh*); it is directed from the subject to a particular person, and thus it is one-sided; it forces the agent to move into action, an action which is irregular in its scope—judging by the reactions of the environment; the core of the action is seeking proximity with the loved.

In the Song of Songs the sole agent of "to love" is a woman, and other verbs are used to describe the attraction of the male protagonist; the uni-directionality seems to be inherent, since the overwhelming incentive to act (getting up from bed, searching the city, finding, grabbing, bringing home) is what typifies the verb "to love," and is the cause of the union. If both are interested in the union, there is no need for action so irregular in its scope.

A notion that has been extensively discussed by scholars is the prevalence in the Bible of male agents of love in comparison to female ones. This has been interpreted as a sign of the hierarchical nature of the love relations (Ackerman 2002; Wolde 2008) or its manliness nature (Brenner 1997, 18). The data from the Song of Songs shows a different picture: it is the woman who loves, and there is no indication for hierarchical concern. By ignoring or setting aside the data of the Song of Songs, scholars misinterpreted the meaning of love, and it became gendered in a skewed manner.

Since women are anyway underrepresented in the Bible, the statistical data regarding their being the agent or subject of the verb "to love" is less revealing, beyond recognizing their underrepresentation.[23]

The one-sidedness of love has also been lamented by scholars (Ackerman 2002, 457; Brenner 1997, 17; Wolde 19), but the expectation for love to be reciprocal is associated with the modern use of the verb, and expresses modern values. Reciprocity was not associated with the biblical verb, and this is not part of the semantics of the biblical word, as I explained above.

So the biblical verb in its mimetic context seems to indicate an obsession that makes the agent overactive in appropriating a uniquely preferred subject. In the Song of Songs the obsession was of feminine erotic nature, which seems to lead to sexual relations. The male protagonist in the Song of Songs seems to comply with the sexual possibility, a compliance which is argued by the verbs other than "love," such as *libavtini* (Song 4:9, "ravished my heart") or *hirhivuni* (Song 6:5, "they have overcome me").

The moralistic aspect associated with love in the modern culture was not there in the mimetic strategy.[24]

In biblical narratives, the sexual association, proximity, and obsessiveness of love transform when expressed in mythic cognition.

In some of the stories we find sexual contexts, but it is very much toned down since, as Brenner indicated, a man loves his wife (and thus sexuality is assumed), but love happens mostly not prior to sex, as in Song of Songs, but after the marriage, and possibly without direct connection to sexuality (Brenner 1997, 16). Elkanah's love of Hannah is such an example, and also Isaac loving Rebekah. Interestingly, whenever a manly love precedes sex, the sex that follows is portrayed as a rape (Amnon and Tamar, Shechem and Dinah), unless the man does not initiate sexual relation, at least not until marriage took place, such as in the case of Jacob loving Rachel.

In contexts other than sexual, "to love" in mythic cognition indicates the preference of a unique individual beyond what he or she deserves according to their social status. This is actualized in terms of endowing of food or clothes, friendship (i.e., a relation that disregards social status) or support. This notion of mythic love is a transformation of the irregularity of the action we saw in the mimetic cognition.

We found a continuum which runs from the private personal narratives, telling about the preference of a particular person (such as Elkanah loving Hannah) all the way to the preference of a category of people (in the story of Solomon loving foreign women), the former changing the course of history because the biblical protagonists are the ancestors of the nation, and the latter being a direct theo-political narrative used to establish current values (i.e. Solomon being punished for this love).

Theoretic cognition expresses itself in a universal manner, which goes beyond a particular time, space, and person. This study focused on texts of legal nature (not necessarily the legal collections in the Bible), which formulate their message in a universal, or a generalized manner. Some of these instructional texts talk about inter-human love (a slave to his master, or a man to one of his wives), and, contrary to narrative texts, the insistence of these text is to keep the social structure (by instructing the husband to go against his love, for example) and not allowing the protagonist to ignore these norms. However, in the majority of legal texts, the Israelites are the most prevailing subject of the verb to love, the object being God.

The command to love God contradicts some aspects of the verb as we have seen earlier: love now is not spontaneous nor coercive, but planned and executed at will; it does not lead the agent to endow favors on the loved one, but on the contrary, the one who loves receives advantages from the loved (God).

Based on Moran's recognition of the hierarchical nature of "love" in the Deuteronomic legal texts, Ackerman studied the use of "love" in narratives, to see if the usage there overlaps with Moran's observations. Ackerman found that "love" in the Bible is one-sided and of hierarchical nature.[25] As we saw above, one-sidedness seems to be inherent in the verb "to love" in its biblical usage. With regard to the hierarchical nature, Ackerman's understanding can be influenced by Moran's, the latter being based on the study of Deuteronomy. Learning from the Deuteronomic-political usage about the personal meaning of love is "going backwards," not chronologically, but in terms of cultural evolution, not starting from the biological to the cultural. Ignoring the Song of Songs data leads scholars to ascribe hierarchy to the basic meaning of "to love" in the Bible, and this understanding is skewed.

There are only a few cases where God is the loving subject, and in those cases the Bible has him love the fathers three times (Deut. 4:37, 10:15, 23:6), the Israelites three times (Deut. 7:8,13, and in a political–narrative context 1 Kgs. 10:9) and once as a reason to love the foreigner, because God loves them (Deut. 10:18). This picture completely changes when the prophetic books are taken into consideration. There, the love of God toward his people is prevailing in both direct description and in metaphoric usage. It is, thus, an innovative move of the prophetic books, which is reshaping of the legal discourse into a narrative one, and by this changing the engagement of the people with these texts, and their accessibility; but discussing this topic goes beyond the limits set for this paper.

When cultural evolutionary categories are employed, a new level of understanding of the ancient sources unfolds. The old typifications of "love" in the Bible as being one-sided and hierarchical are shown now to be only part of the picture, and does not help understand the essential use of the verb and the nature of the phenomenon in the Bible.

5

"The Glory of the Lord Has Risen upon You": Some Observations on the "Glory"-Language of Isa. 56–66 Based on a Cognitive Semantic Approach

Marilyn E. Burton

Cognitive principles

The foundational principle of a cognitive approach to language is that since language is a product of the human mind, and thus inextricably related to human thought processes, it "cannot be properly understood without taking into account the way in which people think" (Van Hecke 2003, 143). Unlike externalist approaches to language, such as structuralism, which hold that language can and should be analyzed entirely on its own terms, without reference to either the human mind or perception, it is the fundamental principle of cognitive linguistic theory that language is inherently tied to human cognition—that lexical meaning, far from being independent of the mind, is a "mental entity" (Gärdenfors 1999, 19)—and that it therefore cannot be studied in isolation from questions of language-speakers' perception of the world around them and the structure of the mental categories into which they organize those things they perceive.

For this reason, a cognitive approach to semantics relies heavily on data gathered from native speakers and, correspondingly, denies the accuracy of the intuitions of non-native speakers. For, no matter how advanced the linguistic knowledge of the second-language learner, it is only to the native speaker that all nuances, connotations, and implications of a lexeme or phrase are fully and intuitively apparent.

In approaching an ancient language such as Classical Hebrew, for which native speakers are no longer available whose intuitions we may consult, the source of our information lies instead in the texts which they left behind. This presents something of a challenge on two counts: first, our ability to accurately extract the necessary data from these texts must remain imperfect insofar as our interpretation of them is not certain; secondly, the corpus of any ancient language is limited, both in volume and in nature.[1] Nonetheless, the endeavor is far from hopeless, and the texts as they stand are a rich source of clues as to the perceptions of the native speaker.[2]

Methodological foundations

The principles of cognitive semantic theory have led to a wide variety of methodologies, and more are under development. Indeed, cognitive semantics is characterized less by any one methodology than by its theoretical tenets, which hold together a diverse collection of approaches. However, the theoretical foundation of cognitive semantics generally leads to certain methodological principles.

First, cognitive semantics is concerned with language-users' cognitive processes, and the ways in which they form and structure their mental categories. Prototype theory addresses this question through the concepts of the centrality (or prototypicality) or peripherality of lexemes to a particular semantic domain. Through consideration of what semantic features may make a lexeme typical or atypical of its domain, it is possible to map out both the position of each term within the domain and the interrelations between the terms. Frame theory also addresses the question of mental categorization, through the identification of a mental "frame" of semantic features against which each member of a domain may be measured.[3] Although these two approaches are distinct, the concepts of "frame" and "prototype" are by no means incompatible—both may simultaneously be fruitfully used to analyze a semantic domain from different angles— for prototypicality is, in itself, a semantic feature which may be included in a frame, and analysis of semantic features through use of a frame aids in determining prototypicality. In the comprehensive study of the semantic domain of כבוד which forms the basis for this chapter, both of these methodological tools were used in the process of mapping out the domain (Burton 2017b). Membership of, and prototypicality within, the domain was determined through examination of lexical frequency and collocation; contextual analysis led to the identification of semantic features—including metaphorical expression—to be included in a frame against which to measure each lexeme. Such a process resulted in a comprehensive picture of the interrelations between the domain's members and the distinctive semantic features of each.

Secondly, cognitive semantics holds that meaning is based in the mind of the language-user, and so maximal objectivity—as opposed to the imposition of the researcher's own subjective perspective—is a crucial methodological feature. Two key methodological features arise from this principle, the first necessarily and the second particularly in the case of an ancient language, where our available data are textual in form.

Bottom-up analysis

Sue Groom, in her monograph *Linguistic Analysis of Biblical Hebrew*, distinguishes between a "top-down" and "bottom-up" approach to semantic analysis (Groom 2003, xxii–xxiii):

> The top-down approach takes a particular theory, such as the existence of semantic fields within the lexicon, and then searches for words which comprise particular fields within the Hebrew data. The bottom-up approach starts with the Hebrew material and conducts a comprehensive survey of all available data to see whether any semantic fields become evident.

In many ways, these two approaches reflect, respectively, an externalist and cognitive perspective—the first tends to allow both the validity of the scholar's own instincts and the applicability of concepts found in one language to another. That is to say, since language may be studied without reference to the mind of the native speaker—i.e., to how native speakers perceive and mentally categorize the world around them— it is appropriate to rely upon one's own instincts and perceptions in approaching it; moreover, and relatedly, since externalist theories are commonly accompanied by a belief in semantic universals, it is not inappropriate to apply a concept or framework from one language—whether or not the scholar's own—onto another. A bottom-up approach, on the other hand, puts the available linguistic data before all else, seeking to avoid imposing a framework upon a text or language, but rather allowing one to arise naturally from the data. Speaking in cognitive terms, this approach focuses on the evidence we have of the native speaker's thought processes—i.e., primarily, the speaker's linguistic output, since language is the greatest window we have into the minds of others.[4] In the case of ancient languages, we are dealing with textual rather than verbal evidence, within which we seek clues as to the way in which the author thought about the world.[5]

When approaching a specific text, a bottom-up approach will in general take a far broader-based corpus as its starting point, and use results derived from analysis of this corpus as a background against which to view the language-use of a particular passage or author. For to attempt to study the language of a given book or passage, without taking fully into account the semantic background within which it was written, runs the risk of biasing the analysis rather dramatically. It is important to know which lexemes were available to a given author, and their usual usage, in order to derive the full significance, by comparison, of which words the author chooses to use and the way in which he or she uses them.

A corpus-based analysis

For maximal objectivity, a comprehensive semantic study should be based upon a large quantity of empirical data. For such a purpose, the extant corpus of most, if not all, ancient languages, including that of Classical Hebrew, is somewhat smaller than would be ideal. It is therefore crucial that we not ignore any relevant data that is available. Maximizing the data set by including the entire extant corpus offers the greatest opportunity for objective, accurate, justifiable results, by factoring in a broader spectrum as well as a greater volume of literature.[6]

This of course raises issues of diachrony, for such corpora tend to extend over a considerable time period and geographic area—the Classical Hebrew corpus, for example, incorporating the biblical texts, inscriptions, texts from Qumran and Ben Sira, spans over a thousand years. In an ideal world, with abundantly available literary data, the corpus analyzed would be synchronic in nature. However, the issues arising from fragmenting the corpus even further by stratifying it according to date—quite apart from the difficulties involved in the dating process itself—in my opinion firmly outweigh the issues arising from treating the corpus as a synchronic whole.

Exegetical application: Isa. 56–66 as a case study

As noted above, I have elsewhere analyzed at length the semantic domain of the Classical Hebrew term כבוד from a cognitive semantic perspective (Burton 2017). Such an exhaustive analysis of a semantic domain across the language as a whole (as represented by the extant corpus) provides a backdrop of "normalcy" against which anomalies in the usage of the domain's language may be observed. Among other things, it exposes some highly distinctive features of the domain's usage in Isa. 56–66. It will be the purpose of the remainder of this chapter to explore some of these features, and consider how they affect our reading of the text.[7] Some of the features discussed below are not in themselves highly significant, but rather contribute to a cumulative picture of the unusual character of the "glory"-language in this passage.[8]

"Trito-Isaiah"

The decision to demarcate the beginning of the text under consideration as the start of chapter 56 of Isaiah is made in line with the traditional divisions perceived in the book. In fact, chapters 56 and 57 do not contain "glory"-language, and do not feature in our discussion; indeed, the majority of the observed anomalies are confined to chapters 60 and following. However, since such instances of "glory"-language as present in chapters 58 and 59 are not contradictory to any of the points made below, but rather agree with them insofar as they contribute anything to our discussion, it seems more reasonable to include them on literary grounds, rather than to exclude them on semantic ones.

The question of the nature of these chapters, like that of almost any part of Isaiah, has provoked considerable discussion; without entering too deeply into this highly complex debate, it will be helpful very briefly to consider the state of scholarship on the so-called Trito-Isaiah. Majority scholarship follows the proposal of Bernhard Duhm that Isa. 56–66 is quite separate and distinct from what comes before, particularly in its focus on the restoration of Israel and on temple practices (Duhm 1892). Authorship in the late sixth or during the fifth century BCE is widely proposed, though there is further dispute concerning whether the chapters are the work of a single author or several; some scholars even retain Deutero-Isaianic authorship, considering the break between chapters 55 and 56 as purely thematic (see for example Holladay 1997; cf. Seitz 2002). Though various accounts of their origins and purpose have been advocated, a number of scholars suggest that these chapters, or at least some thereof, were composed deliberately in the form of a conclusion to the remainder of the book of Isaiah, drawing together themes from chapters 1 to 55 (see for example Beuken 1991; cf. Williamson 1999).

It is not within the scope of this chapter to consider the validity or otherwise of the division between chapters 55 and 56 of Isaiah, or to enter into questions of divisions within, and authorship of the material in the chapters following.[9] Questions of dating are also largely secondary to our analysis, and will be discussed only as and when the issue is raised by the data themselves; no precise date is assumed for the material.

The "glory"-language of Isa. 60–66 is lacking in variety

The semantic domain of כבוד (kavod) boasts at least ten members.[10] These include primarily גאון, צבי, הוד, הדר, תפארת and גאוה (ga'on, tsvi, hod, hadar, tif'eret, ga'avah), as well as, of course, כבוד (kavod) itself.[11] Yet of these terms, only כבוד and תפארת recur in Isa. 56–66, while גאון is found just once. Indeed, הוד, צבי, גאון (aside from the aforementioned single instance) and גאוה are entirely confined to Proto-Isaiah, while הדר is likewise in six of seven of its Isaianic occurrences. This is not due, except perhaps in the case of הוד (which occurs in Isaiah only at 30:30), to the infrequency of these lexemes in Isaiah overall—צבי is found seven times, גאון twelve, and גאוה five in the book. Nor is it due to a general lack of "glory"-language in these chapters—in fact, there are more "glory"-lexemes per chapter on average in Isa. 56–66 than in the book of Isaiah as a whole.[12] Nor can this phenomenon be easily explained with reference to questions of dating, since, while there is indeed a broad tendency for more minor words to be phased out in later texts, all of these lexemes occur, many with high frequency, both in later biblical texts and in postbiblical literature. Rather, it appears to be a choice of the author at this point—whether or not that author is to be identified with the author of any or all of the rest of the book. His reason for doing so—i.e., both for limiting the variety of lexemes and for making use of these lexemes in particular—is a question we shall address below, after considering some of the other distinctive features of the use of "glory"-language in these chapters.

Only in Isa. 60–66 is כבוד given or restored to a nation

One of the semantic features with reference to which the members of the semantic domain of כבוד may be compared is whether they can (as far as our evidence goes) be given by various donors and to various recipients (e.g., by God to humans, by humans to God, by humans to humans, and so forth), and indeed taken by and from the same. In the extant Classical Hebrew literature, the varying types of "glory" show different patterns of behavior in this respect. For example, הדר and הוד are often given but rarely, if ever, taken, while גאון and גאוה are frequently taken but rarely if ever given; this presumably relates to the frequently negative connotations of the latter group of lexemes. כבוד shows in general a more balanced distribution between giving and taking.

When it comes to God giving "glory" to or taking it from nations, however, כבוד is almost exclusively taken away.[13] כבוד is attributed to a nation in seventeen verses in the Hebrew Bible, both to Israel[14] and to foreign peoples.[15] In every one of these contexts, with the exceptions of Isa. 60:13, 61:6, 62:2, 66:11, and 66:12, כבוד is departing from or being stripped from the nation in question—being stripped away, in most cases, either explicitly or implicitly by God.[16] The cause, of course, is in each case their unrighteousness. In Isa. 60–66 alone, כבוד is instead something that may be restored to and retained by Israel, given to her whether explicitly or implicitly at the behest of God.

This reversal of the standard motif in biblical, and indeed classical, Hebrew literature[17] marks a different tone and theological concern—that of the ultimate restoration and glory of Zion and the people of God. We will see this idea again in a number of the points which follow.

Isa. 60:1 demonstrates a unique reaction of humanity to כבוד יהוה

Throughout Classical Hebrew literature, כבוד יהוה—the visible presence of God—provokes an extreme reaction in humans when they perceive it. In the presence of כבוד יהוה, humanity is overwhelmed—unable either to enter the place where the כבוד יהוה is (Exod. 40:35, 2 Chron. 7:2), or to stand upright when faced with it (1 Kgs 8:11). In Ezek. 3:23 and 44:4, it causes the prophet to fall to his face, whether in worship, obedience, humility, or trembling; in worship, the people of Israel also fall prostrate in 2 Chron. 7:3. Even in the absence of the idiomatic phrase כבוד יהוה—when we consider the כבוד of God more generally—the reaction is not dissimilar. 1QH[a] 18:11 and Sir. 42:17 show the inability of God's creatures—even of heavenly beings—to stand before the כבוד of God, while 4Q511 f1:7–8, Ps. 102:16 and Isa. 59:19 illustrate the trembling and passing away of the enemies of God before it. Even the people of God may be seized by trembling in encountering the כבוד of God (4Q377 f2ii:9).[18]

In Isa. 60:1, uniquely, we find a different response:

קוּמִי אוֹרִי כִּי בָא אוֹרֵךְ וּכְבוֹד יְהוָה עָלַיִךְ זָרָח:
    Arise, shine, for your light has come, and כבוד יהוה has risen upon you.

The people of God, when כבוד יהוה comes upon them, do not fall to their faces but, quite to the contrary, arise. This distinctive reaction ties in well with the theme of the restoration of Israel—the presence of God in this eschatological vision is to be an integral part of the new Jerusalem, before which they need no longer tremble.

Isa. 60:2 contains the sole instance outside the Torah in which כבוד *is the subject of the verb* ראה

Throughout the Classical Hebrew corpus, כבוד displays a marked affinity with the verb ראה (*ra'ah*, "to see"), an affinity which ties in naturally with the association of כבוד with light and the visible. כבוד is found ten times as subject of the niphal form ("to appear, be seen"), twelve times as object of the qal ("to see") and twice as object of the hiphil ("to show").[19] It is worth noting that in every one of these cases, it is God's כבוד which is seen or shown, and in many cases it is כבוד יהוה, though the expression is not always used in its idiomatic sense (cf. particularly Isa. 35:2).

In spite of the high frequency with which כבוד occurs with ראה, Isa. 60:2 contains the only biblical instance of כבוד as subject of the verb outside the books of Exodus, Leviticus, and Numbers.[20] An affinity between Isa. 56–66 and the Torah—the Priestly writings in particular—is noted by Williamson (Williamson 1999, 187–88). In this regard, he mentions Isa. 58:8, in which the כבוד יהוה, as rear guard of his people, is portrayed much as the pillar of fire and cloud in Exod. 13–14; likewise the theme of כבוד resting on Jerusalem (60:1–2; 62:2) reflects the theme found in Exodus,

Leviticus, and Numbers of the כבוד יהוה resting on the sanctuary (e.g., Exod. 29:43, 40:34–5; Lev. 9:6, 23; Num. 14:10, 16:19, 17:7, 20:6). Here in Isa. 60:2, then, it seems likely that we have a further example of this tendency to reflect priestly themes.

Only in Isa. 60–66 is תפארת ascribed to God's dwelling place

The lexeme תפארת, when ascribed to things (as opposed to God or people), is in the majority of cases attributed to forms of ornamentation—to anklets, headbands, and crescents (Isa. 3:18), garments (Isa. 52:1), crowns (עטרה: Isa. 62:3, Jer. 13:18; Ezek. 16:12, 23:42), scepters (מקל: Jer. 48:17), and jewels (כלי: Ezek. 16:17, 16:39, 23:26). However, three times in Isa. 60–64 it is attributed instead to the dwelling place of God—his "house" (בית: Isa. 60:7, 64:10) and his "lofty abode" (זבל, *zvul*: 63:15). In the Hebrew Bible, this use of תפארת is unique;[21] indeed, surprisingly, the direct attribution of "glory" (using any lexeme) to God's dwelling place is not prevalent. The usual—almost exclusive—modifier of בית, היכל (when referring to God's house) and related terms in the Hebrew Bible is קודש ("holiness": see Ps. 5:8, 11:4, 43:3, 65:5, 79:1, 93:5, 138:2; Jon. 2:4, Mic. 1:2, Hab. 2:20, Zech. 2:13).[22] Indeed, in both Isa. 63:15 and 64:40 God's dwelling is called "holy" also. The sole passage outside Isa. 60–66 which explicitly calls God's dwelling "glorious" is Hag. 2:3–9, in which כבוד is three times attributed to the temple. Like the Isaianic passage, this text is eschatological in character, speaking of the restoration of the temple through the influx of the wealth of the nations. This resemblance in the nature of the two texts gives us a clue as to the explanation for the use of "glory"-language to talk about God's dwelling place.

Outside the Hebrew Bible—in particular, in the texts from Qumran—describing the temple (both earthly and heavenly) as "glorious" is commonplace. God's heavenly innermost sanctum (4Q400 f1i:4, 4Q405 f14_15i:6, 11Q17 7:4), his dwelling place (1QH[a] 20:3, 24:11), the abode of the luminaries (1QS 10:3), and the temple (Sir. 49:12, 11Q17 10:8) are each ascribed כבוד, while תפארת is attributed to the temple (4Q504 f1_2riv:12), the streets of the holy city (11Q5 22:5), and the city itself (11Q5 22:4). It must be seen that what connects (at least most of) these passages to Trito-Isaiah and to Hag. 2 is their eschatological character.

Why precisely this should be so is a challenging question. We could, of course, say simply that an eschatological vision such as this is beautiful and glorious in character in general and that this is simply extended to the temple. Indeed, such a suggestion is supported by the extraordinarily abundant and superlative use of "glory"-language in texts such as 4Q405 f19. An alternative possibility, however, lies in the intended permanence of the restored and glorified Zion—throughout the Hebrew Bible, God's "glory" comes upon his temple (cf. 2 Chron. 5:14, 7:1–3, Ps. 26:8, 63:3, 96:6, Ezek. 10, 43–4), but it is impermanent and provisional—glory may depart from Israel (1 Sam. 4:21), and the temple become a source of shame (2 Chron. 7:16–22, Ezek. 24:21). Conceivably, the fact that the temple itself may in eschatological texts be called "glorious" suggests that the "glory" which rests upon it is no longer transient.

Isa. 60:19 contains the only association between תפארת and light

When we think of "glory," it tends to be associated strongly with light—it is conceived as something visible, shining, and brilliant. In fact, in Classical Hebrew, this concept is associated predominantly with כבוד—with which it occurs abundantly[23]—rather than with the other members of its domain. הדר and הוד are also occasionally associated with light (1QH^a 13:32, 1QH^a 20:18, Sir. 26:17) and ascribed to the luminous heavenly bodies (Sir. 43:9, 4Q405 f20ii_22:9). In the whole of extant Classical Hebrew literature, however, תפארת just once is found with this association—in Isa. 60:19:

לֹא־יִהְיֶה־לָּךְ עוֹד הַשֶּׁמֶשׁ לְאוֹר יוֹמָם וּלְנֹגַהּ הַיָּרֵחַ לֹא־יָאִיר לָךְ וְהָיָה־לָךְ יְהוָה לְאוֹר עוֹלָם וֵאלֹהַיִךְ לְתִפְאַרְתֵּךְ:

The sun shall no more be for you as light by day, nor for brightness shall the moon give you light; but the Lord will be for you as everlasting light, and your God will be for you as תפארת.

A potential motivation for this unique instance of the association will be suggested in the concluding paragraphs.

Isa. 60:15 is the only place in which God's people are called the גאון of others

גאון is an interesting member of the semantic domain of כבוד, due to its tendency toward negative connotations. Said of both Israel and foreign nations, it is frequently used in contexts of God's judgment to indicate the "arrogance" which sets itself up in opposition to, or rebellion against, God. Ezekiel thrice describes the destruction of the גאון, or עז גאון, of Egypt (Ezek. 30:6, 30:18, 32:12), and twice, with parallel phrasing, of Israel (24:21, 33:28). Zechariah speaks once each of the fall of the גאון of Philistia (9:6) and of Assyria (10:11), and once of that of the Jordan (11:3). Moab, in parallel verses in Isa. 16:6 and Jer. 48:29, is four times labelled with גאון, again in the context of its destruction. This list is not exhaustive.

It is not, however, a consistently negative term, but may signify instead a justifiable, legitimate (source of) "pride." This is particularly the case when applied to God's people in contexts of their restoration;[24] see for example Nah. 2:3:

כִּי שָׁב יְהוָה אֶת־גְּאוֹן יַעֲקֹב כִּגְאוֹן יִשְׂרָאֵל כִּי בְקָקוּם בֹּקְקִים וּזְמֹרֵיהֶם שִׁחֵתוּ:

For the Lord is restoring the גאון of Jacob as the גאון of Israel, for plunderers have plundered them and ruined their branches.

So also Isa. 4:2:

בַּיּוֹם הַהוּא יִהְיֶה צֶמַח יְהוָה לִצְבִי וּלְכָבוֹד וּפְרִי הָאָרֶץ לְגָאוֹן וּלְתִפְאֶרֶת לִפְלֵיטַת יִשְׂרָאֵל

In that day the branch of the Lord shall be (for) צבי and כבוד, and the fruit of the land shall be as גאון and תפארת of the survivors of Israel.

Indeed, the גאון of Israel, when positive, is generally connected with God's land-related gifts (cf. Ps. 45:7).

In Isa. 60:15, uniquely, the restored Zion itself is said to be לגאון for ever. That is, rather than God's people seeking their גאון in the blessings God has given them, here they themselves *are* גאון—while it is not stated explicitly, it is clear that they are the גאון of someone, that someone being the other nations who will flock to the restored Jerusalem. This verse finds its counterpart, or converse, in some sense, in Isa. 13:19, in which the great city of Babylon is called the גאון of the Chaldeans; here the context is that of her downfall at the hand of God, for Babylon has set herself up in arrogance, and those who honor her are misled. In Isa. 60:15, Zion's role as גאון is by the will of God, and the nations' honor to her a form of honor to her King. Thus we see once again that this unique use of "glory"-language is closely tied to the restorative and eschatological character of the text.

Conclusions and implications

The most notable cumulative effect of Trito-Isaiah's distinctive usage of "glory"-language is to tie in with and enhance the chapters' eschatological character. The "glory" that we find here is to be restored to, and no more torn away from, the people of God. Indeed, Zion itself may without sin or presumption be called גאון. The כבוד יהוה will go before God's people and be seen among them as in the time of the Exodus, and their righteousness and cleanliness mean that this presence of God among them is no longer to be feared but met with confidence and rejoiced in.

This brings us back to the issue of the limited range of "glory" vocabulary in these chapters, and the use of (primarily) the lexemes כבוד and תפארת, for which no explanation has as yet been suggested. Consideration of lexical usage is highly significant for understanding authorial intention, and thus for exegesis. For it must be remembered that whenever language is produced, whether written or oral, a choice is made to use one word over another and that in selecting one lexeme, the author is rejecting (however consciously or actively) other syntactically equivalent members of the domain. In the case of written communication, word choice is of course often more conscious and deliberate. Through detailed corpus-based, bottom-up analysis of patterns of word association both within and between semantic domains, as noted earlier, we are able to discover what these alternative possibilities were for the Classical Hebrew author, and to uncover clues as to the way these near-synonyms were both related to and distinguished from each other in the mind of the native speaker, in terms of the standard connotations and common associations of each lexeme.[25] Against this background the lexical choices of the Isaianic (or indeed any) author gain significance, and, by knowing the alternatives between which he was choosing, we are able to make some proposals regarding his motivations for his use of particular vocabulary.

Using the eschatological nature of the chapters as a starting point, I would like to propose two possible reasons why the author might have chosen—deliberately or instinctively—to focus almost exclusively on the lexemes כבוד and תפארת. The first lies in the association between eschatological visions and light. Light imagery in Isa. 58ff. is plentiful, and strongly associated with the themes of restoration and healing, as opposed to the darkness of sin and misery (cf. 58:8–10, 59:9–10, 60:1–5, 19–20, 62:1). Throughout Classical Hebrew, as already noted, כבוד is the "glory"-word which most carries connotations of light, and therefore that which would occur most naturally to the mind of a writer conscious of eschatological visions. While this provides some explanation for the extensive use of כבוד, it cannot also account for the presence of תפארת, which is elsewhere unassociated with light; nonetheless, it may explain the unique association of תפארת with light in Isa. 60:19.

A second potential motivation for the preference given to כבוד is its strong association with divine presence. A key aspect of the restored Jerusalem, of course, is the dwelling of God with his people, a concept widely associated with the expression כבוד יהוה. Thus while in many cases in Isa. 56–66 the idiomatic sense of כבוד יהוה is not present, nonetheless כבוד is likely once again to be the lexeme which most instinctively presents itself to the author's mind.[26]

We have as yet suggested no motivation for the use of תפארת, or for the exclusion of other major "glory"-lexemes, such as צבי, הוד, הדר and גאוה. For the last of these, גאוה, a motivation is not difficult to find, for the term, when applied to man, is consistently negative, bearing connotations of unrighteousness and rebellion; its absence from a text of restoration is thus unsurprising. In the case of הוד, the absence is not specifically from Isa. 56–66 but from the book as a whole—it occurs just once, in Isa. 30:30. Here the most likely explanation relates to the lack of association of הוד with moral behavior, and its entire lack of ascription to nations—making it unconnected to the main themes of Isaiah. The motivation for omitting הדר and צבי, however—both of which occur with considerable frequency in the earlier chapters of Isaiah[27]—is less apparent. Perhaps, however, some hints may be found in considering the standard usage and connotations of the terms.

תפארת, as noted earlier, is strongly associated with ornamentation, and particularly with crowns. This makes it uniquely suitable in the description of Zion in her perfected and adorned state (Isa. 62:3; cf. 52:1). However, another motivation may also be present. It is interesting to note that in most of its earlier instances in Isaiah תפארת bears negative connotations—it is found in connection to the finery of the haughty women of Zion (3:18) which the Lord will take away; to the look of arrogance in the eyes of the king of Assyria (10:12); to Babylon (13:19) and Egypt (20:5), in which the nations falsely boast; to the "proud crown" of the drunkards of Ephraim (28:1, 4); and to an idol of wood (44:13). The reason for this, consistently, is that people are seeking their תפארת in something other than their God. Yet from chapter 46 all is transformed, and the associations consistently positive. Conceivably, we see here a deliberate move to show that now by contrast, in the restored Zion, God's righteous people seek their תפארת only in him and in his gifts to them (cf. Isa 60:19).

הדר, in general, bears connotations of dignity and honor; it is frequently associated with the garments of authority and worthiness—particularly robes (Job. 40:10, Ps.

104:1, Prov. 31:25, 1QS 4:8, 4Q525 f11_12:2). Relatedly, it is linked to the concept of royalty, being attributed to kings and rulers (Ps. 8:6, 21:6, 45:4–5), and to God particularly in his role as warrior leader, in association with his active power (Isa. 2:10, 4Q510 f1:3, 11Q5 26:9). While such themes are not wholly absent from Trito-Isaiah, they are far from dominant—it is God in his role as Savior and Restorer, not Warrior, who predominates in these chapters, while human authority figures do not play a role. This perhaps goes some way to accounting for the absence of הדר in the text.

צבי is the most material of the members of the semantic domain of כבוד, being ascribed in most of its occurrences to the inanimate, and being linked, most notably, to geographic locations, whether to various nations (e.g., Ezek. 25:9) and cities (e.g., Isa. 13:19) or to the Promised Land of Israel (e.g., Jer. 3:19, Ezek. 20:6, Dan. 8:9). Conceivably, its absence here is due to the focus not so much on a concrete geographical location as on an idealized and restored Zion; however, its presence in other eschatological texts, such as Isa. 4:2, would seem to belie such an idea. It may well be that its absence here is either a question of authorial preference, or else simply coincidental, given that צבי is not a highly frequent lexeme in Classical Hebrew.

It is hoped that this chapter has illustrated the value of a cognitive theoretical approach, and of a corpus-based, bottom-up methodology, for the exegesis of biblical and ancient texts, through highlighting the kind of insights which may be gained into a text through detailed and objective analysis of the semantic background against which that text is written. Exegesis based on cognitive methods is still in its infancy in biblical studies, but as this chapter has sought to demonstrate, it promises to enrich our understanding of the thought-world of the people behind the texts.

6

The Influence of Categorization on Translation Meaning

Shelley Ashdown

Introduction

Cognitive science has long addressed the question of what is the basis of cognition. The fundamental operating principle of cognition is categorization (Rosch 1973; Quinn et al. 2003). Harnad states that to cognize automatically also means to categorize (Harnad 2005). Categorization is the principal task of cognition, and as such it operates as the essential means by which we perceive and interpret our life experience (Cohen and Lefebvre 2005). The human mind is dependent on categories to make human life functional (de Blois 2004). Categories do not have to be true but rather functionally effective for their users (Ungerer and Schmid 1996).

People who are herders, farmers, fishermen, Buddhist, Hindu, African Traditional Religionist, Christian, American, African, Asian, and the list goes on, interpret their life experience in a myriad of ways that distinguishes their understanding of the world from others. Because of this, our categories are shaped by knowledge and meaning characteristic to our cultural context whether they come from the hardwired nature of our brain or independently formed by our embodied life experience. Just what goes into a category is quite context dependent. The diversity of languages, peoples, geographies, economies, etc., contributes to the enormous creativity in category formation and content. Categories are innate to human cognition. The study of humanity in recent history is beginning to appreciate how learning about ethnic categories contributes to cross-cultural understanding. And with understanding comes the hope of better oral and written communication.

Category inquiry is useful for the field of translation because of innate human ability to interpret and organize the world in and around key categories that ultimately impact the perceived meaning of a translated text. Cognitive investigation in translation science should be concerned with not only salient categories in the source language text, but also key categories target language members identify with culture-specific values. Members of a target audience use available category knowledge like different colors in a painting to understand and apply the biblical text to daily life. Categorization may be described as a cognitive framework allowing a person to process perception and assign meaning, relevance, and saliency to a text (Kim 2000).

The primary aim of this chapter is to present a functional approach to categorization and its consequences for translation. A suggested paradigm highlights the central role categorization plays in communicating translation meaning across cultures and languages. Discussion will also explore how both cultural exegesis and biblical exegesis are necessary to identify salient categories with meaning specific to a target audience of a translation. The Akan people of West Africa are the example audience, color is the example category, and Zech. 1:8 and 6:1–8 are the example texts for translation. The exegesis of Akan color categories are based on three significant areas: the first, cognitive efficiency defined by key representations; the second, cognitive interpretation defined by key contexts; and the third, cognitive organization defined by key general and concrete levels.

Exegesis of Akan color categories

The population of Akan peoples of West Africa is estimated in Ghana to be 8.3 million. Three major groups include the Asante Twi at 2.8 million located in south central Ghana, Ashanti Province; the Fante Twi at 1.9 million found mostly in south central Ghana, between Winneba, Takoradi, and Obuasi; and the Akwapim Twi at 555,000 located in southeast Ghana, north of Accra.[1] The Akan have a complex worldview which uses color categories as key organizing and meaning-based cognitive structures. The function of these color categories and the possible consequences for translation highlight the role of categorization for interpreting and understanding the biblical text by the Akan audience.

Cognitive efficiency in Akan color representations

People engage in categorizing by evaluating differences and confining together that which they deem similar (Rosch 1978). As a result, categorizing allows associated meaning and significance to quickly aid individual perception with minimal effort. Categorization is an innate tool to make us efficient cognitive processors. Categories have key members/representations that allow a person to automatically access all relevant information in a category to the situation at hand (Ross and Spalding 1994). The tendency in cognitive processing is for a category to be represented by what the perceiver determines are the most typical members. These typical members are referred to as exemplars. Exemplars are key generalizations with the most characteristic category features. People tend to select those category members supporting their worldview and keep them in sharper focus than peripheral category members. Hence, the consequence of cognitive efficiency results in the use of key category representations.

When considering cognitive efficiency, the key question is: What are Akan key representations of color? Certainly Akan people recognize a great many hues, nonetheless three salient color terms are perceived as three broad categories, not only representing the color spectrum, but also symbolically salient in life experience. Akan worldview conceptualizes the universe based on these three colors: white (*fufu*), red (*kokoo* or *kobene*), and black (*tuntum*; Hagan 1970). Each color has a key representation pertaining to one of three fundamental aspects of the universe (see Table 6.1). Female

Table 6.1 Key representations in Akan color categories

	Akan Red Color Category	Akan Black Color Category	Akan White Color Category
Key Representations	FEMALE	NEUTRAL	MALE

represents the red category, male represents the white category, and the black category is represented by the neutral aspect which is sometimes parallel, different from, beyond, or equivalent with male (white) and female (red) exemplars (Bartle 1983). Contained in the female, male, and neutral representations underlying the universe are numerous contexts represented by exemplars specific to each arena.

Cognitive interpretation of Akan color contexts

Categories also have key contexts as a means for cognitive interpretation. The same category will have different key representations with different key meaning in different contexts. Category interpretation can change focus because a person perceives that the point of view has shifted (Barsalou 1987). Category application is highly dependent on contextual knowledge. Cultural influence does make category content context bound (D'Andrade 1990).

The Akan red, white, and black color categories may be applied to five significant contexts selected here to illustrate Akan worldview. In regard to the worldview universal category of Self, there are:

1. Context of the physical Self
2. Context of the spiritual Self
3. Context of Self and social Other

The second group of key contexts has to do with properties of the greater universe referenced here as Other: Context of the physical universe, and Context of the spiritual universe.

In the Akan context of the physical Self, the feminine red category is represented by the red Self (see Table 6.2). Every Akan possesses a red Self since each and every Akan is nurtured in the womb and born of his or her mother. Likewise, in death every human body returns to Mother Nature/Earth. The red physical Self places the Akan as a member in the matrilineage. The context of the spiritual Self is represented by a blood spirit with the inference that an overarching matrilineal spirit binds members of a lineage group together. Any Akan clan member, living or dead, is connected to one's blood spirit by virtue of their matrilineal link. Individual's membership in the matrilineal descent group is a key exemplar for Self in relationship with social Other. The red Self offers possibilities concerning promotion to social offices, property inheritance, and land access—all of which are linked to matrilineal descent customs. Red in the context of the Self and social Other also infers female obligations in Akan

Table 6.2 Five key contexts in the Akan red color category

	Akan Red Color Category	
	Key Category Representation	**FEMALE**
		Key Context Representations
	SELF	
KEY CONTEXTS	1. CONTEXT OF THE PHYSICAL SELF	Red Self
	2. CONTEXT OF THE SPIRITUAL SELF	Blood Spirit
	3. CONTEXT OF THE SELF AND SOCIAL OTHER	Matrilineal descent group
	OTHER	
	4. CONTEXT OF THE PHYSICAL UNIVERSE	Land
	5. CONTEXT OF THE SPIRITUAL UNIVERSE	Mother Nature/Earth

society. Women bear children, provide milk and cook, farm the land and trade crops, and make clay pots.

In the context of the physical universe, land is classed as red. Red is a symbol of both seriousness and danger in earthly life. Dirt is red clay smeared on mourners, and the color red is worn by relatives at funerals. Mother Nature/Earth is the key representation in the context of the spiritual universe. She is the matrilineal grandmother of the ancestors and reflects the role of women as social and economic laborers. This female aspect of the universe infers Mother Nature/Earth and her feminine offspring are the prolific provider of food, children, and other valued commodities. Mother Nature/Earth is fertilized by white and empowered by black. There are opposing dichotomies in relation to the female red, "just as one must get one's feet dirty in the mud of the market to become wealthy, so touching Mother Nature/Earth is serious; one gets defiled, but wealthy" (Bartle 1983, 90). The red category recognizes the importance of female contributions to the clan in fruitful bearing of offspring and economic provision for the matrilineage. But equally as significant is the serious danger inferred by all things red. Red is also the spatially left in the universe.

The black Self represents one of the three physical aspects of a person. It is neither red (female/left) nor white (male/right) but rather neutral in the sense of equivalent yet different, parallel but beyond (see Table 6.3). The black Self is created by the divine breath of life given by the Creator High God Nyame, at the birth of each Akan. He also gives a destiny soul to each newborn operating as a dynamic psychical Self element which animates a person with life and a spiritual personality. An individual is admonished to take care of his or her destiny soul by behaving properly and with good intentions, otherwise one's destiny soul will become soiled resulting in bad luck. The neutral aspect of the black category accounts for the dynamic nature of life. The destiny soul is a changeable element with the capacity to be bribed, ridiculed, and influenced in good or bad ways. Those born on the same day of the week are thought to share a collective destiny soul that places them in a kind of destiny brotherhood or sisterhood.

Table 6.3 Five key contexts in the Akan black color category

	Akan Black Color Category	
	Key Category Representation	**NEUTRAL**
		Key Context Representations
	SELF	
KEY CONTEXTS	1. CONTEXT OF THE PHYSICAL SELF	Black Self
	2. CONTEXT OF THE SPIRITUAL SELF	Destiny Soul
	3. CONTEXT OF THE SELF AND SOCIAL OTHER	Akan tradition
	OTHER	
	4. CONTEXT OF THE PHYSICAL UNIVERSE	Air
	5. CONTEXT OF THE SPIRITUAL UNIVERSE	Ancestors representing Creator Nyame

Tradition represents black in the context of Self and social Other. Tradition is key to a person's history, their potential political power, the past and future (time) as well as ritual. Black mourning clothes may be worn to symbolize a normal life change event and not because it represents sadness. Creator Nyame and the ancestors make tradition possible and sustain it with beliefs in ancestral power, Akan history and memories, and ritual practices.

In the context of the physical universe, air represents neutral space because it operates beyond the realm of direction. Air is central because it is the medium for rain to come from the sky and to make the earth fertile. Air is described as the breath of the universe with its own destiny. Other resemblances to air include sky, motion, fire, heaven, and wind as the medium of predicting rain.

Creator Nyame is the key representation in the context of the spiritual universe. The blackness of Creator Nyame places him beyond reach to know or approach. The created must interact with lesser gods and ancestors for supernatural help. Nonetheless, out of respect, the Akan will speak to Creator Nyame first or second in prayer. In brief prayers just using his name includes all other deities. Akans believe supernatural gods are all in spiritual unity with Creator Nyame, so that if you call one, you call all. The black category accounts for immortality through death and reincarnation either as an ancestral spirit in this life or the next. Air, destiny soul, breath, ancestral spirits, and Creator Nyame are invisible agents operating in a physical universe. Air physically empowers the universe and interacts with the divine energy. It is no wonder that the black category is symbolic of that which is unknown and invisible.

The Akan white category is male with the concept of fluid, a resemblance aspect linking the various contexts together with coherence. Maleness is evident in each person through the white Self. Every child receives a white Self from the white semen fluid of the father at conception. The fertility aspect of white semen fluid infers the capacity to both permeate and purify to give birth. Physical strength as in strength of bones is associated with a father's fluid. In the context of the spiritual Self, white fluids inherited from father supply a child with a morality spirit that seems to account for fertility and personality (see Table 6.4).

Addressing the context of the Self and social Other, whatever contributes to social continuity is white. The morality, personality spirit is tied to Akan social identity so that the white Self is a conscience to honor social tradition. Socially, fertility (white fluid) ensures lineage continuity and purity maintains social ideology. Moral education has traditionally been the responsibility of the father and not the matrilineage. White in the context of Self and social Other infers male social roles in Akan society. Men are concerned with matters of morality and justice in the roles as politicians and community decision makers.

It is no great surprise that water represents the physical universe as it does the right direction. Water takes various forms such as rivers, rain characterized as the semen of the universe, and lakes where blue is considered an intense form of white. Key in the male spiritual universe are river gods who are patrilineal descendants of Creator Nyame. As tutelary deities, river gods inhabit clouds, rain, rivers, lakes, and any water source. Their primary function is to make women fertile including the female Mother Nature/Earth. Water is used for rituals that are concerned with ousting evil spirits associated with illness, crop failure, bad behavior, or just plain bad luck. Other, lesser gods are also classed as white male and these inhabit the rocks, caves, and mountains. It is important to note that the characteristic features of the white category are success and joy since fluid continually makes the universe and all in it fertile.

Cognitive organization of Akan color taxonomy

One way of picturing cognition is to view categories as taxonomies that structure information (Rosch 1978). A person has two needs, with one being "to have the most informative categorization possible" and the other to have a category:

Table 6.4 Five key contexts in the Akan white color category

	Akan White Color Category	
	Key Category Representation	**MALE**
		Key Context Representations
	SELF	
KEY CONTEXTS	1. CONTEXT OF THE PHYSICAL SELF	White Self
	2. CONTEXT OF THE SPIRITUAL SELF	Morality, personality spirit
	3. CONTEXT OF THE SELF AND SOCIAL OTHER	Community leader, politician
	OTHER	
	4. CONTEXT OF THE PHYSICAL UNIVERSE	Water
	5. CONTEXT OF THE SPIRITUAL UNIVERSE	Tutelary deities: river gods

Table 6.5 Key general and concrete levels of Akan color categories

	Akan White Color Category	Akan Red Color Category	Akan Black Color Category
GENERAL TO CONCRETE	*Abstract:* morality, fertility, justice	*Abstract:* kinship, economics	*Abstract:* destiny, power, politics
	Concrete: Water	*Concrete:* Land	*Concrete:* Air

Be as discriminable (or distinctive) as possible. The informativeness desire pushes toward more and more specific categories while the discriminability often leads to higher categories. The informativeness relates directly to one of the primary functions of categories—allowing useful inferences. (Ross and Spalding 1994, 130)

Akan color categories represent categorization by association and this is reflected in the structure of their general and concrete category levels (see Table 6.5). The members of categories by association vary tremendously across cultures and can be regarded as contextual categories (Mandler 2004). At the general level, color is universal; but just what composes the various category levels of color differs across cultures as do the color associations. The task is to identify differences in conceptual associations between the source language and target language in translation.

Exegesis of Zech. 1 and Zech. 6 with color terms

Discussion now turns to the biblical examples from Zech. 1:8 and 6:1–8; before considering Akan interpretation issues for translation. In Zechariah's vision, chariot riders with horse teams of different color patrol the earth in service of their Maker. Their particular function centers on hopeful visions for the post-exilic people of the covenant in the context of rebuilding the temple, and it excludes divine judgment. Here are the text:

Zech. 1:8–11

8 I was attentive that night and saw a man seated on a red (אָדֹם, *adom*) horse that stood among some myrtle trees in the ravine. Behind him were red (אֲדֻמִּים, *adumim*), sorrel (שְׂרֻקִּים, *srukim*), and white (לְבָנִים, *levanim*) horses. 9 Then I asked one nearby, "What are these, sir?" The angelic messenger who replied with me said, "I will show you what these are." 10 Then the man standing among the myrtle trees spoke up and said, "These are the ones whom the Lord has sent to walk about on the earth." 11 The riders then agreed with the angel of the Lord, who was standing among the myrtle trees, "We have been walking about on the earth, and now everything is at rest and quiet."

Zech. 6:1–8

1 Once more I looked, and this time I saw four chariots emerging from between two mountains of bronze. 2 Harnessed to the first chariot were red (אֲדֻמִּים, *adumim*) horses, to the second black (שְׁחֹרִים, *shehorim*) horses, 3 to the third white (לְבָנִים, *levanim*) horses, and to the fourth spotted (בְּרֻדִּים, *berudim*) horses, all of them strong (אֲמֻצִּים, *amutsim*). 4 Then I asked the angelic messenger who was speaking with me, "What are these, sir?" 5 The messenger replied, "These are the four spirits of heaven that have been presenting themselves before the Lord of all the earth." 6 The chariot with the black (הַשְּׁחֹרִים, *hashehorim*) horses is going to the north country; and the white (הַלְּבָנִים, *halevanim*) ones are going after them, but the spotted (הַבְּרֻדִּים, *haberudim*) ones are going to the south country. 7 All these strong (הָאֲמֻצִּים, *ha'amutsim*) ones are scattering; they have sought permission to go and walk about over the earth. The Lord had said "Go! Walkabout over the earth!" So they are doing so. 8 Then he cried out to me, "Look! The ones going to the northland have brought me peace about the northland."

The number of horses differs between the two texts. The first vision, in Zech. 1:8, describes three colored horses with the number three, as analyzed by scholars, is symbolic of their divinely given task to scout all the earth. Three is the smallest number reducible to a beginning, middle, and end; three being a representation of totality (Meyers and Meyers 1987, 112). The red, sorrel, and white horses carry their angelic representatives to see all that is necessary to report back to God.

In the eighth vision of Zechariah (Zech. 6:1–8), there are four chariots, each powered by a different colored horse team. The text itself explains, in 6:5, that the four colored groups of horses have a task that symbolizes Yahweh's control over.

The color of the horses has been associated by some to four quadrants of heaven, red being east, black—the north, white—the west, and spotted being the south (Robinson and Horst 1964). The association of the four colors with four directions is debated among scholars. Ringgren opposes this view; Robinson and Horst confirm it (Robinson and Horst 1964; Ringgren 1985). According to Zech. 6:5, the horses and riders are spirits (רוּחוֹת, *ruhot*) sent out to represent the Lord of heaven and earth. The direction of service given to each team does not offer any information differentiating the task of one team from another; rather it serves to highlight Yahweh's supremacy over the universe. The horse groups of the first vision and the final eighth vision provide an inclusio for the text by framing the sequence of the eight visions (Meyers and Meyers 1987).

Zechariah uses imagery indicative of his time. The reference to night in 1:8 infers the need for traveling undetected, and horses provide the greatest traveling speed at the time. It should be noted, though, that Zechariah presents a positive view of the Persian Empire, its stability, and tolerance (Meyers and Meyers 1987). In both visions the horses and riders are commission by Yahweh. The riders are angels of the Lord whose special function is to bring a portion of divine glory wherever they travel just by their mere presence. These angelic beings assert the omnipresence of Yahweh in the universe and specifically among his chosen people (Bowling 1980). The addition of chariots in the eighth vision of chapter 6 brings to focus the omnipotence of Yahweh using earthly imagery of military muscle and global control (see Table 6.6).

Categorization and Translation Meaning 107

Table 6.6 Cognitive functions of Zech. 1:8 and 6:1–8 horse color categories

	Zechariah Horse Colors				
	Key Category Representation		→	HEAVENLY WINDS/ SPIRITS	
	WHITE	RED	BLACK	SORREL	SPOTTED
Key Representation	West	East	North	—	South
Key Resemblance	COLORED HORSES ARE STRONG אמץ				
Key Context	CONTEXT OF POST-EXILIC HOPE				

There is some debate as to why the list of colors for horses in 6:2–3 differs from those in 6:6–7.[2] In this chapter all the colors mentioned in the two passages, including red (אדם), black (שחר), white (לבן), sorrel (שרק),[3] and spotted (ברד) are considered.[4] אמץ *adom* is discussed later as "strong" and not the equine color term "bay."[5] In Zech. 1:8 and 6:2, *adom* is a hyponym modifying סוס (*sus*, horse) along with *lavan* (לבן), *sarok* (שרק), *barod* (ברד), and *shahor* (שחר). The first vision in 1:8 has the first rider mounted on a אדם (*adom*) horse "standing among the myrtle trees." אדם is normally translated red and encompasses bright red to a reddish brown hue (Kedar-Kopfstein 1988). Horses are obviously not red in the sense of crimson or scarlet but many do have a reddish brown color characterized by chestnut (Brenner 1982). Red earth or red ochre is associated with אדם (Hartley 2011, 114). Red dirt or red clay is a natural stain and is a common geographical feature used by those in the ancient Near East. The semantic range of color hues for אדם is from light brown to dark red and specifies equine chestnut or bay.

Following the first horseman in 1:8 are three groupings of riders made distinguishable by the color of their horses: אדם (chestnut), שרק (sorrel), and לבן (white). There is some debate as to whether שרקם should be translated spotted or some type of solid reddish color. There is no reason to believe שרק should be changed to mean a spotted horse of some type; its meaning quite simply is a reddish brown color delineated in equine terms as sorrel or bay (Brenner 1982). שרק seems to be a secondary color of red with a sheen of reddish brown. An appropriate English gloss would be sorrel or bay (Alden 1997).

לבן is a focal color of bright white but the semantic range encompasses light gray to light yellow. The word is used in regard to the color of goats (Gen. 30:35) suggesting a light color is in the permissible range in addition to white. White or gray could be envisioned for horses delineated as לבן in Zech. 1:8 and 6:3, 6. The LXX uses mostly λευκός to translate לבן. In both cases, the terms for white are associated with the whiteness of things such as garments, teeth, milk, and leprosy; לבן and λευκός symbolize joy and purity (Ringgren 1985, 438).

The prophet saw four color types of horses pulling chariots in the eighth vision in Zech. 6:1–8. These draft horses are referenced according to the colors chestnut, black, white, and piebald/spotted/dappled. שחר, perceived as black, is a term included in the Zech. 6:1–8 passage but missing in Zech. 1:8. This can be adequately explained in terms of the literary use of sevens by Zechariah.[6] Semantically שחר includes dark colors ranging from dark brown to black (Alden 1997).

Most translations of ברד chose a lexeme for multicolored horses such as piebald, dappled, or spotted. Borg suggests that ברד may have referenced a certain kind of species of horses by West Semitic peoples given the extensive color vocabulary of Bedouin shepherds differentiating various hues of livestock (Borg 1999). Even though the use of ברד describes a multicolored horse which then differs from the vision text of four solid colors, Meyers and Meyers believe that within the horses of Zechariah's vision, it is to be understood as spotted or dappled.[7] Piebald is a specific English gloss for animals but descriptions could include horses with patterns of patches or spots, and these spots are white or light colored.

Hartley agrees with Boda as well as Butterworth that אמץ in Zech. 6:3, 7 carries the sense of strong steeds rather than denoting a color aspect of the horses.[8] The basic meaning of אמץ is having strength and power and it refers to a quality one possesses. Oft times this word is used to characterize conflict and even war. Survival and defense in wartime are dependent on one's strength to see it through (Schreiner 1974). Thus, in Zech. 6:3, אמץ modifies all four groups of chariot horses as strong and powerful animals needed to pull a chariot to the ends of the earth.

Exegetical consequences for Akan translation

Every translation at some juncture introduces new meaning with old vocabulary. Without care, the new meaning is sidetracked by existing category representations with its inappropriate inferences. Translation practitioners should question what category knowledge a target language will bring to a passage, the abstract and concrete levels organizing the category, and the values of key representations, key contexts, and key inferences of category knowledge compared to the source language text.

Because Akan color categories encompass so many worldview assumptions, inferences will be made concerning Zech. 1 and 6 so as to influence their interpretation. Essential to the process of meaningful translation is coming to terms with the correlation between Akan color classifications and how this effects perception of events and ultimately the meaning of the written word. The color triad is essential in ordering Akan worldview making it foolhardy to try and replace it or ignore it. In the case of riders on red, black, or white horses, each color category has the meaning potential of physical, spiritual, or social aspects typical of these delineations. The single word "red" triggers multiple meaning potentials typical of the category as do "black" and "white."

Two main questions require attention. First, what aspects of Akan color distinctions seem to support appropriate use of each color in the Zechariah passages? Second, what aspects of Akan color distinctions seem to imply inappropriate meaning to the texts? There are multiple meaning potentials for Akan readers to choose to identify with the biblical riders using colored horses in the Zechariah passages. The task is to discover which meaning is most likely to be associated from Akan worldview to the biblical text.

The colored horses of Zechariah represent all aspects of life for the Akan, including physical, social, and spiritual dimensions. It is the contexts of Self and Other in which key category elements are associated with the Zechariah texts. If the horses/riders represent spirits sent by Creator Nyame, then the four colors could be viewed as

Categorization and Translation Meaning 109

signifying supernatural beings associated with each of the three Akan basic colors. The horse color sorrel in Zech. 1:8 probably would be considered a member of the Akan red category. The horse described as spotted in Zech. 6.3 is more difficult to predict category affiliation. The spotted horse still would be placed in one of the basic colors of the Akan triad but which one is the question. If Akans perceived the spotted horse as mostly white with a few patches, then the white category may come into play. There is no prediction that can be made confidently without field queries.

White, black, and red represent the Akan spiritual universe under the control of Creator Nyame. In a general sense, the horses/riders as winds or spirits in the Zechariah text infer the black, neutral category in which the essence of power is highlighted. These spirits are energized by Yahweh with the ability to move throughout the earth. Creator Nyame is able to send spirits out from each color category as wind, since he is the total of all supernatural beings. As wind, these spiritual beings are invisible and travel quickly. The Akan no doubt would associate these spiritual winds as the animation behind the horses/riders. Air in the black category is the medium of prediction. Perhaps the use of divinely empowered black horses/riders would associate unfolding prophecy or reinforce the Akan belief ancestral spirits and lesser gods monitor the activities of people.

The black horses/riders are likely to be interpreted as ancestral spirits sent by Creator Nyame to survey the people of earth and report on the political climate and distribution of power (see Table 6.7). The tradition of the covenant people was taken

Table 6.7 Key elements of Akan color categories influencing Zechariah meaning

	Interpreting Zechariah through Akan Color Categories			
	Representation of Horses/Riders →			SUPERNATURAL BEINGS
	Key Representation	Key Contexts	Key Inferences	Key Levels Abstract/Concrete
WHITE לבן	Riders are Lesser deities	CONTEXT OF SELF AND OTHER	Condition of Morality AND Fertility	*Abstract*: morality, fertility justice *Concrete*: Water
RED אדם **SORREL** שרק	Riders are Mother Nature/Earth	CONTEXT OF SELF AND OTHER	Condition of Clans/Lineages AND Land	*Abstract*: kin membership, economics *Concrete*: Land
BLACK שחר	Riders are Ancestors	CONTEXT OF SELF AND OTHER	Condition of Political Power	*Abstract*: destiny, power, politics *Concrete*: Air
SPOTTED	POSSIBLY SUBSUMED UNDER THE WHITE CATEGORY			

away in the exile because the destiny soul of the people was deceived away from their destiny as the chosen people of The Promise. Now ancestral spirits are surveying to see whether the past has been put behind and the people of Yahweh are once again ready to move into a divinely blessed future. It is the time right for Israel to inherit the promise of Abraham. It is Israel's destiny to be the people of Yahweh. Be of good cheer, would be the Akans' understanding, in the post-exilic world, the winds of change are coming for Israel to rebuild the temple.

The understanding by Akans that the tradition of the people can somehow be lost creates an enormous dissonance between the Akan worldview and the Zechariah text. It simply is not possible for a people to lose their tradition and still exist as a distinct group of people. This notion would be difficult for the Akan reader. In addition, the existence of a destiny that could be deceived and then lost to the divine is another point of dissonance between Akan worldview and Old Testament worldview. Akan understanding and use of ancestral spirits to interpret the text is contrary to the norms of exegesis.

The red horses/riders may evoke images of the spirit of Mother Nature/Earth sent out to survey the matrilineages of her earthly realm. Each individual has a blood spirit that simultaneously provides individuality and connects the person to increasingly wider matrilineal kin groups until every person shares a degree of matrilineal membership. The totality of red selves culminates in all humanity belonging to Mother Nature/Earth. The spirit of Mother Nature/Earth includes reporting on the physical condition of post-exilic lands. The search is for evidence each clan of Israel has sufficient means of provision and determine what is lacking for economic survival. Is the white universe providing the land with adequate rainfall? Are lesser gods making women fertile? Are lesser gods reversing evil situations such as poverty and agricultural woes?

Akan understanding of spirits from the white category most likely focuses on the supernatural beings of tutelary gods. Akan lesser gods, especially water deities such as river gods, are characterized as "sons of God" (Dickson 1984, 55). Applied in the Zechariah passages, these lesser deities could very well be conceived as divinely commissioned to observe the moral condition of humanity. Unfortunately lesser deities are not recognized by Yahweh. While Akans may rightly understand that the people of Yahweh were sent into exile as a consequence of their sin, the interpretation that lesser gods are concerned with matters of justice and it is they who report the time of Israel's exile had reached a rightful conclusion is not the understanding translators would deem acceptable. The white horses/riders may signal that the continuity of God's people will continue as the people flourish in a new era of spiritual awakening.

Conclusion

The utility for the function of cognition as a theoretical approach to exegesis and translation is the applicability across languages and cultures. Categories are universally organized in terms of an efficient means for interpreting the life experience. These two areas encompassing cognitive efficiency and cognitive interpretation reflect value dimensions. Are valued categories and category values receiving adequate attention by translation practitioners? What can we learn from the power of the color categories Akan people value?

Color speaks.

> Color is held to unify (through percepts and sensations), physical universe and mind. It is the primal "glue," the medium of "inbetweeness" or "tissue" that holds world and mind together: the world of objects being presented to the mind as an array of colored patches. (Saunders 2007)

To the biblical writers, color represented meaning in the Zechariah events. Color in the Akan world organizes and defines meaningful aspects of the life experience.

The triad of red, black, and white is a classificatory system forming the axis of worldview among the Akan. It is a window into the organization of indigenous knowledge that with superb efficiency uses categorization to interpret the world in a tricolor scheme. It is not the sole means whereby the Akan people envision Self and Other; nonetheless, the three color ensemble represents a basic cluster of assumptions about the laws of earthly Other (nature), community Other (society), and supernatural Other (spirits). Each color category is not a bounded, secluded unit of knowledge but operates in a dynamic relationship with the other two color categories. The Akan color triad symbolizes rank and status within the greater society and smaller clan group, provides supernatural presence when evoked, establishes distinctive identities of earthly and supernatural players even to the point of outlining relationships, and denotes specific values associated with a ritual or ceremony.

Many reasons necessitate adjustments to categorical knowledge. People modify their categories with regularity in order to adapt to the changing dynamic of life. The translation community must work toward anticipating the adjustments needed to category knowledge among people as translated Scripture redefines those categories and ultimately reshapes worldview.

7

Imaging Resurrection: Toward an Image Schematic Understanding of Resurrection Beliefs in Second Temple Judaism

Frederick S. Tappenden

Introduction

A methodological problem when studying notions of resurrection in second temple Judaism is the fact that, in many instances, it is not entirely clear how one is to discern or demarcate what constitutes the concept of "resurrection." To be sure, while certain passages stand as prime examples (e.g., Dan. 12:1–3), one can point to several pericopes that may or may not refer to resurrection (depending on one's interpretive stance). The sectarian literature at Qumran is a prime example; despite Émile Puech's two-volume encyclopedic treatment in favor of resurrection belief at Qumran (Puech 1993), others such as John Collins maintain there is no clear reference to resurrection among the sectarian literature (e.g., Collins 2009, esp. 307–10). At a more specific level, what are we to make of a tradition like *Jub.* 23:29–31, which affirms postmortem existence but is variously interpreted as referring to either immortality of the soul or resurrection proper.[1] The Enochic *Book of Watchers* poses a related problem in as much as most scholars uphold this text as early evidence for Jewish resurrection belief despite the fact that no explicit reference to resurrection—however such references might be defined—can be found in it.[2] Concerning the substance of resurrection belief itself, though many texts focus on notions of life and death, how are we to account for those that speak of ethno-geographic (e.g., land and exile) or religio-political motifs (e.g., persecution and injustice). The interrelation of these differing descriptions under the one topic *resurrection* is surely part of the problem here, and any account of second temple Jewish resurrection beliefs must be both fixed and malleable so as to accommodate this topical flexibility.

At the heart of this interpretive problem stands the question: How does one identify the idea or concept of resurrection in a given text? In this chapter I will take some initial steps toward clarifying how the concept of "resurrection" is both fashioned and replicated in a selection of second temple Jewish texts. As I will demonstrate, the traditions examined here evince a recurrent constellation of concepts and image schemata that, when taken collectively as a gestalt, constitute the concept of RESURRECTION.³ The strength and novelty of this thesis is found in the way quite abstract, culturally specific ideas can be grounded in familiar, recurrent patterns of human embodiment. I rely heavily on certain advancements in cognitive linguistics, particularly those that stress the embodied mind and its capacity for meaning creation; I build upon Mark Johnson's affirmation that "there is a growing mountain of empirical evidence from the cognitive sciences that there can be no thought without a *brain* in a *body* in an *environment*" (Johnson 2005, 16, emphasis added). With this contextualized notion of cognition firmly in view, which insists that patterns of thought emerge from and are structured by recurrent patterns of somatic existence, I hope to demonstrate how notions of resurrection can be identified within the diversity of second temple Jewish textual expression.

Problem definition and theoretical framework

The problem of identifying or giving definition to the concept of *resurrection* has not escaped scholarly examination; three interpretive stances are worth examining in brief. One common solution is to isolate individual lexemes and recurrent vocabulary so as to identify *resurrection* at the philological level. John Sawyer, for instance, examines Hebrew literature spanning the second temple through medieval periods, identifying five lexical signs that denote notions of resurrection (these are חיה [*h-y-h*] "to live," קום [*q-w-m*] "to stand," הקיץ or קיץ [*q-y-ts*] "to wake," שוב [*sh-w-b*] "to come back," and ציץ [*ts-y-ts*] "to sprout"; Sawyer 1973). In a similar vein, Jerzy Chmiel builds on Sawyer's work by examining the translation equivalents between the Septuagint and the Hebrew Bible; Chmiel proposes a reduction of the five Hebrew terms down to the two Greek terms ἐγείρω (*egeirō*) and ἀνίστημι (*anistēmi*) (Chmiel 1979). While this approach has the benefit of concretely focusing analysis to a specific set of textual data, it fails to account for the contextual nature of resurrection descriptions. That is to say, identification of resurrection has much to do with literary contexts and the frames employed in rendering such lexemes meaningful.⁴ Moreover, this lexical approach does not address the extent to which notions of resurrection are cultural concepts that are only meaningful within broader social contexts. To these ends, the identification of "resurrection" has less to do with specific lexical signs and more to do with locating a given community's ideals within discursive contexts of meaning. Such a narrow focus, then, precludes overarching meaning-making structures at the expense of individual linguistic units.

A second approach is to reduce the richness of resurrection belief to uniformity at the literary level. One way this has been achieved is by distinguishing that which is literally resurrection from that which is metaphorically resurrection. Consider N. T. Wright's statement:

> YHWH's answer to his people's exile would be, *metaphorically*, life from the dead (Isa 26, Ezek 37); YHWH's answer to his people's martyrdom would be, *literally*, life from the dead (Dan 12). (Wright 2003, 127, emphasis added)

Though Wright suggests elsewhere that a hard distinction should not be made between differing thematic contexts,⁵ the parsing of the period literature into literal and metaphorical categories creates an ontological distinction between that which is "really" resurrection and that which is "secondarily" resurrection.[6] At the same time, literal resurrection is often reduced to recurrent literary motifs (e.g., postmortem corporeality). This approach fails not only in its theoretical distinction between "literal" and "metaphorical" (as we will see), but also in its presumption that uniformity can be identified at the literary level. By seeking unity through narrowly identified motifs (e.g., corporality), such treatments sacrifice cultural nuance at the altar of homogeneity and are therefore reductive in a negative way.

Standing in contrast is the equally problematic tendency to fragment notions of resurrection. Such is the approach taken by James Charlesworth, who sets out a preliminary taxonomy of resurrection texts (Charlesworth 2006a, 237–64. An abbreviated version of the same paper has appeared as Charlesworth 2006b). Examining literature spanning the late second temple through early rabbinic periods, Charlesworth identifies sixteen categories that classify the concept of resurrection, some of which are complementary while others are "mutually exclusive" (Charlesworth 2006a, 260). While Charlesworth rightly stresses cultural and motifical variety, he fails to offer a framework by which to tie such variety together. For instance, several of Charlesworth's categories concern motifs of redemption and vindication, but what have these to do with other categories such as spiritual awakening or the raising of an apocalypticist to heaven?[7] That Charlesworth offers no such framework unfortunately renders his taxonomy ineffective in that it fails to identify what actually classifies something as a resurrection text.

It is perhaps because such an overarching framework might be perceived as reductive that Charlesworth is so silent on the issue.[8] To be certain, such identification is in some sense reductive, though it is not to be shrunken away from. If we are to move forward, we need to be reductive in a good way.[9] To address the problem at hand, I suggest a better analytical approach is one that meets three crucial criteria. First, it must identify recurrent patterns that are general enough to be found across the texts being studied, but also specific enough to warrant distinction and cogency. Second, it must demonstrate how such patterns are able to cut across discursive and topical contexts (e.g., addressing issues of death, persecution/martyrdom, social injustice, exile, etc.). Finally, this analysis also needs to demonstrate how such patterns can give rise to differing (even contrary) understandings of resurrection while still retaining an overarching degree of systematicity.

This chapter will address these concerns, specifically answering the question: What enables a particular text to be interpreted as referring to resurrection? My analysis will not seek to define what a resurrection text is, but rather to illuminate what enables recognition (among modern interpreters) of resurrection within various discursive contexts. Put differently, I aim to explain interpretive flexibility rather than taxonomic classification. Methodologically speaking, my analysis will be textual in nature and will focus on those passages that stand as prime examples of Jewish resurrection beliefs within the pre-70 CE literature[10]—namely, Dan. 12, *2 Macc.* (especially chapter 7), the *Epistle of Enoch*,[11] the *Similitudes of Enoch*, *Enoch's Dream Visions*, *Testament of Moses* 10, and *Psalm of Solomon* 3. Where needed, my analysis will also examine a number of biblical texts so as to identify the traditional world within which such notions are framed.

Theoretically speaking, this analysis is informed by cognitive linguistics, especially the notions of image schemata and conceptual metaphor developed in the work of George Lakoff, Mark Johnson, and Mark Turner.[12] Stressing the embodied nature of human meaning creation (linguistic or otherwise), these theorists argue that language and thought are grounded in recurrent patterns of bodily interaction in the world. *Image schemata* are conceptual structures that are skeletal in nature (i.e., they do not have rich but rather *schematic* content) and which arise experientially as a result of the kinds of bodies we have functioning in the kinds of habitual environments we live in.[13] Such schemata exist at the conceptual level and are what Johnson refers to as gestalts; that is, they are recurrent, organized, and unified wholes (Johnson 1987, 44). Like image schemata, *conceptual metaphors* are also grounded in patterns of human experience (Lakoff and Johnson 1980, 1999, especially pages 16–73; Lakoff and Turner 1989; and also Kövecses 2010); they arise when one, often more abstract, conceptual domain is understood in relation to another, often more concrete, conceptual domain. In an important respect, metaphor structures and characterizes the nature of how the human animal experiences, obtains, and makes sense of the world and its presence therein.[14] That metaphors are conceptual and not merely verbal or poetic points to the functioning of metaphor as a general cognitive capacity; *metaphor* is one of the primary ways human thought is organized and conducted.

The theoretical categories outlined here will be further explored and elaborated as this chapter develops, though at this point I want to stress the key point that stands at the foundation of my argument, namely, because conceptual metaphors are elaborated in relation to image schemata, abstract and particular cultural ideals are thus grounded in recurrent experiences of human embodiment. As I will demonstrate, it is the clustering together, in recurrent ways, of a particular set of image schemata, that enables notions of resurrection to be interpretively identified within a given text. Moreover, while such image schemata are naturally basic and quite general, they can nevertheless be elaborated metaphorically in many different, often divergent, ways. Working toward these points, I hope to demonstrate how and why one reader's expectation of postmortem recompense can also be another's hope of ethno-geographic restoration.

RESURRECTION IS UP—The VERTICALITY image schema

Perhaps the place to begin is with framing resurrection in relation to conceptualizations of LIFE and DEATH. We are justified in starting here for the simple fact that, while resurrection can be identified in relation to notions of social injustice or exile (for example), such descriptions are frequently expressed in the language of life and death. Accordingly, these notions provide entry points into the network of interlocking concepts that structure RESURRECTION. Because human experiences of life and death are so pervasive, several metaphors are required to make sense of such experiences;[15] the following will focus on Hebrew traditions that conceptualize life–death via the VERTICALITY schema.[16]

One of the most pervasive image schemata that Lakoff and Johnson identify is the VERTICALITY schema (also referred to as the UP–DOWN schema—see Diagram 1), of which Johnson provides the following description:

> We grasp this structure of verticality repeatedly in thousands of perceptions and activities we experience every day, such as perceiving a tree, our felt sense of standing upright, the activity of climbing stairs, forming a mental image of a flagpole, measuring our children's heights, and experiencing the level of water rising in the bathtub. The VERTICALITY schema is the abstract structure of these VERTICALITY experiences, images, and perceptions. (Johnson 1987, xiv)

Lakoff and Johnson examine a handful of ways that the UP–DOWN image schema structures human thought (cf. Lakoff and Johnson 1980, 14–21). Of particular note for us are the metaphors LIFE IS UP and CONSCIOUSNESS IS UP, along with their corresponding opposites DEATH IS DOWN and UNCONSCIOUSNESS IS DOWN. Both of these metaphors share an interrelated experiential grounding. Humans experience life, for instance, through active, erect agency in the world. To be a living, healthy human being is to be able to stand up and walk around, while death conversely forces the otherwise erect and active body to fall down and lay limp, thus ceasing active agency. Correlated with this is the human experience of consciousness, which

Diagram 1 Gestalt structure of the VERTICALITY (or UP–DOWN) image schema.

Lakoff and Johnson understand generally as the experience of being able to exercise agency and perceptual awareness in the world (e.g., being asleep or in a coma would be experiences of unconsciousness).[17] Since the state of being awake and able to perceive is experienced in relation to erect agency, the CONSCIOUSNESS IS UP metaphor is rendered meaningful because it corresponds with recurrent embodied experiences. (The same is true of the obverse metaphor UNCONSCIOUSNESS IS DOWN, where conscious perception ceases when one physically lies down and sleeps.) In these ways, the conceptual metaphors LIFE IS UP and CONSCIOUSNESS IS UP arise because of the type of physical bodies that we have functioning in the environmental and habitual contexts in which we live.

The conceptual correlation of LIFE–DEATH with UP–DOWN can be nicely evinced in Hebrew tradition already in many biblical texts. Death, for instance, is repeatedly conceptualized in relation to downward directionality.[18] It is described as something people dig for (Job. 3:21; cf. Amos 9:2), and the Psalmist characterizes death as "downward movement" (ירד, *y-r-d*) into the pit (Ps. 30:10). In Job human death is described as lying down (שכב, *sh-k-b*) and compared to rivers and lakes that dry up (14:10–12);[19] just as the water level is "high" when rivers and lakes are full, so too humans are characteristically "up and erect" when they are alive (comp. 2 Sam. 14:14). Likewise, the dried up water body leaves only the parched ground, as do the deceased leave only the dust of the earth—thus Gen. 3:19, "from [the ground] you were taken; you are dust, and to dust you will return" (cf. Job 34:15; Ps. 22:30).[20] Cosmologically speaking, Sheol exists at the lower strata of world (e.g., Job 11:8; Ps. 139:8; Amos 9:2) and thus is "downward" in relation to the plane of human existence.[21] Like death, accessing Sheol requires that one "descend" into the earth (e.g., Gen. 37:35; Ps. 55:16; Prov. 9:18; Isa. 14:15),[22] while escape requires "ascent" (e.g., Ps. 30:4).[23] It is not surprising that the inhabitants of Sheol, the shades, are consistently described within the context of vertical orientation—either as being located "downward" or (un)able to "rise up."[24]

The correlation of death with downward movement in biblical tradition is also expressed in relation to language of sleeping and waking, which results in metaphorical mappings that are quite familiar in later resurrection contexts. This conceptual mapping consists of the correlation of LIFE–DEATH with AWAKE–ASLEEP such that the more concrete space AWAKE–ASLEEP is blended with the more abstract space LIFE–DEATH (see Diagram 2).[25] Perceptual links are established between these two domains, thus linking paired counterparts within each input and projecting such established cross-space mappings back onto the inputs (e.g., linking death with sleep).[26] In this case, the perceptual connections are structured largely in relation to the VERTICALITY image schema.[27] What emerge in the blended space are the conceptual metaphors LIFE IS BEING AWAKE and DEATH IS SLEEP. Of particular significance is the fact that the blend contains emergent structure that is not found in either of the inputs—i.e., though actually being dead is not the same as being asleep, it is now possible to conceptualize death *as* sleep.[28] This therefore leads to discursive units wherein the dead are said to be "sleeping with their fathers," an idiom used to describe the death of ancestral leaders in the Torah and historical books.[29] By extension, this conceptual structure enables subsequent reasoning about postmortem life—viz., that one is able to "wake" from "death." Neither insignificantly nor surprisingly, the

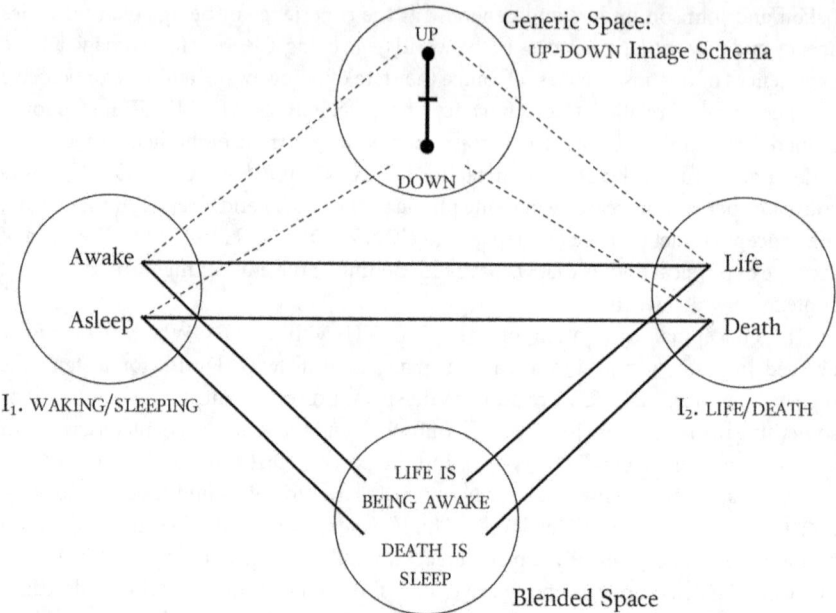

Diagram 2 VERTICALITY metaphor for life and death.

conceptual metaphor LIFE IS BEING AWAKE is pervasive in resurrection discourses. One of our earliest texts to evince this is Dan. 12:2, which looks ahead to a time when many of the "sleepers in the dust of the earth" (מישני אדמת עפר) will be "woken" (קיץ, *q-y-ts*).[30] The same metaphor is also found in *2 Macc.* 12:44–45 and perhaps *1 En.* 92:3, and related conceptions can be found in *1 En.* 100:5–6 and *Ps. Sol.* 3:1–2.[31]

The gestalt nature of the UP–DOWN image schema requires that one must not only identify the elements associated with UP, but also those associated with DOWN. In turn, this requires that we must identify both the activity of rising–falling and the context that occasions such movement, what cognitive linguists identify as the profile–frame relationship (cf. Croft and Cruse 2004, 7–39). Within the period literature we can point to several different frames wherein resurrection is emphasized. Some texts employ the SOCIAL INJUSTICE frame (e.g., *Epistle of Enoch*) while others cast resurrection in the light of the PERSECUTION frame (e.g., *2 Macc.*). Depending on the frame employed, the roles of protagonist(s) and antagonist(s) take on differing values. For example, texts framed by SOCIAL INJUSTICE fill such roles with the values "poor" and "rich" respectively, while the PERSECUTION frame provides values like "martyr(s)" and "wicked ruler(s)."[32] Each frame provides the skeletal gestalt structure with a richer set of contextual nuances, thus enabling the concept of RESURRECTION to take varying and distinct nuances across discursive settings.

For example, the PERSECUTION frame, which is employed in *2 Macc.*, frames resurrection in relation to a series of grotesque Antiochian martyrdoms, thus looking ahead to the regaining of corporeal bodies (e.g., 7:10–11; 14:43–6).[33] This focus upon corporeality demonstrates the extent to which conceptual metaphors such as LIFE IS BEING AWAKE–DEATH IS SLEEP enable emergent meaning not otherwise possible. In biblical tradition the correlation of SLEEP with DEATH was initially in the service of describing death vis-à-vis sleep, though this conceptual metaphor is now extended to enable postmortem speculation concerning renewed life. When extended in this way, the blend of Diagram 2 entails the RESURRECTION IS CONSCIOUSNESS metaphor, where the experience of conscious human agency in the world provides a set of conceptual mappings that inform one's understandings of resurrection. In this way, the RESURRECTION IS CONSCIOUSNESS metaphor enables interpreters to conceptualize resurrection variously, including (but not limited to) the resurrected *state* (i.e., as awake, standing up, even being embodied etc.) or the resurrection *event* itself (e.g., as waking up). There is much interpretive play here, as the conceptual metaphor allows for variance in meaning depending on how certain readers use it.

Another context that frames second temple Jewish notions of resurrection is that of (CELESTIAL) LUMINOSITY, which is expressive of a more general trend toward the clustering of UP-structured concepts with a given frame's protagonists (e.g., the righteous) and DOWN-structured concepts with the antagonists (e.g., the sinners). A prime example is the association of light–darkness with such protagonists–antagonists. From an embodied perspective, light is most commonly experienced during the day and darkness at night, both of which naturally cohere with the LIFE IS BEING AWAKE and DEATH IS SLEEP metaphors. Similarly, light is perceived as coming primarily from the sun and moon (which are orientationally upward) while darkness is found in caves and places that are hidden from the sun and moon (i.e., in the earth, which is down). Within the period literature, the highest resurrection ideal in Dan. 12:3 is that the wise are elevated to shine as celestial bodies/beings. Similar postjudgment luminous elevation is also found in passages that either characterize the protagonists with light terminology or simply speak of them as standing in the light of the Lord, often in contrast to the antagonists (e.g., *1 En.* 58:2–6; 62:15–16; 104.2, *Ps. Sol.* 3:12; *T. Mos.* 10:9; comp. *1 En.* 39:7). The conceptual metaphor at work in such passages is reflective of the more general RESURRECTION IS UP metaphor, here understood via the specific frames LUMINOSITY or even CELESTIAL LUMINOSITY.

One final frame that structures conceptualizations of RESURRECTION via the UP-DOWN image schema is that of ETHNO-GEOGRAPHIC RESTORATION, which correlates LIFE–DEATH with LAND–EXILE. Though the concept of LAND is not readily associated with notions of VERTICALITY, the correlation of LAND with LIFE which stretches back into biblical literature, enables metaphors such as LAND IS LIFE (UP) and EXILE IS DEATH (DOWN). The Deuteronomist, for instance, correlates "life," "land," and "Torah" such that obeying the Lord's commands will bring life and blessing in the land (Deut. 30:11–20).[34] In the Prophets, Ezek. 37:1–14 envisions post-exilic restoration as an instance of dry bones "standing" (עמד, '-*m*-*d*—37:10) such that all God's people will come "up" (עלה, '-*l*-*h*) from the grave and thus return "to the land of Israel" (אל אדמת ישראל—37:12).[35] Similarly, Isa. 26:19 refers to the dead coming to "life" (חיה, *h*-*y*-*h*), "rising" (קום, *q*-*w*-*m*), and "waking" (קוץ, *q*-*w*-*ts*). Within the Isaianic context such references are most likely concerned with ethno-geographic restoration,[36] though in light of the LAND IS LIFE metaphor it is perhaps not surprising that many interpreters—ancient[37] and modern (e.g., Nickelsburg 2006, 31–32)—see this passage as referring to resurrection.[38]

Within subsequent Jewish tradition, just as post-exilic restoration is possible for LAND, so too is postmortem restoration possible for LIFE. When framed in relation to Israel's ethno-geographic identity, the concept of RESURRECTION is expressed via the metaphor RESURRECTION IS RESTORATION TO THE LAND. *Enoch's Dream Visions*, for example, describes the postjudgment reuniting of many who were dispersed and destroyed (*1 En.* 90:33). Similarly, in several other texts the recipients of resurrection are the members of Israel herself vis-à-vis foreign rulers/oppressors (e.g., Dan. 12:1–3; *2 Macc.*; *T. Mos.* 10:7–10). In these texts both eschatological resurrection and ethno-geographic restoration are structured by the same UP–DOWN schema, which allows these ideas to not only signify each other, but also enables later interpreters to find one in the other.

I have demonstrated that the UP–DOWN image schema is pervasive within second temple Jewish notions of resurrection. All the metaphors examined thus far are expressive of the very general conceptual metaphor RESURRECTION IS UP, a conceptual mapping that has very little meaning on its own. However, when framed in relation to differing aspects of second temple Jewish experience (e.g., erect human agency [consciousness], ethno-geographic restoration [land], etc.), the metaphor can be specified so as to find distinct meanings across discursive contexts.

RESURRECTION IS GOAL—The PATH image schema

Another image schematic structure, which functions at both a macro and micro level in structuring notions of resurrection, is the PATH schema (or SOURCE–PATH–GOAL schema). At times both the PATH and VERTICALITY schemata work in correlation with one another (e.g., the linking of UP with GOAL, as we will see). In an important respect, however, the PATH schema supplements its VERTICALITY counterpart so as to enable conceptual structure not made possible by the latter. As with UP–DOWN, the SOURCE–PATH–GOAL schema functions as a gestalt structure—i.e., the schema has a basic set of interdependent elements that all work in concert with one another (e.g., a source, a trajector, a path etc.—see Diagram 3).[39] Like all image schemata, the PATH schema is pervasive within human experience; thus Johnson states:

> Our lives are filled with paths that connect up our spatial world. ... Some of these paths involve an actually physical surface that you traverse, such as the path from your house to the store. Others involve a projected path, such as the path of a bullet shot

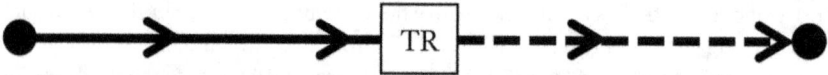

Diagram 3 Gestalt structure of the PATH (or SOURCE–PATH–GOAL) schema. Adapted from Lakoff and Johnson 1999, 33.

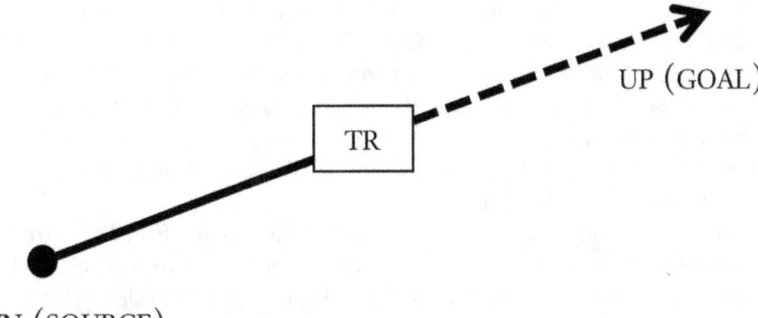

Diagram 4 Integrated PATH and VERTICALITY schematic structure.

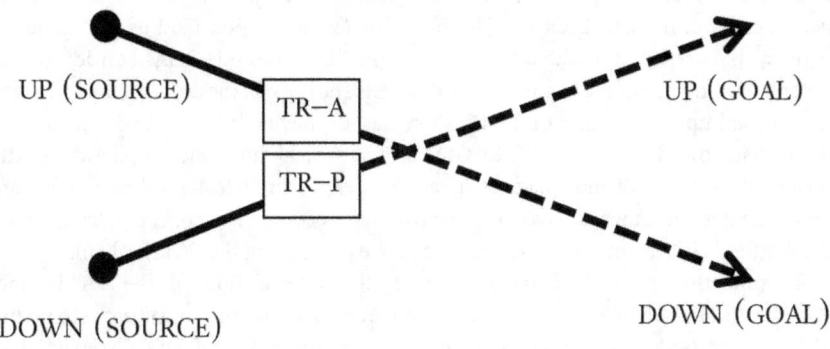

Diagram 5 Reciprocal protagonist (TR–P) and antagonist (TR–A) PATHs.

into the air. And certain paths exist, at present, only in your imagination, such as the path from the Earth to the nearest star outside our solar system. (Johnson 1987, 113)

Though no one in the Greco-Roman world would ever conceive the path a bullet would travel, they would certainly perceive the path of an archer's arrow, or of a thrown stone. Johnson is here illuminating an image schematic structure that is commonly shared by the human animal across cultural contexts.

Macro SOURCE–PATH–GOAL structure

At the macro level, the PATH schema provides the concept of RESURRECTION with a more robust structure than the VERTICALITY schema alone permits. This robustness is akin to the difference between a one- and two-dimensional object; where the VERTICALITY schema enabled conceptions along a single axis (orientated vertically), the PATH structure creates a second, horizontal axis. The most common expression of the PATH schema is via the structuring of time as progressing toward a looming divine visitation. For example, Daniel looks ahead to "the time of the end" (ובעת קץ—11:40)[40] in which a great judgment will take place (12:1–3). Several other texts likewise point to similar teleological judgments, which is reflective of the same schematic structuring (e.g., *Enoch's Dream Visions* [esp. *1 En.* 90:20–7]; the *Epistle of Enoch* [esp. *1 En.* 99:11–102:3]; the Enochic *Book of Similitudes* [esp. *1 En.* 51; 62]; *Ps. Sol.* 3:11–12; and *T. Mos.* 10).

In some instances the source and goal elements of the PATH structure are characterized by values such as *present conflict* and *judgment* (respectively). Other texts, however, scale the PATH structure to a much larger degree, thus identifying the present distress as a single point on the path toward the end. Such is the case in *2 Macc.*; the martyrdom of the seven brothers and their mother in chapter 7 is particularly worth noting. In 7:23, the mother of these seven brothers asserts that the creator of the world, who has "formed" (πλάσσω [*plassō*]) humankind, "will give breath and life back to you again" (τὸ πνεῦμα καὶ τὴν ζωὴν ὑμῖν πάλιν ἀποδίδωσιν [*to pneuma kai tēn zōēn humin palin apodidōsin*]—v. 23). Of note is the mother's focus upon God as the "creator" (κτίστης [*ktistēs*]—v. 23), who is seen as restoring life in the end (GOAL) on account of his creative impetus in the beginning (SOURCE). The hope of these Antiochian martyrs is premised upon the assertion that history has an inevitable outcome, a teleological drive that flows from SOURCE to GOAL, and which thus renders physical death meaningless in light of anticipated resurrection (7:9). Such a teleological feature further demonstrates the inherent sense of purpose that accompanies conceptualizations of RESURRECTION, which is doubtless tied to the presence of the PATH schema.[41]

Beyond the mere structuring of time, the interrelation of the PATH and VERTICALITY schemata creates tight correlations between the constituent elements. This is expressed in two ways: (1) through the correlation of DOWN-structured concepts (i.e., perceived experiences of distress such as death, exile, and injustice) with the SOURCE element, and (2) the correlation of UP-structured concepts (e.g., renewed life, ethno-geographic restoration, and just recompense) with the GOAL element. What results is a PATH structure that is, conceptually speaking, VERTICALLY inclined so as to denote sequential movement from DOWN (SOURCE) to UP (GOAL) via PATH (see Diagram 4). As we have noted above, the roles of protagonist(s) and antagonist(s) are filled with either UP- or DOWN-structured values, respectively. With this in mind, the gradient structure that we have just outlined is, of course, described from the point of view of the protagonist(s) and an obverse path must also projected for the antagonist(s). The resultant structure is vertical sequential movement wherein opposing role-value figures traverse reciprocal paths, one toward GOAL (UP), the other toward GOAL (DOWN). (This is sketched in Diagram 5.)

The reciprocal nature of this gradient structural interrelation facilitates the concept of reversal, expressed via the conceptual metaphor RESURRECTION IS REVERSAL and thus enabling the elevation of the protagonists vis-à-vis the abasement of the antagonists. The structure is readily apparent in the *Epistle of Enoch* (esp. *1 En.* 99:11–102:3), where the righteous enjoy postmortem recompense/reward, including luminous existence (104:2), while the unrighteous/sinners go down to Hades into darkness and great judgment (103:7–8). Similarly, Dan. 12:1–3 holds that some will be raised "to everlasting life" (לחיי עולם, *lehayey 'olam*) and others to "shame and everlasting disgrace" (לחרפות לדראון עולם, *laharafot ledir'on 'olam*).

We should of course note that ideas of anticipated judgment and postmortem reversal are not exclusive to resurrection contexts, but are also found in other Jewish afterlife reflections from the same period (e.g., Wis. 5).[42] Such conceptual overlap doubtless contributes to the interpretive problem described at the outset of this chapter. Despite these similarities, we have demonstrated a tight connection between the path and VERTICALITY schemata in structuring conceptualizations of RESURRECTION. These tight correlations enable a variety of frames, themselves rooted in different kinds of second temple Jewish experiences, to produce a variety of expressions of resurrection (e.g., death/martyrdom [RESTORED LIFE IS GOAL], ethno-geographic restoration [RESTORATION TO THE LAND IS GOAL], or even social injustice [JUST RECOMPENSE IS GOAL]). All are reflective of the more general RESURRECTION IS GOAL metaphor.

Micro SOURCE–PATH–GOAL structure

In addition to offering an overarching framework (at the macro level) whereby UP- and DOWN-structured concepts can be organized, the SOURCE–PATH–GOAL schema is also used to structure a specific kind of resurrection ideal: the idea of postmortem transformation. In this regard, the PATH schema is employed twice in constructing the concept of RESURRECTION—once at the macro level to provide an overarching framework, and again at the micro level to enable the concept of CHANGE in relation to postmortem form.

As noted already, texts such as Dan. 12:3, *1 En.* 104:2, and *T. Mos.* 10:9–10 frame their resurrection ideals with celestial categories. In Dan. 12 celestial association is reserved only for the wise, whereas in *1 En.* 104 it is for the righteous and in *T. Mos.* 10 it is an ethno-geographic hope. In Dan. 12:3 the comparison is made with the stars and luminous heavens, and is specifically characterized by temporal length (i.e., shining forever).[43] Because angels are at times described with such luminary imagery (e.g., Job 38:7; *1 En.* 86:1, 3; 90:21), this comparison may be understood in terms of angelic likeness and even angelomorphic transformation. Very similar language is used in *1 En.* 104:2, where the comparison is directly correlated with heavenly beings in the Ethiopic text (cf. 104:4, 6).[44] By contrast, in *T. Mos.* 10:9 God will raise his people and fix them in the "heaven of the stars," a celestial elevation that is specifically contrasted with Israel's enemies on earth (10:10).

The introduction of CELESTIAL LUMINOSITY within resurrection conceptualizations results in the metaphor RESURRECTION IS CELESTIAL LUMINOSITY, which differs significantly from the aforementioned RESURRECTION IS CONSCIOUSNESS metaphor. That said, both metaphors have strong elements of VERTICALITY built into them (as noted above), and they also presuppose the concept of POSTMORTEM CHANGE. In the CELESTIAL LUMINOSITY metaphor, the envisaged change is more imaginative and radical in as much as premortem human bodies neither shine like stars nor do they exist in the heavens. Alternatively, the CONSCIOUSNESS metaphor leans in the direction of the reconstituted human body, which requires the changing of the decomposed corpse into a corporeal state.

Thus, while the CELESTIAL LUMINOSITY and CONSCIOUSNESS metaphors result in very different resurrected states, both presuppose postmortem transformation.

From an embodied perspective, experiences of change are ubiquitous within human life patterns. The human body experiences change in mundane tasks such as sitting up (change of position) and walking across the room (change of location). Throughout the course of life, the process of human maturation is marked by many physical (e.g., growth, fitness conditioning, puberty, etc.) and social (e.g., shifting social circles, relationships, marriage, work, etc.) changes, and the process of growing from a baby into an adult is both immediately experienced and observed in others. One of the most common and basic experiences of change is that of using force to manipulate an object from one shape into another, such as a potter molding clay into a bowl.[45]

Given both the ubiquitous and complex nature of such experiences, several different metaphors are used by the human animal to conceptualize change.[46] One of the most basics is the CHANGE IS MOVEMENT metaphor, which is premised on the PATH image schema, thus enabling CHANGE to be conceptualized as movement from one location to another. Additionally, the states from which and into which human beings exist are commonly conceptualized via the CONTAINER schema (see Diagram 6), which is orientated along a simple IN–BOUNDARY–OUT axis.[47] When conceptualized in this way, both locations and states are understood as containers that can be either moved "into" or "out of."[48] With respect to CHANGE, both the PATH and CONTAINER schemata work interdependently with each other so as to form a CHANGE gestalt structure (see Diagram 7). Here the SOURCE and GOAL roles of the PATH schema are characterized by contrasting CONTAINERS. These CONTAINERS represent differing states/locations (i.e., A and B), and the TRAJECTOR represents the subject undergoing the change in question. What results is a conceptual structure that facilitates the movement of a TRAJECTOR from one container (STATE/LOCATION A) to another (differing) container (STATE/LOCATION B).[49]

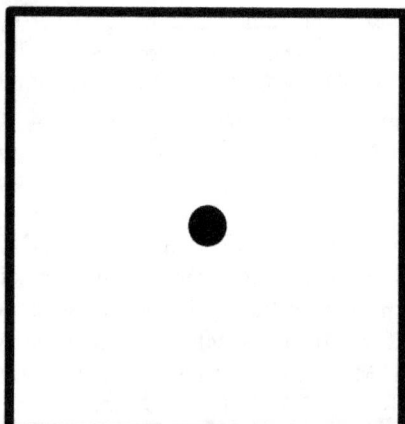

Diagram 6 The CONTAINER (or IN–OUT) schema. Adapted from Lakoff and Johnson, 1999 32.

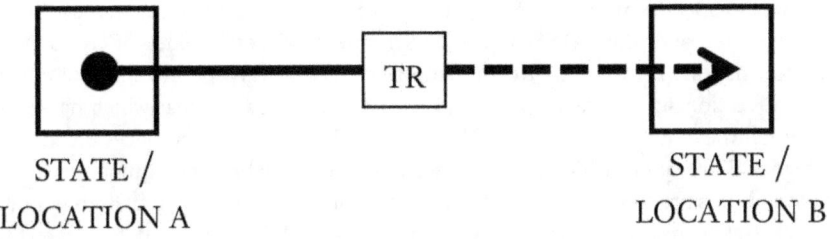

Diagram 7 The CHANGE gestalt.

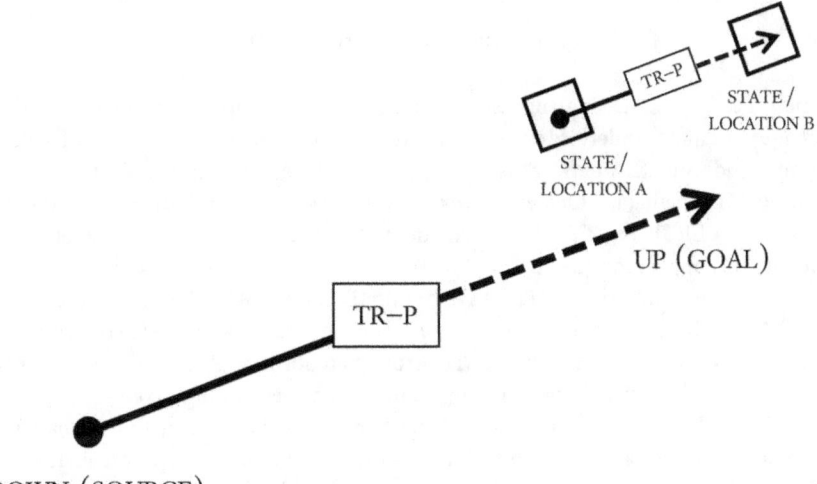

Diagram 8 Integrated micro-PATH structure.

Returning to conceptions of RESURRECTION, the CHANGE IS MOVEMENT metaphor functions at a micro level in as much as it structures the goal element of the larger SOURCE–PATH–GOAL schema (see Diagram 8). As such, the CHANGE IS MOVEMENT metaphor characterizes the UP-structured protagonist associations in two significant ways, which can be nicely demonstrated with respect to the CELESTIAL LUMINOSITY frame. On the one hand, the CHANGE IS MOVEMENT metaphor expresses a change of location such that the elevated protagonists are no longer on earth but in the heavens (e.g., Dan. 12:3; *1 En.* 104:2 [cf. v. 6]; *T. Mos.* 10:9–10). In this regard, the change in question is characterized by movement (i.e., a trajector moving along the path toward the goal [celestial placement]). In a more categorical way, however, the same metaphor can also be extended to refer to stative or transformative change. Conceptually speaking, this CHANGE is both locative (i.e., point A *to* point B) and stative (i.e., state A *into* state B) change, thus producing descriptions of both celestial ascent *and* celestial transformation.

Similar change dynamics can also be demonstrated for the RESURRECTION IS CONSCIOUSNESS metaphor, though the meaning that arises from the

CONSCIOUSNESS frame vis-à-vis the CELESTIAL LUMINOSITY frame differs. On the one hand, the CONSCIOUSNESS frame produces the idea of "restorative transformation" (i.e., restoration of the natural body), which gives rise to understandings of resurrection such as redemption and a kind of setting right that which has gone awry. On the other hand, the CELESTIAL LUMINOSITY frame produces the idea of categorical alteration, which is usually seen as transformation into a more desirable state and thus produces notions of an improved and even beatific future. Both notions are central to resurrection modes of thought, and while they are both somewhat inherent in these two types of change, it is helpful to contrast them in this way.

Summary and conclusions

The preceding discussion suggests that a network of recurrent and interdependent image schemata undergirds various expressions of resurrection beliefs in second temple Judaism. This network is specifically structured by both the VERTICALITY and PATH schemata, which each provides differing structural elements. On the one hand, the VERTICALITY schema provides notions of directional movement (i.e., up, down) and opposition (i.e., up vs. down), as well as experiential links with concepts such as LIFE–DEATH, LIGHT–DARK, and HEAVEN–EARTH. On the other hand, the PATH schema introduces elements of sequence (i.e., from source to goal), purpose (i.e., achievement of goal), change (i.e., from state/location A *into* state/location B), and reversal (i.e., switching of up and down—achieved through combination with VERTICALITY). The interrelation of the two schemata is not a simple matter of overlay but rather a dynamic blending, resulting in a gradient conceptual structure that enables sequential vertical movement for either the protagonist (upward movement) or the antagonist (downward movement) trajectors. The overall structure has been sketched in Diagram 9.[50] As is apparent, the structure itself is quite general, even abstract. In this way, we have identified a recurrent cluster or network of concepts that is (a) coherent in and of itself and which (b) displays certain internal interrelations that give rise to different components of meaning while still being (c) general enough as to not be tied to or dependent on any one set of resurrection motifs and/or themes. Contextual specificity is achieved through differing cultural frames (e.g., PERSECUTION, SOCIAL INJUSTICE etc.), which are metaphorically elaborated so as to flesh-out such skeletal structure with richer and more robust sets of information.

To demonstrate this point we can examine the conceptual metaphor RESURRECTION IS UP. As noted above, this metaphor is very general and has little meaning on its own. When framed in relation to UP-structured concepts, however, the metaphor gives rise to varying and even divergent conceptualizations. The focus in *2 Macc.* upon corporeality, for instance, is doubtless an expression of the RESURRECTION IS CONSCIOUSNESS metaphor, which projects elements of the one domain NATURAL LIFE (e.g., walking, talking, earthly body etc.) onto the other domain RISEN LIFE such that risen bodies are understood as reconstituted natural bodies. Conversely, the focus on celestial ascent in the *Epistle of Enoch* is reflective

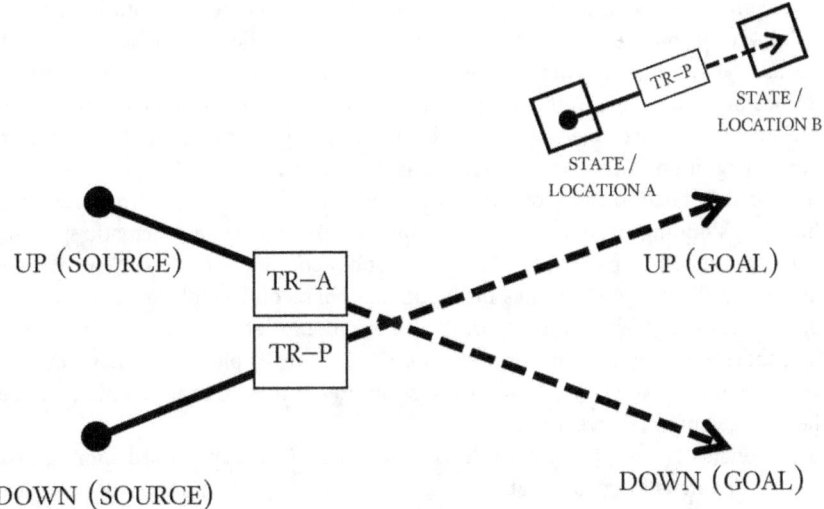

Diagram 9 Gestalt RESURRECTION schematic structure.

of the RESURRECTION IS CELESTIAL LUMINOSITY metaphor and thus envisions postmortem life vis-à-vis astral (even angelic) categories. Despite the fact that these two metaphors reflect the general RESURRECTION IS UP metaphor, they nonetheless give rise to differing resurrection descriptions.

We can also note that some texts are able to trigger several different, even divergent, metaphors simultaneously, thus resulting in differing interpretations of the same text. Dan. 12:1–3 is a prime example. Many scholars find in 12:2 the affirmation of bodily resurrection, a point that is made on the grounds of intertextual associations with Deutero- and Trito-Isaiah.[51] Verse 2, however, does not address the issue of risen form and instead only speaks of the activity of rising: that is, many who "sleep" will "awake" (cf. Collins 1993, 392). Here we have the concept of RESURRECTION being framed via the DEATH IS SLEEP metaphor, and while readers can use the LIFE IS CONSCIOUSNESS metaphor to infer corporeality in Dan. 12:2, such an interpretation is not explicitly warranted. Indeed, the very next verse upholds celestial ascent as the highest postmortem ideal.[52] The assertion that the wise will be granted heavenly luminosity calls forth the RESURRECTION IS CELESTIAL LUMINOSITY metaphor and thus projects astral categories onto the envisioned risen form. That the language of this text triggers both conceptual metaphors not only betrays the richness of the literary unit, but also exposes the degree to which differing readers are able to frame a text like Dan. 12:1–3 via differing (though interrelated) conceptual metaphors.

As we have seen, notions of resurrection are thoroughly contextual, conceptual, and metaphorical, all of which promises a way beyond the limitations of the scholarly approaches examined at the outset of this chapter. On the one hand, identification of resurrection is not reducible to mere lexical signs (such as ἐγείρω [egeirō], ἀνίστημι [*anistēmi*], קוּם [*q-w-m*], or קוּץ [*q-w-ts*]), for discursive contexts—both literary and social—are formative and determinative for the comprehension of such signs. On the other hand, any attempt to distinguish between "literal" and "metaphorical" notions of resurrection is theoretically problematic. Resurrection is an imaginative category; it is constructed by and reflective of the poetic or figurative nature of human cognition (Gibbs 1994). Accordingly, resurrection is *always* metaphorically elaborated in relation to more basic, common somatic experiences. The strength of this study's findings is found in the identification of a recurrent schematic structure that is grounded in patterns of human embodiment, and which is then extended metaphorically to various frames and/or domains of second temple Jewish experience (e.g., ethno-geographic restoration, postmortem life, etc.). It is this process of metaphorical elaboration that accounts for Charlesworth's pluralistic taxonomy, and which also offers an explanation for the clustering of these disparate notions under the one category, "resurrection."

In conclusion, the present study is a necessary first step toward more clearly defined understandings of what enables *resurrection* to be identified within various textual traditions. My analysis has not been exhaustive. Further attention should be given to those texts that envision resurrection not as "rising up" but rather as "giving back" (e.g., *1 En.* 51:1; cf. Bauckham 1998, 269–89), an image that may be premised on the PROXIMITY (or NEAR–FAR) schema.[53] I suggest that the PROXIMITY schema works interdependently with its VERTICALITY and PATH counterparts, further enriching the concept of RESURRECTION within second temple Jewish thought. In addition to this textual work, further theoretical reflection should press Lakoff's descriptions of categorization, particularly with respect to the idea of radial categories (Lakoff 1987, especially pages 91–114). Within cognitive linguistics, radial categorization provides an explanation for the presence of polysemy. Working from the principle of metaphorical elaboration, various and even divergent word-usages can be demonstrated to relate to one another through chains of meaning. As an extension, radial categorization may provide a more robust way of linking various notions of resurrection that moves beyond this study's unidirectional procedure of somatic ground.

Acknowledgments

The author would like to thank the Canadian Society of Biblical Studies, which awarded the 2011 Founders Prize to an earlier draft of this chapter, and also the Fonds de recherche du Québec—société et culture, whose support enabled the final editing and dissemination of this research. This chapter appeared as portions of Tappenden 2016 (used by permission of SBL Press).

8

Liturgical Linguistics: Toward the Syntax of Communicating with the Superhuman Agent in Judaism

Tamás Biró

Linguistics and the cognitive science of religion

Linguistics was likely the first discipline in the humanities to take a cognitive turn. For this reason alone, the case of linguistics might be of interest to the cognitive scientist of religion. One may learn much from the way linguists turned their viewpoints from historical ("language as an aspect of the nation's history," in the nineteenth century) and social ("language as an arbitrary social code," structuralism in the first half of the twentieth century) to neurological ("language as a biological phenomenon," from Chomsky 1957 onwards, especially in Chomsky 1968). At the same time, linguistics was not reduced to psychology but managed to preserve its century-long scholarly traditions.

An apparent connection between linguistics and religion is the fact that human language can be seen as the universal code behind cultural phenomena, such as religion. To tell the truth, however, a linguist is unable to interpret the vague and general concept of "language" as the main medium of the mind, used in many later-twentieth-century literary and philosophical theories, and which probably go back to the refuted Sapir-Whorf hypothesis. For a linguist, language is understood in its narrow sense, nowadays also including sign languages, but excluding both nonverbal forms of communication and conceptual thinking, which are transferred to the realm of psychology. Language is the verbal system that is used to encode a certain message, which itself is shaped by non-linguistic factors.

Nevertheless, communication in its narrower, linguistic sense also takes place in a religious context. This chapter focuses on the textual aspect of liturgy, which is unquestionably a linguistic product, a string of well-formed sentences in any given language(s)—at least in rabbinical Judaism, the religion to be dealt with here. We shall claim that prayer is a special situation of inter-agent communication, namely, when the addressee is a (culturally postulated) superhuman agent (henceforth: SHA). Additionally, the structure of Jewish liturgy will be demonstrated to be analyzable using standard linguistic methodology. This analysis will not be complete, but may represent the first steps in a new research program, the aim of which is to place liturgy among the cultural products that can be analyzed using concepts from generative syntax.[1]

This attempt is by far not the first to use a generative linguistic approach to religious rituals, the most noteworthy precedents being the work of Frits Staal (Staal 1979), and of Lawson and McCauley (Lawson and McCauley 1990). Without taking a stance on whether rituals have meaning (semantics), we shall focus on form (syntax) exclusively. In linguistics, syntax is primarily concerned with the linear (temporal) order of constituents within a structure, such as words in a phrase or phrases in a sentence. As we adhere to this definition of syntax, our description of traditional Jewish liturgy, as it appears in contemporary Ashkenazi prayer books, will resemble more Staal's work than Lawson and McCauley's model.[2] Nonetheless, a more systematic structuralist analysis of the material, together with recent developments in linguistics and in the cognitive science of religion, offer new insights on religious rituals.

Prayer as communication with SHAs

A dominant idea within the cognitive science of religion has been viewing religious phenomena as special cases of their everyday counterparts, with adding a "twist," that is, involving the culturally postulated SHAs. Gods, spirits, and ancestors are agents violating certain ontological expectations, and rituals are actions involving such "counterintuitive" agents.[3] Hence, the methodology or approach employed to analyze nonreligious phenomena will also work for religious ones. The knowledge accumulated on recalling memorable events in one's life can also be applied to the way details of religious rituals are remembered (Whitehouse 1995; McCauley and Lawson 2002); the thematic roles describing participants in actions in linguistics can also serve as a model for ritual actions (Lawson and McCauley 1990; McCauley and Lawson 2002); and the syntactic structures of everyday speech can also be identified in a liturgical context, as the current chapter shall argue.

If SHAs are seen as agents in a society by its members, even if special ones, then they participate in the life of that society in a similar way to any other agent—notwithstanding their special (counterintuitive) features. If a fellow-agent (such as a child) can be fed, then a god can also be fed: this special act is called "food sacrifice." If a fellow agent can be swung round to my point with flattery, then similar techniques (*mutatis mutandis*) should also work with the spirits. Certain nasty forms of behavior hurt ancestors, just as they would humans—with the difference that it is much harder to hide from ancestors than from living people.

Therefore, if a fellow agent can be spoken to—in order to convince her, to praise her, or to ask her a favor—then a SHA must also be capable of being addressed. Speaking to a SHA is called, at least in the Judeo-Christian tradition, a prayer. Indeed, a prayer, either institutionalized with a fixed text or spontaneous, is a linguistic product: a text with an inner overall structure, built up of syntactically well-formed sentences, each of which contains meaningful and grammatical words. A prayer is, therefore, a form of speech, namely, the special situation when the usual verbal communication is applied to a SHA as the addressee.

If it is so, we expect to be able to employ linguistic methodology to analyze the structure of liturgies. As a special form of speech, prayers should be produced by the same mental processes, while minor differences can only be found as far as some of the extra-linguistic factors (the identity of the addressee, the context, and the message) are unusual. But as the mental "representations" to be realized as either everyday speech or as prayers are translated using the same mental processes, the resulting structures should also be identical. In other words, prayer is a form of language (or communication) organized along the same cognitive, mental, and social principles as nonreligious language.

In addition, one may conjecture that it is the linguistic structure that makes certain forms of liturgy evolutionarily stable. In a culture with a high degree of oral transmission (due to either low literacy rates or a lack of affordable books), these familiar structures make prayers simpler to learn, to remember, and to reproduce (cf. the results of Mandler and Johnson on recalling stories: Mandler and Johnson 1977). This simplicity also motivates one to reproduce these forms of liturgy frequently. If written transmission is present in the culture, the linguistic nature of prayers makes the institutionalization of prayers possible in the form of prayer books. While the Jewish culture has since very long included a strong written component, orality also played a significant role, especially at times and places where not all congregants (let alone, children learning how to pray) owned a private prayer book.

If linguistic structure is indeed important for the evolutionary stability of liturgies, a further point can be clarified. Namely, one could object that the above-mentioned train of thought about prayers being a form of speech applies to spontaneous prayers only, whereas regularly repeated, fixed, and institutionalized liturgies transmitted for centuries, with which we shall deal, are rather literary works: even if the basic layer used to be linguistic once, nonlinguistic factors have shaped its form. One can argue that the long editing process aimed at meeting some aesthetic or theological criteria results in an artificial structure, similar to the syntax of many poems that would be ungrammatical outside poetry. This objection may be legitimate. And yet, observe that a poem would be illegible, hence evolutionarily unstable (it would not outlive its author) if its syntax were too far away from the syntax of everyday language. Similarly, I assume, the structures of artificially edited liturgies cannot be too far away from the structures naturally emerging in communication.

In what follows, we shall analyze the main structure of Jewish liturgy, which is a highly fixed system, with a long tradition. To be more exact, we shall focus on the *Ashkenazi nusah*, the liturgy of the Jews in most of Europe, historically north of the Mediterranean region. As a principle, the only addressee of prayers in Judaism can be God, the only SHA tolerated in this theological system. The message to be transmitted might be a statement (such as the acknowledgment of God's sovereignty), a request, or praise.

At the same time, Jewish liturgy is also biblical exegesis, but ritually performed. On the one hand, the Jewish prayer book contains various biblical texts, fulfilling different functions, as we shall see. On the other, the core of the synagogue service will be shown to be the *Amida*, which is seemingly a postbiblical text, a series of blessings, but in fact it is a performative interpretation of the Pentateuch: its recitation corresponds to the daily and holiday sacrifices prescribed in the Torah, as justified by a rabbinical interpretation of Deut. 11:13. In sum, this chapter addresses the syntax of ritual exegesis in Judaism.

Constituents in syntax

Before we begin analyzing the structure of the Jewish liturgy, let us survey some of the techniques widely used in linguistics (more precisely, in syntax), without going into excessive detail.

Both the starting point and the goal in modern linguistics are to delineate the set of grammatical utterances: in syntax, specifically, the set of (potential) grammatical sentences within a given language. At the beginning, this set is not defined explicitly: it is precisely the goal to construct a grammar, that is, a (more or less) formal system that is able to predict whether a sentence is grammatical or ungrammatical. For that purpose, the native speaker's grammaticality judgments help in collecting the data: using the competence of a native speaker, the linguist is first given many grammatical sentences, as well as ungrammatical ones.[4]

Then, based on these data—and, if needed, asking the native speaker for new grammatical judgments again and again—the linguist starts building a model that should account for them. First, the constituents of each sentence are determined in order to understand its nonlinear but tree-like structure. A typical example for the importance of this nonlinear syntactic structure is the following pair of sentences:

(1) a. John ate French fries with mayonnaise.
    b. John ate French fries with a fork.

Seemingly, the two sentences are very similar: a subject, a verb, an object and a *with*-phrase—importantly, in this linear order. And yet, from their meaning we know that the *with*-phrases must have different roles. In (1a) the phrase "with mayonnaise" belongs to the object, while in (1b) the parallel phrase "with a fork" is an instrument of the verb. The sentence structures are then:

(2) a. John ate (French fries with mayonnaise)$_{object}$
    b. John ate (French fries)$_{object}$ (with a fork)$_{instrument}$

Linguists argue for a given structure based on different constituency tests, whose aim is to identify the constituents (the phrases), but often also their category. We now review some of these tests, so that we can subsequently also apply them to analyze the structure of liturgy.

The simplest test is "substitution" or "replacement." Two words belong to the same category if they can be replaced with each other. The meaning can change not more than the difference in the meanings of the words involved. Note that if "with mayonnaise" is replaced in (1a) with the words "with a fork," then more changes in meaning take place, because not only does the substance of the sauce accompanying the French fries change, but an instrument of eating also enters the sentence.

For instance, take now the following sentences:

(3) a. I loved that girl.
 b. I kissed that girl.
 c. John loved that girl.
 d. This man loved that girl.
 e. I loved Mary.
 f. I smiled.

First, the whole sentence should be seen as one constituent, called "Sentence" or S. Comparing (3a) to (3b) proves that the words *loved* and *kissed* belong to the same category: let us dub this category "Verb" or V. Similarly, sentences (3a), (3c), and (3d) display the interchangeability of "I," "John," and "this man": linguists usually label this category "Noun Phrase" (NP). Similarly, "that girl" and "Mary" constitute also NPs, due to the comparison of sentences (3a) and (3e). (One can easily construct sentences proving that "this man," "that girl," "I," "John," and "Mary" indeed belong to the same category.) Finally, sentence (3f) demonstrates that the transitive verb and its object form one constituent (termed a "Verb Phrase" or VP) that is equivalent to an intransitive verb.[5]

Consequently, the structure of the sentences under (3) can be summarized using the following tree structure:

(4)

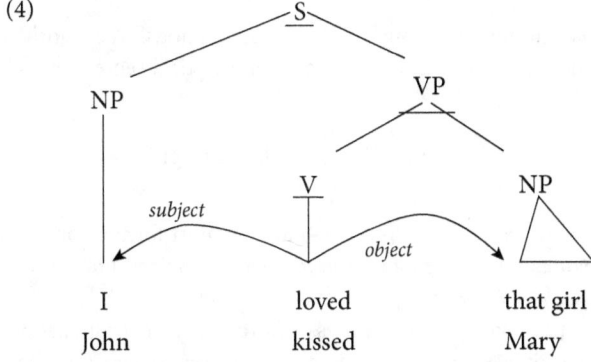

Another frequently employed constituency test is "movement," such as the "fronting" in the following pair of sentences:

(5) a.   I loved that girl.
    b. That girl I loved

Here, the fact that the words "that girl" can move together to the front of the sentence is an argument for these words forming one single constituent. Furthermore, sentence (5a) is seen as the basic structure, from which the NP is moved to the front in sentence (5b), leaving behind an empty position called a "trace," which becomes important in certain syntactic theories. This movement is an example of the (in)famous Chomskyan transformations. Hence, the structure of sentence (5b) is most often argued to be as follows:

(6)

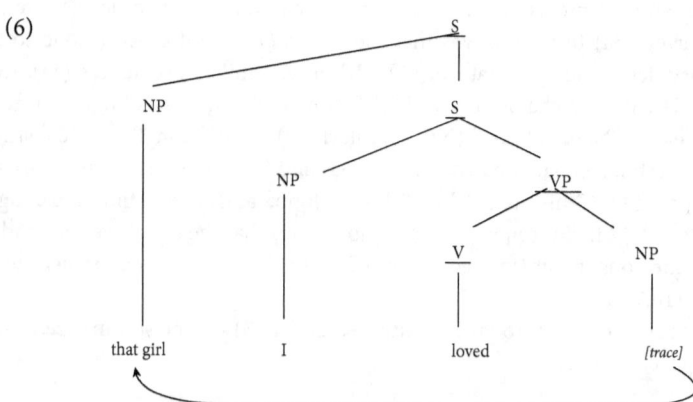

A third, frequently used test is observing "elliptical constructions." A constituent is left out, but is recoverable or inferable from the context in elliptical sentences such as the following ones:

(7) John loved that girl, but Jack didn't [that is: ... love that girl].

The combination of words left out in elliptical sentences must form a constituent. Hence, sentence (7) provides another proof for the verb with its object (but without its subject) forming a phrase.

A further test is "coordination": if combinations of words can be coordinated using *and*, then they must each form a constituent; moreover, these constituents must belong to the same category. The * precedes an ungrammatical sentence:

(8) a. John (loved Mary) and (hated Ann).
 b. (Going to a movie with Mary) and (kissing Ann) are enjoyable activities.
 c. * I ate French fries (with a fork) and (with mayonnaise) and (with my friend).
 d.
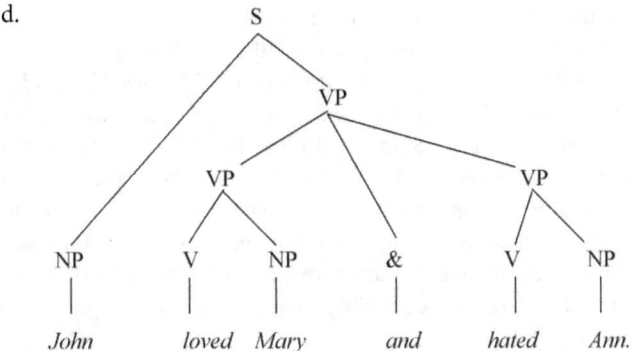

The ungrammatical sentence (8c) demonstrates that coordinated constituents must belong to the same category and must play the same role.[6] Tree (8d) displays a possible analysis of sentence (8a).

A similar test is the "stand-alone" test. See the following examples of answers without a subject:

(9) a. — What did you do yesterday?
  — Worked on my new project.
 b. — What did you do yesterday?
  — * Worked on.

The fact that "Worked on" is an ungrammatical answer in (9b) is an argument for this word combination not being a constituent, unlike "Worked on my new project" in (9a), which is a VP. The "stand-alone" test is not accepted by every linguist as a sufficient proof for the constituency of some word combination, but at least might be used as an additional argument.

In general, many of these constituency tests are theory dependent, as shown by the fact that syntactic theories often differ in the exact structure they assign to a given sentence. Furthermore, the applicability of a test is sometimes unclear, because the resulting sentence might be correct, but in a different context or with a slightly different meaning. In brief, these tests can be used to argue in favor of a certain structure, but *a priori* theoretical considerations and preferences are also important, resulting in rapidly changing analyses in syntax. Finally, the intuition based on the meaning of the words and of the sentence—a factor coming from beyond syntax proper—is also crucial in determining the constituents.

The constituency tests just discussed help us establish the less obvious, mid-level units (phrases and clauses) of a sentence between the word level and the sentence level. Phrase structure grammars aim at defining the set of grammatical sentences in the language being studied by specifying exactly how words are joined together to form phrases, and how phrases in turn form clauses and sentences. Traditional phrase structure grammars do so with the help of rewrite rules.

Let us now return to trees (4) and (6). They illustrate how an S can be composed of an NP and a VP ("an S *can be rewritten* with an NP followed by a VP," formally: S → NP + VP). This NP, which is an immediate "daughter" of an S and a "left-sister" of a VP, is the subject of the sentence. Similarly, a VP consists of a V and an NP (the object) in the case of a transitive verb, and of a single V in the case of an intransitive verb. Note that the order of the constituents is also very important, unless the word order is free in the given language. Without entering details, observe also that (6) shows how S can be rewritten in another way as well: as an NP followed by an S (formally: S → NP + S), which is a recursive rewrite rule as the mother category is reproduced among the daughters.

In all of these rewrite rules, one of the daughter constituents is the "head": it carries the "essence" of the mother node. The heads (the VP and the V) are underlined in trees (4) and (6). At the same time, all the other constituents are "complements" of the head, so the subject is a complement of VP, and the object is a complement of V.[7] Even within an NP such as "French fries with mayonnaise," one can distinguish between the head "French fries" whose complement is "with mayonnaise."

Seen from a bottom-up perspective, the head receives its complement(s) in order to form a more complex unit. In particular, the verb is the head constituent of the head constituent of the sentence: it gradually receives its arguments (which might also be complex) in order to build up the whole sentence. Heads play a central role in most of the recent syntactic theories, and they will do so even in our model.

In the next section we shall attempt to apply the methodology and concepts just introduced to Jewish liturgy.

Structure of Jewish liturgy—a generative linguistic approach

On data collection

Collecting the primary data is more difficult in the case of liturgy than in the case of a living language. We do not have liturgical "native speakers" who would be able to produce a broad array of liturgical "sentences," and judge liturgical constructions for their grammatical correctness. Instead, we have the fixed liturgy with a given amount of variation: morning, afternoon, and evening services, each of which performed on weekdays, Shabbat days, and various holidays. Although we will not make use of it here, another source of variation could be the different customs observed among various Jewish communities (regional and local *minhagim* [customs]), assuming they still belong to the same "liturgical language," and do not constitute "dialects" with slightly different grammars. Studying innovations in the Jewish liturgy, such as the inclusion of a new song at the end of the service, or the liturgy of the modern Israeli holidays, might also contribute to the study of structural subtleties in the future. Still, the set of collected "grammatical sentences" stays much more restricted than in syntax.

Even more problematic is the fact that we do not have negative evidence, that is, information about certain structures being ungrammatical. These negative evidences are crucial in syntax. If linguists do not find a certain construction in a corpus, they still can ask the native speaker whether the construction is correct. Languages without an available native speaker, such as ancient languages, may be analyzed using generative grammar only if the corpus is so large that the lack of evidence for some structure can be regarded as evidence for the lack of that structure.

Yet, we can accept reflections by contemporary practitioners and remarks in rabbinical sources as the intuition of "native speakers," and we can take those into consideration. Remember the competence approach to religious rituals advanced by Lawson and McCauley, which "takes participants' intuitions about the forms of a symbolic-cultural system's products as part of the subject matter under study and as a body of evidence against which to test theoretical proposals" (Lawson and McCauley 1990, 173, n. 1). Some unattested liturgies could more probably be the tradition of a hypothetical or an unknown community than some other unattested liturgies. A learned observant Jew may have some intuition on this, like a native speaker performing a *wug*-test (differentiating between a nonsense word that could be a word in her language, and a string of sounds that severely violates the laws of that language) (Berko 1958). Therefore, remarks by a congregant or information in the rabbinic literature might sometimes help us corroborate a hypothesis.

Nonetheless, not everything should be accepted automatically. The native speaker of a language often has many misconceptions about his own speech, either due to prescriptive rules learned in school and imposed by the society, or due to the lack of sufficient self-observation. As Frits Staal puts it: "It does not pay to ask elephants about zoology, or artists about the theory of art" (Staal 1979, 4). If asked explicitly, many native speakers would judge incorrect an elliptical sentence, such as the one under (7), even if they would utter and write such sentences daily. Consequently, our goal is to develop our analysis with as few references to "native" opinions as possible, since we aim at analyzing the syntactic structure of the Jewish liturgy itself, and not its perception by the observant Jew.

Another point worth emphasizing is that we do not want to understand the historical development of the liturgy, but its synchronic structure, even if connections can always be made. As in generative linguistics, we do not claim that the synchronic analysis sheds light onto diachronic developments, and conversely, the synchronic structure reflects cognitive processes and need not be consistent with known historical facts. Sometimes the connection between the synchronic structure and historical development is evident; in other cases it is conceivable; very often, however, the system is reanalyzed at a certain point in history, and diachronically unrelated features are blended in the (conscious or unconscious) mind of the next generation.

Even though syntax is supposed to be independent of semantics, the structure in the meaning of the sentence commonly influences the linguist whose goal is to determine the structure of the form of the sentence. Meaning influences the applicability of syntactic tests, and most importantly, meaning gives important hints to the syntactic analysis. Therefore, we will have to refer to the "meaning" of the liturgy—to the role of certain texts in theology or in the ritual practice[8]—even if our goal is to understand its form.

In brief, the sparseness of the data may somehow undermine the methodological soundness of the present exploratory study. I do hope, however, that future work can collect enough data and develop a systematic methodology to overcome these flaws.

An overview of the Jewish liturgy

The basic structure of the main Jewish communal services, as well as of a para-liturgical ritual, the monthly blessing of the Moon (*Kiddush levana*) is given in (10). The experts should forgive me for many simplifications.

(10)
Weekday				
Shacharit (morning):	*Pesukei de-zimra*	*Shma*	*Amida*	*Aleinu*
Mincha (afternoon):	*Ashrei*	—	*Amida*	*Aleinu*
Maariv (evening):	*Ve-hu rachum*	*Shma*	*Amida*	*Aleinu*
Shabbat				
Maariv (Friday evening):	*Kabbalat Shabbat*	*Shma*	*Amida*	*Aleinu*
Mincha (Shabbat afternoon):	*Ashrei, U-va le-Tsion*	*Torah*	*Amida*	*Aleinu*
Kiddush levana				
(Blessing of the new moon):	Psalms, blessings etc.			*Aleinu*

There are three daily prayers in Judaism: *Shacharit* is the morning service, *Mincha* is the afternoon service, and *Maariv*[9] is the evening prayer. The Shabbat and holiday services follow the same structure, but are significantly longer.[10]

Each of these services has a fourfold structure, with the second part of a regular weekday *Mincha* (afternoon) service being empty. They all begin with an introductory part, typically composed of psalms and other (mostly biblical) poetic compositions. The morning *Pesukei de-zimra* ("Verses of praise") is a longer string of psalms and other biblical texts, *Ashrei* is Ps. 145 preceded by two and followed by one verse from other psalms, and *Ve-hu rachum* is Ps. 78:38 and 20:10. *U-va le-Tsion* is a compilation based on the Prophets, their *Targumim* (Aramaic translations), Psalms and Chronicles, while *Kabbalat Shabbat*, even if officially a separate service preceding the Friday night *Maariv*, contains six psalms, followed by a sixteenth-century poem (*Lecha dodi* by Shlomo Alkabetz), followed by Ps. 92 and 93.

After this introduction, the morning and evening services go further with a section entitled *the Shma and its blessings*. The *Shma* contains three texts from the Torah (Deut. 6:4–9, 11:13–21, and Num. 15:37–41), whose recitation twice a day is a separate explicit commandment (cf. Deut. 6:7). The *Mishna* (*Ber.* 1:4) adds that in the morning two blessings are recited before the *Shma* and one afterwards, whereas in the evening two blessings precede and two blessings follow it. In many communities outside Israel, a third blessing is added after the evening *Shma*. As the *Shma* has to be recited in the morning and in the evening, but not in the afternoon, the section *the Shma and its blessings* is not found in the *Mincha* service. Here, however, we find Torah readings at certain occasions, such as on Shabbat and fast days (including *Yom Kippur*).

The third part of each service is the *Amida*,[11] the core of each service: it is a string of a varying number of blessings to be recited silently by the individual and on certain occasions it is repeated by the cantor.[12] At this point we do not enter into the details of the *Amida*, but it will play an important role in our analysis of the Jewish liturgy later.

Finally, a closing section concludes the prayer. This last section always contains a text beginning with the words *Aleinu leshabeach* ("It is our duty to praise ... ") composed most probably around the first century CE. *Aleinu* might be preceded and followed by other texts (from the rabbinic literature, from Psalms etc.), but their detailed analysis is also left to future work.

The Shabbat morning service is not shown in (10). It is composed of the same major parts as the weekday morning service (even if certain parts become much longer or very different), but two major elements are added between the *Amida* and the *Aleinu*: the weekly or holiday-specific Torah reading and a *Musaf* ("supplementary service"). The weekly portion is read from a Torah scroll containing the five books of Moses, which is followed by the corresponding portion from the Prophets and a few blessings; furthermore a few texts accompany the carrying of the scroll from the Ark to the platform where it is read, as well as its carrying back. Once the scroll has been brought back, the congregation recites the *Musaf Amida* silently, which is then repeated by the cantor if a quorum of ten adult Jewish males (traditionally) is present. The *Musaf* is an additional service on Shabbat, the beginning of a new Jewish month and holidays, complementing the three daily services (i.e., the daily three times of reciting the *Amida*). It corresponds to the supplementary offerings in the Temple on these special occasions, as is explicitly mentioned in the *Musaf* text. After the *Musaf Amida* has been repeated, the closing section with the *Aleinu* concludes the Shabbat morning service.

Thus, the Shabbat morning service is in fact two services: theoretically Shacharit and Musaf are separate services, but in practice, they are combined into one. We shall come back to this paradox.

A structural analysis

The major constituents presented in (10) are already the result of some analysis. For instance, the fact that the long string of psalms at the beginning of the morning service can be replaced by two sentences, and so we obtain a grammatical service (namely, the weekly *Maariv*, or evening prayer),[13] is an argument that these psalms form one constituent. Thus the linguistic substitution test could be applied readily to liturgy.

What is an immediately surprising result of this analysis is that the *Shma* (in the morning and evening services) and the Torah reading of the Shabbat (and fast days) *Mincha* (afternoon service) seem to belong to the same category. Observe how they can be replaced with each other, similarly to the way we argued earlier for "John," "I," and "this man" to be equally NPs in sentences (3). Let us call this category *Lectio*.[14] Even though a congregation just reciting the *Shma* looks very different from a congregation just reading the Torah, the parallels are numerous. In both cases, texts from the Pentateuch are read—the Hebrew term employed for both is קריאה (keri'a, reading): קריאת שמע (keri'at Shma, the reading of the Shma) and קריאת תורה (keri'at Torah, the reading of the Torah)—preceded and followed by blessings, and the preceding blessing headed by the call to the congregation *Barkhu* "Bless the Lord!" A major difference between the *Shma* and the Torah reading is that the *Shma* is an obligation of the individual, while the Torah reading is an obligation of the community. Yet, this difference is already semantic (pertaining to the interpretation) and not syntactical (pertaining to the observable form).

The next step is to identify larger components. Here, I must admit that I am influenced by linguistic theories. Many of the contemporary syntactic models prefer binary branching trees to flat structures. That is, a mother node may have at most two daughters, resulting in higher trees, with more levels. Nonetheless, the reader is not expected to be fully convinced by the arguments in the following couple of paragraphs and may vote for a flat structure in which all of the constituents in (10) are sisters and daughters of the top node S (standing here for "Service"):

(11)

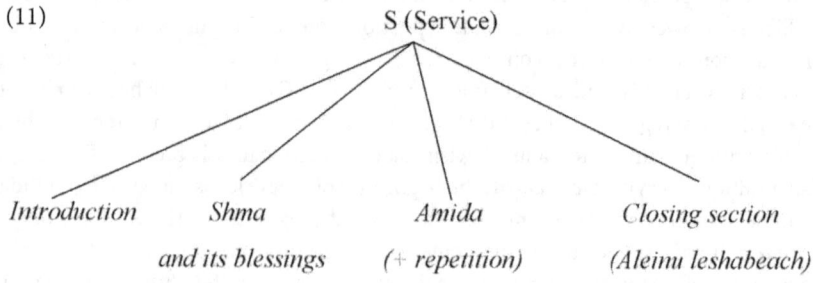

If, however, one prefers a binary tree with each node having two daughters at most, then we can argue as follows.

First, let us look at the structure of *Kiddush levana* (the blessing of the growing Moon in the first half of each liturgical month) whose structure is also shown in (10), but has been ignored as yet. Its structure can be clearly divided into two parts: the blessing itself embedded in a series of psalms and other texts forms the first part, and the *Aleinu* (omitted in some traditions) forms the second part. Hence, we have an example where the three first parts of the analyzed daily services are replaced with one unit in *Kiddush levana*.

Another argument for the first three components forming one constituent employs the stand-alone test, illustrated above by the sentences in (9). There are a few occasions, such as most services of *Yom Kippur*, but also the Friday afternoon *Mincha* in some congregations, when *Aleinu* is omitted.[15] Thus we obtain a "standing alone" service without the closing part, which should also form a single constituent, as it happened in sentence (9a). In fact, *Aleinu* is omitted in all these cases because a number of services are held consecutively and uninterruptedly, so their shared closing section follows only the last service. That is, we obtain a situation similar to the coordination in sentences (8a) and (8b), and the fact that only constituents of the same category may be coordinated is an additional argument for the first three parts forming one constituent. Let us label this constituent, which contains the Introduction, the *Shma* and the *Amida* but not the Closing section (*Aleinu*), Main.

The next step is to decompose the constituent Main into its two daughters: the "Introduction," as well as another constituent, containing the *Shma* (the *Lectio*) and the *Amida*, to be called "Core." In other words, the Introduction does not form one constituent with the *Shma*. One argument for this is the rule that there can be a break between the Introduction and the *Shma*, but not between the *Shma* and the *Amida*. The occurrence of the different types of *Kaddish*, which serve as dividers between parts of the service, reinforces this hypothesis. Additionally, there is also an argument based on distribution: the *Mincha* (afternoon prayer) of the *Yom Kippur* service lacks not only its closing part, but also the introductory part, and consists only of the Torah reading and of the *Amida*. In Ashkenazi tradition, its introductory part moves to the next service, *Neila*, which is a special prayer held only on *Yom Kippur*. Therefore, referring again to the stand-alone test, we conclude that the *Lectio* and the *Amida* must form a single constituent.

In sum, we have obtained the following structure:

(12)

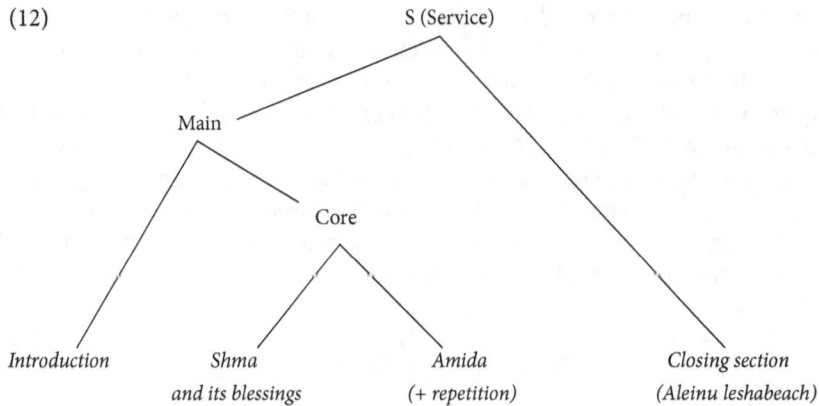

A last major point to be solved in the overall structure of Jewish liturgy is the place of the Torah reading and of Musaf ("supplementary service") in the Shabbat morning service, or in any other service containing Musaf or Torah reading at its end. As explained, Musaf is an additional prayer inserted on special occasions commemorating the additional sacrifice offered once in the Jerusalem Temple on these special days. Consequently, and following the traditional view, we can see the relation of the Shacharit (morning) service and of Musaf as similar to the coordination in a sentence like (8a): "*John loved Mary and hated Ann.*" Tree (8d) suggests the two VPs to be sisters and their shared subject to be a sister of their combination. In a similar way, I propose the *Aleinu* following the Musaf to be the shared Closing section of Shacharit and Musaf (refer to the tree in (13) below, ignoring temporarily the *Torah reading*). The Musaf *Amida* projects a Core node without a *Lectio*, which in turn projects a Main node without an Introduction. This bare Musaf Main node will be the right-sister of the Shacharit Main node (covering an Introduction, a *Lectio* and the morning *Amida*), keeping in mind that only constituents of the same category might be coordinated. Finally, the constituent composed of these two Main nodes is complemented by their shared Closing section to form the top node, Service.

Let us now turn to the Torah reading in the Shabbat morning service. One could propose to analyze it as the *Lectio* complementing *Musaf*, paralleling the Torah reading during certain *Mincha* (afternoon) services on (10). Then, a Torah reading that comes after the *Amida* of *Shacharit* (morning) must always be a consequence of the subsequent *Musaf*. Yet, Torah reading follows the *Amida* of *Shacharit* without an ensuing *Musaf* on regular Mondays and Thursdays, as well as on the holidays of *Chanukah* and *Purim* and public fast days; all these instances could not be analyzed in the offered way. Similarly, *Musaf* cannot be viewed as the complement of the Torah reading, because *Musaf* can be recited independently of Torah reading, for instance if no quorum of ten men is present.

Observe, however, that the Torah reading follows the *Amida* only in the cases when *Shma* precedes the *Amida*. This happens typically in the morning services, but also in the evening service on the holiday of *Simchat Torah* ("rejoicing of the Torah").[16] In the *Mincha* (afternoon) service, which does not contain the *Shma*, the Torah reading can take the regular place of the *Lectio* before the *Amida*. If, nevertheless, more constituents of the *Lectio* type have to be inserted, such as both *Shma* and Torah reading, then only one can fill that slot, while the other one[17] is moved to the edge, higher in the tree, similarly to the tree in (6). Therefore, a second node Main is created with two daughters: the usual node Main and a slot for the Torah reading. Using syntactic terminology, the second *Lectio* can be said to have been raised higher in the tree. On Shabbat, this second node Main will then be coordinated with the *Musaf*'s node Main.

To summarize, the Shabbat morning service is proposed to look as follows:

(13)

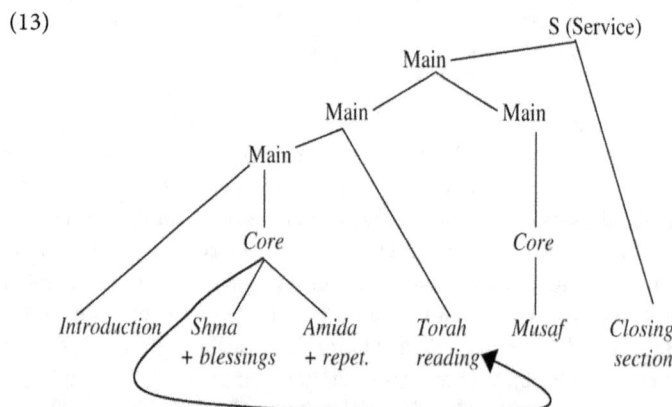

Heads and complements

Thus far, we have not yet raised the question which constituent in the structural analysis is the head and which one is the complement among the daughters of a certain node. But it also remains unclear how to interpret the head–complement relationship, at all, in liturgical syntax.

According to the most widespread definition used in linguistics, the head is the constituent that determines the category of the mother node. Put it simply, the head of a VP is another VP or a V, and the head of an NP is an N (noun). Presently, however, we do not have a system elaborate enough to introduce a more abstract set of categories, as it is the case in syntax. We are still a step earlier: we should use our intuition in order to obtain a first model that can be developed further in future research. On an informal level, and combining syntax and semantics, the head constituent may be said to bear the main meaning of the larger unit, whereas the complement adds something to the meaning of the head.[18] Complements often fill in slots left empty in the meaning of the head. For instance, a complement joining a noun may be an adjective or another noun in apposition or a relative clause, while a complement joining a verb can be the verb's direct or indirect object, or its subject. If the head is left out, much more of the structure's meaning is lost than if one omits the complement.[19]

Therefore, as we can see in (12), Main must be the head whose complement is the Closing section. *Aleinu* is peripheral to what precedes it. One would not recite *Aleinu* only, without a service, but one may omit *Aleinu*, as it happens on *Yom Kippur*. Similarly, the Introduction makes no sense without the Core; therefore, Core is the head within Main, and the Introduction is the complement. Finally, the *Amida* must be the Core's head, because it can never be omitted, unlike the *Shma* and its blessings.[20] Indeed, a *Mincha* service does not contain the *Shma*.

Furthermore, those who know Jewish liturgy would unquestionably accept the semantic claim that *Amida* is the essence of a service. *Amida* is also called *Tefilla*, that is, "prayer," for it is the *a priori* prayer. It is the *Amida* that systematically contains the main elements of a prayer: the acknowledgment of God's attributes, requests, and praises. Moreover, *Maariv* and *Shacharit* services are held in the time span in which the morning and evening *Amida* can be recited. Outside this time span, it would not make sense to have a service. Nevertheless, as this time span does not coincide exactly with the period in which the evening and morning *Shma* must be recited, it sometimes happens that the congregant does not fulfill the commandment of reciting the *Shma* in the framework of the service. Then, the service is held as usual, but the recitation of the *Shma* within the service is considered just as mere Torah study, and not as the fulfillment of the commandment of reciting the *Shma* (*mBer.* 1:2). Therefore, the observant Jew repeats the *Shma* in its proper time, which ritual, however, is not considered a service. Hence, the *Amida* without the (proper) recitation of the *Shma* generates a service, but not vice versa.

To summarize, the *Amida* acts as the verb in the sentence. According to the tree in (4), the verb is joined by its object as a complement to form a VP, which is then joined by the subject as another complement to form an S. Similarly, in the tree in (12) the *Amida* is first joined by the *Lectio* (most often the *Shma* and its blessings) to create a Core, then by the Introduction to have a Main, and finally by the Closing section to form a Service. In certain situations, the slots of the *Lectio*, of the Introduction or of the Closing section are left empty, but without an *Amida*, no service can take place.

The remaining part of this section intends to theoretically underpin this analysis. How can the head–complement relationship be interpreted in liturgy? Here, we borrow an idea from "story grammars."

The idea of "story grammars" goes back to Rumelhart, who viewed the cognitive task of understanding and recalling a story as a problem similar to sentence parsing: "Just as simple sentences can be said to have an internal structure, so too can stories be said to have an internal structure. (…) the notion of 'well-formedness' is nearly as reasonable for stories as it is for sentences" (Rumelhart 1975, 211). With the aim of having computers understand stories, the ensuing research line revived Propp's structuralist approach (Propp 1968), but using the formal framework (the notion of "rewrite rules") of the early generative syntax, and supporting the computational models with psychological experiments. So, for instance, Mandler and Johnson (Mandler and Johnson 1977) demonstrate that these structures are used by both children and adults for encoding and recalling stories. For much later developments and practical computational applications, see for example Halpin et al. (2004), or the closely related Mueller (2003), or the conferences organized by the AMICUS project.[21]

In what follows, I rely on Rubin (Rubin 1995, 28–31), as was first put into the context of the cognitive science of religion by Pyysiäinen (Pyysiäinen 2004, 154). We have seen earlier that a sentence is composed of a NP followed by a VP; that is, the tree structures in (4) and (6) prove that the rewrite rule S → NP + VP is part of the grammar of English. Likewise, observed stories can be divided into a setting and an episode. Hence, the corresponding story grammar contains the rule Story → Setting + Episode. Further analysis shows that episodes in certain genres or traditions should include either one or three attempts before the goal is reached, hence two further rules are Episode → Attempt + Goal and Episode → Attempt + Attempt + Attempt + Goal. To the best of my knowledge, these story grammars relied on early versions of generative grammars, for which reason they did not involve head–complement relationships. Nonetheless, Rubin observes that ballads often do not have settings (Rubin 1995, 303), whence it becomes obvious that the Episode must be the head of the Story, and the optional Setting is its complement. An episode or the action is the "essence" of the story in the same way as is the verb in a sentence; whereas the setting supplies additional information, similar to the object, to the subject, or to the locative and temporal adjuncts of the verb.

Therefore, the proposition is to view the complements in Jewish liturgy also as the "settings" that define the "context" to the action, which in this case is the action of praying, of reciting the *Amida*. What contexts are defined here? The psalms of the Introduction and the (poetic) compositions in the Closing section set the *Sitz-im-Leben* of the prayer, providing a smooth transition between the profane and the sacred. The Introduction helps the congregant reach a mental state adequate for the prayer, while *Aleinu* brings him back to everyday life but also furnishes him with a final positive message, such as messianic hopes. Another role of the lengthy Introduction—overtly acknowledged—is to wait for latecomers, thus the Introduction also sets the social context, not only the psychological one.

The role of the constituent that we have called *Lectio*, which includes both the *Shma* and the Torah reading, is significantly different. Unlike the Introduction and the Closing section, it serves as the fulfillment of important precepts, such as reading the *Shma* twice a day. Therefore, the closest complement to the *Amida* sets the theological setting: the commandments, but also the central theological concepts concentrated extremely densely in Deut. 6:4–9, the idea of reward and punishment expressed in the second part of the *Shma* (Deut. 11:13–21), as well as the historical perspective, also central to Judaism, appearing in the third section (Num. 15:37–41). For Torah reading, the previous elements are all present again: even if a particular weekly portion might contain theological, halakhic, and historical elements in varying proportions, the very fact that the Torah scroll becomes central to a part of the service maximally recalls all these elements in any Jew with sufficient background education.

So far, we have argued for the complements in the previously presented tree structure in (12) of the Jewish liturgy to be analogous to the setting in story grammars. But how does the *Amida* become the episode?

Blessings—why?

The *Amida* is a series of blessings with a fixed text, varying in number from seven to nineteen, depending on the occasion. At the beginning of this chapter, I argued that prayer is a form of speech act whose aim is to communicate (to hand over information, to petition, to praise or flatter the other, to acknowledge something) with another agent that happens to be superhuman. Now, we are about to conclude that this speech act is presented in the form of blessings in Judaism.[22]

What are blessings and how have they assumed such a central role in Judaism? The Jewish blessings start with the following words: "Blessed are you Lord, our God, King of the universe," and continue depending on the concrete blessing, mentioning an attribute of God, what he does or what he has done. Now this form raises the question how a human can bless the superhuman. To answer it, we should review the role of prayers in Judaism.

As an exegesis to the biblical clause "and you shall serve Him with/within your whole heart" (Deut. 11:13), on several occasions, rabbinic literature calls prayer (*tefilla*) "the service with/within the heart."[23] Here the early rabbinic sources remain open to interpretation: Does the word *tefilla* refer to prayer in general, or to the established *Amida*? To be sure, traditionally, the occasions of reciting the *Amida* correspond to the sacrifices (and other actions) performed in the Temple (cf. Maimonides *Mishne Tora, Hilkhot Tefilla* 1:5–6), and the *Musaf Amida* explicitly refers to the biblical passages describing the special offerings on that day. Consequently, reciting the *Amida*, a series of blessings composed in postbiblical Hebrew, becomes performative biblical exegesis.

Put it differently, the *Amida* took over the role of the sacrifices after the destruction of the Jerusalem Temple. A temple sacrifice, originally, is a form of feeding another agent, namely, the SHA. Using the action representation scheme proposed by McCauley and Lawson (McCauley and Lawson 2002), a sacrifice can be seen as a feeding action where the human person is the agent and the SHA is the beneficiary.[24] Notice that here we have a surprising reversed parent–child relationship: even though God is often seen in Western theology as the "Heavenly Father," in a sacrifice the SHA acts as the baby who is fed by the parents.

These observations help us better understand the role of blessings in Judaism. First, the basic (nonreligious, everyday) action corresponding to the ritual action of blessing should be identified. I propose to see blessings as a form of helping. Namely, if "X blesses Y," then what happens is that "X helps Y, but beyond the human capacities of X." In other words, I would like to give you a hand, but for some reason, this is not feasible. Therefore, I turn to the realm of magic and religion, and I help you by blessing you, that is, by involving superhuman agency. Reasons why I cannot help you in the regular sense may be that you want to achieve some goal not depending exclusively on human actions (to grow crops, to defeat the enemy etc.), or because I would like to help you beyond my own life.

Consequently, a prototypical example of this *first type of blessing* is when the old Isaac blesses his son (whomever); but also—to come back to Jewish liturgy—when a person of priestly origin (a kohen) blesses the congregation on certain occasions, or when the father blesses his children on Friday night. The patriarch blessing his offspring before he passes away also shows why superhuman agency should be involved: after one's death, one is unable to help their descendants further, in the nonreligious sense. This first type of blessing can be called *superhuman instrument blessing*, since the SHA is nothing but the thematic instrument of the action. Both the thematic agent and the thematic recipient (beneficiary) of the blessing action are human agents.

In the second phase, the thematic roles are changed slightly, and the SHA turns to be more active. Instead of being invited by a human, the SHA becomes the initiator of the blessing, probably as a result of the blessed person's righteous behavior. So, in the narratives of God blessing Abraham we encounter a "superhuman agent blessing." The result is the same, the person receiving the blessing is helped and given everything nice and good; but the thematic agent is now identical with the thematic instrument, which is the SHA, the only participant in the action who possesses the skills necessary to ensure the efficacy of the blessing. Only the thematic beneficiary is still a human.

In the third phase, finally, the thematic roles are totally reversed, as in the reversed parent–child relationship in feeding (sacrificing to) the SHA. When David blesses God (1 Chron. 29:10, which is the prototypical text for all Jewish blessings; see also 1 Kgs. 1:48), a "superhuman beneficiary blessing" takes place. The everyday act of helping loses all of its meaning in this third phase, for King David certainly cannot know how he could help God; only the form, the mental representation of the action of helping is used in a religious context, similar to the situation when a SHA is fed by a human.[25] In fact, in both instances the human acts toward the SHA, because he or she expects some sort of reciprocity: if I feed or help the SHA (whatever the meaning, i.e., the effect on the SHA of this action is), I might have her goodwill thereby.

To summarize, the idea of the prayers being "the service within the heart" makes sense from a cognitive science of religion viewpoint. Notwithstanding the minor difference between feeding somebody and helping somebody,[26] both prayer and Temple service are actions with a "reversed agent-beneficiary relationship": the agent giving is the human being, while the beneficiary receiving is the SHA. This reversal is surprising because usually God is regarded as the Father who feeds and helps his (her) children, while the small child feeding or helping the strong parent is unusual and incomprehensible. Nevertheless, the action with a reversed argument structure might be a form of *imitatio dei* whose aim is to create a psychological bond to the SHA, beyond the expectation of reciprocity.

Conclusion

Prayer is a twisted form of communication, the situation when the addressee is a SHA. But this twist aside, it builds on everyday cognitive capacities, in particular, communicative and linguistic ones. This observation motivated us to attempt to apply linguistic methodology to uncover the structure of liturgy. A structural analysis of Jewish liturgy has been proposed, employing elements of the generative syntax in the 1970s and 1980s. The level of abstractness of contemporary linguistics might have been counter-productive in these first experimental steps toward a generative syntax of liturgy.

As yet, it is unclear whether the similarities discovered in the structure of English sentences and in the structure of Jewish liturgy are only the result of the similar methodology employed, or whether they also demonstrate the existence of similar (or of the same) underlying cognitive structures. Although our starting point was hypothesizing the latter, it would be premature to consider this hypothesis as already proven by the previous sections. Generative trees could also describe galactic structures and military hierarchies, computer file systems, and family relations: these examples share nothing more than the cognitive structure in the brain of the scholar describing them. Yet, I conjecture that the linguistic methodology presented is applicable to liturgies even beyond the point that can be reached by comparing any two unrelated fields. The earlier sections of this chapter only scratched the surface of syntactic theory, but decades of research on numerous phenomena in countless languages by thousands of syntacticians produced a much deeper understanding of language. An equally thorough study of various liturgical systems in a wide range of religious traditions should also result in more principled analyses. In turn, similarities between the principles underlying the linguistic system and the liturgical system would be an argument for the connection of the two domains. Subsequently, further research should discover more significant arguments for the working hypothesis that religious phenomena are but special, "twisted" cases of everyday phenomena.

In the proposed approach, the head of a larger constituent is the action whose setting is defined by the complements. We argued that blessings in Jewish liturgy form the nucleus-head of the prayer. The speech act in this type of blessing is the action of helping, with the thematic agent being a human person and the beneficiary being God. This action becomes the head of the structure, which is added a complement setting the theological context (the *Lectio*: the *Shma* and its blessings in the morning and evening service, and Torah reading on certain days in the afternoon) to form a larger unit that we called the Core. The Core itself is the head in a larger unit, the Main, which in turn is the head of the unit Service. Using linguistic terminology, Core, Main, and Service are projections of the lowest head, *Amida*. The Introduction is a complement within the Main, while the Closing section is a complement within the Service, and both set the social and psychological contexts of the action expressed by the whole structure.

The results presented here are only the first steps toward a comprehensive syntax of liturgy. Details will most probably be reconsidered in the light of future research. The theory must be further developed, first by proposing new tests identifying the constituents and their relationship, and by elaborating on the relationship between the constituents. In practice, the fine details of the structure of Jewish liturgy must be worked out (including the structural role played by the various versions of *Kaddish*), and the inner structure of each major constituent should also be expounded. Yet, applying this methodology to other religions is even more important, in order to observe what is universal and what varies among different cultures and liturgical traditions. What are the "principles" and what are the "parameters" in the syntax of (communicative) rituals? Finally, accumulating sufficient experience, we will be able to tackle the central question of the cognitive science of religion: how can these observations be explained using general cognitive principles? For instance, in an analogous way to the results of Mandler and Johnson (Mandler and Johnson 1977) on recalling stories, we may ascertain the assumption that liturgies following language-like syntax are easier to recall and are therefore evolutionarily more stable.

9

Forgiveness of the Sinless: A Classic Contradiction in 1 Jn in the Light of Contemporary Forgiveness Research

Rikard Roitto

Forgiveness in 1 Jn is an enigma, which has generated countless scholarly discussions. One such discussion concerns the limit of forgiveness in 1 Jn:

> If someone sees his brother sinning a sin not unto death, he shall ask and give him life—to those sinning not unto death. There is sin unto death. I do not talk about that [sin], that he should pray [for the brother]. All wrongdoing is sin, and there is sin not unto death. (1 Jn 5:16–17)

What is the difference between "sins unto death," which one should pray for, and "sin not unto death," which one is not obliged to pray for, in 5:16–17?

Another enigma is how can 1 Jn state both that community members who claim to be free from sin have got it wrong (1:8–2:2) and that community members cannot sin (3:6, 9; 5:18):

> If we say that we do not have sin, we deceive ourselves and truth is not in us. If we confess our sins, he is faithful and righteous to forgive us the sins and cleanse us from every wrongdoing. (1 Jn 1:8–9)
>
> Everyone who remains in him does not sin. Everyone who sins has neither seen him nor known him. ... Whoever does sin is of the Devil ... Everyone born of God does not do sin, since the seed of him remains in him, and he cannot sin, since he is born of God. (1 Jn 3:6, 8a, 9)

Why must community members confess sins (1:8–10) and pray for the sins of other "brothers" (5:16–17), although they do not and cannot sin (3:6, 9; 5:18)?

In this chapter, I evaluate some typical number of scholarly answers to the questions above in the light of contemporary research on forgiveness and a number of related fields in the behavioral sciences.[1] I argue that scholars have used their intuitions about forgiveness in order to find solutions to the problems—sometimes for better, sometimes for worse. Then I suggest a novel interpretation based on forgiveness studies and behavioral sciences. This interpretation will emphasize that 1 Jn's aim is to form the identity and the practical communal life of the community, and that the discourse on forgiveness is an aspect of this ambition. My suggestion in the final section of this chapter is that although the statements may be considered self-contradictory from a theological point of view (emic perspective), the contradictory statements nevertheless, from an functionalist viewpoint, can be understood as promoting a balance of social practices that helped the Johannine community to prevail (etic perspective).

In the late nineteenth century, commentators such as Brooke Foss, Westcott, and Alfred Plummer assumed that 1 Jn handles primarily the saving forgiveness of individuals.[2] Beginning with Robert Law in 1909, however, several scholars have interpreted 1 Jn's discourse about sinlessness and forgiveness as "vehement polemic" against a historical situation of conflict with secessionists (Law 1909, 226. Later also for example Brown 1979, 124–27; Dodd 1946, 78–81; Swadling 1982). I consider this scholarly development a progress, since such interpretations appreciate the group dynamic functions of the text's theology of forgiveness. In the 1990s, however, Judith Lieu and Terry Griffith rightly argued that this kind of situational interpretation could not capture the character of 1 Jn fully, since the theology of 1 Jn is not solely a mirror of a schism, but aims to build the identity of the Johannine community more broadly (Lieu 1991; Griffith 1998). Griffith perhaps goes too far when he claims that any reference to a historical crisis is unnecessary in order to understand the letter. Lieu is more balanced:

> However serious the schism, the polemic against specific views and claims of opponents does not control the letter or its thought. The so-called "moral debate" is not explicitly related to the schismatics and so should not be interpreted purely as a reaction against them. (Lieu 1991, 15–16)

Neither Lieu nor Griffith interprets 1 Jn as a timeless theological treatise, but rightly understands the theology of forgiveness and non-forgiveness of community members as interwoven with the goal of maintaining a meaningful identity of the community. In 1 Jn, forgiveness and acceptance by God equals belonging to the community and vice versa (e.g., 1:7; 2:19; 3:14, cf. Griffith 1998, 265–66). I will follow their lead, and therefore socio-cognitive research on forgiveness and identity formation will be the most valuable tools in our interpretation.[3] As psychologist and forgiveness researcher Michael McCullough would say, theologies of forgiveness often have important group dynamic functions (cf. McCullough 2008, 202–23).

The limits of forgiveness: Sin unto death and sin not unto death

We begin by using behavioral research on forgiveness and identity formation to evaluate different scholarly interpretations of what sins are impossible (1 Jn 3:9) and "unto death" (5:16–17) for a Johannine community member.

Habitual and occasional sins

Brooke Foss Westcott suggests in his commentary from 1886 that what the author really means to say in 1 Jn 3:6, 9 is that those who are born of God do not sin habitually, over and over again (Westcott 1886, 104). This interpretation is comparable to the theology of the *Psalms of Solomon*, where the righteous "stumbles" but does not commit "sin after sin" (*Pss. Sol.* 3:5–8, cf. 9:5–7; 13:7–10; 16:11). Although Westcott's understanding has not convinced scholars in the last decades (e.g., Kubo 1969), it remains popular.[4] The main argument for this view is that the author uses the present tense, which is a durative tense, when he claims that those who remain in Christ do not and cannot sin in 1 Jn 3:6, 9, but the aorist tense, which is a punctiliar tense, when he writes about what happens if someone sins in 2:1. This argument rests on subtleties and ignores that the present tense is used about sinning brothers in 1:8 and 5:16 (Dodd 1946, 79; Kubo 1969).

Nevertheless, it is not difficult to understand why this suggestion remains popular in spite of scholarly objections. It is utterly unrealistic to assume that there has ever been a social group where not even occasional moral transgressions existed, particularly if the norms of the group include helping brothers in material need (3:16–18). As Johannes Heinrich August Ebrard writes, "It would be a frightful and most depressing utterance, that whosoever sins in any sense whatever, has no part in Christ" (Ebrard 1850, 228). On the other hand, any group that allows habitual transgression of group norms is bound to dissolve or change into something else.

This problem was well explored in game theoretical computer simulation on cooperation and forgiveness, pioneered by Robert Axelrod (Axelrod 1997). Game theoretical models, which have been most influential in contemporary forgiveness research (McCullough 2008, 88–101), show that limited forgiveness seems to be the most successful cooperation strategy. Axelrod simulated different strategies, representing cooperating individuals, in iterated series of cooperation. In these simulations, it was possible to gain extra resources at the cost of one's cooperation partner by defecting (cheating, stop cooperating), but if both players defected, they both gained less resources than if they had both cooperated. The result of his initial simulations was that a simple strategy called "tit for tat" was more successful than all other strategies: do whatever the other player did to you in the last round. That is, cooperate as long as the other player cooperates, but if the other player defects, retaliate by defecting in the next round. This strategy gave both fruitful cooperation with cooperative partners and protection against nasty cheats. The result suggests that any social species needs to combine the capacity to cooperate with the capacity to cut cooperation with non-cooperative partners.

However, "tit for tat" is not forgiving, but retaliation without hesitation. Does this mean that forgiveness is socially irrational? Axelrod realized that the simulations lacked something that could be likened to mistakes and moral weakness. Therefore he added "noise," that is, mistakes, to the simulations. Under these conditions, strategies called "forgiving tit for tat" and "contrite tit for tat" came out as winners rather than "[non-forgiving] tit for tat." Forgiving tit for tat "forgives" a defector once or twice before retaliation. That is, it continues cooperation one or two times before it stops cooperating.

As opposed to the ordinary tit for tat strategy, this strategy can handle occasional mistakes without terminating cooperation too quickly. Therefore this strategy is able to gain more resources in cooperation with flawed partners. Contrite tit for tat is a "repentant" strategy. It cooperates one or two rounds after making a mistake even if the other player retaliates, in order to turn the other player back into cooperative mode. This strategy is able to avoid endless feuds. Yet, even in simulations with noise, ever-forgiving strategies did not do that well, since they never protected themselves from exploitation by nasty strategies. These results are also supported by studies on real people. Most people forgive to a certain extent, but not unconditionally, and people are more willing to forgive those who repent and apologize (Mullet and Michèle 1999). We humans have an emotional setup that helps us maintain a balance between forgiveness and retaliation (d'Aquili 2001). The same principle is valid on a cultural level. Groups endorsing cultural ideals that balance cooperation, forgiveness, and punishment of transgressors will do better than one-sidedly forgiving or one-sidedly retaliating cultures (Wilson 2002, 189–218). This last point is important, since 1 Jn reflects a cultural phenomenon.

According to social identity theory, every group is motivated to maximize its (a) collective self-esteem and (b) distinctiveness (Tajfel and Turner 1979; Haslam et al. 1998). These are cognitive (rather than material) resources that groups aim to maximize. Now, group members who deviate by transgressing group norms can undermine both self-esteem and distinctiveness (Hogg et al. 2005). If the group's self-esteem is based on moral superiority, as it clearly is in 1 Jn, group members who sin undermine this self-image and the experiences of moral distinctiveness. Consequently, it can be quite destructive for the social identity of a group to harbor habitual deviators. It can even be satisfying for the group to exclude deviators, since exclusion manifests the identity of the group and maintains its boundaries (Marques et al. 2001).

Therefore, Westcott's suggestion is realistic in a very general sense. The interpretation of 1 Jn that God—and thereby the community—forgives occasional sinners, but excludes those who sin habitually without any sign of remorse, is socially realistic, simply because it is reasonable to act that way in any group. Westcott seems to have used his human intuitions about interpersonal forgiveness to find a realistic interpretation of the reality behind the text, even though the differentiation between habitual and non-habitual sin has little support in the rhetoric of the text itself. Although Westcott distorts the theological and rhetorical point to which the text aims, he is probably right in the sense that the real Johannine community excluded those who habitually deviated from group norms, but only after giving them chances to change their ways.[5]

Intentional and unintentional sins

A less common but still interesting interpretation, suggested by Johannes Heinrich August Ebrard in 1850, is that the author of 1 Jn distinguishes between intentional and unintentional sin (Ebrard 1850, 226–28, 233–34).[6] 1 Jn 3:6, 9 would then mean that they cannot sin intentionally, and 1:8–2:2 would mean that they should confess and be absolved from unintentional sins. Therefore, sins unto death and sins not unto death in 5:16 refer to intentional and unintentional sin, respectively. This interpretation is also supported by the distinction between intentional and unintentional transgressions in

Jewish tradition (e.g., Lev. 4:13–14; Num. 15:27–31; 1QS VIII.21–24; *mKer.* 1.2) and similar distinctions in Greco-Roman discussions on forensic rhetoric (e.g., Aristotle, *Rhet.* II.3; Cicero, *Inv.* II.5).[7] Nevertheless, there is no mention of intentional and unintentional sin in 1 Jn.

Ebrard's distinction between voluntary and involuntary acts speaks directly to how we humans tend to judge the moral value of other people's actions. Humans have a unique innate capacity to understand the motivation and knowledge behind other people's actions. This capacity is often called "theory of mind," since we can imagine what is going on in other people's minds (Leslie 1995). The process where we ascribe intentions, character traits, and motives to other people in order to explain their actions is called "attribution" by social cognition scholars (Augoustinos 2006, 149–85). Jean Piaget, in his pioneering work on the child's development of morality, saw that as children mature, they develop their capacity to judge the moral value of an action depending on the agent's underlying motivations and intentions (Piaget 1932). More recent cognitive studies on forgiveness show that adults are generally more willing to forgive those who wrong them if they believe that the offender did not do it intentionally (Mullet and Michèle 1999).

Therefore, although the author of 1 Jn does not theologize intentionality, it is quite reasonable that the members of the historical Johannine community shared our intuition that intentional transgressions are more serious than unintentional ones. The distinction is innate in the human mind and it was a part of Jewish, Greek, and Roman moral discourses. We may assume that Ebrard, just like Westcott, was inspired by his moral intuitions in his interpretation.

Grave and minor sins

Some interpreters have suggested that the author of 1 Jn intends to distinguish particularly grave sins, sins unto death, from other sins. 1:8–2:2 and 5:16–17 would then deal with less grave sins, but 3:6, 9 and 5:18 with sins so grave that it is impossible to "remain in him" (3:6). There is an abundance of suggestions as to which these sins are (for a survey see Brown 1982, 615–17), but most famous is perhaps the interpretation by Tertullian, who in the early third century suggested that "murder, idolatry, fraud, apostasy, blasphemy; and, of course, too, adultery and fornication" are sins unto death while other sins are forgivable (*Pud.* 19; cf. Scholer 1975, 236–38).[8]

Tertullian's interpretation fits our general intuitions about how forgivable a transgression is. The gravity of an offense is one of the factors that affect how willingly people forgive (Mullet and Michèle 1999).[9] That is perfectly rational, since if cooperation with someone has been costly, it might become costly again in the future. It is no wonder that many interpreters have tried to resolve the tensions in 1 Jn by limiting forgiveness to less severe sins.

Tertullian's suggestion assumes a scenario of an individual before God. However, if we are to take the aim of 1 Jn—identity formation—seriously, gravity should be understood from a group perspective and not an individual perspective. We should look for transgressions that affect the identity of the whole group, not just the salvific status of the individual, and that is what we will do next.

In-group and out-group sins

An interpretation, which appreciates the community building goal of 1 Jn, is that sins "unto death" are sins which cause exclusion from the community with God and thus also with the Johannine community (the expression "passed from death to life," 3:14, describes the spiritual status of the community). Many modern commentators since Robert Law's study *The Tests of Life*, published in 1909, have suggestions in this direction.[10] Such a definition is of course redundant unless the content of the sins is elaborated. Some define the content of sin unto death in a very rigid manner, so that only the most vicious fit the criteria. Robert W. Yarbrough, for instance, defines sins unto death as having "a heart *unchanged* by God's love in Christ and so *persist* in [sinful] convictions and acts and commitments" (Yarbrough 2008, 311, emphasis added. Similarly, Köstenberger 2009, 467–68). Collin G. Kruse suggests that the sins that a true community member cannot commit (3:9) equal ἀνομία in 3:4, which he understands as rebellion against God (Kruse 2003. Similarly, Griffith 1998). While such definitions may bring comfort to a worried soul, they do not appreciate how the text of 1 Jn describes sins that are signs of being "of the Devil" (3:8).

David M. Scholer, in his essay from 1975, rightly summarizes the sins that are described by 1 Jn as sins which exclude you from "remaining" in the group in two categories: (a) "murder," which equals hating other group members and not helping them (3:11–18), and (b) "lying," that is, claiming a false Christology (2:22–23; Scholer 1975).[11] From an individualistic soteriological perspective, Scholer's understanding may be perceived as harsh, but from a group perspective, it is quite reasonable that hate, unhelpfulness, and false teachings constituted the limit of group belonging. According to social identity theory (discussed above), groups tend to see transgressions that undermine the identity of the group as more severe than other transgressions. Group members who identify strongly with the group tend to act and interpret the social situation on the group level, so that the interests of the group are also the interests of the committed group member (Tajfel and Turner 1979). Severity is then understood from a group perspective, where the good of the group is the most important concern, not the good of individuals.

The two kinds of sin identified by Scholer are of highest concern from a group perspective. First, a group that appreciates "love" as an obligation to help each other in practical matters (3:17) would inspire cooperation and intimacy and thus strengthen the identity of the group. Second, in a group that is able to maintain a fairly coherent theological narrative, it is easier to maintain cognitive certainty among the group members. According to social identity theory, the sense that the group is distinct and has a meaning is very important in order to maintain commitment among the members of the group (Haslam et al. 1998). One important aspect of the group identity of the Johannine community was their theological narrative. When people in a group share similar narratives, they support each other emotionally and thus feel cognitively certain about the truth of these narratives. However, when some group members claim other narratives, this emotional support is weakened and cognitive uncertainty increases (Festinger et al. 1950; Moscovici 1976). As a consequence, there is a risk that commitment to the group decreases. Therefore, from a group perspective it is quite understandable that alternative teachings that undermine cognitive certainty within the group would merit exclusion from the group. In short, both categories of sin identified by Scholer would weaken the group, and it is therefore in the interest of the community that these sins would merit reproach and in some cases even exclusion.

If we analyze the culture, or the identity, of the Johannine community from the perspective of the culture itself, rather than its members, we see a cognitive system that has to fulfill two conditions in order to survive. First, the culture must spread to new brains (evangelization). Second, the culture must protect itself from destruction. (The personification of culture is merely illustrative. A culture is, needless to say, not an intentional agent.) István Czachesz has used social network theory to show that one of the reasons early Christianity spread well was that its members were successful at creating "weak links," that is, contacts with people other than those with whom one interacts every day ("strong links," for example the household; Czachesz 2011a, 129–54). Through these weak links, the message of Christianity could spread into new contexts. However, Czachesz does not discuss the other side of the coin—that information potentially flows both ways through a social link (Centola and Macy 2007).[12] Any social links could potentially influence group members in the wrong direction. I would suggest that the non-forgiveness of false teachers functions as a way to cut off potentially dangerous information flows from social links, and that non-forgiveness of unhelpful group members is a way to protect positive links within the community from destruction. In short, by claiming that God has no community with false teachers and those who destroy relations within the group, the culture and identity of the Johannine community became more apt for long-term survival.

Sinlessness, yet confession of sins

There is a tension in 1 Jn between ideal and reality in the self-perception of the community. For example, all group members are described as characterized by love (1 Jn 4:19; 5:1). Only those who love and act accordingly remain group members (2:10; 3:14; 4:12, 16; 5:2–3). Those who do not love other group members do not belong to the group (3:10, 14; 4:8, 11, 20). Yet love and its practical consequences are often described as an obligation rather than a fact (3:11, 16, 23; 4:21) and the text even directly exhorts the community to love (4:7),[13] thus implying that there is still need for moral improvement.

The claims of sinlessness in 1 Jn accentuate the tension between ideal and reality. The text claims that all group members are perfect and impeccable. Those who are born of God do not and cannot sin, since the seed of God is in them (3:6, 9; 5:18). In fact, those who fail to live up to the standards are by definition not group members (2:4, 9, 11). When the text describes a group of people who apparently have left the community, the judgment is that they never belonged to the group, not even while they were in it (2:19). If being born of God causes a state of moral perfection (2:5; 4:14, 17–18), the only logical conclusion is that deviants could not even have entered that state.

Yet the text insists that group members who claim not to sin are liars (1:8–10). Everyone must confess their sins publicly,[14] and they are urged to pray for sinning group members (5:14–17). The contradiction is particularly accentuated in 5:16–18, where the instruction to pray for each other's sins stands right beside the claim of sinlessness.

Countless attempts have been made to solve this contradiction. After all, it is reasonable to assume that an author (or final redactor) clever enough to compose 1 Jn was also clever enough to understand that the text contains an apparent contradiction.[15] We may even assume that the author has a purpose in doing so. We will now evaluate these scholarly attempts in the light of research on forgiveness and identity formation.

Struggles within

Alfred Plummer argues in his commentary from 1886 that the contradictions in 1 Jn merely reflect "that internal contradiction of which everyone who is endeavouring to do right is conscious" (Plummer 1886, 124). He then relies on Paul's description of a similar struggle in Rom 7:20 as a template to understand the tensions in 1 Jn. Further, Plummer thinks 1 Jn means that "the Divine nature imparted on the believer" is the entity that cannot sin (Plummer 1886, 127). Later commentators have not been impressed by this interpretation, since 1 Jn does not mention any struggle between flesh and Spirit within a person (e.g., Smalley 1984, 160–61).

Greek and Roman philosophers often conceptualized the inner life of a person as a struggle between different impulses. Plato postulated a tripartite soul (*Rep.* 436b); Aristotle discussed how rational thought and passions had to be coordinated in order to achieve virtue (*Eth. Nic.* VII.1–10); Seneca regarded passions as destructive forces that reason had to conquer (*Ira*). Some Jewish thinkers, for instance Philo (e.g., *Decal.* 142–153) and the author of 4 Maccabees (e.g., 3.2–5), had been impressed by Hellenistic thought on passions and rationality (Aune 1994). However, we must remember that not all Jews conceptualized the inner life of a person in this fashion. The traditional Jewish discourse on the inner life of a person was much more holistic and less precise (Stacey 1956). 1 Jn surely knows how to talk about virtues (e.g., love, 3:10), knowledge (e.g., 2:3), emotions (e.g., fear, 4:18), spiritual influence (e.g., 3:6–10), and other attributes of the mind of humans as the cause of behavior, but there is no developed concept of a struggle between different parts of this inner life in 1 Jn. One is either "of the Devil" or "of God" (3:8–9), but not simultaneously.[16]

Should we conclude that the real community members of 1 Jn did not experience a struggle between moral and immoral impulses, since we do not find this kind of vocabulary in the Johannine tradition? I think not. The last decades of research on the human brain has shown that the brain reacts subconsciously to social situations at several levels and creates a multitude of emotional and cognitive impulses, which it then has to coordinate (Gross 2008). It is part of our biology, not only of our culture, to coordinate contradicting impulses. Therefore, there is no reason to think that the brains of Johannine community members were any different in this regard. We may thus assume that the members of the real Johannine community experienced both moral and immoral impulses. They most probably interpreted the moral impulses as signs that "the seed of him [i.e. God] remains" (3:9) in them and caused them to act morally. If so, they were probably concerned about immoral impulses since they implied that they were "in the dark" (2:11) and "of the Devil" (3:8). The complicated human process of making moral decisions was probably conceptualized as the difference between being influenced by the seed of God or not. Thus, Plummer's suggestion has a point. Nevertheless, his by all means correct description of the experience of being human cannot do justice to the way 3:6, 9 describes the condition of those born by God.

It is evident that Plummer is only concerned with the perspective of the individual when he discusses struggles within. He does not ask about the social function of the theology of forgiveness, although 1 Jn describes reality on the group level when it divides humanity into two categories. What social effects does it bring to associate deviant impulses and behaviors with being of the devil? We will return to this below.

Imperatives in disguise

Georg Strecker resolves the tensions within 1 Jn in his commentary from 1989 by arguing that the statements about moral perfection in 1 Jn 3:6, 9 are meant to be a forceful way to urge the community to act morally—moral imperatives in indicative disguise (Strecker 1996, 96–97, 102–03). He points out that the statements about perfection occur in the hortative context of 1 Jn 3, which indicates that the purpose of these statements is to set forth the ideal which the community should reach for. Moreover, the purpose of the letter, as expressed in 2:1, is to urge them not to sin. The obvious problem with this interpretation of 3:6, 9 is, of course, that the clauses are indicative, not imperative or hortative subjunctive (Smalley 1984, 161).

The indicative tense does not have to be such a decisive objection, though. The suggestion that the indicative has the rhetorical force of an imperative captures the conflation of causality and moral judgment in human attribution processes. A few illustrative examples: when Proverbs claims "The wise of heart heeds[17] commandments" (Prov. 10:8), the statement about what the wise person is like is intended to exhort the reader to heed commandments. Epictetus introduces one of his discourses by defining a human as "a rational and mortal being" (Diatr. II.9). As the discourse continues, it becomes obvious that the statement that a human *is* rational, really functions as a statement about what a human ideally *should be*. Paul, too, uses this kind of rhetorics quite straightforwardly: "If we live by the Spirit, let us also be guided by the Spirit" (Gal 5:25).

This conflation of indicative and imperative has to do with how processes of attribution (see discussion above) function in our minds. The statement in 1 Jn that "whoever is born of God does not commit sin" (3:9) is an attribution: The attribute "born of God" is imagined to cause the behavior "does not commit sin." Now, in everyday life we use attribution processes not only to explain why people act in certain ways, but also to judge the moral value of other people's actions. If we think that someone gives money out of love, we think it is good. If we believe money is given in order to manipulate and gain advantages, we judge the action as bad. Attributions are often done ad hoc; for instance, if someone crashes my car, I might be so upset that I refuse to accept that it was an accident and attribute evil intent to the person who caused the crash (Nichols and Knobe 2007; Cushman et al. 2008). Since indicative attribution statements are simultaneously imperatives and moral judgments, indicative statements about the connection between attributes and actions can also be used rhetorically in order to convince people to act in certain ways, just like 1 Jn and many other ancient texts do (Roitto 2011, 74–106).

We may therefore assume that the first readers of 1 Jn were able to interpret these statements as statements about what they should be like, just like Strecker suggests. Nevertheless, to only emphasize the hortative function does not fully capture the flexible nature of attribution statements. In our minds, they function as statements, ideals, and moral demands.[18]

Idealistic versus realistic self-perception

Another interesting solution, suggested by Henry Alford in 1861, is that the claims about sinlessness are descriptions of an ideal, indeed a real spiritual state, while the exhortation to confess sins reflects the practical reality of the everyday struggle to remain in that state (Alford 1878, 465–70). This solution was significantly developed in 1958 by Ignace de la Potterie, who suggests that the ideal is their spiritual potential, that which they are in the eyes of God (Potterie 1971).[19] The ideal is realized, yet eschatological; already now and still not yet.[20] Lyonnet shows how numerous Jewish texts expect perfection given by the Spirit in the eschatological future (e.g., *1 En.* 5.8; *Pss. Sol.* 17.32–33; *T. Levi* 18.9; *Jub.* 5.12; 1QS IV.20–23; *4 Ezra* 9:31). There is an important difference in 1 Jn compared to most of these eschatological texts, however: In 1 Jn the eschatological expectation is not only future but also present (cf. Kubo 1969). "We have passed (μεταβεβήκαμεν [*metabebēkamen*]) from death to life" (3:14; cf. Jn 3:18; 5:24; 8:51). Therefore demand and realization stand side by side in 1 Jn.

Lyonnet is right in arguing that the realized eschatological framework in 1 Jn accentuates the tension between ideal and reality. However, this tension is not unique to groups with strong eschatological convictions. On the contrary, these tensions can be readily explained by how we humans conceptualize social identities. According to self-categorization theory, which is a development of social identity theory, we conceptualize social identities as categories (Turner et al. 1987). We humans do not only think of categories as a number of elements that fulfill a number of minimal criteria. Most of the categories in our mind also have a prototype, that is, an idea about the ideal or typical member of that category (Rosch 1978). For example, we think of robins and sparrows as more prototypical birds than penguins. This is also true for social categories. Within social groups with a shared identity, there is a (more or less) shared imagination of the prototypical group member. This prototype is not merely the mean of all group members, but an ideal (Hogg et al. 2004). This in-group prototype functions both at the group level and at the individual level. At the group level, the prototype is the group's shared imagination of what they are, and when they contrast themselves to other groups, they contrast the prototype with the stereotype of the out-group. In this way, the in-group prototype can be a source of collective self-esteem. When an individual group member identifies with a group, the prototype functions as an ideal self and the group member becomes motivated to act in a way that coheres with this prototype (Doojse 1999). In this way the social identity prototype is both an indicative and an imperative. We can therefore assume that the idealistic descriptions of sinlessness in 3:6, 9; 5:18 are expressions of the group's identity prototype. This prototype is experienced both as a description of what the group is and as a prescription for group members.

As discussed above, most groups tolerate that group members deviate from the in-group prototype to a certain extent, but when the deviation becomes a threat to the self-esteem, the distinctiveness, or the cooperation of the group, deviators are reproached, marginalized, and perhaps even excluded from the group (see Hogg et al. 2005; Marques et al. 2001). In this perspective, the rhetorical exaggeration in 3:9 is a problem, since it does not allow for any deviance from prototypical ideals at all.

I would like to suggest that the claim to incapability of sin in 3:9 has two simultaneous social effects. First, it creates a sense of superiority and distinctiveness in relation to other groups. As Judith Lieu has shown, 1 Jn forms the identity of the Johannine community by contrasting "us" to "them" (Lieu 2008). Second, the exaggeration in 3:9 functions as instrument of social control within the group. By claiming that group members are impeccable, it is *possible* for the socially influential to marginalize others for just about any offence. We may assume that this did not happen most of the time (1:8–10; 5:15–17), but the imagination expressed in 3:9 made it possible. In other words, the claim to perfection maximized how flexibly the group could choose what should be considered a sin "unto death" (5:16–17). As Michael McCullough points out, religions (and other cultures) must be flexible in how they balance forgiveness and non-forgiveness in order to be able to handle all kinds of social situations (McCullough 2008, 220–23).

Rhetorical exaggeration

Finally, we briefly consider a situational solution to the problem. In 1946 Charles Harold Dodd suggested that 1 Jn 1:8–2:2 and 3:1–10 fight two different heresies, one group who thinks it is immune to sin, and another who thinks that sin is not an issue any longer, since the group is in a spiritual state (Dodd 1946, 80–81).[21] This suggestion does not explain theologically why the author chooses to contradict himself. Rather, Dodd seems to imagine that the author is swept away by eagerness to counter heresies to the extent that he forgets to be consistent. "In combating [heresy], the author uses all the resources of antithesis to set forth the essential polarity of ethical religion" (Dodd 1946, 80).

Although Dodd's suggestion might be too speculative, since he assumes two different opponents, he pinpoints an important group-dynamic insight: groups tend to define themselves as the contrast of competing groups. In self-categorization theory (see above), this is called the "meta-contrast principle" (Oakes 1990). Since the purpose of the letter is to form the identity of the group, it is quite reasonable to appreciate that the letter contains a rhetoric that demarcates the group from those who do not belong to the group in order to enhance the experience that the group is meaningful.

Forgiveness and sinlessness from a group perspective

In the final section of this chapter, I will draw on the theory of cultural evolution to articulate a new proposal about the role of forgiveness in 1 Jn. Throughout the evaluation of different scholarly interpretations of forgiveness and sinlessness in 1 Jn, I have insisted that forgiveness is not only a matter between God and individuals in 1 Jn. Rather, forgiveness by God is integrated with community belonging and social identity formation. Therefore, it is reasonable to assume that the good of the group, particularly the good of the group's shared identity, defines the limit of forgiveness in 1 Jn. In other words, forgiveness is not only a matter of salvation, but also a matter of boundary maintenance in the community.

More precisely, 1 Jn's theology of forgiveness and non-forgiveness was instrumental in preservation of both (a) the cognitive constructs (beliefs) that defined the identity of the group, (b) and the real community, those who were bearers of this cognitive construct. By this suggestion, the culture of the Johannine community is analyzed as the primary unit that is optimized for survival and the community members are understood as instrumental in the survival of this culture. This suggestion is counterintuitive, since we are used to see it the other way around: The community should be seen as instrumental to the individual. However, by putting the culture of the group at the center of our analysis, we arrive at a new understanding of the aim of the text, which is to form and maintain the identity of the community. David Sloan Wilson argues that evolutionary selection applies to cultures, not only to individuals. Some cultural patterns will be better at spreading and protecting themselves than others, and will therefore be more widely distributed in a population (e.g., Wilson 2002, 115–22). He argues that how a culture handles forgiveness and punishment is of particular importance to a culture's fitness and that one of the most powerful advantages of Christianity throughout the centuries is the flexibility with which it has handled issues of forgiveness (e.g., Wilson 2002, 189–218).

Although we cannot know how successful the historical Johannine community was, we get the impression that 1 Jn was able to create a flexible balance between forgiveness and demands of good behavior that enabled the community both to cooperate and to protect itself from destructive social forces. On the one hand, the community emphasized the possibility of forgiveness, which ensured continued cooperation. Those who were willing to confess their sins (1:8–2:2), could continue to participate in the "fellowship" (κοινωνία, 1:7), and community members were encouraged to pray and thus mediate God's forgiveness (5:14–17). On the other hand, the community limited forgiveness, so that behaviors that undermined the continuity and meaning of the community were not accepted. Those who undermined the cognitive certainty of the community's faith in Christ were marginalized, just like those who did not practice love and did not help those in need. The contradiction in 1 Jn is a rhetorically skillful way to express this balance.[22]

Yet that is not all. The contradiction has other important social functions, as well. Claiming sinlessness as their true identity, as unrealistic as it is, has several group dynamic effects. First, it creates a positive social identity, which gives both self-esteem and distinctiveness in relation to competing groups. Second, it functions as an imperative ideal to strive for. Third, claiming that true group members are sinless, while at the same time holding on to the possibility of forgiveness, creates flexibility in the limits of group belonging, which is necessary for long-term thriving.

In short, there is good reason to think that 1 Jn, precisely through its contradictory statements, created a culture of forgiveness and non-forgiveness that was beneficial for the continuity of the community. We may therefore suspect that whoever wrote 1 Jn was sensitive to the complex needs of the Johannine community when he wrote the way he did. The theology of forgiveness in 1 Jn may be frustrating if we treat it as a theological system, but if we think of theology as a way to enable sharing of religious life and identity in a community, we can appreciate how 1 Jn manages to achieve just that with its inconsistent theology.

10

Christian Beginnings and Cultural Evolution

István Czachesz

How did early Christianity spread to distant regions of the Roman Empire and why did it survive the other popular religions of its time, including the cults of Mithras and Isis? This question has been asked at least since Adolf von Harnack's *The Expansion of Christianity* (Harnack 1906; cf. Frend 1984; Räisänen 2010; Stark 1996, 2004; Markschies 2006), and scholars discussed a variety of historical, political, theological, and socioeconomic details to answer it. In this chapter I will use evolutionary theory to reconsider the question of the success of the Christian movement. I will examine, in particular, how the interaction of social network formation and theological innovation helped the emergence and spread of earliest Christianity, focusing especially on the first century CE. In the given timeframe, it would be perhaps more accurate to call the people in whom I am interested "Jesus followers" or "Christ followers." Still I decided to call them simply the "earliest Christians," keeping in mind that Christianity as we know it from Late Antiquity onward did not yet exist in those early days.

Evolutionary theory and its extensions

When Charles Darwin created the theory of evolution, he was mainly concerned with the history of biological species. Importantly, Darwin was not yet aware of the existence of genes and understood very little of how traits of the organisms are inherited. In contrast, the so-called neo-Darwinian theory of evolution (e.g., Mayr 2001) takes genes as the main actors of evolution, looking into how genes are passed on and how the relative frequency of genes changes in populations. In biological evolution, traits are inherited through genes: traits of an individual (such as height) will show up in the individual's offspring because genes that caused the trait to develop in the parents will also cause it to develop in the offspring. If the respective trait increases the chances of the organism to leave offspring (i.e., its reproductive fitness), we can expect the genes underlying the trait to be present in greater numbers in the next generation. This is how *natural selection* works.

Can we extend the theory of evolution, and the model of natural selection in particular, to study cultural transmission? Richard Dawkins (Dawkins 2006) famously suggested that cultural traits are inherited via so-called *memes*, which are small pieces of cultural information that can be passed on independently from each other. Examples of memes are "tunes, ideas, catch-phrases, clothes fashions, ways of making pots or of building arches" (Dawkins 2006, 192). The concept of the meme has been criticized on different accounts (cf. Kundt 2011), such as the practical problem of isolating memes (is Buddhism a meme?), their material implementation (what do memes consist of?), and the fidelity of their transmission. Addressing the latter problem, Dan Sperber (Sperber 1996, 2000) argued that pieces of culture are not copied with high enough fidelity so that something like natural selection could act on them; the stability of cultural traits is due to psychological biases rather than to the faithfulness of copying. According to Sperber (see below), among the range of possible forms a cultural bit can take there are optimal forms dictated by psychological factors, which he calls "attractor positions." We can add that by "cultural evolution" scholars almost always mean the natural selection of cultural traits (i.e., traits are inherited because they increase the reproductive fitness of the organism), even though natural selection is only one of several mechanisms of evolution. It has been argued that both Sperberian "attraction" and natural selection can take place among bits of culture and the two models are complementary (McElreath and Henrich 2007; Czachesz 2018b).

We can add yet another twist to evolutionary theory, asking if evolution can take place among groups rather than individuals. The notion of group selection (Wilson and Wilson 2007, 2008) suggests that some genes can contribute traits that are neutral or even disadvantageous for the reproductive success of the individual but get transmitted because they benefit the group. The notion of group selection is burdened by at least two problems. First, anyone who benefits from cooperation in a group but manages to contribute to it less than others will automatically acquire a fitness advantage and thus the gene (or meme) that made him or her behave in such a way will be passed on with greater frequency; that is, cheaters will be represented in ever-greater numbers in the population, undermining cooperation. According to David Sloan Wilson and Edward O. Wilson (Wilson and Wilson 2007, 2008), sufficiently strong selection on the group level will prevent the spread of such free-riding. The other problem concerns the group as a unit: What is a social group and are groups producing offspring or die out in sufficiently great numbers to be units of selection? Below I will return to the concept of the group.

Putting the two above-mentioned extensions of evolutionary together, we can speak of cultural group selection (e.g., Richerson and Boyd 2005; Stone et al. 2006). According to the theory of cultural group selection, a social group can thrive better than other groups because it has some knowledge or technology that the others do not. As a consequence, the group might survive natural circumstances that the others do not, it can physically annihilate other groups, less successful groups can merge into successful ones, or a group can learn pieces of culture that helped a more successful group. We can think of examples of cultural group selection among religious groups in Greco-Roman antiquity: a group can make more proselytizes, or the beliefs, rituals, and artifacts of a group that thrives better can be copied by less successful groups. On the analogy of neo-Darwinian evolutionary theory, we can think of a group's "success" simply as passing on its beliefs, behavior, or artifacts at higher rates than other groups do. Let us note that bits of culture can also spread irrespective of what they do for the group—e.g., ideas can be catchy without the group thriving better as a consequence of holding them. We will return to this distinction below.

Above I mentioned the problem that the group-level selection of genetically inherited traits is undermined by the spread of genes that cause individuals to draw benefits from cooperation without contributing to it. In cultural group selection, a similar problem exists insofar as individuals can use some knowledge or innovative technology to take advantage of other group members. However, cultural traits can also be shared by many group members through horizontal or oblique transmission. Although in prehistorical societies knowledge was typically passed on within families (Shennan 2002, 38–42), and this was arguably still the case to some degree in antiquity, it is also the case that many ideas, beliefs, behaviors, and technologies spread within the same generation, and we call this *horizontal transmission*. The notion of *oblique transmission*, in turn, means that a trait is passed on from one generation to the other without remaining in the family. Whereas individuals with high reproductive success pass on their genes only to their offspring, ideas or knowledge that makes someone successful can be passed on to an entire population quickly. Moreover, many ideas and technologies involve cooperation and group-level action to begin with. Cultural group selection thus can be a viable theory even if genetic group selection remains controversial and not well understood.

Let us summarize our main points about evolutionary theory and its extensions.

1. Modern evolutionary theory focuses on the spread of genes in populations. One of the reasons for the spread of a gene is that it causes traits that increase the reproductive success of an organism. This process is called natural selection.
2. Evolutionary theory can be extended to the study of culture with some important caveats. The cultural equivalents of genes are called memes, which are distinct bits of culture. What memes are and how they work are debated.
3. Memes (but also genes) can spread irrespective of their effect on the organism. This can be examined in terms of evolutionary theory or in terms of Dan Sperber's cultural epidemiology.
4. The idea of evolution (and natural selection, in particular) can be extended to groups. In terms of cultural group selection, some groups thrive better than others due to their cultural (rather than genetic) characteristics. Groups that are less successful can disappear but they can also borrow successful cultural knowledge.

Weak social ties in earliest Christianity

While discussing group selection, we were confronted by an important conceptual problem: What is a social "group"? In this section, I will use social network theory (Kolaczyk 2009; Prell 2011) to define the notion of a group. In a social network, individuals are represented as nodes of a network, and social ties between individuals as links. In a social network, not every node has the same number of ties: some nodes have more connections than others; such nodes are also called "hubs." Furthermore, sets of nodes sometimes have more connections to other nodes within the same set than connections to other nodes in the network that are not members of the set. In the language of network theory, we call the subset of nodes connected in this way a "cluster." We can use the notion of a network cluster to define a group in a non-essentialist sense. In any real social network, there will be more or less densely connected clusters, which, in turn, might have varying degrees of connectedness with other clusters in the network. This corresponds to the fact that a social group might be barely recognizable or might be very clearly isolated from the rest of society.[1]

The sociologist Mark Granovetter (Granovetter 1973, 1983) suggested that if two people are connected by a *strong* social tie (to put it simply, they are friends), it is likely that their respective social networks will largely overlap: many of A's friends and acquaintances will be also B's friends or acquaintances. In terms of our definition, they will be part of the same network cluster and thus of the same social group. As a consequence, two people connected by a strong tie will be likely to share the same opinions, habits, and knowledge. The strength of an interpersonal tie is characterized by the amount of time, emotional intensity, intimacy (mutual confiding), and reciprocal services in the relationship. Conversely, if two people are connected by a *weak* social tie (i.e., by acquaintance rather than friendship), the number of their shared friends and acquaintances will be significantly smaller. In other words, they are likely to belong to different clusters of the network and thus to different social groups.

The major importance of weak links, Granovetter argued, is that they can serve as "bridges," that is, as the only links between two clusters of social networks. On the one hand, if two individuals A and B are connected by a strong tie, information (such as the latest gossip) can spread on their overlapping friendship networks in many different ways, sometimes including the link between A and B and sometimes via other routes. On the other hand, if A and B are connected by a weak tie, it is possible that they have no friends or acquaintances in common, and even their friends do not have any friends or acquaintances in common, and so forth. In this case, any information that originates with A's friends will reach B's friends only after it has first arrived from A to B at some point: the weak link between A and B will be a bridging weak link, connecting two social networks that would be otherwise unconnected. Granovetter's theory of weak links has been tested in a number of empirical studies. An important domain of application has been the advantage of weak links in the job market. Granovetter found empirical evidence that people find new jobs with the help of individuals to whom they are connected by weak links (acquaintances), because they provide new information more often than close friends and relatives, who tend to be in possession of the same information as the jobseeker.

An analysis of various documents of earliest Christianity suggests that the Jesus movement generated weak social ties in many ways (Czachesz 2011a, b).[2]

Itinerancy

First, the gospels encourage the formation of weak social ties by relativizing the importance of traditional social bonds and idealizing itinerancy. Although it has been debated whether such motifs in the sources truly represent social reality, at least we can say that they advertised mobility as an ideal. Ample references to actual mobility are found in the epistles of Paul, who tirelessly founded and visited Christian communities throughout Asia Minor and Greece. He maintained regular contact with Christians in Antioch, which probably served as his home base (Gal. 2), and at least occasionally visited Jerusalem (Gal. 1–2), the center of Palestinian Christianity. Many of his epistles end with a list of greetings (Rom. 16; 1 Cor. 16), in which Paul and members of the community where the letter was written send their greetings to individuals in the community to which the letter is addressed. Since Paul moved about so much, he was prevented from maintaining many strong social ties, but it enabled him to develop a great number of weak ties with individuals in a variety of geographical and social locations. In his epistles, Paul also refers to other visitors and itinerants. He had a number of deputies (such as Silas, Timothy, and Titus) who traveled, carried messages, and delivered (possibly also co-authored) his letters. Other apostles traveled as well, some of them even taking their spouses with them (1 Cor. 9:5). Yet another group of travelers are identified as Paul's adversaries or "false apostles" (Gal. 1:6; 2:4; 3:1; 2 Cor. 11). These other missionaries probably also had helpers and built social networks similar to Paul's. For example, in his Second Epistle to the Corinthians, Paul denounces some of his adversaries for carrying "letters of recommendation" (2 Cor. 3:1), which could actually contain the same kind of reference that Paul himself gives to Titus in the very same epistle (2 Cor. 8:16–24).[3]

The Didache allows us a glimpse into the problem of itinerancy toward the end of the first century. As a rule of the thumb, *Did. 11* prescribes that only guests whose teaching agrees with the contents of that document (allegedly summarizing the teaching of the twelve apostles) should be received by the communities. What is more surprising is the serious rules about the entertainment of visitors. Guests recognized as "apostles" and "prophets" were expected to stay for only one day (!), which could be extended by another day, if necessary. Someone who remained for three days was identified as a false prophet. Apostles and prophets could take bread with them as needed until they found new accommodation, but one who took money was regarded as a false prophet. Ordinary travelers were permitted to stay for up to three days. There were also rules for officials and travelers who wished to settle in a community, but there was no medium-term visiting status. Apostles could not settle at all in the community: "a settled-down apostle is an ex-apostle," as John Dominic Crossan put it (Crossan 1998, 376).

Charity

Another means of maintaining weak links in earliest Christian communities was the widespread practice of charity. Again, Paul's epistles provide the earliest concrete evidence on this matter. In the "gentlemen's agreement," made in Antioch between Paul and the apostles Peter, James, and John (Gal. 2:6–10), the apostles ask Paul "to remember the poor," which he is "eager to do." Collecting money for the poor of Jerusalem remains an important concern during his work in other congregations (1 Cor. 16:1; 2 Cor. 9; Gal. 2:10). In the famous passage about the Lord's Supper (1 Cor. 11), Paul expresses his concern about the poor going hungry while the rich get drunk at community meals. A historically less reliable but nevertheless quite informative passage in Acts 6 describes the election of "deacons," whose task is to assist at the table, that is, to provide food for the poor of the Jerusalem community. Evidence about Christian charity is also abundant in the second century AD. A particular form of charity involved fasting to save money, which was then spent on charity (Hermas, *Similitudes* 5.3; Aristides, *Apology* 15). The importance of charity for the development of Christianity has already been noted by scholars, who assumed that it was an attractive feature for potential sympathizers and converts. Rodney Stark specifically emphasized the significance of Christian charity towards outsiders, considering it as a revolutionary step in the ancient world (Stark 1996, 212). Whereas ties shaped by charity within the communities could be either strong or weak, charity toward outsiders or across communities (such as the collection in Greece and Asia Minor for the poor in Jerusalem) facilitated the formation of numerous weak links within Christianity, as well as between Christianity and its social environment.

Women

We have to mention a third important source of weak ties in earliest Christianity, that is, the inclusion of women. Whereas the data is often too sparse to allow for more than speculative reconstructions, it is beyond dispute that women, in general, were present in more significant, emancipated, and diverse roles in Christianity than in most contemporary religions. For example, the apocryphal Acts of the Apostles regularly mention women as the first followers of the apostles in different places, portraying women from the upper class as influential patronesses of Christian communities (Davies 1980; Bremmer 1995; Czachesz 2009b). Both the "Gnostic" Mary (not always clearly identifiable with one of the women by that name in the New Testament) in the *Gospel of Philip*, the *Gospel of Mary*, and other writings, as well as Thecla in the *Acts of Paul and Thecla* are represented as female apostles. It is, however, not so much the prominent position, but rather the massive participation of women in the movement that carries more weight for my argument. In this respect, the repeated mention of a great number of widows in the earliest documents also deserves attention. The widows of "the Hellenists" and "the Hebrews" (the first term referring to either non-Israelites or Greek-speaking Jews) are mentioned in Acts 6, and something like a class or office of widows is described in 1 Tim. 5. Widows are also mentioned in a favorable light in Mk 12:40–44 and in the Gospel of Luke (2:36–38; 4:26; 18:1–8). Outside the New Testament, Tertullian reports the existence of an "order of widows" in Carthage around 200 AD (*De monogamia* 11.1; *De praescriptione* 3.5). Lucian of Samosata (*Life of Peregrinus Proteus* 12) notes with surprise the active participation of widows in Christianity. Various other sources indicate that widows were well cared for in Christian communities (Hermas's *Shepherd* I.50.8 etc.; *Acts of Peter* 8, 21; *Acts of John* 30–36).

The participation of women in earliest Christianity is especially relevant for the study of social networks because there are significant differences in the ways men and women use their relationship systems. For example, empirical studies show that women have more friends on networking websites and contact them more often than men (Thelwall 2008; Szell and Thurner 2013). Further, women react to stress by reinforcing social ties, which has also been found in females of various animal species and must have deep evolutionary roots (Repetti 1989; Taylor et al. 2000; Mazure 2003).

How can we connect these empirical results to the study of women's position and relationships in earliest Christianity? Although early Christian sources contain many references to women's influence on the social networks of the movement, it is often difficult to establish their historical accuracy. For example, both the Pastoral Epistles (esp. 1 Tim. 5:3–16) and Celsus (Origen, *Against Celsus* 3) suggest that women were engaged in active networking, the latter source identifying shops and households as the main contexts of their activity (Origen, *Against Celsus* 3.55). Suspicions could be raised by the fact that women's purported gullibility as well as their proneness to spread superstition and silly religious ideas were stock material in the rhetoric against new religions (Balch 1981, 65–80; Osiek et al. 2006, 220–25). Further, the portrait of leading women in the canonical and apocryphal Acts of the Apostles was probably colored by entertaining details. Yet, women's roles in managing households and coordinating social events between households in Greco-Roman antiquity are well documented, and there is no reason to doubt that these roles served the network formation of the Christ movement (Osiek et al. 2006, 144–63). So even after accounting for rhetorical accesses and fictional elaborations (e.g., Osiek et al. 2006, 220–43) it seems safe to assume that some elite women had special influence on Christianity as patronesses and leaders (partly derived from their positions in Jewish and Greco-Roman institutions) as well as women had access to households in ways men (especially strangers) did not.

Implications

What are the implications of these findings for the social networks of the Jesus movement and the early Church?

First, an obvious and direct application of weak-link theory is that the development of weak links supported the spread of the movement: its message reached various distant social and geographical locations—whereas it would have spread slower if information had been only circulating among friends and within families. Via weak links, the movement was able to leapfrog to new social groups before it became fully established in a certain location. To put it differently, instead of moving from door to door, the movement spread simultaneously in different cities and socioeconomic niches. The existence of Christian communities in such distant places as Jerusalem, Damascus, Corinth, and Rome around the middle of the first century, only two decades after the probable time of Jesus's death, with their respective traditions, theological debates, and internal factions, as attested by Paul's epistles, was a remarkable achievement.[4] Mithraism, to mention a contemporary religious cult, progressed stepwise from Rome, where it probably started in the later part of the first century, into Germania and the Danube region, from where it then spread to the rest of the empire during the second century (Beck 2006, 182–83).[5]

Second, weak links facilitated the interconnection of diverse cultural and socioeconomic groups, without forcing a uniform set of values, beliefs, and attitudes on them. The lack of a uniform mold for every believer helped the spread of the movement tremendously, yet weak connections of several kinds generated bridging links that connected variants with each other. If we compare Christianity with some of its competitors, the differences become evident. Judaism, in spite of all its diversity, imposed requirements on people that were overly tied to ethnicity and seemed difficult or undesirable for most outsiders in most social and cultural settings to fulfill. The popular Hellenistic and Roman cults of the time were typically tailored to particular socioeconomic niches. The cult of Mithras, for example, relied on the army and the administration for its expansion, and shows a very uniform picture across time and space (although the old hypothesis that it was a soldiers' religion has been substantially revised, Beck 1996; Clauss 2000). From a very early stage, in contrast, the Jesus movement and emergent Christianity posited high requirements, while recruiting members from a wide range of social and geographic locations, appealing (in its diverse forms) to Jewish peasants in Galilee as well as urban elites in Corinth (Rom. 16:23).

Third, as a consequence of its socioeconomic and cultural diversity, and the use of weak links rather than a general mold to keep together such a diverse membership, Christianity was able to incorporate various points of view. In the New Testament we can already find an unprecedented variety of socioeconomic and cultural perspectives, including the world of rural society and wisdom tradition in the synoptic gospels; urban social milieus and popular philosophy in the epistles of Paul and the *Gospel of John*; and the thoughts of aspiring intellectuals, such as the author of Acts (probably identical with the author of the Gospel of Luke); not to mention the Gnostic, ascetic, apocalyptic, millenarian, charismatic, and many other branches of early Christianity. Such diversity of backgrounds and visions allowed Christianity to conquer almost every social and cultural segment found in Late Antiquity. More importantly, a social network in which diverse groups were connected by weak links fostered the improvement of cognitive abilities that made it possible for people to assume and appreciate different points of view. This was a hard process, which is evident from the fierce theological battles already attested to in the earliest sources.

Fourth, the social network structure of earliest Christianity facilitated the emergence of memorable and attractive beliefs. On the one hand, the inclusion of various social and ethnic groups yielded a mixture of different traditions and increased the chance for really innovative ideas to emerge. On the other hand, the accelerated migration of ideas across social and geographical distances resulted in frequent memorization and recall and supported the selection of memorable and cognitively attractive beliefs. Below I will elaborate on this point in more detail.

So far we have described the benefits of weak social ties with respect to the stability of the social group and the spread of religious beliefs. Of course, the social network structure of the early Church also had various implications for individual believers. The frequency of weak social ties and the diversity of the movement explain many aspects of what Rodney Stark dubbed the "miniature welfare state" of early Christians (Stark 2004, 30–31). Although I do not doubt that such benefits for the individual existed, and ultimately resulted in a more successful propagation of the attached belief system, as well, I believe that social network theory offers a more economic explanation for a range of phenomena, among which higher welfare is only one in many consequences.[6]

Theological innovation

How well an idea can be remembered will influence its success, whether it helps the individual who holds it or not (i.e., irrespective of the effect of the idea on the fitness of people who hold the idea). As we have seen above, anthropologist Dan Sperber suggested that the success of some ideas can be explained by them taking optimal forms as dictated by psychological factors. Sperber called such optimal forms *attractor positions*.[7] For example, people believe in ghosts and spirits in many (and perhaps all) cultures around the world. In terms of the Sperberian model of cultural epidemiology, this is explained by the fact that the idea of a ghost conforms to innate psychological structures. Let us elaborate on this claim in some detail (cf. Czachesz and Theißen in this volume).

Innate or *maturationally natural* ontological categories are shared across cultures. It is important to note that they are not necessarily identical with categories that people use to describe the world when we ask them (or categories that philosophers use). Maturationally natural ontology develops in children under a wide range of external circumstances and enables people to respond to information in the environment quickly and efficiently (Atran 1989; McCauley 2000, 2011; Barrett 2008). For example, we know that animals move, humans speak, and tools are designed for some purpose and can interact with them accordingly, without testing those features on every individual instance of them. Maturationally natural ontological categories include HUMAN, ANIMAL, PLANT, ARTIFACT, and (natural) OBJECT. A donkey that talks (e.g., *Acts of Thomas* 39–41 and 68–81) or a statue that hears what people speak violates expectations about animals and artifacts, respectively. However, if such violations are multiplied, the advantage diminishes. As a consequence, *minimally counterintuitive* ideas are passed on across generations at higher rates than either ordinary or maximally counterintuitive items (Boyer 1994a, 2001; Barrett and Nyhof 2001; Boyer and Ramble 2001).[8] For example, the formation of the mainstream idea of Jesus's death and resurrection can be explained by the dominance of a minimally counterintuitive version, whereas ebionite and docetic alternatives were too "ordinary" or excessively counterintuitive, respectively, and had little chance to be widely circulated (Czachesz 2007c, e).

The memorability of an idea or motif is also influenced by its emotional content (Laney 2004; Norenzayan and Atran 2004; Porubanova and Shaver 2017). For example, healing miracles feature people who desperately seek healing (e.g., Mk 2:1–12) and parents who seek help for their sick or dead children (e.g., Mk 1:21–43). We also read about extreme (e.g., lameness, blindness), repulsive (e.g., "leprosy"), or spectacular (e.g., "demoniacs") symptoms and diseases. Many of the vivid details in the stories are likely to elicit empathy, fear, and disgust. Further, after such a start, healing stories are likely to evoke emotions of relief when difficulties are miraculously overcome in the end. Apocalyptic texts also contain many emotionally laden details, including the representation of the human body in hell (Czachesz 2012, 157–80).

In general, more memorable ideas spread quicker and persist longer. Minimally counterintuitive traits seem to influence especially long-term retention (Czachesz 2012, 158–63). However, this general advantage is nuanced by other factors. For example, religious beliefs are organized into mythological narratives or theological systems. In a given text, the amount of ideas violating ontological expectations has to be limited in order that the text as a whole has good chances to be remembered (Norenzayan and Atran 2004; Norenzayan et al. 2006). Institutionally supported forms of religious literature can overcome any such limitation: specially trained theological experts maintain textual traditions that would not have a chance to survive otherwise. Social class and education also influence what ideas and texts people are exposed to and what they deem worth transmitting. In Greco-Roman elite literacy, the excessive use of miracles was not accepted. Thucydides required that no fables, however entertaining, should be included in a work of history (*On the Peloponnesian War* 1.22). Lucian of Samosata ridiculed authors who seek the favor of the reader by filling their texts with miraculous and fantastic details (*On Writing History; True History* 1-4). When Josephus and Philo report or discuss miracles in their works, they take a skeptical, or at least reflective, stance (Delling 1958, 291-309; Moehring 1973; Duling 1985, 9-19; Eve 2002, 3-85).

Finally, ideas spread along social connections and the structure of social networks has an important role in the success of new ideas. As we have seen above, weak links in social networks catalyze innovation and enable the circulation of new ideas. Early Christianity consisted of tight clusters (local communities) connected by weak links (contacts by letters and visitors), a network structure that provided plenty of opportunity for the exchange, modification, merging, and sifting of ideas.

Theological ideas as symbolic identity markers

An important problem with network clusters that are connected by weak ties is that the boundaries of the overall social formation (loose association of clusters) are unclear. How does the community in Achaia, perhaps consisting of Roman veterans and Greek artisans, worshipping a Christ who looks to them like Dionysus or Asclepius, recognize its identity with the Torah-observant, Aramaic-speaking group in Syria, whose Jesus is maybe more like a Jewish prophet? The portraits I am drawing here are of course purely hypothetical, yet such differences were certainly not unknown of in ancient Christianity, and Paul's epistles offer plenty of evidence for similar cases.

Sociologists and social psychologists recognized before some decades that symbols can create group identities in surprisingly flexible and efficient ways. *Social identity theory* has shown that membership in randomly assigned groups, where members are made to believe they share some aesthetic values, for example, can motivate high levels of solidarity with other in-group members (Tajfel 1982; Tajfel and Turner 2001). *Deviance labeling theory* argues that members of dominant social groups attach labels to dominated groups (Becker 1997; Bernburg et al. 2006). Moreover, people are willing to accept such labels and behave accordingly: labels can actually make people deviants. Stigmatization is a related phenomenon: stigmas deeply affect people's self-esteem and behavior. Even more surprisingly, negative labels often become important symbolic markers for the group members: terms such as "black," "queer," or "Paki" are points in case from recent Western history. From antiquity, one can mention "Cynic,"

"Pharisee," and the very term *Christianos* (Horrell 2007). Unfortunately, symbolic markers create not only strong feelings of solidarity, but also irrationally hostile emotions toward outsiders. Religious wars and ethnic violence are obvious examples, but we can also mention street gangs and football hooliganism as everyday examples. Why are symbolic markers so important? Why are people willing to die for symbols, including national banners and stigmatizing labels? And why do people feel strong hostile emotions toward others, who might be very similar to themselves in every respect, only because they are members of another symbolically marked group?

Understandably, these issues are being studied intensely by scholars in many fields, but are not the subject of this chapter. Among many possible approaches, we will continue to use evolutionary theory, with particular attention to gene-culture coevolution. Most evolutionary theories of human psychology proceed from the scenario of humans having evolved in small groups of hunter-gatherers and assume that humans lived in such societies until the advent of agriculture, some ten to fifteen thousand years ago. Peter J. Richerson and Robert Boyd (Richerson and Boyd 2005), however, suggested a different developmental path. They argued that ethnographic evidence supports the scenario that hunter-gatherers lived in much larger societies even before agriculture started. For example, some North American hunter-gatherer societies (such as the Kwaikiutl) had large, permanent settlements already before the arrival of Europeans. At other times, even though settlements were small, bands maintained large-scale cooperative networks, with a clear sense of who belongs to the tribe even without ever seeing each other or meeting at one place (Richerson and Boyd 2005, 226). Richerson and Boyd concluded that humans probably lived in societies of several thousand members with multi-level organization for a long time before the advent of agriculture.

Instead of relying on face-to-face interaction and a bookkeeping of mutual favors, large-scale societies depend on peaceful interaction between unrelated strangers. This can be achieved by the use of symbolic markers, such as the exchange of gifts, marriage rules, shared artistic and design elements, shared history and mythology, and joint ceremonies. Symbolic markers, of course, do not only mark in-group and out-group, they also mark various divisions that exist within such a large society and contribute to its smooth functioning. These markers evolved as technological innovations in first instance: societies that were able to run large-scale cooperation more efficiently won out over other societies and passed on this know-how. Again, ethnographic evidence shows that the extinction of societies must have been a frequent phenomenon in the past (Richerson and Boyd 2005, 208–09). This did not necessarily mean that every member of a group died: migration and assimilation into a more successful group were important factors.

Since symbolically marked, large-scale societies existed for a long time, genetic evolution shaped the human mind so that we can easily find our ways in them. The better adapted our ancestors were to life in their societies, the more chance they had to leave healthy offspring.[9] As a result, we have strong, innate dispositions to use symbols as markers of social groups. First, we maintain an essentialist view of groups, that is, we have a deep intuition that there are actually indelible essential differences between members of different groups. Second, we tend to learn from members of our own group rather than from members of other groups, which ensures that subsequent generations become sufficiently similar and selection can take place at all. Third, we expect that in-group members will return our altruistic behavior, similarly as our early ancestors could rely on such reciprocity in small-scale societies. Fourth, we tend to be hostile with the symbolically marked out-group: our ancestors come from symbolically marked groups that won more battles than others.

What are the implications of an innate, group-oriented psychology for the success of religious innovations, in general, and earliest Christianity, in particular? In the first stage of the Jesus movement, members of the group were able to maintain face-to-face interaction. Although "the name" (Mt. 10:22; Mk 13:13; Jn 15:21; Acts 4:30; 10:43; 1 Cor. 1:10 etc.) or "the way" (esp. Acts 9:2; 19:9.23; 22:4; 24:14) were used to refer to the movement, such shared symbols and self-designations were not functioning as symbolic markers, strictly speaking. Symbolic marking became essential when the movement started to grow in numbers (exceeding about 150 members, cf. Dunbar 2009), and at the same time reached distant geographical locations. This expansion was due to various kinds of mobility that I described in my discussion of social networks above. Among the innovative ideas that emerged and spread on the early Christian's social networks, there were symbolic identity markers, which helped identification across social and geographic distance.

A decisive move was the geographic expansion of the movement in the middle of the first century, documented in Paul's epistles (see above). Not surprisingly, symbolic markers were especially important for Paul, whose innovative ideas, more than anyone else's, influenced the formation of Jesus's image as a highly symbolic, divine figure. Paul was actively involved in defining the boundaries and identity of the movement, and in finding efficient symbolic markers. In Gal. 3:28, for example, he attempts to mitigate the strong psychological motivations attached to symbolically marked group memberships, such as being a "Jew," "Hellene," "free," "slave," "male," or "female," and argues that these identities are made obsolete by the new group membership "in Jesus Christ." Paul also paid much attention to ceremonial markers, such as baptism and the Eucharist, which contributed to the formation of a shared identity. The development of efficient symbolic markers, in turn, helped to mobilize innate prosocial psychological dispositions, which prepared the way for the long-term success of early Christianity.

Whereas religious beliefs, ceremonies, and artifacts are often adapted as symbolic markers, some religious ideas are better suited as symbolic markers than others, and many elements of religion do not function as symbolic markers at all. A tentative list of what makes religious ideas good symbolic markers includes the following four requirements.

1. The first requirement of a symbolic marker is *discriminability*. Symbolic markers have to be easy to identify. Arguably, an oppressed group must use markers that are easy to identify by insiders, but not by outsiders.
2. *Memorability* will be important at least for the initial success of symbolic markers. The marker that is used by more people will win in the long run, simply because it will enable more people to find exchange partners or undertake joint action.

3. The third requirement is *symbolic potential*. People often attach interpretations to symbolic markers: coats of arms, banners, and even simple markers have stories and explanations attached to them, often with etymological elements.
4. The fourth requirement is the ease of *identification*. The aesthetic and semantic features of the symbols themselves and the interpretations attached to them influence how easy people find it to use them for marking their groups.

From Paul's epistles we know that some early Christians arrived to communities with letters of recommendations (see above). Apart from relying on previously existing personal contacts, even letters had to contain symbolic identity markers. Creedal and liturgical formulas could fulfill such a role, for example.[10] We can imagine that visitors participated in rituals; however, there could be substantial variation in the ritual practices. The knowledge of some formulaic passages could serve as ways to identify the stranger as a fellow Christian. Stories could be important, as well, although variation was probably great in what stories people knew and in what particular form. The display of emotions in the right context could provide further means to check a stranger's devotion. Symbolic identity markers were probably used as a network of clues, where not each and every reference had to be got right, but a certain overall picture had to emerge.[11]

Subjective religious experience and theological ideas interact in many ways (Czachesz 2015). First, theological ideas are used to make sense of subjective experience. Certain states of mind, sensations, emotions, and other elements of internal life are interpreted as experiences of superhuman realities. Religious beliefs can shape subjective experience as it arises (Azari and Birnbacher 2004). Second, religious beliefs become integrated into autobiographical narratives. Autobiographical memory is modified during rehearsal (such as telling stories or only thinking about past events) and by new experience. Theological ideas can interact with the believer's identity as maintained in the autobiographical self. Third, the interpretation of one's actions can change so that one feels actions initiated by superhuman agents (gods, spirits, demons) rather than by the self. The integration of theological ideas into the self by one or more of the above-mentioned mechanisms adds a new dimension to symbolic identity markers because they will be laden with a variety of subjective elements. When believers communicate such subjective details they will be recognized and identified by other group members (who hold similar beliefs and have similar subjective experience) but such details will be difficult to fake by an outsider. In this way, the expressions of subjective experience and the respective theological concepts will mark identity reliably and decrease the possibility of free-riders entering the group and using its resources without serious commitment.

There are many passages in the New Testament that emphasize the personal, subjective nature of the believers' relationship with God and use important theological concepts to express this relationship. Baptism is dying and rising with Christ (Rom. 6:1–14); the believers' bodies are members of Christ (1 Cor. 6:15); the Church is his body (1 Cor. 12; cf. Eph. 4:15–16); the relation between the Lord and the Church is like the relation between man and wife (Eph. 5:31–32). The mystical language of the Gospel of John describes the relation of Jesus to the Father as well as the believer's relationship to God (Bultmann 1941, 294). This is expressed, for example, in Jesus's saying, "I know my own and my own know me, just as the Father knows me and I know the Father" (Jn 10:14). The apocryphal *Acts of John* elaborates further on this mystical relationship: "But if you hear and listen to me, then you shall be as I am, and I shall be what I was, when I have you like me with myself" (ὅταν σὲ ὡς ἐγὼ παρ' ἐμαυτῷ) (*Acts of John* 100, trans. J.K. Elliott). Some of these experiences and the related theological concepts probably varied across Christian communities. For example, the self-understanding of Johannine Christianity included their sense of opposition to other Christian groups. Even within the Johannine community there could be further social clustering (Theissen 1988). As we discussed above, symbolic identify markers could be used to maintain groups of varying sizes and complexities. Some identity markers could be used only by "Johannine" (or Pauline, Montanist, Gnostic etc.) Christians, whereas others served identification in on a higher level of social organization.

Texts and theological innovation

In previous sections of this chapter, we have considered the interaction of social network structures and theological innovation in the success of earliest Christianity. However, for this theory to be useful in the interpretation of texts, we also have to show how the above-mentioned processes are connected to the texts as cultural artifacts. This is necessary for both exegetical applications and the further elaboration of the theory itself. After all, we have access to the ideas of early Christians mostly through the texts they left behind. The information we gain from texts is all the more important since other clues to early theological development from archaeological evidence and external textual references are marginal to nonexistent. The connection of early Christian texts to early Christian groups is a much-discussed problem that we cannot analyze in all of its details. At this place we are interested in the question of how evolutionary theory sheds new light on the formation of texts as a consequence of social network formation and theological innovation.

In his *Darwin's Cathedral*, evolutionary biologist David Sloan Wilson (Wilson 2003, 213–18) suggested that the formation of local gospel traditions can be seen in light of cultural evolution. In particular, Wilson viewed the gospels written for local communities as adaptations to selective pressures, which consist of the socioeconomic situation, cultural background, and needs of a community. An important function of the gospels was to provide communities with rules of behavior according to their specific local needs. Recently Petri Luomanen (Luomanen 2017) argued that the long-term success of (some of) the gospels required that they appeal to a large number of communities. In particular, Luomanen suggested that the gospels had to contribute to the formation of a distinct social identity of the emerging religious movement. He identified four aspects ("discourses") of the texts that are relevant for such a purpose and analyzed Q, Mark, and Matthew with the help of these aspects.

What kind of evolutionary theorizing do Wilson's and Luomanen's respective theories exactly apply to explain the genesis and circulation of the gospels? First, let us note that Wilson's idea of the gospels showing adaptive responses is formulated from the replicator's perspective. However, the replicator (a gene or a cultural meme) does not necessarily have to do anything for the organism to spread, except cause itself copied. Further, as Luomanen argues (Luomanen 2017, 116), Wilson's idea was inspired by his encounter with historical-critical theories about the formation of the gospels. However, although form-criticism contains an element of evolutionary logic (some pieces of tradition spread because their use is preferred in some typical situation of life), this is hard to argue about entire gospels, which came to being (according to redaction-criticism) by piecemeal editorial operations rather than by (random) variation and selection.

Second, if we were to put Wilson's idea back into a truly selectionist context, we could say that (bits of) gospel texts underwent mutation and selection and became adapted to local niches (of regional versions of Christianity), just as various species in the family of cats became adapted to respective natural habitats. Extending this analogy to Luomanen's version of the theory, we could imagine a generalist species of felines that manages to spread to a wide range of habitats—just as a successful Christian text finds its way to many communities. Further, Luomanen's version of the idea emphasizes the universal appeal and relevance of texts, thus invoking Sperber's epidemiological model rather than cultural evolution. This is not a problem, as such: as we noted above, some scholars have defended the synergic potential of Sperberian epidemiology and cultural evolution.

Third, Luomanen's focus on the contribution of texts to social identity formation brings in yet another kind of evolutionary reasoning, that is, cultural group selection, which we introduced in the first section of this chapter and utilized in our discussion of symbolic identity markers. According to this theory, inherited (i.e., learned) bits of culture can cause groups survive better: the groups having that cultural bit will outcompete other groups, which will either disappear or learn the respective cultural bit. Could texts play the role of advantageous cultural bits in ancient Christianity? In terms of redaction-criticism, it was the authors who edited the gospels according to what they perceived to be the needs of their respective communities—thus the formation of the text did not depend on their actual effect on the respective groups. The redaction of the gospels, however, can be seen as the source of guided (Lamarckian) variation.

For cultural group selection to shape the gospels, we would have to assume that the survival of a community depended substantially on the gospel it used. Further, the gospels must be limited in their circulation—otherwise all communities would use a mix of gospels and there would be no difference in their respective chance of survival depending on the gospel they use. Let us consider the following parallel. Voluntary associations in antiquity used regulations (but each had only one set of rules). If some association thrived better, other associations might have lost membership and dissolved, or some associations could decide to adopt the successful group's regulation. Probably a selection of regulations in this way could occur in many generations. Of course we could allow for the borrowing or gradual adjustment of only selected rules (e.g., it is better to appoint a treasurer this way rather than that way), but that is not what the assumed selection process between gospels claims. Would a community disappear because they used Q but not Matthew? Or would they drop Q and adopt Matthew because they thought the use of the latter benefited the other group? It is likely that communities collected multiple gospels over time. It is unlikely, however, that they easily threw out what they already had.

What about the particular aspects of the texts that influence the success of the group, which Luomanen calls "discourses" (Luomanen 2017, 126)? Let us put aside "attractiveness" and "credence" as they belong to Sperberian epidemiology rather than cultural group selection. The remaining three aspects are the influence of the text first on network formation (and the free-rider problem), secondly, on identity formation, and in the third place, on rituals. Apart from the difficulties of this taxonomy (as acknowledged by the author), it is indeed likely that the factors highlighted by Luomanen influenced the formation and maintenance of Christian communities. Yet it is not clear whether the text *caused* the respective behaviors and beliefs or simply *reflected* existing behaviors and beliefs, as redaction-criticism would assume. It is relatively easy to identify issues related to network formation, identity, and rituals in the texts. It is less straightforward to explain how groups derived such beliefs and behaviors from the text. We have mentioned the example of voluntary associations above. As many local Christian communities probably operated as voluntary associations, they also had to have regulations. (For example, the Pauline epistles or the Didache can give us an impression of the rules and the debates about them.) Although the gospels were likely read out aloud and their content influenced the behaviors and beliefs of the communities, it remains to be seen that their effect was strong and direct enough to account for group selection.

From our discussion of texts in the context of cultural group selection (based on the models suggested by Wilson and Luomanen) we can conclude that longer texts are not very likely to function as effective memes (i.e., units of inheritance influencing cognitive and behavioral traits) on the timescale of a few decades. In other words, the gospels probably did not cause the formation of local and shared identities during the first few decades of the history of early Christianity. Whether texts had a long-term effect on Christianity is an entirely different question, which we cannot, however, discuss at this point.

I suggest that texts and social identities were connected by a different process. In each local community, sayings, stories, creedal formulas, liturgical passages, and other pieces of tradition were preserved that either survived in memory due to their cognitive and emotional nature or served as important symbolic identity markers. As a consequence, these pieces of tradition were used in great numbers when longer textual units were created. Thus many of the extant texts probably contain theological concepts, sayings, liturgical fragments, and stories that served as symbolic identity markers in the beginning. Conversely, after longer texts existed and were circulated, symbolic identity markers could be borrowed from the passages and concepts in the text.

Conclusion

The success or failure of religious innovations depends on a variety of factors. The reconstruction of historical details alone might or might not allow us to identify the most relevant of them. Instead of relying on alternative narrative reconstructions of the past, in this chapter I described three aspects of the emergence and spread of religious movements that allow for the elaboration of abstract models that explain the respective levels of success that religious traditions achieve. I identified the structure of social networks as the most important factor, which, in turn, influenced the generation of memorable ideas and the use of religious elements as symbolic identity markers. In early Christianity, weak social ties enabled large-scale cooperation across geographically and sociologically distant groups and individuals. As a consequence, the social composition and structure of the movement favored the emergence of innovative theological ideas. Some of these ideas functioned as powerful symbolic identity markers, which further enhanced solidarity in cooperative associations of varying sizes between groups. Finally, both memorable ideas and social identity markers found their ways in great numbers into literary compositions.

Notes

Introduction

1. For a survey of the problem see Smart (2014).
2. For a recent survey see Czachesz (2017b).
3. For a reconsideration of these factors in light of cognitive approaches see Czachesz and Theissen's contribution to this volume.
4. For a survey of recent developments in the cognitive science of religion, see Schjødt and Geertz (2017).
5. Levy (2012, 146–51) discusses the case of European Jewish history.

Chapter 1

1. Optionally, one could reserve the term "cognigram" for the scientific representation of cognitive processes that underlie the production and use of an artifact or text and introduce the term "cognigraph" to refer to the counterpart of a cognigram, denoting the corresponding processes in people's minds. In this essay, we use the term "cognigram" for both aspects of the cognitive model.
2. The term "evangelical" is understood here as in British and American usage, and not a synonym of "Lutheran."
3. The recurrence of contextual semes, which connect the semantic elements of discourse, assures textual homogeneity and coherence. In a basic sense, isotopy "allows the semantic concatenation of utterances," see Greimas (1974, 60).
4. According to Bartlett, a schema is "an active organization of past reactions, or of past experiences" (p. 201). Schemata play a crucial role in reacting to environmental stimuli: "Together with the immediately preceding incoming impulse, it [the schema] renders a specific adaptive reaction possible" (p. 207).
5. For recent surveys of the field, see Draper (2004); Kirk and Thatcher (2005); Kelber (2007, 2014).
6. Without using cognitive science explicitly, this has been previously suggested by Theißen (1998).
7. This is the thesis of H.J. Held in Barth and Held (1963).
8. Note that we can analyze such connections between the two books independently of the question of a possible common authorship.
9. Some of these approaches are covered by Haynes and MacKenzie (1999).
10. See the introduction to the section "Cognitive factors at the diachronic transmission of texts: How texts change in oral and literate transmission."
11. Greimas extended the concept of isotopy also to such larger units of textual organization. Cf. Greimas (1983, 219–20).
12. For an application of cognitive linguistics to the interpretation of the parables of the New Testament, see Massa (2000).

13 We have to note that many scientific concepts are counterintuitive, as well, and we also use metaphorical language to explain them and talk about them.
14 In his introduction to the volume, Ruben Zimmermann suggests that the traditional taxonomy of subdivisions should be abandoned. A cognitive approach, however, seems to validate the subdivisions by pointing to the differences in the ways the source and target domains of the parable incorporate counterintuitive imagery.
15 For convenient overviews, see Callaway (1999), Sheppard (1999).
16 For a concise introduction see Jefferson et al. (1987).
17 In Jewish and Roman Catholic traditions there is a tendency to provide some interpretations of canonical texts which have special authority—although this authority is lesser than the authority of the canonical texts.
18 For example, the 59th canon of the Council of Laodicea (c. 360 CE) says, "No psalms composed by private individuals nor any uncanonical books (ἀκανονιστά) may be read in the church, but only the Canonical Books (τὰ κανωνικά) of the Old and New Testaments." The canon does not forbid the reading of other writings in private: the non-acceptance of a writing as canonical thus does not imply that such writing would be suppressed.
19 "Do not add to it or take anything from it" (Deut. 13:1, cf. 4:2). The canon formula originated in legal texts. At the end of the Ten Commandments in Deuteronomy we can find the following clause: "and he added no (more)" (Deut. 5:22). The text, which probably resulted from the final stage of redaction, intended to avoid further additions to the Ten Commandments. Cf. Lang 1995, 442. For similar prohibitions in a Graeco-Roman context, see Gamble (1995, 122–25), Czachesz (2009a).

Chapter 2

1 Material from the book is reproduced here by permission.
2 Damasio is often referred to, for example, Rottschaefer (1998, 162), Peterson (2003, 89–91), Gärdenfors (2005, 87–93). For criticism against Damasio, see Griffiths (1997, 228–47).
3 This is evidenced by varying types of research that point to a number of interesting features: the neural system of the mammalian brain seems to be "experience expectant," there are certain sensitive periods in the development of human sensory systems and language, synapse selection occurs during the first years and is particularly active in the prefrontal cortex during late childhood. Crucial moral *biological* development thus seems to take place at a fairly late stage and interacts with cultural influence. For a discussion with references see Haidt (2001, 827).
4 As such it is *self-conscious*, but also "the ultimate self-praising emotion"; see Haidt (2003, 863).
5 Haidt talks of compassion, but I prefer to use empathy, and employ this term here, too.
6 That is, awe, elevation, fear, guilt, contempt, anger, and disgust. See Looy (2004, 223), Damasio (1994, 129–39).
7 The understanding of sentimental structures comes from van der Dennen (1987).
8 It goes without saying that, while ethnocentrism and xenophobia may have evolved due to adaptive values at some stages and in certain contexts, other circumstances make such behavior maladaptive. See McEvoy (2002, 42–45).

9 A few examples may suffice: Campbell and O'Brien (2005) while doing away with the traditional sources, argue for two partly parallel narratives: an exodus narrative ending at the deliverance at the sea and a sanctuary narrative going all through the book of Exodus. However, they regard the section 19:2–24:15 as "a well-structured capsule," stressing "the priority of relationship with regard to law, and the narrative context or independence of the capsule" (p. 83). Within this capsule, we find the "Book of the Covenant," i.e., 20:22–23:33 (p. 152). Bernard M. Levinson argues for the Covenant Code as originally independent from the Sinai pericope, being integrated as a supplement to the Decalogue at a later stage. Following Otto Eissfeldt, Levinson (1997, 153, n. 17; 2004, 281–83) points to the redaction critical implications of the combination of "words" and "ordinances" in Exod. 24:3a, thus integrating the Decalogue (20:1: "All these words…") and the Covenant Code (21:1: "These are the ordinances…"). Levinson (2004) dismisses Van Seters's attempt to reestablish a J source, including the Covenant Code, although dating it during the exile, thus regarding the Covenant Code later than Deuteronomic law. Cf. Levinson 1997. Kratz 2000, (138–39) argues similarly, stating, "in substance it is pre-Priestly and pre-Deuteronomic, and subsequently pre-Deuteronomistic" (p. 144).

10 For a convenient summary of customary law see Viberg (1992, 15–17).

11 Jackson (Jackson 1989, 199) hypothesizes "a customary origin for the content of the individual rules, and a scribal, court origin for the literary structure."

12 The similarities in content and order are so overwhelming that direct dependence is required. Hypotheses of mediating Canaanite codes (e.g., Alt 1953, 278–332) lack any evidence whatsoever (Van Seters 2003, 8–46; Levinson 2004, 288–89). A theory of literary dependence seems plausible (cf. Levinson 1997, 7–8; Wright 2003).

13 Wright (2009, 301) considers this possibility, but finds that in view of the references to Egypt true foreigners are intended. However, the fact that the Covenant Code neither refers explicitly to exile and exodus nor to slavery in Egypt, but to the experience of being a foreigner and a migrant, suggests a situation before the exodus narrative was established and a social context like the one we would envisage in Judah at the time of Assyrian occupation of the northern kingdom.

14 The theory of two sources behind Deuteronomic law, i.e., the Covenant Code and a "Privilege Law" (cf. Lohfink) is considered unnecessary by others (Levinson 1997, 8).

15 A fact that is emphasized by Levinson in his criticism (2004, 297–315).

16 This observation concerns not only altar laws and questions of worship, but the consequences of the administration of justice; only cases permitting secular justice may be tried locally, whereas cases requiring cultic justice are prohibited as a result of centralization. This also means that royal justice is not supreme (Levinson 1997, 98–143, especially 124). See also Levinson (2008, 2010), Stackert (2007).

17 Levinson finds the gist of the narrative to be "the work of a pre-exilic editor who sought to legitimate the introduction of a new set of laws and to sanction Josiah's cultic and political initiatives" (p. 10).

18 Laws of Hammurabi 47:61–62.

19 The formula is identical in the Covenant Code (Exod. 22:20; 23:9).

20 They amount to more than a repetition of standard *topoi*, as we find that the preceding section (24:6, 10–15) similarly develops the Covenant Code instructions on usury. This elaboration contains prohibitions of certain items as pledges, specifying the manner in which pledges may be taken and exhibits a concern for the poor, repeating the importance of returning a poor man's clothing before sundown. The

21 triad (immigrants, orphans, and widows) is referred to by some of the prophets, accusing the people for being faithless to the covenant: Jer. 7:6; 22:3; Ezek. 22:7 (cf. 22:29); Zech. 7:10; Mal. 3:5.
21 Cf. Deut. 2:23; 3:6; 7:26; 13:15, 17; 20:17.
22 The term is also used twice in Genesis (43:32; 46:34) to convey the Egyptian view of Hebrews and shepherds as unclean. In Exod. 8:26 the Egyptians are assumed to regard the sacrifice of the Hebrews as abominable.
23 Cf. Deut. 7:25–6; 12:31; 14:3; 17:1; 18:9, 12; 20:18; 22:5; 23:8 (ET 23:7; here the verb תעב [ta'av] is used); 23:19 (ET 23:18); 24:4; 25:16; 27:15.
24 Milgrom suggests a root meaning of darken, contaminate, or stain. The variability of the term is emphasized by Humbert (1960), who argues that it cannot be restricted to a particular type of sacred language.
25 Further on we find interesting nuances, however. While Ammonites, Moabites, and people of mixed heritage are never to be included in the congregation (23:3–4 [ET 2–3]), this does not apply to Edomites and Egyptians, whose descendants may be assimilated in the third generation (23:8–9 [ET 7–8]). The motivations for the two exceptions are very different, but still representing two types of empathy: Edomites are brothers; Israelites were once immigrants in Egypt. While leniency toward Edomites appeals to closer kinship than in the case of other peoples, nothing of that sort motivates leniency toward Egyptians. As the harsh judgment on Ammonites and Moabites is motivated by their enmity in the narrative of Bileam, we might have expected resentment toward the Egyptians as former masters. Instead, we find the oft-repeated reference to the shared experience of being an ethnic minority, being immigrants in an exposed situation. The text explicitly commands Israelites not to "abominate" (תעב, ta'ev) these two groups. Fear of foreigners is clearly mitigated by empathy and reinforced by disgust.
26 Still maintained by, for example, Kratz (2000, 110–11), Levine (2003, 16–17).
27 Knohl has the idea of a Holiness School throughout several centuries. For a discussion with further references, see Kazen (2011 64–70).
28 The relationship between Deut. 14:3–19 and Lev. 11 is a moot question. The concise character and homogeneous terminology of the Deuteronomic variant is evident, but Lev. 11 develops the category of שרץ (sherets) further. See, for example, Meshel (2008), Kazen (2008), Kazen (2011, 72 –80; Kazen 2015, 457 –59).
29 We should note the parallel endings: Lev. 26 is in many ways similar to Exod. 23 and Deut. 28. According to Kratz (2000, 110), "the Holiness Code… reformulates Deuteronomy in the spirit and style of the Priestly writing."
30 Both Kratz (Kratz 2000, 110–11) and Levine (Levine 2003, 11, 18) thus believe that the priestly writers redacted Deuteronomy, although they regard the Holiness Code as the beginning of the literary development of Leviticus. Cf. Levine (2003, 13–15).
31 Cf. Kratz, after 515 BCE (Kratz 2000, 326); Levine, during exile or after waves of return following 538 BCE (2003, 15); Nihan, late 5th century BCE (Nihan 2004, 105–22). This is much later than Milgrom's far too early dating (Milgrom 1991, 34; Lev. 17–22, 1345–64). Knohl's dating of the Holiness Code is likewise too early and too precise, although giving room for overlapping and extended processes (1995, 204–16).
32 For the blind, cf. Deut. 27:18.
33 This claim is insistently frequent in the Holiness Code (Lev. 17:8, 10, 12, 13, 15; 18:26; 20:2; 22:18; 24:16, 22), carried on in Numbers (Num. 9:14; 15:14–16, 26, 29–30; 19:10; 35:15) and found in the Passover narrative in Exodus, too (Exod. 12:19, 48–49), all

considered to be H redactions (Nihan 2011). It is, however, conspicuously absent from Deuteronomy (except in the farewell speech of Moses, Deut. 31:12; possibly 29:11 may be interpreted in this way, too).

34 Deut. 14:21. The Holiness Code does, however, admit one difference: immigrants may become "eternal" slaves of Israelites, without the year of release applying (Lev. 25:45).
35 As Nihan points out, other mentions of גרים (*gerim*) in P occur in sections that are often considered to be H redactions.
36 For example, Lev. 18:10; 19:33–4; 25:6, 35.
37 Laws that P traces from the covenant with Noah.
38 Lev. 19:2, 37; 20:7–8, 22–6; 22:31–3.
39 Lev. 17:10; 18:29; 20:2; 24:16; cf. Num. 15:30.
40 Milgrom (2000a, 1345) argues that since תועבה (*to'evah*) in Lev. 18 is used separately only to characterize one prohibition (18:22), while several times summarizing all the prohibitions in the closing exhortation, this points to the incorporation of an older list of sexual prohibitions (18:6–23) into two reworded exhortations (18:1–5, 24–30).
41 Moses is criticized for his foreign wife (Num. 12:1); Israelite men are led into idolatry by Moabite women (Num. 25). In the Holiness Code one may note a somewhat reverse case in the story of the blasphemer with an Egyptian father (Lev. 24:10–23).
42 Cf. Exod. 23:27.
43 Parts of the subsequent warnings as well as the Song of Moses have a similar intent (Deut. 29:16–28; 32:15–25).
44 Instead of the more common תעבה (*to'evah*) or קוץ (*quts*) as in Lev. 20:22, we here find the verb געל (*ga'al*). This verb is not used elsewhere in the Pentateuch, but occurs in Jeremiah and Ezekiel. Cf. Milgrom (2000b, 2301–02). The fact that the subject changes from God to the people suggests, however, that "expel" is not the best translation, but that a notion of physical disgust is present. In any case it is inconsistent to swap between "expel" and "loathe."
45 Following Hoffmann, Milgrom (2000a, 1361; 2000b, 2272–343) assigns 26:1–2, 33b–35 and 43–44 to H$_R$, the post-exilic final redactor (H itself is considered pre-exilic by Milgrom). These sections talk about the Sabbath and presuppose the exile. However, in view of the use of the verb געל (*ga'al*) both within and outside of these passages, I think the discrepancies with preceding sections of the Holiness Code cannot be solved by the excision of a few verses. Rather, this chapter exhibits quite a different perspective.
46 For the sacrifice of three birds, see Collins (2002, 227, 228, 230). See also Milgrom (1991, 834), with a reference to Otten (1961, 130) (not seen).
47 RS 1.009, line 8; 24.256, line 5–6; 24.249, line26; 24.250+, line 2, 7–8; 1.003/18.056, line 5–6, 27, 36 (?), 40; 1.001, line 21–22; 19.013, line 7–8. Pardee (2002).
48 1 En 10:4–5; cf. 11QT 26:13. Douglas (2003).
49 Also, v. 34 fixes it to once a year, which might suggest that the rite had not previously been fixed to a certain time. Milgrom (1991, 1061). Cf. Wright (1987a, 17–21).
50 Shurpu vii 53–70, in Reiner (1958). Cf. the role of the steppe in the Namburbi texts, (Maul 1994, 48, 93, 124, 387).
51 The Qumran sectarians seem to have been opposed to this. The statement that no youth may sprinkle is heavily reconstructed (4Q269 8 ii, 6 and 4Q271 ii, 13); the crucial *na'ar* is missing in both but conjectured! The translation of 4Q277 1 ii, 7 is furthermore debated. It is, however, reasonable to accept Baumgarten's suggestion that עלול (*'alul*) is a variant for עולל (*'olal*) i.e., child (Baumgarten 1999, 118). In any case it is clear that other Qumran texts consider only priests competent for the task, see 4Q276; 4Q277.

52 For a recent study on this rite see Dietrich (2009). Cf. the brief but comprehensive discussion in Tigay (1996, 472–76).
53 This is one of Dietrich's points in his review of previous research (Dietrich 2009, 29–64).
54 There are good arguments for interpreting the rite as a reenactment of the murder, an elimination rite, transferring the impurity of bloodguilt from arable land to a desert place. Cf. Milgrom (1981), Wright (1987b), Tigay (1996).
55 The relationship between the asylum laws in Exod. 21:12–14, Deut. 19:1–13 and Num. 35:9–34 cannot be discussed here; see Stackert (2007, 31–112). Many scholars agree with Stackert that the passage in Numbers is H's composition or redaction, for example Knohl (1995, 179–80), Milgrom (2000a, 1344) (probably); Nihan (2004, 118, n.167). According to Achenbach, however, Num. 35 belongs to a late stage of theocratic redaction with a focus on holiness and presupposes the asylum law in Deuteronomy (Achenbach 2003, 598–600, 638).
56 See *Vendidād* 3.14; 5.27–38; 7.1–9; 8.14–19.
57 See, for example, *Vendidād* 3.8–9, 12–15, 36–9; 6.44–51; 8.4–13.

Chapter 3

1 An earlier and slightly different version of this article has been published as Gudme (2012).
2 Milgrom writes that the blood "is returned to God via the altar" (Lev. 1–16, 156), but as Lundager Jensen notes there is nothing in the Hebrew Bible text that indicates that the blood is actually returned to or even given to Yahweh when it is dashed on the altar (Jensen 2000, 273, note 17).
3 Lev. 17:10–14, which is part of the Holiness Code, says that the life of the flesh is the blood, and that the blood makes atonement for the Israelites because it is the life. It is doubtful, however, that one can presuppose an element of atonement in all blood rites in the Hebrew Bible (see Milgrom 1991, 704–13; Gilders 2004, 12, 24–25).
4 See Stowers (1998, 179–94), for a good critical discussion of this claim. Stowers focuses on the role of sacrificial blood in Greek religion in particular.
5 Baruch J. Schwartz concedes that "'life' is associated with 'blood' outside of Israel as well," but he does not give any examples of this (Schwartz 1991, 56, note 2). Schwartz maintains that the meaning of the blood in a sacrificial context is unique to the Hebrew Bible, but see the discussion in Stowers (1998).
6 For a good analysis of this passage see Johnston (2013, 7–14). Johnston writes: "It is only by means of the blood—a striking emblem of the vigorous life they have left behind forever—that they temporarily become capable of normal human converse" (p. 8). In a recent article, Bridget Martin suggests, that the reason for why some of the dead in *Odyssey* XI drink from the blood and others abstain is that the ones who abstain are the honored dead who are well taken care of and supplied with funerary sacrifices and therefore do not need the blood (Martin 2014, 1–12).
7 With a single exception, the translation of ψυχή is "life" rather than "soul"; I follow Homer, *Iliad*, trans. G. P. Goold; 2 vols. LCL (Cambridge, MA: Harvard University Press, 1985).
8 McCarthy insists that even though *Iliad* XIV, 518 does equate blood with soul and life, it is merely as "a figure of speech based on the common observation that blood and life go together" ("The Symbolism of Blood and Sacrifice," 172). I fail to see why the

Iliad's identification of blood with life is metaphorical, whereas the Hebrew Bible's is not.

9   Interestingly, the Homeric Greek term for soul/life-force (see above), *psychê*, is etymologically connected with *psychein*, which means to blow or breathe. See Bremmer (2010, 14).
10 For more Greek examples see Stowers (1998 and 1995, 300–06).
11 I am indebted to Professor Philip C. Schmitz, who inspired me to think along the lines of conceptual metaphors with an excellent lecture on Phoenician perceptions of the afterlife, presented at the Mainz International Colloquium on Ancient Hebrew (MICAH) in October 2011.
12 Lakoff and Johnson (1999, 16–44), Slingerland (2008a, 151–218).
13 Following the style of Lakoff and Johnson, capital letters are used to denote concepts and conceptual metaphors that are cross-mapped with one another. In this case, the source-domain concept UP is being cross-mapped with the target-domain concept MORE in such a way that the source-domain gives definition or understanding to the target-domain: thus the conceptual metaphor, MORE IS UP. See further: Lakoff and Johnson (1999, 58).
14 A similar notion seems to present in the Ugaritic epic of *Aqhat* (KTU 1.18 IV:24–25), where a dying man's breath, his life-breath (*npšh*), is compared with the wind (*rh*); see Margalit (1989, 130).
15 I am grateful to Professor Hans Jørgen Lundager Jensen for pointing this connection out to me and for lending me his copy of La Barre's book.
16 In this connection there is an interesting passage in Eccl. 3:21 about where the "spirit" (רוח) goes after death. It seems that Qoheleth is saying that, contrary to common belief, the spirit of man may descend downwards to the earth like the spirit of animals and not ascend upwards. If life-breath comes from Yahweh as it is described in Gen. 2, then presumably the *right* way to go would be up just like the burnt fat that ascends from the altar. But perhaps Qoheleth is questioning that the life-force of man actually does come from Yahweh.

Chapter 4

1   Modern here meaning modern humans (*Homo sapiens*), as opposed to other humans.
2   Donald actually talks about four transitions, the first being from ape to human (Donald 1991, 149), but I will not relate to the first transition here.
3   See also a nice description of hominids in the mimetic stage by Jeremy Lent in: https://jeremylent.wordpress.com/2010/07/28/mimetic-culture/.
4   Donald here does not agree with Feldman Barrett's theory, which is based on the predictive brain theory; Feldman Barrett sees concepts as preceding language, and it entails that mythic cognition as a cognitive strategy precedes language. I agree with Feldman Barrett here, but did not, of course, change the quote from Donald.
5   It is not the first time that Donald's theory is used for explaining texts. This has been done by Eelco van Es in his dissertation on George Herbert's poetry (Es 2012).
6   This might be what Lisa Feldman Barrett calls a "cascade of emotions" (Feldman Barrett 2017, 84–112). I plan to elaborate on this in a future work.
7   For blending see Fauconnier and Turner (2002), but there are other processes in play, such that have been identified and described in the cognitive science or religion and in cognitive approaches to culture. I refer to concepts such as the ratcheting

(Tomasello 1999), metaphorizing (Lakoff and Johnson 1980), advantages of the counterintuitivity (Boyer 1994a); Barrett and Nyhof (2001, 69–100), conditions for learning (see his contribution in this volume "Christian Beginnings and Culture Evolution"), fractalic thinking (Czachesz 2012b, 3–28), and others, but I will not elaborate on all these in this chapter.

8   General statements can also be found in wisdom literature, but I will not study these here, because of their special nature which asks for a separate study.

9   I am not studying in this chapter the question of the inclusion of the Song of Songs in the biblical corpus, which is usually answered by the assigning a metaphoric meaning to it by the canonizers; rather I am presenting an analysis of the text itself.

10 I am translating the cohortative imperfect in the suggestive modality to indicate that the protagonist is driven into action.

11 It is not clear what the word נפש means in the biblical context. It is explained in the dictionaries as life, self, sentient aspect, or soul (cf. Gesenius 1990, 558–60: "נפש"). In any case, it is this aspect of the person which does the "loving."

12 An example of personification is the idiom "mother earth"; recursion is "successively apply[ing] an operation to its own result" (Czachesz 2012b, 5), and this cognitive process (together with others) is responsible for our understanding of the nation as a family, for example. Metaphorizing is behind our understanding of the leader as a father. All these are just examples of how the familiar interpersonal relations are applied to relations within larger social units, whose members are not really familiar. For this notion in relation to nationalism see Anderson (1991, 5–7).

13 See the discussion of אפים in Bar-Efrat (1996, 51).

14 With this in mind, it is interesting to look again at Zakovich (1975, 292–94) (Hebrew) who talks about the connection between the Samson stories and the Song of Songs; the similarities between the Song of Songs and the Samson stories to which Zakovich points have to do with language use, but he also points to the mimetic nature of Samson's sexuality in comparison to the one of his wives.

15 One may argue, and correctly, that the stories of the Patriarch are also constructing imagined history for the sake of explaining current social situation; the difference is that the stories in the political books relate to dynasties and official rulers, and do not claim ethnic ancestry.

16 The only woman who is a unique person among those loved by Solomon is Pharaoh's daughter. Of her it is said in chapter 3 that Solomon married her but it does not say that he loved her. When saying that Solomon loved foreign women, the daughter of Pharaoh is mentioned again as a particular person, but this seems like an editor's hand.

17 I am following Kazen's presentation of the scholarship and his conclusions (Kazen 2011, 51–70): it is generally accepted that the legal collections interpolated into the Bible are the Covenant Code (Exod. 22:20–23:33), embedded within the revelation narrative (19:2–24:15); the Cultic Laws (Lev. 1–16); the Holiness Code (Lev. 17–26); parts of Deut. 12–26; also of legal nature, as well as including the verb "to love," are the verses in Jos. 22:5 "Only take heed to do the commandment and the law, which Moses the servant of the Lord commanded you, to love the Lord your God," and 23:11 "take good heed therefore unto yourselves, that you love the Lord your God."

18 The six cases where god loves are Deut. 4:37, 7:8, 7:13, 10:15, 10:18, 23:6; in the prophetic and wisdom literature there are many more cases where God loves (e.g.,

him who follows righteousness, Prov. 15:9). I see it as a unique characteristic of these literatures, which merit a separate research.
19 The verses where people love are Exod. 20:6, 21:5; Lev. 19:18,34; Deut. 5:10, 6:5, 7:9, 10:12,19, 11:1,13,22, 13:4, 15:16, 19:9, 21:15,16, 30:6,16,20; Jos. 22:5, 23:11.
20 It is important to recognize that God loves, because some studies in the past emphasized the submissive nature of love (of a slave to a master), but if we talk about God loving, then love cannot be only submissive.
21 This is found ten times: Deut. 6:5; 10:12; 11:1, 13, 22; 19:9; 22:5; 23:11; 30:16, 20.
22 For a possible explanation of such a reversal see Biro's contribution in this volume.
23 Ackerman (2002, 441–42): "I believe it is not possible to explain the one-sided usage of *'aheb* or *'ahaba* within the interpersonal accounts simply by appeal to the Bible's preferred perspectival... the Bible is an almost exclusively male-oriented [and] typically tells us only men's perspectives on things."
24 About the development of morality and love see, for example, Illouz (2012), 22.
25 So did Wolde, apparently independently (Wolde 2008, 19).

Chapter 5

1 That is, the texts, however extensive, inevitably are not fully representative of the language as it was spoken, since (a) they are likely to cover specific subject-matter, deemed worthy of recording, such as religious, legal, or financial texts, or literary works, and (b) the language used is likely to be more literary and formal in character than that of the spoken word.
2 For a fuller discussion of the issues involved in the adaptation of a cognitive approach to an ancient language see Burton (2017a).
3 For a helpful introduction to each of these concepts see Geeraerts (2010), particularly Chapter 5: "Cognitive Semantics." For a discussion of their application in the field of biblical studies see Burton (2017b).
4 Of course, verbal language is not the sole means by which cognitive processes may be communicated; visual, tactile, and other forms of communication also play a role, but nonetheless verbal communication is not only the clearest, but also the main form available, particularly in the context of ancient languages.
5 For a detailed discussion of the practical outworkings of this principle, see Burton (2017a).
6 It should be noted that neither a bottom-up analysis nor a corpus-based approach requires a cognitive theoretical framework to underpin it; it is perfectly possible to arrive at both methodological tools from an externalist position, when a highly systematic and exhaustive analysis is sought. However, an externalist theoretical framework will not lead so naturally or so necessarily to a methodology of this kind. The purpose of this chapter is not to argue that a cognitive methodology is *inherently* distinct from a non-cognitive one (though most often, in practice, it will be), but rather to demonstrate, having accepted the fundamental cognitive principle that linguistic meaning should be sought in the mind of the speaker, the necessary methodological consequences of this theoretical underpinning, particularly in the context of the study of ancient languages.
7 The full list of relevant verses, containing one or more of the lexemes belonging to the semantic domain of כבוד, is as follows: כבוד: Isa. 58:8; 59:19; 60:1, 2, 13; 61:6; 62:2;

66:11, 12, 18, 19 (x2). תפארת: Isa. 60:7, 19; 62:3; 63:12, 14, 15; 64:10. גאון: Isa. 60:15. The domain as defined consists solely of nouns—of lexemes which are near-synonyms of, and syntactically substitutable for, כבוד itself. There are, of course, numerous semantically related lexemes from other grammatical classes, a number of which occur in Isa. 56–66, the examination of which would likely shed further light on the overall use of "glory"-language in these chapters. This unfortunately remains a subject for a larger study.

8   Here and throughout this paper, "glory" (in quotation marks) is used for ease of reference to refer to any or all lexemes belonging to the semantic domain of כבוד, and bears no specific semantic implications. It is not to be understood as semantically equivalent to the English concept of glory, or to any individual Hebrew term.

9   This is not to suggest that questions concerning authorship are not of relevance to the cognitive semantic project. Indeed, in an ideal situation, with unlimited available data and accurate information as to its source, we would be able to categorize all linguistic samples by place, date and author, and analyze the distinctions between language from different sources. The disregard for authorship (and dating) of Trito-Isaiah in this chapter is a purely practical one—not only is the question so disputed as to make any certainty unattainable, but even were we to be confident in identifying the author of a given verse or passage, the quantity of data available on a single author would be so small as to lose almost all significance.

10 The membership and boundaries of the semantic domain of כבוד I have analyzed and defined at length elsewhere (Burton 2017b), and space here does not allow for a full reiteration of method and results. Regarding the number of members, I say "at least" since at the boundaries of the domain lie certain lexemes of indeterminate membership status; there are also likely to be a number of more minor lexemes which properly belong to the domain but which, due to their infrequency, may not objectively be firmly identified as such.

11 For the reader unfamiliar with the Hebrew vocabulary of glory, I offer the following glosses; these must be treated with caution, since no gloss accurately conveys the nuance of the term translated: תפארת (beauty), הדר (honor), הוד (status), צבי (splendor), גאון (pride) and גאוה (haughtiness). For more on this choice of glosses, see Burton (2017b). Of the ten members of the domain firmly identified, I have excluded here גאות, עז and תהלה, for the following reasons: גאות is too infrequent for data concerning its distribution to be statistically significant, and thus its precise relationship to the domain is ambiguous. עז is more commonly glossed as "strength," and while I have argued at length elsewhere for its inclusion within the domain of כבוד (see Burton 2017b), its complex position spanning two domains renders it a nonstandard member, and for simplicity we exclude it from this chapter. תהלה, according to my analysis, belongs to a distinct (sub-)domain on the periphery of the domain of כבוד, and has thus been excluded from this chapter for the same reason.

12 The book of Isaiah boasts ninety-five instances, collectively, of the lexemes mentioned in this paragraph; twenty of these are in Isa. 56–66.

13 Indeed, "glory" in general is far more commonly taken by God from nations than bestowed upon them.

14 Isa. 5:13; Mic. 1:15; children of Israel: Isa. 17:3; "my people": Jer. 2:11; Jacob: Isa. 17:4; Ephraim: Hos. 9:11; the Israelites: Ps. 106:20; Jerusalem: Isa. 60:13; 61:6; 62:2; 66:11, 12.

15 Moab: Isa. 16:14; Kedar: Isa. 21:16; Lebanon: Isa. 35:2; 60:13; the nations: Isa. 61:6; the inhabitant of Dibon: Jer. 48:18; Pharaoh and his multitude: Ezek. 31:18.

16 The exceptions to this are Ps. 106:20 and Jer. 2:11, in which God's people give away their own כבוד.

17 In just one other place in the entire Classical Hebrew corpus is כבוד received by God's people: this is at 2Q20 f1:3, a manuscript containing fragments of Jubilees (Jub. 46:2). Here we find the Egyptians giving כבוד to the sons of Israel on account of Joseph. The only other text of relevance is Sir. 49:5, which reads: ויתן... כבודם לגוי נבל נכרי (He [God] gave... their כבוד to a foolish, foreign nation). This is an intriguing verse, for it is the only time in Classical Hebrew literature that any foreign nation is ascribed כבוד in a context where they do not lose it; indeed, God gives it to them, in an apparent reversal of the sentiment of Isa. 60–66.

18 It is often difficult to make a clear distinction between כבוד יהוה—signifying the presence of God itself—and the כבוד of God as an attribute. In many cases, particularly in the extra-biblical material, the idiomatic sense of כבוד יהוה is present even in the absence of the precise phrase.

19 Niphal: Exod. 16:10; Lev. 9:6, 23; Num. 14:10; 16:19; 17:7; 20:6; Isa. 60:2; 4Q369 f1ii:3; 4Q457b 2:6; qal: Exod. 16:7; Num. 14:22; 2 Chron. 7:3; Ps. 63:3; 97:6; Isa. 35:2; 40:5; 62:2; 66:18, 19; Ezek. 3:23; 4Q504 f1_2Riv:8; hiphil: Exod. 33:18; Deut. 5:24.

20 This is also the only biblical instance in which כבוד as subject of the verb ראה is not explicitly said to be כבוד יהוה, though the previous verse makes it plain that the idiomatic sense is nonetheless present here.

21 The only other texts connecting תפארת to the temple are 1 Chron. 22:5 and 2 Chron. 3:6; in the former, תפארת is not attributed to the temple, but rather the temple itself is called לתפארת—i.e., a source of תפארת—throughout the lands; in the second, תפארת is in fact attributed to the temple, but is specifically tied to the precious stones which constitute its ornamentation.

22 Aside from the texts mentioned below, the only instance I have been able to find in which another abstract descriptor modifies these terms is Ps. 84:1, which speaks of God's dwelling as יְדִיד ("lovely, beloved").

23 Cf. Isa. 60:1; Ezek. 4:10; 43:2; Sir. 42:16; 4Q511 f1:7; and 1QH[a] 20:15. The list is far from exhaustive.

24 It is not entirely clear whether the גאון of nations other than God's own may be positive in connotation; the clearest example is Ezek. 16:49, where the גאון of Sodom does not seem to be her crime in and of itself, Sodom's crime being rather her lack of compassionate use of her גאון and of her other forms of wealth.

25 Of course, our definition of "native speaker" must be limited by the nature of the available texts—collectively, these were highly literate, educated, and religious members of the Hebrew community. To what degree their perceptions of the world were the same as those of the population in general is impossible to determine.

26 The question of knowing what "instinctively presents itself" to the mind of another is, of course, a tricky question; word association tests have shown that, for any cultural or linguistic group, certain lexemes are more likely to be produced in response to a stimulus lexeme than others. Where a strong cognitive association exists (such as that among British English speakers between "salt" and "pepper"), one member of the pair evokes the other with high frequency (according to the Birkbeck word association norms, "pepper" evokes "salt" 54.2 percent of the time [Moss and Older 1996, 91]). In the absence of native speakers on whom to perform such experiments directly(!), evidence of similar cognitive associations may be found through analysis of word associations in the texts themselves. In the case of Classical Hebrew, both parallel terms and other forms of word pairing yield compelling evidence of what were "instinctive" word associations for the authors of

the texts. The claim that כבוד, in this eschatological context, is likely to be the lexeme that most instinctively presents itself to the Isaianic author's mind is based on my own analysis of the associations of the Classical Hebrew כבוד-domain with God (cf. Burton 2017b).

27 הדר: Isa. 2:10, 19, 21; 5:14; 35:2; 53:2; צבי: Isa. 4:2; 13:19; 23:9; 24:16; 28:1, 4, and 5.

Chapter 6

1. The Asante Twi, Akwapim Twi, and Fanti Twi speak Akan languages referred to as Twi. These languages are from the Niger-Congo linguistic family and are mutually intelligible. There are currently three standardized orthographies for Asante Twi, Akwapim Twi, and Fante Twi; there is also a unified Akan orthography which was created during the 1980s. See Lewis (2009).
2. BHS suggests haplography because of homoearcton. The vision of the scribe jumped from the ה of the red horses to the ה of the black horses which in turn eliminated the red horses phrase in verse 6.
3. Sorrel horses have copper-red shade of chestnut for hair coat color with mane, tail, and ear edges the same color as the body or lighter.
4. Both the MT and LXX have the same translations of color terms.
5. Bay horses have hair coat color characterized by a reddish brown body color with black mane, tail, and ear edges.
6. Hartley writes, "MT's reading three colour terms in Zech. 1:8 gains additional support from the literary pattern of sevens present in Zechariah's eight visions. The first (1:8-17) and the last visions (6:1-8), in which there are horses of different colours, form an *inclusio* for the vision reports. In the first vision there are three groups of horsemen; each group of horses is identified by a different colour, and in the last vision four chariots are drawn by teams of horses, each team having a differing colour. In addition, 'land,' occurs three times in the first vision and four times in the eighth vision. Since emending Zech. 1:8 MT in order to have four groups of horses of differing colours in the first vision would disrupt this pattern, the MT is accepted as having both strong textual and literary support" Hartley (2011, 74).
7. Meyers and Meyers offer a plausible explanation for using in the Zechariah text. It may be there was a limited pool of lexical terms for colors and Classical Hebrew did not have a fourth basic term that could be used in regard to horses (Meyers and Meyers 1987).
8. Hartley explains, "The only two existing collocations in which אמץ may function as a possible colour lexeme in ancient Heb occur in Zechariah's eighth vision (6:3, 7). In that case אמץ is a colour lexeme used for identifying the team of horses drawing one of the chariots as chestnut" (Hartley 2011, 217). However, it is possible to achieve a sound reading in both texts by exegeting as a form of the well-attested root "strong ones" Boda (2005), Butterworth (1992).

Chapter 7

1. *Jub.* 23:29-31 is commonly held by exegetes as proposing something closer to the idea of immortality of the soul rather than resurrection (cf. Cavallin 1974, 38). The immediate context of 23:22-32, however, does not mention a final judgment

2. or definitive break in history (though compare with 5:13–16; 10:7; 23:11), thus causing some to de-eschatologize the passage and instead see it as anticipating future judgment (thus Wright 2003, 143–44). Alan Segal takes a middle ground, arguing "a sort of resurrection is blended with a sort of immortality of the soul, though neither one of them is a typical example of that belief" (Segal 2004, 355).
2. The description of the inhabitants of the fourth hollow not rising in *1 En.* 22:13 seems to imply that the inhabitants of the other three hollows will rise, though this is conjectural. Because resurrection seems to presume some kind of postmortem intermediary state for the dead (which *1 En.* 22:13 perhaps betrays), many exegetes thus see the *Book of Watchers* as presuming resurrection. Nonetheless, this text does not explicitly mention resurrection, even in the description of the great judgment in chapters 1–5. Proponents include Cavallin (1974, 41–42), Segal (2004, 279), Wright (2003, 157), Nickelsburg (2006, 169–70), and Cavallin (1974, 41–42).
3. Following the convention outlined in Lakoff and Johnson (1980), conceptual metaphors are articulated via the capitalized formula A IS B (or A ARE B), where A and B refer to the conceptual domains being cross-mapped. This stylistic notation should not be understood as a statement in its own right (e.g., RESURRECTION IS UP), but rather as a symbolic description of cross-domain mappings: the target domain (RESURRECTION) is mapped to the source domain (UP), with the mapping represented by the copula (IS)—see also Lakoff and Johnson 1999, 58. Similarly, lexical signs should be distinguished from the concepts for which they represent (e.g., verticality is a lexical sign; VERTICALITY denotes the concept behind the sign). Exceptions to this rule include standard scholarly abbreviations (e.g., BCE, CE, etc.) as well as discipline-specific shorthand (e.g., HB, NT, etc.).
4. So noted by James H. Charlesworth, who argues "the concept of resurrection… can be detected only by examining exegetically a cluster of words in a particular context" (Charlesworth 2006a, 238).
5. The point is made in addressing what he refers to as the fallacious either/or distinction between individual resurrection and national restoration (Wright 2003, 116).
6. Similar language is used by other scholars too, particularly in relation to Dan. 12:2 though often without the same insistence on bodily resurrection—e.g., see Collins (1993, 395), Cavallin (1974, 26), and Day (1996, 240).
7. The closest that Charlesworth comes to offering such a unifying framework can be found at the conclusion of his article where he offers the single maxim: "The varieties and differing taxonomies of resurrection beliefs represent not a system but an expression of *the common human hope that God will have the last word and the future of the righteous will be blessed*" (Charlesworth 2006a, 261 [emphasis added]). This unifying thread is, unfortunately, more reflective than critical, offering little to our understanding of what actually constitutes a resurrection text.
8. I am here conjecturing, though Charlesworth does note that configurations too narrowly construed have led to divergent scholarly opinions concerning (for example) the Qumran sectarian material (Charlesworth 2006a, 237–39).
9. On productive reductionism, see Slingerland (2008b), McCauley (2013, 11–32).
10. Accordingly, I will not examine literature such as the Qumran sectarian documents (which are contested on the issue of resurrection), texts that refer to non-resurrection postmortem existence (e.g., Wisdom), nor Puech's reconstructed Hebrew Ben Sira fragment (cf. Puech 1990, 81–90). Other notable exclusions include the *Testaments of the 12 Patriarchs* (which in their present form are Christian texts that date from

the second century CE) and the Enochic *Book of Watchers* (which perhaps refers to resurrection but not explicitly enough to warrant examination here [see note 2 above]).

11 I include the *Epistle of Enoch* here despite the fact that the surviving Greek fragments (in contrast to the Ethiopic) lack explicit reference to resurrection.

12 Additionally, this chapter is also influenced by Gilles Fauconnier and Mark Turner's theory of conceptual blending, particularly in my examination of the cross-space mappings that establish the conceptual metaphors examined below (see especially Diagram 2). See Fauconnier and Turner (2002).

13 On image schemata, see Johnson (1987), Lakoff and Johnson (1999), especially pages 16–44. For an excellent and succinct introduction to image schemata, see Evans (2006, 176–205).

14 Accordingly, the cognitive view of metaphor concerns, as Zoltán Kövecses notes, the whole system of human embodiment: "Language, culture, body, mind, and brain all come together and play an equally crucial role in our metaphorical competence" (Kövecses 2010, 321).

15 Thus Lakoff and Turner, "Life and death are such all-encompassing matters that there can be no single conceptual metaphor that will enable us to comprehend them" (Lakoff and Turner 1989, 2).

16 This is by no means the only way in which notions of life and death are conceptualized in Hebrew tradition. An important counterpart to the UP–DOWN conceptualizations noted here is the structuring of LIFE–DEATH by the LIFE–FAR or PROXIMITY schema, such that life is conceptualized as proximity to YHWH. Such conceptualizations are readily apparent within biblical tradition. In Ps. 73:27–8, for instance, the Psalmist insists that "those far (רחוק, *rahoq*) from you will perish (*yovedu* יאבדו,)... but for me, nearness (קרבת, *qirvat*) to God is good" (cf. vv. 17 and 23–6). The correlation of PROXIMITY (specifically FAR) with DEATH is reflective of the metaphors LIFE IS NEARNESS TO YHWH and DEATH IS DISTANCE FROM YHWH.

17 It must be stressed that this is a pragmatic or functional understanding of (un)consciousness and thus should not be understood either as a technical definition of consciousness, nor as a limitation to the scope of what constitutes conscious experiences (e.g., I do not intend to preclude the existence of conscious states while one sleeps).

18 It should be noted that death is described in various ways in biblical tradition, many of which have been examined in Johnston (2002, 23–46).

19 Though the date of Job is disputed, I do not construe this text as affirming any kind of postmortem rising of the dead. Job 19:25–7 should thus be read against the backdrop of Job's broader attitude toward death (including the immediate passage) and therefore does not refer to resurrection (cf. Wright 2003, 105).

20 The same lifecycle referred to in Gen. 3:19 is also described in Job 14:1–2, where the course of human life is likened to a flower that grows and then withers. This blend clearly correlates and contrasts life/vitality/erectness with death/inaction/lowness via the same UP–DOWN image schema.

21 Alongside שאול (*she'ol*) we should note other underworld terminology such as אבדון (*avadon*), בור (*bor*), שחת (*shahat*), באר (*be'er*), and occasionally ארץ (*'erets*), all of which have an explicit downward orientation. For a full discussion of these terms, see Johnston (2002, 83–5).

22 Compare also the description in Num. 16:29–33 that, should the ground open up, one would be *swallowed* (בלע, *b-l-'*) *down* (ירד, *y-r-d*).

23 This is particularly expressed in passages where the cosmological mapping is blended with experiences of pain/suffering, such that Sheol and its various synonyms stand for despair or trouble, from which yhwh will *raise up* the afflicted (e.g., Ps. 40:3).
24 See Isa. 14:9; 26:14, 19; Ps. 88:10; Job 26:5; Prov. 2:18; 9:18; 21:16.
25 Earlier versions of Diagram 2 are published in Tappenden (2012).
26 Blending theory was developed by Gilles Fauconnier and Mark Turner over many publications, but chiefly presented in their 2000 monograph, *The Way We Think*. This theory examines the ways human beings conceptually integrate differing domains of thought with one another. To some extent, metaphor stands as a prime example of conceptual blending, as the features of one domain of thought (known as the Source Domain) are mapped onto (or integrated with) certain features of another domain of thought (the Target Domain). But conceptual blending is concerned with more than just a linear process of Source-to-Target-Domain mappings. According to Fauconnier and Turner, blending happens dynamically and integratively as conceptual domains are simultaneously blended with one another so as to produce emergent meaning not found in either of the two input spaces alone. Thus, blending happens through the organization of conceptual networks that always consist of at least two input spaces (i.e., the domains being blended), one general space (which establishes cross-space correlations), and one blended space (where emergent structure is created).
27 For the sake of clarity and brevity I have not represented all the cross-space mappings at work in the blend mapped in Diagram 2. To be certain, the content and conceptual correlations between the two input spaces mapped in Diagram 2 are quite robust and extend beyond the generic linking of UP and DOWN counterparts. For example, the Waking–Sleeping space contains elements such as Bed, Physical Body, and even the activity of Going to Sleep, all of which are respectively correlated with elements in the Life–Death space such as Grave, Physical Body, and the activity of Dying. While these correlations are made, at least in part, due to the shared VERTICALITY structure—Bed–Grave (DOWN) and Awake–Alive (UP)—these two inputs are mapped on to a richer set of correlations than mere verticality alone. For a more thorough description of the blend, and of blending theory generally, see Tappenden (2012), and also Tappenden (2016, 33–39). In those previous publications, the same blend mapped in Diagram 2 is examined with an eye toward the emergent metaphor RESURRECTION IS CONSCIOUSNESS (also discussed in this chapter, below). This metaphor systemically relates to the LIFE IS BEING AWAKE/DEATH IS SLEEP metaphors in as much as the same mental spaces blend together so as to create alternative components of meaning. Taken together, we see how the one conceptual mapping (Diagram 2) enables emergent structure that can render varying yet interdependent conceptual metaphors.
28 In biblical tradition, several contexts that use "sleep"-related language likewise have correlations with death—see, for example, various usages of שכב (sh-k-b; e.g., Ezek 32:21, 27, 30), ישן (y-sh-n; e.g., Jer 51:39, 57), שנה (sh-n-h, shenah; e.g., Job 14:12), and the opposite קוץ (q-w-ts), which in Jer. 51:39, 57 is used to denote the impossibility of waking from the dead.
29 For example, Jacob (Gen. 47:30), Moses (Deut. 31:16), David (e.g., 2 Sam. 7:12; 1 Kgs 2:10), Solomon (1 Kgs 11:43 / 2 Chron. 9:31), and several other monarchs.
30 In the LXX, both the Old Greek and θ' retain the same metaphor with only a slight alteration in the Old Greek's rendering of קוץ (q-w-ts).
31 In addition to other UP–DOWN language in *2 Macc.* 12:44–5, those who have died are said to have "fallen asleep" (κοιμάομαι [*koimaomai*]—12:45). In *1 En.* 93:2, the

description of the righteous one waking and walking in the way of righteousness may be a collective singular speaking of resurrection, though this is disputed (cf. Stuckenbruck 2007, 227–29). In *1 En.* 100:5–6, the focus seems to be upon those righteous who have already died and are now awaiting a future judgment; this passage is reflective of the DEATH IS SLEEP metaphor, though it does not mention a correlated future waking (cf. Nickelsburg 2001, 501; Stuckenbruck 2007, 442–43). In *Ps. Sol.* 3 the language of sleeping and waking frames the entire passage. Though it is not used to describe resurrection specifically, emphasis throughout the psalm is placed upon both being awake (vv. 1–2) and the value of life (vv. 9–12). Further, the description of the Lord as "awake" (γρηγόρησιν [*grēgorēsin*]—v. 2) coheres well with the psalm's focus on life, light, and other UP-orientated images.

32 Such frames and their values are, of course, culture specific and thus demonstrate variance. I have proposed here typical values (e.g., the poor and the rich); in actuality we see at times many synonymous values existing within a single frame. For example, the *Epistle of Enoch*, which is framed to a great extent by the SOCIAL INJUSTICE frame, refers to the protagonists and antagonists variously (e.g., protagonists: righteous, wise, suffering ones etc.; vis-à-vis antagonists: sinners, foolish, rich etc.).

33 One should not, of course, make too much of such presumed postmortem corporeality, for it is doubtless tied to the martyriological situation that *2 Macc.* addresses. Corporeal resurrection is envisaged in this book as a response to the horrible and gruesome deaths that are described, and such cannot be disconnected from the narratological world of the text.

34 While Deut. 30:16 correlates "life," "land," and "Torah," the converse is upheld in vv. 17–18 where disobedience and the worship of other gods are said to lead to death and a truncated stay in the land. Moses continues by paralleling life/blessing and death/curse (v. 19), and he explicitly connects "land" with "life" in v. 20. Unlike the LIFE IS BEING AWAKE metaphor discussed above, here the UP–DOWN image schema does not tie the various conceptual domains together (i.e., LIFE–DEATH and LAND–EXILE) but is rather projected from one domain (LIFE) onto the other (LAND). (The UP–DOWN structure is also projected onto the concept TORAH OBSERVANCE.) This is what Fauconnier and Turner refer to as a single scope blend (Fauconnier and Turner 2002, 126–31).

35 Israel is also described in 37:12 as coming "up" (עלה '-*l-h*) from the grave.

36 Donald C. Polaski has recently argued that this verse is not only consonant with the broader chapter (and therefore not a later interpolation), but that the focus of the passage is squarely upon the restoration of Israel. Thus Polaski: "The most telling piece of evidence… is the focus of ch. 26 on corporate bodies, including 'national' groupings [comp. 26:2, 9, 10, 11, 15, 16–18, and 20–1]" (Polaski 2001, 214). Several other exegetes concur with Polaski's assessment (e.g., Doyle 2000, 304–05 and Collins 1998, 25).

37 In the Septuagintal traditions, for instance, the focus is more explicitly on the act of rising (note the renderings ἀναστήσονται [*anastēsontai*] and ἐγερθήσονται [*egerthēsontai*] for the MT יחיו [*yihyw*] and יקומון [*yequmun*]). Wright suggests that during the Hellenistic period this passage was understood as referring to resurrection (Wright 2003, 116–18). Alternatively, the MT's third reference to those who will live again ("awake and sing for joy, oh dwellers of the dust" [הקיצו ורננו שכני עפר, *haqitsu veranenu shokney 'afar*]) is translated "and those in the earth/land will rejoice" (καὶ εὐφρανθήσονται οἱ ἐν τῇ γῇ [*kai euphranthēsontai hoi en tē gē*]). Given this shift away from the actual description of "rising," at least one

modern commentator has argued that the Greek text looks ahead to those who will survive the judgment in the land (cf. Cavallin 1974, 106–07).

38   Such a tendency is compounded by the presence of other motifs and themes that are representative of later resurrection descriptions (e.g., the affirmation of cosmic catastrophic destruction [Isa. 24], the promise that yhwh will destroy death [Isa. 25:8]), which in turn betray other image schemata that structure resurrection conceptualizations (see discussion below).

39   For an overview of the PATH schema, see Lakoff and Johnson (1999, 32–34). My Diagram 3 is adapted from Lakoff and Johnson (1999, 33).

40   Collins rightly sees this as referring primarily to the anticipated end of the present crisis (i.e., the Antiochian conflict) but also as drawing upon a "mythic pattern," attested within Hebrew tradition, which is concerned with the destruction and restoration of Israel (Collins 1993, 389). Not surprisingly, such a mythic pattern is littered with tight correlations between UP–DOWN and SOURCE–PATH–GOAL image schematic structures. An excellent example is Isa. 14:1–20, which speaks of Judah's return from exile. The passage stresses the abasement (e.g., ירד, *y-r-d* and נפל, *n-ph-l*—14:11–12, 15) of the king of Babylon, a kind of setting right of the cosmic order such that the exiles who were once under foreign rule will one day return from exile and be themselves rulers (14:2). The entire passage is premised upon an UP–DOWN interplay where the downfall of the king of Babylon is juxtaposed with the elevation of Israel to a place of political independence. This restoration manifests the HAVING CONTROL IS UP/BEING SUBJECT TO CONTROL IS DOWN metaphors (cf. Lakoff and Johnson 1980, 15), articulated here in relation to the metaphor (RETURN TO THE) LAND IS UP (cf. 14:1). This entire UP–DOWN drama is envisioned as a promised future event (GOAL), and thus is yet to come (14:1). Though Isa. 14 is not explicitly identifiable within Dan. 12:1–3, the shared coupling of the UP–DOWN and SOURCE–PATH–GOAL image schemata constitutes the shared mythic ideal of future redemption in the face of current calamity.

41   Lakoff and Johnson note that one of the primary metaphors that the human animal uses to conceptualize purposes is the PURPOSES ARE DESTINATIONS metaphor, which is built upon the PATH schema (Lakoff and Johnson 1999, 52–53). The primary experiences from which this metaphor arise are, as Lakoff and Johnson suggest, embodied experiences such as "reaching destinations throughout everyday life and thereby achieving purposes (e.g., if you want a drink, you have to go to the water cooler)" (Lakoff and Johnson 1999, 53). In *2 Macc.*, and other period literature too, martyrdom is acceptable precisely because natural death is not an end in and of itself. Rather, natural death is only one step along the temporal path (i.e., PATH) toward resurrection (i.e., GOAL). The same idea is found in other period literature too (e.g., Collins rightly notes that "Daniel 10–12... provides a *rationale* for martyrdom.... The hope for salvation is beyond death" [Collins 1993, 403, emphasis added]).

42   Wis. 5 presumably looks ahead to a judgment where the righteous and the wicked will receive their respective recompense. The text does not speak of resurrection, but does affirm the immortality of the righteous (cf. Cavallin 1974, 126–34; Nickelsburg 2006, 112–15).

43   In Dan. 12:3 it is said that the wise will be "like" (כ, *k*) the stars and the brightness of the sky (v. 3a, b); the כ, *k* here is certainly comparative but could also be understood, using Williams's categories, as an assertive expression of identity (i.e., ontological change—Williams [1976], §§256 and 261). The Greek translations of Dan. 12:3

retains the same comparative quality—the Old Greek uses ὡς (*hōs*—v. 3a) and ὡσεί (*hōsei*—v. 3b), θ' uses only ὡς (*hōs*—v. 3a, b).

44 Similar to Daniel, in the *Epistle* the righteous are said to shine and appear "like" (ὡσεί [*hōsei*]) the stars of heaven (104:2), and later called "companions" of the angels of heaven (104:6, Ethiopic text only). The references to angels in 104:4 and 6 are only found in the Ethiopic text—for v. 6, Stuckenbruck attributes the omission to *homoioarcton* (Stuckenbruck 2007, 568); for v. 4 the situation is more difficult, though Stuckenbruck suggests the reference to angels was found in the Greek *Vorlage* (Stuckenbruck 2007, 566–67).

45 Lakoff and Johnson highlight this experience, providing examples such as changing a log into a canoe, or changing lead into gold (Lakoff and Johnson 1999, 208–09).

46 For example, CHANGE can be understood in terms of directionality (TURNING), substitution (REPLACEMENT), and forceful alteration (MAKING)—see especially Lakoff and Johnson (1999, 206–11).

47 Like the other schemata examined here, the CONTAINER schema arises from human embodiment; thus according to Johnson, "Our encounter with containment and boundedness is one of the most pervasive features of our bodily experience.... From the beginning, we experience constant physical containment in our surroundings (those things that envelope us). We move in and out of rooms, clothes, vehicles, and numerous kinds of bounded spaces. We manipulate objects, placing them in containers (cups, boxes, cans, bags etc.). In each of these cases there are repeatable spatial and temporal organizations. In other words, there are typical schemata for physical containment" (Johnson 1987, 21). My Diagram 6 is adapted from Lakoff and Johnson (1999, 32).

48 This builds upon Lakoff and Johnson's STATES ARE LOCATIONS metaphor, where they define "locations" as "bounded regions in space. Each bounded region has an interior, an exterior, and a boundary" (Lakoff and Johnson 1999, 180). Earlier in the same work, Lakoff and Johnson explicitly define the CONTAINER schema as denoting "a bounded region in space" (Lakoff and Johnson 1999, 31). In my analysis I am stressing the CONTAINER image schematic structure of the STATES ARE LOCATIONS metaphor.

49 So Lakoff and Johnson, who characterize the CHANGE IS MOVEMENT metaphor as "a change of state as a movement from one bounded region in space to another" (Lakoff and Johnson 1999, 183–84).

50 The schematic structure mapped here should not be taken as a definitive articulation of what constitutes second temple Jewish resurrection thinking. It rather functions as a recurrent gestalt structure that underscores many understandings of resurrection. It should be noted, as I do here in the conclusion, that this structure stands alongside (and even blends with) other resurrection descriptions so as to constitute only one mode of resurrection thinking among many. That said, while the schematic underpinnings of the motifs and themes examined in this chapter perhaps constitute the primary ways that resurrection is conceptualized in pre-70 CE Jewish thinking, we must remain open to other developments and nuances.

51 The association centers primarily on the use of the word "abhorrence" (דראון, *deraʾon*), which in the HB occurs only in Dan. 12:2 and Isa. 66:24. In its Isaianic context the focus is specifically on dead corpses, which cues many exegetes to intertextually read Dan. 12:2 as referring to corporeal resurrection (e.g., Cavallin 1974, 27). Others stress the presumed Isa. 26:19 backgrounds, which speaks of dead bodies rising (e.g., Nickelsburg 2006, 38). We should not forget, however, that

intertextual connections are not fixed but are always constructed by the reading community. If one removes the Isaianic background, such corporeal conclusions cannot be sustained. Despite this, still others find in Dan. 12:2 references to corporeality without relying upon Isaianic traditions; so Wright, who strongly asserts "there is little doubt that [Dan. 12:2–3] refers to concrete, bodily resurrection" (Wright 2003, 109).

52 The argument could of course be made that Dan. 12:3 deals more with the concept of exaltation rather resurrection, and while this may indeed be the case, we should not make too firm of a distinction between the two.

53 This chapter has only briefly touched on this point (see note 16). It is worth noting, however, that notions of PROXIMITY are inherent in many of the traditions examined in this chapter; for example, resurrection often results in the reconciliation of protagonists with the Lord (e.g., *2 Macc.* 7:33; *1 En.* 62:14, 16), with one's family (e.g., *2 Macc.* 7:29), and even with the broader kin-group (e.g., *1 En.* 90:33).

Chapter 8

1 For a traditional generative linguistic analysis of the structure of musical compositions see Jackendoff and Lerdahl (1982).

2 Lawson and McCauley (1990) in fact adopt the concept of *thematic roles* from Chomskyan syntax, which belong rather to the syntax–semantics interface, and not so much to syntax proper. Representing these roles as nodes in a tree is Lawson and McCauley's unprecedented innovation. In fact, linguistics employs trees to derive the temporal order of the words in a sentence: the linear word order in a sentence corresponds to the *left-to-right* order of the final nodes (the "leaves," which are the words) in the syntactic tree describing that sentence. We shall see ample linguistic examples in the section "Constituents in syntax." Conversely, it is the *vertical* (top-down) dimension which maps the temporal order of the rituals in the trees of Lawson and McCauley. In short, the way Lawson and McCauley adopt and adapt linguistic notions and formalisms to religious rituals is not as faithful as Staal's and mine.

3 *Counterintuitive* here understood in the technical sense suggested by Boyer (2002).

4 Note the importance of negative data, that is, of ungrammatical sentences: without them, there would be no way to restrict the grammar. Namely, a grammar according to which "just anything goes" (according to which any sentence is grammatical) would perfectly predict the grammaticality of a data set including only positive data (grammatical sentences).

5 According to textbooks, the safest way to perform the substitution test is to replace constituents using pro-forms: replace NPs with pronouns, prepositional phrases (PPs) with pro-adverbs (such as *here* or *then*), and VPs with pro-verbs (such as *does, did*).

6 A sentence such as "(John loved) and (Jack hated) that girl" seems to prove that the subject and the verb (but not the object) would form one constituent. This conclusion contradicts the basic structure proposed in (4) in which the object joins the verb *before* the subject. The solution is to suppose that in both clauses the object is moved to the right periphery of the sentence, leaving behind a trace, similar to what happens in sentence (5b) and in (6). Hence, the proposed structure is: "((John (loved [trace]) and (Jack (hated [trace])) that girl)."

7   Linguists differentiate between mandatory *complements* and optional *adjuncts*. In the case of a transitive verb, for instance, the subject and the object are complements, whereas time and location are adjuncts. Syntactic theories propose different structural representations for complements and for adjuncts. For the present purpose, however, this differentiation will not bring us any further, and so we shall ignore adjuncts. So we shall do, moreover, with respect to several further subtleties and abstract concepts introduced by contemporary syntax.

8   The word "meaning" is used here only to develop the parallelism to linguistic methodology. I do not want to enter the issue of "ritual meaning" in general: as emphasized earlier, we presently focus solely on form.

9   Also called *arvit*.

10 Besides the details of all parts, certain further elements are also neglected for the sake of simplicity. These are among others Hallel and the different versions of Kaddish. Working out all these details, which are probably of interest only to a reader familiar with Jewish liturgy, should be the subject of a larger work to be written in the future. Probably the *Artscroll Siddur* is nowadays the most comprehensible and most easily available Jewish prayer book (*siddur*) with English translation and explanations, but any other traditional Ashkenazi prayer book for everyday use (i.e., not a *machzor* for holidays) might help the reader follow the details of our discussion.

11 Also called as *Shemone Esrei* or *Tefilla*.

12 The cantor repeats the *Amida* and includes certain additions into it if a quorum of ten adults (a *minyan*) is present, but not during the *Maariv*. On Friday evening, however, a "short summary" of the *Amida* follows the individual's silent prayer.

13 Further minor changes have to be applied here and there, similarly to the conjugation changes in sentences (3a) and (3c), if those sentences were written in the present tense or in a different language.

14 The term *Lectio* refers to catholic liturgy, which follows an overall structure similar to (10): introduction (including the *ritus paenitentiales*), lectio (*liturgia verbi*), "sacrifice" (Eucharist in Christianity; cf. to the *Amida*'s corresponding to the Temple sacrifice in Judaism), and the closing parts.

15 Observe that if these *Yom Kippur* services are seen as elliptical structures, then the omission of *Aleinu* can also serve as an argument for *Aleinu* being a constituent in itself.

16 The *Simchat Torah hakafot* form an expanded version of the Torah reading liturgy, even though a few communities do not actually read from the Torah scroll on that evening. Note, moreover, that the same observation applies to reading from further biblical books (*Esther, Lamentations* etc.) on different occasions (such as Purim or *Tisha be-Av*) always following the evening *Amida*, and before the Closing section. This practice contrasts reading the *haftara* (passage from the Prophets) following the Torah reading but before the *Amida* of Mincha on fast days (including *Yom Kippur*).

17 Further research might determine which factor drives the choice: Is the Torah reading moved and not the *Shma*, because the Torah reading is longer, or because it is less frequent, or because of practical reasons (it is a communal liturgy unlike the Introduction, the *Shma*, and the silently recited *Amida*)? Similar answers can be given to the question why the two units are not coordinated (put together between the Introduction and the *Amida*): they are very different both in terms of length and the way they take place. An English sentence displaying a similar right movement pushed by the more ponderous of the two objects (the verb's closest sisters) may be: "I saw you yesterday night in the movie and the girl with the white scarf." Note,

finally, that emic answers to these questions exist, for example in halakhic sources, but belong rather to the data to be explained by the cognitive scholar of religion, than to the explanation itself.

18 The history of syntax contains several cases where a structure was re-analyzed in terms of what its head is. For instance, traditional analyses of Noun Phrases viewed the noun as the head, while the determiner (the article, the possessive, the numeral) was believed to be a complement (viz., the specifier). Nowadays, however, the determiner is argued to be the head of the structure, which is hence re-baptized a "Determiner Phrase" or DP, and whose complement is the noun, cf. Abney (1987).

19 Many of contemporary theories of syntax employ abstract heads which are leaves in the syntactic tree that do not correspond to any pronounced word of the sentence. This first attempt to formulate a syntax of liturgy, however, follows simpler, earlier theories. Future work might also argue for a more abstract structure in the case of liturgy, adopting several concepts and ideas of contemporary syntactic theories.

20 Having a service in the evening might have developed from a communal recitation of the evening *Shma* (*bBerakhot* 4b; Idelsohn 1995, 118–19), and hence, the *Maariv Amida* was originally optional. Nevertheless, the fact that the evening *Amida* later became a universal custom (e.g., Maimonides *Mishne Tora, Hilkhot Tefilla* 1:6), hence in practice compulsory, supports its role as the head of the service: the Jewish community must have felt that without an *Amida* the evening service would not have the status of a service. This view is further corroborated by the practice of early *Maariv* services in the summer. This service, including all its parts, is held in order to be able to recite the *Amida* in community before it is too late for children, even if the timing is too early to fulfill the commandment of reciting the evening *Shma*. Therefore, each person must repeat the *Shma* later at home, in its due time, but this recitation is not a service anymore. To conclude, the *Amida* has long been regarded as the central element of the evening service.

21 AMICUS stands for *Automated Motif Discovery in Cultural Heritage and Scientific Communication Texts*. For more information, refer to their website at http://amicus.uvt.nl/.

22 A more detailed analysis of the text shall reveal how different communicative goals are embedded into the form of a blessing, but here we skip this question due to lack of space.

23 Cf. e.g., *yBerakhot* 29ab; *bTa'anit* 2a; *Mek. de rabbi Simeon b. Yohai* 23:25; Maimonides' *Mishne Tora, Hilkhot Tefilla* 1:1. Note the story of Daniel supporting the biblical exegesis in the *Mek. de r. Simeon b. Yohai*, which clarifies the terminology: for the early rabbis, the word *tefilla* here could refer to an established daily prayer, such as the *Amida*, and replaced the service (*avoda*) taking place in the Jerusalem temple, and thus impossible in the diaspora.

24 Lawson and McCauley (1990, 125). The action representation scheme of McCauley and Lawson (2002) has its roots in the thematic roles used in syntax, whose goal is to encode the logical (as opposed to the syntactic) relationship between the elements of a sentence. In the simplest English sentence, the thematic role of the "agent" is realized as the subject of the sentence, the role of the "patient" is syntactically the object, while the "beneficiary" or "recipient" is the indirect object, and so forth. Further thematic roles might be "location," "goal," "instrument" etc. In passive voice, however, the patient becomes the subject of the sentence. Furthermore, different languages might express certain thematic roles using various syntactic constructions (e.g., "I like you" is in French "Tu me plais": the same thematic roles are expressed

by reversing syntactically the subject and the (indirect) object). For a more detailed discussion, refer to Biró (2013).
25 A classic example for the decoupling of syntax and semantics is Chomsky's famous sentence: "Colorless green ideas sleep furiously." This sentence has not been underlined by my computer's spell checker, nor by its grammar checker, for it contains perfect English words (though, some would prefer "colourless"), and its syntax follows the syntactic rules of English. Consequently, even if a structure violates one mental level (for instance, it is void of meaning), it may be perfect on another level (its syntactic structure is acceptable).
26 Actually, feeding is a special case of helping, namely, helping somebody eat.

Chapter 9

1 There are excellent surveys of scholarly suggestions in most scholarly commentaries, for example Brown (1982, 411–16, 610–19), Kruse (2000, 126–23, 193–94). The innovation of this chapter is that I evaluate the proposal in the light of behavioral research.
2 Westcott (1886, 23–26, 104–108), Plummer (1886, 82–84, 124–28), when expounding 1:8–10 and 3:6–9, write solely of the relation between the individual and God.
3 The "heuristic" use of the behavioral sciences to structure our interpretation of history is well established, see for example Philip F. Esler, "Social-Scientific Models in Biblical Interpretation" in *Ancient Israel: The Old Testament in Its Social Context*, ed. Philip F. Esler (London: SCM, 2005), 3–14; Theissen 2007, 20–32.
4 NIV translates 3:6 "*keeps on* sinning" and 3:9 "*will continue to* sin… *go on* sinning" (emphasis added).
5 Practices of public confession (1:9) and intercession (5:16–17) were probably vital in these processes.
6 This interpretation has since been quite rare, see Marshall (2008, 226–28).
7 Ebrard does not himself point out that the distinction between intentional and unintentional sin was important in Jewish halakha, but some later commentators do, for example Schnackenberg (1992, 249–50), Stephen Smalley (1984, 297–98). However, Schnackenberg and Smalley rightly do not think that the text of 1 Jn supports the conclusion that the author has intentional sin in mind.
8 Cf. the Holiness Code, where sexual immorality (e.g., Lev. 18:24–30), idolatry (e.g., Lev. 19:31; 20:1–3) and bloodshed (e.g., Num. 35:33–34) are considered particularly grave; see Klawans (2000, 26–30).
9 It should however be noted that the severity of a transgression tends to affect the willingness to forgive less than, for instance, the degree of intentionality and repentance.
10 Law, *Tests of Life*, 141, suggests that sins unto death are sins of those who "severed themselves from Christ *and from the Christian community*" (emphasis added). Similarly for example Brown (1982, 617–19), Painter (2002, 317–20), Scholer (1975), Smalley (1984, 297–99).
11 His analysis is similar to Law, *Tests of Life*, who thinks that the three "tests" of a Christian in 1 Jn are practices of righteousness, love, and belief.
12 Centola and Macy show that in cases of "complex contagion" where people typically need to be exposed to an idea repeatedly in order to become convinced, the number

13 In 4:7, ἀγαπῶμεν [agapōmen] may be understood as either indicative or subjunctive, but most translations assume that it is subjunctive.
14 In 1:9, ὁμολογῶμεν [homologōmen] probably refers to public confession, see Brown (1982, 208).
15 Redactional theories (I. Howard Marshall, *Epistles of John*, 27–31, for an overview) may be used to explain the contradiction between 1:8–10; 5:16–17 and 3:6, 9; 5:18. However, even if the text has been redacted, the final redactor probably did not leave the text with a contradiction by stupidity or accident. Therefore, redactional theories cannot explain why the final redactor allowed the contradiction to stand. Cf. Schnelle (2010, 180–81).
16 Cf. 1QS III.13–IV.26. The parallel is not perfect, however, since 1QS IV.23–4 mentions briefly that the Spirit of Truth and the Spirit of Error struggles in man. Still, each individual is entirely dominated by one of the spirits and is not described as experiencing this struggle.
17 NRSV translates יִקַּח (*yikakh*) "will heed," probably in order to capture that the Hebrew imperfect indicative can be used to express an intention or a wish, see Gesenius (1910), §107.4.(a).
18 To be fair, Strecker (1996, 102–03) does write briefly that the statement in 3:9 is an ideal, although without coordinating it clearly with the hortative function.
19 The chapter originally appeared in French. The preface of the English translation wrongly states that the chapter was written by Lyonnet.
20 1 Jn clearly has an eschatological expectation (2:8, 17–18).
21 Dodd's suggestion has a precursor in Law, *Tests of Life*, 222–30, who argues that 1 Jn engages in polemic exaggeration in 3:6, 9.
22 Cf. *mAbot*. 3:16: "The world is judged by grace, yet all is according to the excess of works."

Chapter 10

1 Further, groups can be defined for different purposes and people are usually members of multiple groups. In terms of network theory, any group to which I belong is only a subset of the interconnected nodes of my friends and acquaintances and their friends and acquaintances.
2 On the importance of strong social ties see Duling (2013).
3 I do not go into details about the possibility that 2 Cor. might contain two or more letters. See Thrall (2000, 47–50).
4 Note that the notion of "distance" has to be considered in terms of traveling opportunities. For example, maritime connections reduced distance taken in this sense.
5 The beginnings of Mithraism are hotly debated and it is not my task here to discuss alternative hypotheses.
6 Stark (1996, 20–21) himself refers to social network theory and suggests that Christians had "open networks." A major difference between the Stark's notion of

open networks and my use of "weak ties" is that open network links are directed from within Christianity toward outsiders. In my theory, weak social ties are found within the Christian movement itself.

7 The concept of attractors is borrowed from system theory: some cultural bits occupy "attractor positions" in the space of possible combination of traits. Thus "attraction" in Sperber's theory does not mean that people find some cultural forms "attractive" (as some popular interpretations of the theory suggest), although this can be the consequence of some cultural concept or behavior occupying an attractor position. The deeper analysis of the concept of attractors is beyond the scope of this chapter.

8 Various contextual factors modulate the effect of counterintuitiveness, including narrative context (Gonce et al. 2006; Upal et al. 2007), imagery (Slone et al. 2007), cultural background (Boyer and Ramble 2001), and the involvement of agency (Steenstra 2005; Porubanova et al. 2014).

9 Well-documented genetic adaptations to culture include the shape of the human larynx (an adaptation to language) and the ability to digest milk in adults (at least in many populations).

10 For the ritual use of formulas see (Uro 2013b, 67–72, 2016, 170–75).

11 The concept of symbolic identity markers is related to the theory of costly signaling (Irons 2001; Bulbulia and Sosis 2011) but there are also differences between them. Signaling theory does not deal with large, anonymous groups, although "charismatic signaling" is an attempt in that direction.

Bibliography

Abney, Steven Paul (1987), *The English Noun Phrase in Its Sentential Aspect*. PhD Dissertation, MIT.
Achenbach, Reinhard (2003), *Die Vollendung der Tora: Studien zur Redaktionsgeschichte des Numeribuches im Kontext von Hexateuch und Pentateuch*. Wiesbaden: Harrassowitz.
Achenbach, Reinhard, Rainer Albertz, and Jakob Wöhrle, eds (2011), *The Foreigner and the Law: Perspectives from the Hebrew Bible and the Ancient Near East*. Wiesbaden: Harrassowitz.
Ackerman, Susan (2002), "The Personal Is Political: Covenantal and Affectionate Love ('aheb, 'ahaba) in the Hebrew Bible." *Vetus Testamentum* 52(4): 437–58.
Alden, Robert L. (1997), "שחר," in Willem Van Gemeren (ed.), *New International Dictionary of Old Testament Theology and Exegesis*, vol. 4, 83–84. Grand Rapids, MI: Zondervan Publishing House.
Alford, Henry ([1861] 1878), *The Greek Testament*, vol. 4. 5th edn. Boston, MA: Lee & Shepard.
Alt, Albrecht (1953), *Kleine Schriften zur Geschichte des Volkes Israels*, vol. 1. München: C.H. Beck'sche Verlagsbuchhandlung.
Anderson, Benedict (1991), *Imagined Communities: Reflections on the Origin and Spread of Nationalism*. Revised Edition. London and New York: Verso.
Anonymous (2010), "Cognitive Neuroscience: How Self-Touch Relieves Pain." *Nature* 467(7315): 503.
Arrindell, Willem A., Mary J. Pickersgill, Harald Merckelbach, Angélique M. Ardon, and Frieda C. Cornet (1991), "Phobic Dimensions: III. Factor Analytic Approaches to the Study of Common Phobic Fears: An Updated Review of Findings Obtained with Adult Subjects." *Advances in Behaviour Research and Therapy* 13: 73–130.
Atran, Scott (1989), "Basic Conceptual Domains." *Mind & Language* 4(1–2): 7–16.
Atran, Scott (1990), *Cognitive Foundations of Natural History: Towards an Anthropology of Science*. Cambridge: Cambridge University Press.
Augoustinos, Martha, Iain Walker, and Ngaire Donaghue (2006), *Social Cognition: An Integrated Introduction*. 2nd edn. Thousand Oaks, CA: SAGE.
Aune, David E. (1994), "Mastery of the Passions: Philo, 4 Maccabees and Earliest Christianity," in Wendy E. Helleman (ed.), *Hellenization Revisited: Shaping a Christian Response within the Greco-Roman World*, 125–58. Lanham, MD: University Press of America.
Axelrod, Robert (1997), *The Complexity of Cooperation: Agent-Based Models of Competition and Collaboration*. Princeton, NJ: Princeton University Press.
Azari, Nina P., and Dieter Birnbacher (2004), "The Role of Cognition and Feeling in Religious Experience." *Zygon: Journal of Religion & Science* 39(4): 901–17.
Bainbridge, William Sims (2006), *God from the Machine: Artificial Intelligence Models of Religious Cognition*. Cognitive Science of Religion Series. Lanham, MD: AltaMira Press.
Balch, David L. (1981), *Let Wives Be Submissive: The Domestic Code in 1 Peter*. Chico, CA: Scholars Press.

Bandura, Albert (1999), "Moral Disengagement in the Perpetration of Inhumanities." *Personality and Social Psychology Review* 3: 193–209.
Bar-Efrat, Shimon (1996), *I Samuel: Introduction and Commentary*. Tel-Aviv and Jerusalem: Am Oved and Magnes. Series: Mikra LeYisraʾel, A Biblical Commentary for Israel.
Barrett, Justin L. (2004), *Why Would Anyone Believe in God?* Cognitive Science of Religion Series. Walnut Creek, CA: AltaMira Press.
Barrett, Justin L. (2008), "Coding and Quantifying Counterintuitiveness in Religious Concepts: Theoretical and Methodological Reflections." *Method & Theory in the Study of Religion* 20(4): 308–38.
Barrett, Justin L., and Milanie A. Nyhof (2001), "Spreading Non-natural Concepts: The Role of Intuitive Conceptual Structures in Memory and Transmission of Cultural Materials." *Journal of Cognition and Culture* 1(1): 69–100.
Barsalou, Lawrence (1987), "The Instability of Graded Structure: Implications for the Nature of Concepts," in Ulric Neisser (ed.), *Concepts and Conceptual Development: Ecological and Intellectual Factors in Categorization*, 101–40. Cambridge: Cambridge University Press.
Barsalou, Lawrence W. (1999), "Perceptual Symbol Systems." *Behavioral and Brain Sciences* 22(4): 577.
Barsalou, Lawrence W. (2003), "Abstraction in Perceptual Symbol Systems." *Philosophical Transaction of the Royal Society B Biological Sciences* 358(1435): 1177–87.
Barsalou, Lawrence W. (2008), "Grounded Cognition." *Annual Review of Psychology* 59(1): 617–45.
Barsalou, Lawrence W., and Katja Wiemer-Hastings (2005), "Situating Abstract Concepts," in Diane Pecher and Rolf A. Zwaan (eds), *Grounding Cognition: The Role of Perception and Action in Memory, Language, and Thought*, 129–64. New York: Cambridge University Press.
Barsalou, W. Lawrence, W. Kyle Simmons, Aron K. Barbey, and Christine D. Wilson (2003), "Grounding Conceptual Knowledge in Modality-Specific Systems." *Trends in Cognitive Sciences* 7(2): 84.
Barth, Gerhard, Guenther Bornkamm, and Heinz Joachim Held (1963), *Tradition and Interpretation in Matthew*. Translated by Percy Scott. London: SCM Press.
Bartle, Philip F. W. (1983), "The Universe Has Three Souls: Notes on Translating Akan Culture." *Journal of Religion in Africa* 14: 55–114.
Bartlett, Frederic (1932), *Remembering: A Study in Experimental and Social Psychology*. Cambridge: Cambridge University Press.
Bauckham, Richard (1998), *The Fate of the Dead: Studies on the Jewish and Christian Apocalypses*. Supplements to Novum Testamentum, 93. Leiden: Brill.
Baumgarten, Joseph M. (1999), "D. Tohorot," in Joseph M. Baumgarten, Torleif Elgvin, Esther Eshel, Erik Larson, Manfred R. Lehmann, Stephen Pfann, and Lawrence H. Schiffman (eds), *Qumran Cave 4, XXV: Halakhic Texts*, 79–122. Discoveries in the Judaean Desert, 35. Oxford: Clarendon Press.
Bechtel, William, Adele Abrahamsen, and George Graham (2001), "Cognitive Science: History," in Neil J. Smelser and Paul B. Baltes (eds), *International Encyclopedia of the Social & Behavioral Sciences*, 2154–58. Amsterdam: Elsevier.
Beck, Roger (1996), "The Mysteries of Mithras," in John S. Kloppenborg and Stephen G. Wilson (eds), *Voluntary Associations in the Graeco-Roman World*, 176–85. London: Routledge.
Beck, Roger (2006), "On Becoming a Mithraist: New Evidence for the Propagation of the Mysteries," in Leif E. Vaage (ed.), *Religious Rivalries in the Early Roman Empire:*

Competition and Coexistence among Jews, Pagans and Christians, 175–94. Waterloo and Lancaster: Wilfrid Laurier University Press.

Beck, Roger (2006), *The Religion of the Mithras Cult in the Roman Empire: Mysteries of the Unconquered Sun*. Oxford and New York: Oxford University Press.

Becker, Howard S. (1997), *Outsiders: Studies in the Sociology of Deviance*. 3rd edn. New York and London: Free Press.

Bering, Jesse M. (2002), "Intuitive Conceptions of Dead Agents' Minds: The Natural Foundations of Afterlife Beliefs as Phenomenological Boundary." *Journal of Cognition and Culture* 2(4): 263–308.

Bering, Jesse M. (2006), "The Folk Psychology of Souls." *Behavioral and Brain Sciences* 29(5): 453–62.

Bering, Jesse M. (2011), *The Belief Instinct: The Psychology of Souls, Destiny, and the Meaning of Life*. London: Nicholas Brealey.

Berko, Jean (1958), "The Child's Learning of English Morphology." *Word* 14: 150–77.

Bernburg, Jón Gunnar, Marvin D. Krohn, and Craig J. Rivera (2006), "Official Labeling, Criminal Embeddedness, and Subsequent Delinquency: A Longitudinal Test of Labeling Theory." *Journal of Research in Crime & Delinquency* 43(1): 67–88.

Beuken, Willem A. M. (1991), "Isaiah Chapters LXV–LXVI: Trito-Isaiah and the Closure of the Book of Isaiah," in John A. Emerton (ed.), *Congress Volume Leuven 1989*, 204–21. Leiden: Brill.

Biale, David (2007), *Blood and Belief: The Circulation of a Symbol between Jews and Christians*. Berkeley: University of California Press.

Biró, Tamás (2013), "Is Judaism Boring? On the Lack of Counterintuitive Agents in Jewish Rituals," in István Czachesz and Risto Uro (eds), *Mind, Morality and Magic: Cognitive Science Approaches in Biblical Studies*, 120–43. Durham: Acumen.

Boda, Mark J. (2005), "Terrifying the Horns: Persia and Babylon in Zechariah 1:7–6:15," *Catholic Biblical Quarterly* 67: 22–41.

Borg, Alexander (1999), "Linguistic and Ethnographic Observations on the Color Categories of the Negev Bedouin," in Alexander Borg (ed.), *The Language of Color in the Mediterranean: An Anthology on Linguistic and Ethnographic Aspects of Color Terms*, 121–47. Stockholm: Almqvist and Wiksell International.

Bowden, Hugh (2010), *Mystery Cults of the Ancient World*. Princeton, NJ: Princeton University Press.

Bowling, A. (1980), "לאך," in Robert L. Harris, Gleason Archer, and Bruce K. Waltke (eds), *Theological Wordbook of the Old Testament*, vol. 1, 464, 465. Chicago, IL: Moody.

Boyer, Pascal (1994a), *The Naturalness of Religious Ideas: A Cognitive Theory of Religion*. Berkeley: University of California Press.

Boyer, Pascal (1994b), "Cognitive Constraints on Cultural Representations: Natural Ontologies and Religious Ideas," in Lawrence A. Hirschfeld and Susan A. Gelman (eds), *Mapping the Mind: Domain Specificity in Cognition and Culture*, 391–411. Cambridge, Eng.: Cambridge University Press.

Boyer, Pascal (2002), *Religion Explained: The Human Instincts That Fashion Gods, Spirits and Ancestors*. London: Vintage.

Boyer, Pascal, and Charles Ramble (2001), "Cognitive Templates for Religious Concepts: Cross-Cultural Evidence for Recall of Counter-Intuitive Representations." *Cognitive Science* 25(4): 535–64.

Boyer, Pascal, and Pierre Liénard (2006), "Why Ritualized Behavior? Precaution Systems and Action Parsing in Developmental, Pathological and Cultural Rituals." *Behavioral and Brain Science* 29(6): 595–612.

Bremmer, Jan N. (2010), "The Rise of the Unitary Soul and Its Opposition to the Body. From Homer to Socrates," in Ludger Jansen, Christoph Jedan, and Christoph Rapp (eds), *Philosophische Anthropologie in der Antike*, 11–29. Frankfurt: Ontos Verlag.
Bremmer, Jan N. (1995), "Pauper or Patroness: The Widow in the Early Christian Church," in Jan N. Bremmer and Lourens P. Van Den Bosch (eds), *Between Poverty and the Pyre: Moments in the History of Widowhood*, 31–57. New York and Ithaca, NY: Snow Lion Publications and Routledge.
Brenner, Athalya (1982), *Colour Terms in the Old Testament*, JSOTSup 21. Sheffield: A and C Black.
Brenner, Athalya (1997), *The Intercourse of Knowledge: On Gendering Desire and 'Sexuality' in the Hebrew Bible*. Biblical Interpretation Series 26. Leiden: Brill.
Brown, Raymond E. (1979), *The Community of the Beloved Disciple: The Life, Loves and Hates of an Individual Church in New Testament Times*. London: Geoffrey Chapman.
Brown, Raymond E. (1982), *The Epistles of John*. Anchor Bible 30. Garden City, NY: Doubleday.
Bulbulia, Joseph A., and Richard Sosis (2011), "Signalling Theory and the Evolution of Religious Cooperation." *Religion* 41(3): 363–88.
Bultmann, Rudolf Karl (1985 [1941]), *Neues Testament und Mythologie: Das Problem der Entmythologisierung der neutestamentlichen Verkündigung*. Beiträge zur evangelischen Theologie. Munich: Chr. Kaiser.
Burton, Marilyn E. (2017a), "Cognitive Methodology in the Study of an Ancient Language: Impediments and Possibilities," in Keith Dyer and Tarsee Li (eds), *From Ancient Manuscripts to Modern Dictionaries: Select Studies in Aramaic, Hebrew, and Greek*, 213–26. Piscataway, NJ: Gorgias Press.
Burton, Marilyn E. (2017b), *The Semantics of Glory: A Cognitive, Corpus-Based Approach to Hebrew Word Meaning*. Studia Semitica Neerlandica 68. Leiden: Brill.
Butterworth, Mike (1992), *Structure and the Book of Zechariah*, JSOTSup 130. Sheffield: Sheffield Academic Press.
Callaway, Mary C. (1999), "Canonical Criticism," in Stephen R. Haynes and Steven L. McKenzie (eds), *To Each Its Own Meaning: An Introduction to Biblical Criticisms and Their Applications*. Louisville, KY: Westminster John Knox Press.
Campbell, Anthony J., and Mark A. O'Brien (2005), *Rethinking the Pentateuch: Prolegomena to the Theology of Ancient Israel*. Louisville, KY: Westminster John Knox.
Cavallin, Hans Clemens Caesarius (1974), *Life after Death: Paul's Argument for the Resurrection of the Dead in 1 Cor 15; Part 1: An Enquiry into the Jewish Background*. Coniectanea Biblica: New Testament Series, 7. Lund: Gleerup.
Centola, Damon, and Michael Macy (2007), "Complex Contagions and the Weakness of Long Ties." *American Journal of Sociology* 113: 702–34.
Chalupa, Aleš (2015), "GEHIR – Generative Historiography of Religion Project." *Masaryk University of Brno*. http://gehir.phil.muni.cz/.
Charlesworth, James H. (2006a), "Prolegomenous Reflections toward a Taxonomy of Resurrection Texts (1QH^a, 1En, 4Q521, Paul, Luke, the Fourth Gospel, and Psalm 30)," in Ian H. Henderson and Gerbern S. Oegema (eds), *The Changing Face of Judaism, Christianity, and Other Greco-Roman Religions in Antiquity*, 237–64. Studien zu den Jüdischen Schriften aus hellenistisch-römischer Zeit, 2. Gütersloh: Gütersloher Verlagshaus.
Charlesworth, James H. (2006b), "Where Does the Concept of Resurrection Appear and How Do We Know That?" in James H. Charlesworth, et al. (eds), *Resurrection: The*

Origin and Future of a Biblical Doctrine. Faith and Scholarship Colloquies Series, 1–21. New York: T & T Clark.

Childs, Brevard S. (1979), *Introduction to the Old Testament as Scripture*. Philadelphia: Fortress Press.

Chmiel, Jerzy (1979). "Semantics of the Resurrection," in Elizabeth A. Livingstone (ed.), *Studia Biblica 1978: I. Papers on Old Testament and Related Themes*, 59–64. Journal for the Study of the Old Testament: Supplement Series, 11; Sheffield: Dept. of Biblical Studies, University of Sheffield.

Choksy, Jamsheed (2005), *Purity and Pollution in Zoroastrianism: Triumph over Evil*. Austin: University of Texas Press.

Cholewiński, Alfred (1976), *Heiligkeitsgesetz und Deuteronomium: Eine vergleichende Studie*. Analecta Biblica, 66. Rome: Biblical Institute Press.

Chomsky, Noam (1957), *Syntactic Structures*. The Hague: Mouton.

Chomsky, Noam (1968), *Language and Mind*. New York: Harcourt, Brace & World.

Clark, Andy (2001), *Mindware: An Introduction to the Philosophy of Cognitive Science*. New York and Oxford: Oxford University Press.

Clark, Andy, and David J. Chalmers (1998), "The Extended Mind." *Analysis* 58(1): 7–19.

Clauss, Manfred (2000), *The Roman Cult of Mithras: The God and His Mysteries*. New York: Routledge.

Cohen, Henry, and Claire Lefebvre (2005), *Handbook of Categorization in Cognitive Science*, 1st edn. New York: Elsevier Science.

Collins, Billie Jean (2002), "Necromancy, Fertility and the Dark Earth: The Use of Ritual Pits in Hittite Cult," in Paul Mirecki and Marvin Mayer (eds), *Magic and Ritual in the Ancient World*, 224–41. Leiden: Brill.

Collins, John Jean (1993), *Daniel: A Commentary on the Book of Daniel*. Hermeneia. Minneapolis, MN: Fortress Press.

Collins, John Jean (1998), *The Apocalyptic Imagination: An Introduction to Jewish Apocalyptic Literature*, 2nd edn. Grand Rapids, MI: Eerdmans.

Collins, John Jean (2009), "The Angelic Life," in Turid Karlsen Seim and Jorunn Økland (eds), *Metamorphoses: Resurrection, Body, and Transformative Practices in Early Christianity*. Ekstasis: Religious Experience from Antiquity to the Middle Ages, vol. 1, 291–310. Berlin: Walter de Gruyter.

Cosmides, Leda, and John Tooby (1987), "From Evolution to Behavior: Evolutionary Psychology as the Missing Link," in John Dupré (ed.), *The Latest on the Best: Essays on Evolution and Optimality*, 277–306. Cambridge, MA: MIT Press.

Cosmides, Leda, and John Tooby (1994), "Origins of Domain Specificity: The Evolution of Functional Organization," in Lawrence A. Hirschfeld and Susan A. Gelman (eds), *Mapping the Mind: Domain Specificity in Cognition and Culture*, 85–116. Cambridge; New York: Cambridge University Press.

Croft, William, and D. Alan Cruse (2004), *Cognitive Linguistics*. Cambridge Textbooks in Linguistics. Cambridge: Cambridge University Press.

Crossan, John Dominic (1998), *The Birth of Christianity: Discovering What Happened in the Years Immediately after the Execution of Jesus*. San Francisco, CA: HarperSanFrancisco.

Cushman, Fiery, Joshua Knobe, and Walter Sinnott-Armstrong (2008), "Moral Appraisals Affect Doing/Allowing Judgments." *Cognition* 108: 281–89.

Czachesz, István (1995), "Narrative Logic and Christology in Luke-Acts." *Communio viatorum* 37(2): 93–106.

Czachesz, István (2003), "The Gospels and Cognitive Science," in Alasdair A. MacDonald, Michael W. Twomey, and Gerrit J. Reinink (eds), *Learned Antiquity: Scholarship and Society in the Near East, the Greco-Roman World, and the Early Medieval West*, 25-36. Groningen Studies in Cultural Change, 5. Leuven: Peeters.

Czachesz, István (2007a), "'As God Counselled Socrates': Commission Narratives in Cognitive Perspective," in Géza G. Xeravits and Péter Losonczi (eds), *Reflecting Diversity: Historical and Thematical Perspectives in the Jewish and Christian Tradition*, 13-23. Münster and London: LIT Verlag.

Czachesz, István (2007b), "Early Christian Views on Jesus' Resurrection: Toward a Cognitive Psychological Interpretation." *Nederlands Theologisch Tijdschrift* 61(1): 47-59.

Czachesz, István (2007c), "Kontraintuitive Ideen im urchristlichen Denken," in Gerd Theißen and Petra von Gemünden (eds), *Erkennen und Erleben: Beiträge zur psychologischen Erforschung des frühen Christentums*, 197-208. Gütersloh: Gütersloher Verlagshaus.

Czachesz, István (2007d), "Magic and Mind: Toward a Cognitive Theory of Magic, with Special Attention to the Canonical and Apocryphal Acts of the Apostles." *Annali di Storia dell'Esegesi* 24(1): 295-321.

Czachesz, István (2007e), "The Transmission of Early Christian Thought: Toward a Cognitive Psychological Model." *Studies in Religion. Sciences Religieuses* 36(1): 65-84.

Czachesz, István (2008), "The Promise of the Cognitive Science of Religion for Biblical Studies." *CSSR Bulletin* 37(4): 102-05.

Czachesz, István (2009a), "Rewriting and Textual Fluidity in Antiquity: Exploring the Sociocultural and Psychological Context of Earliest Christian Literacy," in Jitse H. F. Dijkstra, Justin E. A. Kroesen, and Yme B. Kuiper (eds), *Myths, Martyrs, and Modernity: Studies in the History of Religions in Honour of Jan N. Bremmer*, 425-45. Leiden: Brill.

Czachesz, István (2009b), "Wordt Vervolgd: Apocriefe handelingen van de apostelen." *Schrift* 241(41/1): 31-34.

Czachesz, István (2010a), "Passion and Martyrdom Traditions in the Apocryphal Acts of the Apostles," in Andreas Merkt, Tobias Nicklas, and Joseph Verheyden (eds), *Gelitten, Gestorben, Auferstanden*, 1-20. Tübingen: Mohr Siebeck.

Czachesz, István (2010b), "Explaining Magic: Earliest Christianity as a Test Case," in Luther H. Martin and Jesper Sørensen (eds), *Past Minds: Studies in Cognitive Historiography*, 141-65. London: Equinox.

Czachesz, István (2010c), "Long-Term, Explicit Memory in Rituals." *Journal of Cognition and Culture* 10: 321-33.

Czachesz, István (2011a), "Women, Charity and Mobility in Early Christianity: Weak Links and the Historical Transformation of Religions," in István Czachesz and Tamas Biró (eds), *Changing Minds: Religion and Cognition through the Ages*, 129-54. Leuven: Peeters.

Czachesz, István (2011b), "Theologische Innovation und Sozialstruktur im Urchristentum: Eine kognitive Analyse seiner Ausbreitungsdynamik (Theological Innovation and Social Structure in Earliest Christianity: A Cognitive Analysis of the Dynamics of Its Expansion)." *Evangelische Theologie* 71(4): 259-72.

Czachesz, István (2012), *The Grotesque Body in Early Christian Discourse: Hell, Scatology, and Metamorphosis*. Sheffield: Equinox.

Czachesz, István (2013a), "The Evolution of Religious Systems: Laying the Foundations of a Network Model," in Armin W. Geertz (ed.), *Origins of Religion, Cognition and Culture*, 98-120. London: Equinox.

Czachesz, István (2013b), "Jesus' Religious Experience in the Gospels: Toward a Cognitive Neuroscience Approach," in Petra von Gemünden, David G. Horrell, and Max Küchler (eds), *Jesus – Gestalt und Gestaltungen: Rezeptionen des Galiläers in Wissenschaft, Kirche und Gesellschaft: Festschrift für Gerd Theissen zum 70. Geburtstag*, 569–96. Göttingen: Vandenhoeck & Ruprecht.

Czachesz, István (2015), "Religious Experience in Mediterranean Antiquity: Introduction to the Special Issue." *Journal of Cognitive Historiography* 2(1): 5–13.

Czachesz, István (2017a), *Cognitive Science and the New Testament: A New Approach to Early Christian Research*. Oxford and New York: Oxford University Press.

Czachesz, István (2017b), "Cognitive Science Approaches in Biblical Studies," in Christopher R. Matthews (ed.), *Oxford Bibliographies in Biblical Studies*. New York: Oxford University Press. doi:10.1093/obo/9780195393361-0238.

Czachesz, István (2018a), "Ritual and Transmission," in Risto Uro, Juliette J. Day, Richard E. DeMaris and Rikard Roitto (eds), *The Oxford Handbook of Early Christian Ritual*, 115–33. Oxford: Oxford University Press.

Czachesz, István (2018b), "Evolutionary Theory on the Move: New Perspectives on Evolution in the Cognitive Science of Religion." *Unisinos Journal of Philosophy* 19(3): 263–71.

Czachesz, István, and Risto Uro, eds (2013), *Mind, Morality, and Magic: Cognitive Science Approaches in Biblical Studies*. BibleWorld. Durham: Acumen.

Czachesz, István, and Tamás Biró (2011), *Changing Minds: Religion and Cognition through the Ages*. Groningen Studies in Cultural Change. Leuven: Peeters.

Dalley, Stephanie (1991), *Myths from Mesopotamia: Creation, The Flood, and Others*. Oxford: Oxford University Press.

Damasio, Antonio R. (1994), *Descartes' Error: Emotion, Reason, and the Human Brain*. New York: Grosset/Putnam.

Damasio, Antonio R. (1999), *The Feeling of What Happens: Body and Emotion in the Making of Consciousness*. New York: Harcourt Brace.

Damasio, Antonio R. (2003), *Looking for Spinoza: Joy, Sorrow, and the Human Brain*. Orlando: Harcourt.

D'Andrade, Roy (1990), "Some Propositions about the Relations between Culture and Human Cognition," in James W. Stigler, Richard A. Shweder, and Gilbert Herdt (eds), *Cultural Psychology: Essays on Comparative Human Development*, 65–129. Cambridge: Cambridge University Press.

d'Aquili, Eugene G., Stephanie K. Newberg, and Verushka deMarici (2001), "The Neuropsychological Correlates of Forgiveness," in Michael E. McCullough, Kenneth I. Pargament, and Karel E. Thoresen (eds), *Forgiveness: Theory, Research, and Practice*, 91–110. New York: Guilford Press.

Davies, Stevan L. (1980), *The Revolt of the Widows: The Social World of the Apocryphal Acts*. Carbondale and London: Southern Illinois University Press; Feffer & Simons.

Dawkins, Richard (2006), *The Selfish Gene* (30th anniversary edition). Oxford: Oxford University Press.

Day, John (1996), "The Development of Belief in Life after Death in Ancient Israel," in John Barton and David J. Reimer (eds), *After the Exile: Essays in Honour of Rex Mason*, 231–57. Macon, GA: Mercer University Press.

Deacon, Terence (1997), *The Symbolic Species: The Co-evolution of Language and the Human Brain*. London: Penguin Books.

de Blois, Reinier (2004), "Lexicography and Cognitive Linguistics: Hebrew Metaphors from a Cognitive Perspective," *DavarLogos* 3: 97–116.

Delling, Gerhard (1958), "Josephus und das Wunderbare." *Novum Testamentum* 2: 291–309.
de Vaux, Roland (1964), *Les sacrifices de l'ancien testament*. Les cahiers de la Revue Biblique 1. Paris: Gabalda.
de Waal, Frans B.M. (1996), *Good Natured: The Origins of Right and Wrong in Humans and Other Animals*. Cambridge, MA and London: Harvard University Press.
de Waal, Frans B.M. (2006), *Primates and Philosophers: How Morality Evolved*. The University Center for Human Values Series. Princeton, NJ and Oxford: Princeton University Press.
Dickson, Kwesi A. (1984), *Theology in Africa*. Maryknoll, NY: Orbis.
Dietrich, Jan (2009), *Kollektive Schuld und Haftung: Religions- und rechtgeschichtliche Studien zum Sündenkuhritus des Deuteronomiums und zu verwandten Texten*. Orientalische Religionen in der Antike, 4. Tübingen: Mohr Siebeck.
Dodd, Charles H. (1946), *The Johannine Epistles*. MNTC. London: Hodder and Stoughton.
Donald, Merlin (1991), *Origins of the Modern Mind: Three Stages in the Evolution of Culture and Cognition*. Cambridge, MA: Harvard University Press.
Donald, Merlin (1993), "Précis of Origins of the Modern Mind: Three Stages in the Evolution of Culture and Cognition." *Behavioral and Brain Sciences* 16(4): 737–48.
Doojse, Bertjan, Naomi Ellemersand, and Russell Spears (1999), "Commitment and Intergroup Behaviour," in Naomi Ellemers, Russel Spearsand, and Bertjan Doojse (eds), *Social Identity: Context, Commitment, Content*, 84–106. Oxford: Blackwell.
Douglas, Mary (1993), "The Forbidden Animals in Leviticus." *Journal for the Study of the Old Testament* 59: 3–23.
Douglas, Mary (1995), "Poetic Structure in Leviticus," in David P. Wright, David N. Freedman, and Avi Hurvitz (eds), *Pomegranates and Golden Bells: Studies in Biblical, Jewish, and Near Eastern Ritual, Law, and Literature in Honor of Jacob Milgrom*, 239–56. Winona Lake, IN: Eisenbrauns.
Douglas, Mary (2003), "The Go-away Goat," in Rolf Rendtorff and Robert A. Kugler (eds), *The Book of Leviticus: Composition and Reception*, 121–41. Leiden: Brill.
Downing, F. Gerald (1992), "A Paradigm Perplex: Luke, Matthew and Mark." *New Testament Studies* 38(1): 15–36.
Downing, F. Gerald (2000), *Doing Things with Words in the First Christian Century*. Sheffield: Sheffield Academic Press.
Doyle, Brian (2000), *The Apocalypse of Isaiah Metaphorically Speaking: A Study of the Use, Function and Significance of Metaphors in Isaiah 24–27*. Bibliotheca Ephemeridum Theologicarum Lovaniensium, 151. Leuven: Leuven University Press.
Draper, Jonathan A., ed. (2004), *Orality, Literacy, and Colonialism in Antiquity*. Atlanta, GA: Society of Biblical Literature.
Duhm, Bernhard (1892), *Das Buch Jesaia Übersetzt und Erklärt*. Gottingen: Vandenhoeck und Ruprecht.
Duling, Dennis C. (1985), "The Eleazar Miracle and Solomon's Magical Wisdom in Flavius Josephus's 'Antiquitates Judaicae' 8.42–49." *The Harvard Theological Review* 78(1–2): 1–25.
Duling, Dennis C. (2013), "Paul's Aegean Network: The Strength of Strong Ties." *Biblical Theology Bulletin* 43(3): 135–54.
Dunbar, Robin I. M. (1987), "Sociobiological Explanations and the Evolution of Ethnocentrism," in Vernon Reynolds, Vincent S.E. Falger, and Ian Vine (eds), *The Sociobiology of Ethnocentrism*, 48–59. London: Croom Helm.

Dunbar, Robin I. M. (2009), "The Social Brain Hypothesis and Its Implications for Social Evolution." *Annals of Human Biology* 36(5): 562–72.

Ebeling, Gerhard (1947), *Kirchengeschichte Als Geschichte der Auslegung der Heiligen Schrift*. Tübingen: J.C.B. Mohr (Paul Siebeck).

Eberhart, Christian A. (2002), *Studien zur Bedeutung der Opfer im Alten Testament: Die Signifikanz von Blut- und Verbrennungsriten im kultischen Rahmen*. Neukirchen-Vluyn: Neukirchener Verlag.

Eberhart, Christian A. (2011), "Sacrifice? Holy Smokes! Reflections on Cult Terminology for Understanding Sacrifice in the Hebrew Bible," in Christian A. Eberhart (ed.), *Ritual and Metaphor: Sacrifice in the Hebrew Bible*, 17–32. Resources for Biblical Study 68. Atlanta, GA: Society of Biblical Literature.

Ebrard, Johannes Heinrich August (1850), *Biblical Commentary on the Epistles of St. John*. Edinburgh: T&T Clark.

Eidinow, Esther (2011), *Luck, Fate, and Fortune: Antiquity and Its Legacy*. Oxford and New York: I.B. Tauris.

Es, Eelco van (2012), *urning the Self: George Herbert's Poetry as Cognitive Behaviour*. PhD dissertation, Rijksuniversiteit Groningen

Esler, Philip F. (2005), "Social-Scientific Models in Biblical Interpretation," in Philip F. Esler (ed.), *Ancient Israel: The Old Testament in Its Social Context*, 3–14. London: SCM.

Evans, Vyvyan, and Melanie Green (2006), *Cognitive Linguistics: An Introduction*. Mahwah, NJ: L. Erlbaum.

Eve, Eric (2002), *The Jewish Context of Jesus' Miracles*. Journal for the Study of the New Testament Supplement, 231. Sheffield: Sheffield Academic Press.

Eve, Eric (2016), *Writing the Gospels: Composition and Memory*. London: SPCK.

Eysenck, Michael W., and Mark T. Keane (2005), "Approaches to Cognitive Psychology," in Michael W. Eysenck and Mark T. Keane (eds), *Cognitive Psychology: A Student's Handbook*. Vol. 5, 1–30. Hove and Hillsdale, NJ: L. Erlbaum Assoc.

Fauconnier, Gilles, and Mark Turner (2002), *The Way We Think: Conceptual Blending and the Mind's Hidden Complexities*. New York: Basic Books.

Faulkner, Jason, Mark Schaller, Justin H. Park, and Lesley A. Duncan (2004), "Evolved Disease Avoidance Mechanisms and Contemporary Xenophobic Attitudes." *Group Processes & Intergroup Relations* 7: 333–53.

Feldman Barrett, Lisa (2017), *How Emotions Are Made: The Secret Life of the Brain*. Boston, MA: Houghton Mifflin Harcourt.

Festinger, Leon, Stanley Schachterand, and Kurt W. Back (1950), *Social Pressures in Informal Groups: A Study of Human Factors in Housing*. New York: Harper & Brothers.

Fishbein, Harold D. (2002), *Peer Prejudice and Discrimination: The Origins of Prejudice*. 2nd edn. Mahwah, NJ: Lawrence Erlbaum Associates.

Fodor, Jerry A. (1983), *The Modularity of Mind: An Essay on Faculty Psychology*. Cambridge, MA: MIT Press.

Frend, William H. C. (1984), *The Rise of Christianity*. London and Philadelphia, PA: Darton, Longman & Todd and Fortress Press.

Froehlich, Karlfried (1978), "Church History and the Bible." *Princeton Seminary Bulletin* 1(4): 213–24.

Frye, Northrop (1982), *The Great Code: The Bible and Literature*. New York: Harcourt Brace Jovanovich.

Gamble, Harry Y. (1995), *Books and Readers in the Early Church: A History of Early Christian Texts*. New Haven, CT: Yale University Press.

Gärdenfors, Peter (1999), "Some Tenets of Cognitive Semantics," in Jens S. Allwood and Peter Gärdenfors (eds), *Cognitive Semantics: Meaning and Cognition*, 19–36. Amsterdam: John Benjamins.

Gärdenfors, Peter (2005), *Tankens vindlar: Om språk, minne och berättande*. Nora: Nya Doxa.

Geeraerts, Dirk (2010), *Theories of Lexical Semantics*. Oxford: Oxford University Press.

Geertz, Armin W. (2010), "Brain, Body and Culture: A Biocultural Theory of Religion." *Method & Theory in the Study of Religion* 22: 304–321.

Gesenius, H. Wilhelm F. (1990), "נפשׁ", *Gesenius' Hebrew and Chaldee Lexicon to the Old Testament Scriptures: Numerically Coded to Strong's Exhaustive Concordance, with an English Index of More Than 12,000 Entries*. 7th edn. Grand Rapids, MI: Baker Publishing Group.

Gesenius, Wilhelm (1910), *Gesenius' Hebrew Grammar*. Edited and enlarged by Ezekiel Kautzsch. 2nd edn. Oxford: Clarendon Press.

Gibbons, Ann (2010), "Tracing Evolution's Recent Fingerprints." *Science* 329(5993): 740–42.

Gibbs, Raymond W., Jr. (1994), *The Poetics of Mind: Figurative Thought, Language, and Understanding*. Cambridge: Cambridge University Press.

Gibbs, Raymond W., Jr. (2004), Paula Lenz Costa Lima, and Edson Francozo. "Metaphor Is Grounded in Embodied Experience." *Journal of Pragmatics* 36: 1189–210.

Gilders, William K. (2004), *Blood Ritual in the Hebrew Bible: Meaning and Power*. Baltimore, MD: The Johns Hopkins University Press.

Gonce, Lauren O., M. Afzal Upal, D. Jason Slone, and Ryan D. Tweney (2006), "Role of Context in the Recall of Counterintuitive Concepts." *Journal of Cognition and Culture* 6(3): 521–47.

Granovetter, Mark S. (1973), "The Strength of Weak Ties." *American Journal of Sociology* 78(6): 1360–80.

Granovetter, Mark S. (1983), "The Strength of Weak Ties: A Network Theory Revisited." *Sociological Theory* 1: 201–33.

Greimas, Algirdas Julien (1974), "Dialogue with Herman Parret," in Herman Parret (ed.), *Discussing Language: Dialogues with Wallace L. Chafe, Noam Chomsky, Algirdas J. Greimas, M.A.K. Halliday, Peter Hartmann, George Lakoff, Sydney M. Lamb, Andre Martinet, James Mccawley, Sebastian K. Saumjan, and Jacques Bouveresse*, 55–79. The Hague: Mouton.

Greimas, Algirdas Julien (1983), *Structural Semantics: An Attempt at a Method*. Winfried Nöth, Handbook of Semiotics. Lincoln: University of Nebraska Press.

Griffith, Terry (1998), "A Non-Polemical Reading of 1 John: Sin, Christology and the Limits of Johannine Christianity." *Tyndale Bulletin* 49: 253–76.

Griffiths, Paul E. (1997), *What Emotions Really Are: The Problem of Psychological Categories*. Chicago, IL and London: University of Chicago Press.

Groom, Susan (2003), *Linguistic Analysis of Biblical Hebrew*. Carlisle: Paternoster.

Gross, James J. (2008), "Emotion Regulation," in Michael Lewis, Jeannette M. Haviland-Jones, and Lisa Feldman Barrett (eds), *Handbook of Emotions*, 497–512. 3rd edn. New York: The Guilford Press.

Grünwaldt, Klaus (1999), *Das Heiligkeitsgesetz Leviticus 17–26: Ursprüngliche Gestalt, Tradition und Theologie*, Beihefte zur Zeitschrift für die alttestamentliche Wissenschaft, 271. Berlin and New York: Walter de Gruyter.

Gudme, Anne Katrine de Hemmer (2012), "Der er ingen vampyrer i Det Gamle Testamente: Blod, liv og konceptuelle metaforer," in Søren Holst and Christina Petterson (eds), *Den store fortælling: Festskrift til Geert Hallbäck*, 173–84. Copenhagen: Forlaget Anis.

Guthrie, Stewart Elliott (1993), *Faces in the Clouds: A New Theory of Religion*. New York: Oxford University Press.

Guthrie, Stewart Elliott (2013), "Early Cognitive Theorists of Religion: Robin Horton and His Predecessors," in William McCorkle (ed.), *Mental Culture: Classical Social Theory and the Cognitive Science of Religion*, 33–51. Montreal and Kingston: McGill-Queens University Press.

Haacker, Klaus (1981), "Leistung und Grenzen der Formkritik." *Theologische Beiträge* 12: 53–71.

Haenchen, Ernst (1968), *Der Weg Jesu*. 2nd edn. De Gruyter Lehrbuch. Berlin: de Gruyter.

Hagan, George P. (1970), "A Note on Akan Colour Symbolism." *Research Review of the Institute of African Studies* 7: 8–14.

Haidle, Miriam N. (2009), "How to Think a Spear?" in Sophie A. de Beaune, Frederick L. Coolidge, and Thomas Grant Wynn (eds), *Cognitive Archaeology and Human Evolution*, 57–73. New York: Cambridge University Press.

Haidle, Miriam N. (2014), "Building a Bridge: An Archeologist's Perspective on the Evolution of Causal Cognition." *Frontiers in Psychology* 5: 1472, doi:10.3389/fpsyg.2014.01472.

Haidt, Jonathan (2001), "The Emotional Dog and Its Rational Tail: A Social Intuitionist Approach to Moral Judgment." *Psychological Review* 108: 814–34.

Haidt, Jonathan (2003), "The Moral Emotions," in Richard J. Davidson, Klaus R. Scherer, and H. Hill Goldsmith (eds), *Handbook of Affective Sciences*, 852–70. Oxford: Oxford University Press.

Halpin, Harry, Johanna D. Moore, and Judy Robertson (2004), "Towards Automated Story Analysis Using Participatory Design." *Proceedings of the 1st ACM workshop on Story representation, mechanism and context, International Multimedia Conference*. 75–83, New York: ACM Press.

Harnack, Adolf von (1906), *Die Mission und Ausbreitung des Christentums in den ersten drei Jahrhunderten*, vol.1. 2nd edn. Leipzig: J.C. Hinrichs.

Harnad, Stevan (2005), "To Cognize Is to Categorize: Cognition Is Categorization," in Henry Cohen and Claire Lefebvre (eds), *Handbook of Categorization in Cognitive Science*. 1st edn, 20–43. New York: Elsevier Science.

Hartley, John E. (2011), *The Semantics of Ancient Hebrew Colour Lexemes*, Ancient Near Eastern Studies: Supplement 33. Leuven: Peeters.

Haslam, Alexander S., John C. Turner, Penelope J. Oaks, Craig McGarty, and Katherine J. Raynolds (1998), "The Group as a Basis for Emergent Stereotype Consensus." *European Review of Social Psychology* 8: 203–39.

Haynes, Stephen R., and Steven L. McKenzie (1999), *To Each Its Own Meaning: An Introduction to Biblical Criticisms and Their Applications*. Louisville, KY: Westminster John Knox Press.

Heusch, Luc de (1962), "Cultes de possession et religions initiatiques de salut en Afrique." *Annales du Centre d'etudes des Religions*, 2: 226–44.

Hoffmann, Dirk L., Chris D. Standish, Marcos García-Diez, P. B. Pettitt, J. Andy Milton, et al. (2018), "U-Th Dating of Carbonate Crusts Reveals Neandertal Origin of Iberian Cave Art." *Science* 359(6378): 912–15.

Hogg, Michael, A. Dominic Abrams, Sabine Otten, and Steve Hinkle (2004), "The Social Identity Perspective—Intergroup Relations, Self-Conception, and Small Groups." *Small Group Research* 35: 246–76.

Hogg, Michael, A. Kelly, S. Fielding, and John Darley (2005), "Fringe Dwellers: Processes of Deviance and Marginalization in Groups," in Dominic Abrams, Michael A.

Hoggand, and José M. Marques (eds), *The Social Psychology of Inclusion and Exclusion*, 161–90. New York: Psychology Press.

Holladay, William L. (1997), "Was Trito-Isaiah Deutero-Isaiah After All?," in Craig C. Broyles and Craig A. Evans (eds), *Writing and Reading the Scroll of Isaiah: Studies of an Interpretive Tradition*, 2 volumes. Supplements to Vetus Testamentum 70, 2, 193–217. Leiden: Brill.

Horrell, David G. (2007), "The Label Χριστιανος: 1 Peter 4:16 and the Formation of Christian Identity." *Journal of Biblical Literature* 126(2): 361–81.

Houston, George W. (2014), *Inside Roman Libraries: Book Collections and Their Management in Antiquity*. Chapel Hill: The University of North Carolina Press.

Houston, Walter (1993), *Purity and Monotheism: Clean and Unclean Animals in Biblical Law*. Journal for the Study of the Old Testament Supplement Series, 140. Sheffield: JSOT Press.

Houston McNeel, Jennifer (2014), *Paul as Infant and Nursing Mother: Metaphor, Rhetoric, and Identity in 1 Thessalonians 2: 5–8*. Early Christianity and Its Literature 12. Atlanta, GA: SBL Press.

Howe, Bonnie (2006), *Because You Bear This Name: Conceptual Metaphor and the Moral Meaning of 1 Peter*. Biblical Interpretation Series 81. Boston: Brill.

Howe, Bonnie, and Joel B. Green, eds (2014), *Cognitive Linguistic Explorations in Biblical Studies*. Berlin: De Gruyter.

Humbert, Paul (1960), "Le substantif *toʿēbā* et le verbe *tʿb* dans l'Ancien Testament", *Zeitschrift für die Alttestamentliche Wissenschaft* 72: 217–37.

Hutchins, Edwin (1995), *Cognition in the Wild*. Cambridge, MA: MIT Press.

Idelsohn, Abraham Z. (1995), *Jewish Liturgy and Its Development*. New York: Dover.

Illouz, Eva 2012, *Why Love Hurts: A Sociological Explanation*. Cambridge: Polity Press.

Irons, William (2001), "Religion as a Hard-to-Fake Sign of Commitment," in Randolph M. Nesse (ed.), *Evolution and the Capacity for Commitment*, 292–309. New York: Russell Sage Foundation.

Jablonka, Eva, and Marion J. Lamb (2005), *Evolution in Four Dimensions: Genetic, Epigenetic, Behavioral, and Symbolic Variation in the History of Life*. Cambridge, MA: MIT Press.

Jablonka, Eva, and Marion J. Lamb (2007), "Précis of Evolution in Four Dimensions." *Behavioral and Brain Sciences* 30(4): 353–65.

Jackendoff, Ray S., and Fred Lerdahl (1982), *A Generative Theory of Tonal Music*. Cambridge, MA: MIT Press.

Jackson, Bernard S. (1989), "Ideas of Law and Legal Administration: A Semiotic Approach," in Ronald E. Clements (ed.), *The World of Ancient Israel: Sociological, Anthropological and Political Perspectives*, 185–202. Cambridge: Cambridge University Press.

Jackson, Bernard S. (2006), *Wisdom-Laws: A Study of the* Mishpatim *of Exodus 21: 1–22:16*. Oxford: Oxford University Press.

Jefferson, Ann, David Robey, and David Forgacs (1987), *Modern Literary Theory: A Comparative Introduction*. London: Batsford.

Jensen, Hans Jørgen Lundager (1998). *Gammeltestamentlig Religion: en indføring*. Frederiksberg: Forlaget Anis.

Jensen, Hans Jørgen Lundager (2000), *Den fortærende ild: Strukturelle analyser af narrative og rituelle tekster i Det Gamle Testamente*. Århus: Aarhus Universitetsforlag.

Johnson, Mark (1987), *The Body in the Mind: The Bodily Basis of Meaning, Imagination, and Reason*. Chicago, IL: The University of Chicago Press.

Johnson, Mark (2005), "The Philosophical Significance of Image Schemas," in Beate Hampe (ed.), *From Perception to Meaning: Image Schemas in Cognitive Linguistics*, 15–33. Cognitive Linguistics Research, 29. Berlin: Mouton de Gruyter.

Johnson, William A. (2000), "Toward a Sociology of Reading in Classical Antiquity". *The American Journal of Philology* 121(4): 593–627.

Johnston, Philip S. (2002), *Shades of Sheol: Death and Afterlife in the Old Testament*. Downers Grove, IL: InterVarsity Press.

Johnston, Sarah Iles (2013), *Restless Dead: Encounters between the Living and the Dead in Ancient Greece*. Berkeley: University of California Press.

Kammers, Marjolein P. M. (2010), Frédérique de Vignemont, and Patrick Haggard. "Cooling the Thermal Grill Illusion through Self-Touch". *Current biology* 26(20): 1819–22.

Kaufmann, Yehezkel ([1937–1948] 1960), *The Religion of Israel: From Its Beginnings to the Babylonian Exile*. Translated and abridged by Moshe Greenberg. Chicago, IL: The University of Chicago Press.

Kazen, Thomas (2008), "Dirt and Disgust: Body and Morality in Biblical Purity Laws," in Baruch J. Schwartz, David P. Wright, Jeffrey Stackert, and Naphtali S. Meshel (eds), *Perspectives on Purity and Purification in the Bible*. LHB/OTS, 474, 43–64. New York: T & T Clark.

Kazen, Thomas (2011), *Emotions in Biblical Law: A Cognitive Science Approach*. Hebrew Bible Monographs 36. Sheffield: Phoenix Press.

Kazen, Thomas (2015), "Purity and Persia," in Roy E. Gane and Ada Taggar-Cohen (eds), *Current Issues in Priestly and Related Literature: The Legacy of Jacob Milgrom and Beyond*, 435–62. Atlanta, GA: Society of Biblical Literature.

Kedar-Kopfstein, Benjamin (1988), "דם," in Robert L. Harris, Gleason Archer, and Bruce K. Waltke (eds), *Theological Wordbook of the Old Testament*, vol. 3, 234–50. Chicago, IL: Moody Publishers.

Keil, Frank C. (1979), *Semantic and Conceptual Development: An Ontological Perspective*. Cognitive Science Series, 1. Cambridge, MA: Harvard University Press.

Kekes, John (1992), "Disgust and Moral Taboos." *Philosophy* 67: 431–46.

Kelber, Werner H. (1983), *The Oral and the Written Gospel: Hermeneutics of Speaking and Writing in the Synoptic Tradition, Mark, Paul and Q*. Philadelphia, PA: Fortress Press.

Kelber, Werner H. (2007), "Orality and Biblical Studies: A Review Essay." *Review of Biblical Literature* 9: 1–24.

Kelber, Werner H. (2008), "The Oral-Scribal-Memorial Arts of Communication in Early Christianity," in Tom Thatcher (ed.), *Jesus, the Voice, and the Text: Beyond the Oral and Written Gospel*, 235–62. Waco, TX: Baylor University Press.

Kelber, Werner H. (2014), "Orality and Literacy in Early Christianity." *Biblical Theology Bulletin* 44(3): 144–55.

Kelly, Michael H., and Frank C. Keil (1985), "The More Things Change…: Metamorphoses and Conceptual Structure." *Cognitive Science: A Multidisciplinary Journal* 9(4): 403–16.

Kim, Uichol, Young-Shin Park, and Donghyun Park (2000), "The Challenge of Cross-Cultural Psychology: The Role of the Indigenous Psychologies." *Journal of Cross Cultural Psychology* 31: 63–75.

Kirk, Alan, and Tom Thatcher (2005), *Memory, Tradition, and Text: Uses of the Past in Early Christianity*. Semeia Studies. Atlanta, GA: Society of Biblical Literature.

Klawans, J. (2000), *Impurity and Sin in Ancient Judaism*. New York: Oxford University Press.

Knohl, Israel (1995), *The Sanctuary of Silence: The Priestly Torah and the Holiness School*. Minneapolis, MN: Fortress.

Knuuttila, Simo, and Juha Sihvola (1998), "How the Philosophical Analysis of Emotions Was Introduced," in Juha Sihvola and Troels Engberg-Pedersen, (eds), *The Emotions in Hellenistic Philosophy*, 1–19. The New Synthese Historical Library, 46. Dordrecht, Boston, MA, and London: Kluwer Academic Publishers.

Kohlberg, Lawrence (1971), "From Is to Ought: How to Commit the Naturalistic Fallacy and Get away with It in the Study of Moral Development," in Theodore Mischel (ed.), *Cognitive Development and Epistemology*, 151–235. New York and London: Academic Press.

Kohlberg, Lawrence, Charles Levine, and Alexandra Hewer (1983), *Moral Stages: A Current Formulation and a Response to Critics*. Contributions to Moral Development, 10. Basel: Karger.

Kolaczyk, Eric D. (2009), *Statistical Analysis of Network Data: Methods and Models*. New York and London: Springer.

Körtner, Ulrich H. J. (1994), *Der Inspirierte Leser : Zentrale Aspekte Biblischer Hermeneutik*. Göttingen: Vandenhoeck & Ruprecht.

Köstenberger, Andreas J. (2009), *A Theology of John's Gospel and Letters*. Biblical Theology of the New Testament. Grand Rapids, MI: Zondervan.

Kövecses, Zoltán (2005), *Metaphor in Culture: Universality and Variation*. Cambridge and New York: Cambridge University Press.

Kövecses, Zoltán (2010), *Metaphor: A Practical Introduction*. 2nd edn. Oxford: Oxford University Press.

Kratz, Reinhard G. (2000), *The Composition of the Narrative Books of the Old Testament*. London and New York: T & T Clark.

Kruse, Colin G. (2000), *The Letters of John*. Pillar New Testament Commentary. Grand Rapids, MI: Eerdmans.

Kruse, Collin G. (2003), "Sin and Perfection in 1 John." *Australian Biblical Review* 51: 60–70.

Kubo, Sakae (1969), "1 John 3:9: Absolute or Habitual?" *Andrews University Seminary Studies* 7: 47–56.

Kundt, Radek (2011), *Contemporary Evolutionary Theories of Culture and the Study of Religion*. London and New York: Bloomsbury Academic.

La Barre, Weston (1984), *Muelos: A Stone Age Superstition about Sexuality*. New York: Columbia University Press.

Lakoff, George (1987), *Women, Fire, and Dangerous Things: What Categories Reveal about the Mind*. Chicago, IL: The University of Chicago Press.

Lakoff, George (1993), "The Contemporary Theory of Metaphor," in Andrew Ortony (ed.), *Metaphor and Thought*, 202–51. Cambridge: Cambridge University Press.

Lakoff, George, and Mark Johnson (1980), *Metaphors We Live By*. Chicago, IL: University of Chicago Press.

Lakoff, George, and Mark Johnson (1999), *Philosophy in the Flesh: The Embodied Mind and Its Challenge to Western Thought*. New York: Basic Books.

Lakoff, George, and Mark Turner (1989), *More Than Cool Reason: A Field Guide to Poetic Metaphor*. Chicago, IL: University of Chicago Press.

Lambert, Wilfred G. (1993), "Donations of Food and Drink to the Gods in Ancient Mesopotamia," in J. Quaegebeur (ed.), *Ritual and Sacrifice in the Ancient Near East*. Orientalia Lovaniensia analecta 55, 191–201. Leuven: Uitgeverij Peeters en Departement Oriëntalistiek.

Lancaster Patterson, Jane (2015), *Keeping the Feast: Metaphors of Sacrifice in 1 Corinthians and Philippians*. Early Christianity and Its Literature 16. Atlanta, GA: SBL Press.

Laney, Cara, Hannah V. Campbell, Friderike Heuer, and Daniel Reisberg (2004), "Memory for Thematically Arousing Events." *Memory and Cognition* 32(7): 1149–59.

Lang, B. (1995), "Kanon," in Manfred Görg, Bernhard Lang, and Beatrice Rauschenbach (eds), *Neues Bibel-Lexikon*, 440–50. Zürich: Benziger.

Larson, Jennifer (2016), *Understanding Greek Religion: A Cognitive Approach*. London: Routledge.

Law, Robert (1909), *The Tests of Life: A Study of the First Epistle of St. John*. Edinburgh: Clark.

Lawson, E. Thomas, and Robert N. McCauley (1990), *Rethinking Religion: Connecting Cognition and Culture*. Cambridge: Cambridge University Press.

Leslie, Alan M. (1995), "A Theory of Agency," in Dan Sperber, David Premackand, A. James Premack (eds), *Causal Cognition: A Multidisciplinary Debate*, 121–41. Oxford: Clarendon Press.

Levine, Baruch A. (1974), *In the Presence of the Lord: A Study of Cult and Some Cultic Terms in Ancient Israel*. SJLA, 5. Leiden: Brill.

Levine, Baruch A. (2003), "Leviticus: Its Literary History and Location in Biblical Literature," in Rolf Rendtorff and Robert A. Kugler (eds), *The Book of Leviticus: Composition and Reception*, 11–23. Leiden: Brill.

Levinson, Bernard M. (1997), *Deuteronomy and the Hermeneutics of Legal Innovation*. New York and Oxford: Oxford University Press.

Levinson, Bernard M. (2004), "Is the Covenant Code an Exilic Composition? A Response to John Van Seters," in John Day (ed.), *In Search of Pre-Exilic Israel*. Journal for the Study of the Old Testament Supplement Series, 406, 272–325. London and New York: T & T Clark International.

Levinson, Bernard M. (2008), *"The Right Chorale": Studies in Biblical Law and Interpretation*. FAT, 54. Tübingen: Mohr Siebeck.

Levinson, Bernard M. (2010), *Legal Revision and Religious Renewal in Ancient Israel*. Cambridge: Cambridge University Press.

Levy, Gabriel (2012), *Judaic Technologies of the Word: A Cognitive Analysis of Jewish Cultural Formation*. Bristol, CT: Equinox Publishing. http://site.ebrary.com/id/10745269.

Lewis, Ioan M. (2005), *Ecstatic Religion: A Study of Shamanism and Spirit Possession*. London and New York: Routledge.

Lewis, Paul, ed. (2009), *Ethnologue: Languages of the World*. 16th edn. Dallas, TX: SIL International.

Liénard, Pierre, and Pascal Boyer (2006), "Whence Collective Rituals? A Cultural Selection Model of Ritualized Behavior." *American Anthropologist* 108(4): 814–27.

Lieu, Judith (1991), *The Theology of the Johannine Epistles*. NT Theology. Cambridge: Cambridge University.

Lieu, Judith (2008), "Us or Them? Persuasion and Identity in 1 John." *Journal of Biblical Literature* 127: 805–19.

Looy, Heather (2004), "Embodied and Embedded Morality: Divinity, Identity, and Disgust." *Zygon* 39(1): 219–35.

Lundhaug, Hugo (2010), *Images of Rebirth: Cognitive Poetics and Transformational Soteriology in the Gospel of Philip and the Exegesis on the Soul*. Leiden and Boston, MA: Brill.

Luomanen, Petri (2017), "Morality and the Evolution of Christianity," in Petri Luomanen, Anne Birgitta Pessi, and Ilkka Pyysiäinen (eds), *Christianity and the Roots of Morality*, 115–39. Leiden and Boston, MA: Brill Academic Publishers.

Luomanen, Petri, Ilkka Pyysiäinen, and Risto Uro, eds (2007), *Explaining Christian Origins and Early Judaism: Contributions from Cognitive and Social Science*. Biblical interpretation series. Leiden and Boston, MA: Brill.

Malley, Brian (2004), *How the Bible Works: An Anthropological Study of Evangelical Biblicism*. Walnut Creek, CA: AltaMira Press.

Mandik, Pete (2001), "Representation: Introduction," in William Bechtel, Pete Mandik, Jennifer Mundale, and Robert S. Stufflebeam (eds), *Philosophy and the Neurosciences: A Reader*, 331. Oxford: Blackwell.

Mandler, Jean M. (2004), *The Foundations of Mind*. Oxford: Oxford University Press.

Mandler, Jean M., and Nancy S. Johnson (1977), "Remembrance of Things Parsed: Story Structure and Recall." *Cognitive Psychology* 9(1): 111–51.

Margalit, Baruch (1989), *The Ugaritic Poem of AQHT*. Beihefte zur Zeitschrift für die alttestamentliche Wissenschaft 182. Berlin: Walter de Gruyter.

Markschies, Christoph (2006), *Warum hat das Christentum in der Antike überlebt? Ein Beitrag zum Gespräch zwischen Kirchengeschichte und Systematischer Theologie*. Leipzig: Evangelische Verlagsanstalt.

Marques, José M., Dominic Abramsand, and Rui G. Serôdio (2001), "Being Better by Being Right: Subjective Group Dynamics and Derogation of Ingroup Deviants When Generic Norms Are Undermined." *Journal of Personality and Social Psychology* 81: 436–47.

Marshall, Ian H. (2008), *The Epistles of John*. NICNT. Grand Rapids, MI: Eerdmans, 1979.

Martin, Bridget (2014), "Blood, Honour and Status in Odyssey 11." *Classical Quarterly* 64: 1–12.

Martin, Luther H. (2003), "Cognition, Society and Religion: A New Approach to the Study of Culture." *Culture and Religion: An Interdisciplinary Journal* 4(2): 207–31.

Martin, Luther H. (2015), *The Mind of Mithraists: Historical and Cognitive Studies in the Roman Cult of Mithras*. New York: Bloomsbury Academic.

Massa, Dieter (2000), *Verstehensbedingungen von Gleichnissen: Prozesse und Voraussetzungen der Rezeption Aus Kognitiver Sicht*. Texte und Arbeiten zum Neutestamentlichen Zeitalter 31. Tübingen: Francke.

Maul, Stefan M. (1994), *Zukunftsbewältigung: Eine Untersuchung altorientalischen Denkens anhand der babylonisch-assyrischen Löserituale (Namburbi)*. Baghdader Forschungen, 18; Mainz am Rhein: Verlag Philipp von Zabern.

Mayr, Ernst (2001), *What Evolution Is*. New York: Basic Books, Perseus Books Group.

Mazure, Carolyn M., and Paul K. Maciejewski (2003), "The Interplay of Stress, Gender and Cognitive Style in Depressive Onset." *Archives of Women's Mental Health* 6(1): 5–9.

McCarthy, Dennis J. (1969), "The Symbolism of Blood and Sacrifice." *Journal of Biblical Literature* 88: 166–76.

McCauley, R. N. (2011), *Why Religion Is Natural and Science Is Not*. New York: Oxford University Press.

McCauley, Robert (2013), "Explanatory Pluralism and the Cognitive Science of Religion: Why Scholars in Religious Studies Should Stop Worrying about Reductionism," in Dimitris Xygalatas and William W. McCorkle, Jr. (eds), *Mental Culture: Classical Social Theory and the Cognitive Science of Religion*, 11–32. Durham: Acumen.

McCauley, Robert N. (2000), "The Naturalness of Religion and the Unnaturalness of Science," in Frank C. Keil and Robert A. Wilson (eds), *Explanation and Cognition*, 61–85. Cambridge, MA: MIT Press.

McCauley, Robert N., and E. Thomas Lawson (2002), *Bringing Ritual to Mind: Psychological Foundations of Cultural Forms*. New York: Cambridge University Press.

McCullough, Michael (2008), *Beyond Revenge: The Evolution of the Forgiveness Instinct*. San Francisco, CA: Josey Bass.

McElreath, Richard, and Joseph Henrich (2007), "Modeling Cultural Evolution," in Robin I. M. Dunbar and Louise Barrett (eds), *Oxford Handbook of Evolutionary Psychology*, 571–85. Oxford and New York: Oxford University Press. http://philpapers.org/rec/DUNOHO.

McEvoy, Chad Joseph (2002), "A Consideration of Human Xenophobia and Ethnocentrism from a Sociobiological Perspective," *Human Rights Review* 3(3): 39–49.

McKnight, Edgar V. (1985), *The Bible and the Reader: An Introduction to Literary Criticism*. Philadelphia, PA: Fortress Press.

McNamara, Patrick N. (2009), *The Neuroscience of Religious Experience*. New York: Cambridge University Press.

Meshel, Naphtali (2008), "Pure, Impure, Permitted, Prohibited: A Study of Classification Systems in P," in Baruch J. Schwartz et al. (eds), *Pectives on Purity and Purification in the Bible*, 32–42. Library of Hebrew Bible/Old Testament Studies, 474. New York: T & T Clark.

Meyers, Carol L., and Eric M. Meyers (1987), *Haggai, Zechariah 1–8*, Anchor Bible 25B. New York: Doubleday.

Milgrom, Jacob (1981), "The Paradox of the Red Cow (Num. xix)." *Vetus Testamentum* 31: 62–72.

Milgrom, Jacob (1991), *Leviticus, 1–16: A New Translation with Introduction and Commentary*. Anchor Bible 3. Garden City, NY: Doubleday.

Milgrom, Jacob (2000a), *Leviticus, 17–22: A New Translation with Introduction and Commentary*. Anchor Bible 3a. Garden City, NY: Doubleday.

Milgrom, Jacob (2000b), *Leviticus, 23–27: A New Translation with Introduction and Commentary*. Anchor Bible 3b. Garden City, NY: Doubleday.

Milgrom, Jacob (2003), "H_R in Leviticus and Elsewhere in the Torah," in Rolf Rendtorff and Robert A. Kugler (eds), *The Book of Leviticus: Composition and Reception*, 24–40. Leiden: Brill.

Mirguet, Francoise (2016), "What Is an 'Emotion' in the Hebrew Bible? An Experience That Exceeds Most Contemporary Concepts." *Biblical Interpretation* 24: 224–65.

Mithen, Steven J. (1996), *The Prehistory of the Mind: A Search for the Origins of Art, Religion, and Science*. London: Thames and Hudson.

Moehring, Horst R. (1973), *Rationalization of Miracles in the Writings of Flavius Josephus*. Berlin: Akademie Verlag.

Moll, Jorge, Roland Zahn, Ricardo de Oiveira-Souza, Frank Krueger, and Jordan Grafman (2005), "The Neural Basis of Human Moral Cognition." *Nature Reviews. Neuroscience* 6: 799–809.

Moscovici, Serge (1976), *Social Influence and Social Change*. London: Academic Press.

Moss, Helen, and Lianne Older (1996), *Birkbeck Word Association Norms*. Hove: Psychology Press.

Mueller, Erik T. (2003), "Story Understanding through Multi-Representation Model Construction," in George S. Hirst and Sergei Nirenburg (eds), *Proceedings of the HLT-NAACL 2003 workshop on Text Meaning*, vol. 9, 46–53. Morristown, NJ: Association for Computational Linguistics.

Mullet, Étienne, and Girad Michèle (1999), "Developmental and Cognitive Points of View on Forgiveness," in Michael E. McCullough, Kenneth I. Pargament, and Carl E. Thoresen (eds), *Forgiveness: Theory, Research and Practice*, 111–32. New York: Guilford Press.

Navarrete, Carlos David, and Daniel M.T. Fessler (2006), "Disease Avoidance and Ethnocentrism: The Effects of Disease Vulnerability and Disgust Sensitivity on Intergroup Attitudes." *Evolution and Human Behavior* 27: 270–82.

Nemeroff, Carol, and Paul Rozin (1994), "The Contagion Concept in Adult Thinking in the United States: Transmission of Germs and of Interpersonal Influence." *Ethos* 22(2): 158–86.

Nemeroff, Carol, and Paul Rozin (2000), "The Making of the Magical Mind: The Nature and Function of Sympathetic Magical Thinking," in Karl Sven Rosengren, Carl N. Johnson, and Paul L. Harris (eds), *Imagining the Impossible: Magical, Scientific, and Religious Thinking in Children*, 1–34. Cambridge and New York: Cambridge University Press.

Nichols, Shaun, and Joshua Knobe (2007), "Moral Responsibility and Determinism: The Cognitive Science of Folk Intuitions." *Noûs* 41: 663–85.

Nickelsburg, George W. E. (2001), *1 Enoch: A Commentary on the Book of 1 Enoch, Chapters 1–36; 81–108*. Hermeneia Series. Minneapolis, MN.: Fortress.

Nickelsburg, George W. E. (2006), *Resurrection, Immortality, and Eternal Life in Intertestamental Judaism and Early Christianity*. Harvard Theological Studies, 56. Cambridge, MA: Harvard University Press.

Nihan, Christophe (2004), "The Holiness Code between D and P: Some Comments on the Function and Significance of Leviticus 17–26 in the Composition of the Torah," in Eckart Otto and Reinhard Achenbach (eds), *Das Deuteronomium zwischen Pentateuch und Deuteronomistischen Geschichtswerk*, 81–122. Forschungen zur Religion und Literatur des Alten und Neuen Testaments 206. Göttingen: Vandenhoeck & Ruprecht.

Nihan, Christophe (2011), "Resident Aliens and Natives in the Holiness Legislation," in Reinhard Achenbach, Rainer Albertz, and Jakob Wöhrle (eds), *The Foreigner and the Law: Perspectives from the Hebrew Bible and the Ancient Near East*, 111–34. Beihefte Zur Zeitschrift Fur Altorientalische Und Biblische Rechtsgeschichte. Wiesbaden: Otto Harrassowitz.

Norenzayan, Ara (2013), *Big Gods: How Religion Transformed Cooperation and Conflict*. Princeton, NJ: Princeton University Press.

Norenzayan, Ara, and Scott Atran (2004), "Cognitive and Emotional Processes in the Cultural Transmission of Natural and Nonnatural Beliefs", in Mark Schaller and Christian S. Crandall (eds), *The Psychological Foundations of Culture*, 149–69. Mahwah, NJ: Lawrence Erlbaum Associates Publishers.

Norenzayan, Ara, Scott Atran, B. Jason Faulkner, and Mark Schaller (2006), "Memory and Mystery: The Cultural Selection of Minimally Counterintuitive Narratives." *Cognitive Science* 30(3): 531–53.

Norin, Stig (2006), "John Van Seters, *A Law Book of* [sic] *the Diaspora: Revision in the Study of the Covenant Code*." *Svensk Exegetisk Årsbok* 71: 237–39.

Oakes, Penelope J. (1990), "The Categorization Process: Cognition of the Group in the Social Psychology of Stereotyping," in Dominic Abrams and Michael A. Hogg (eds), *Social Identity Theory: Constructive and Critical Advances*, 28–47. London: Harvester Wheatsheaf.

Oeming, Manfred (2006), *Contemporary Biblical Hermeneutics: An Introduction*. Aldershot and Burlington, VT: Ashgate.

Öhman, Arne (2000), "Fear and Anxiety: Evolutionary, Cognitive, and Clinical Perspectives," in Michael Lewis and Jeannette M. Haviland-Jones (eds), *Handbook of Emotions*, 2nd edn, 573–93. New York: Guildford.

Okasha, Samir (2015), "Population Genetics," in Edward N. Zalta (ed.), *The Stanford Encyclopedia of Philosophy*. Stanford, CA: The Metaphysics Research Lab, http://plato.stanford.edu/archives/fall2015/entries/population-genetics/.

Ong, Walter J. (1982), *Orality and Literacy: The Technologizing of the Word*. London and New York: Methuen.
Ong, Walter J., and John Hartley (2012), *Orality and Literacy: The Technologizing of the Word*. London and New York: Routledge.
Osiek, Carolyn, Margaret Y. MacDonald, and Janet H. Tulloch (2006), *A Woman's Place: House Churches in Earliest Christianity*. Minneapolis, MN: Fortress Press.
Otten, Heinrich (1961), "Eine Beschwörung der Unterirdischen aus Boğazköy." *Zeitschrift für Assyriologie* 54: 114–57 (not seen).
Otto, Eckart (1994), *Theologische Ethik des Alten Testaments*. Theologische Wissenschaft: Sammelwerk für Studium und Beruf, Band 3,2. Stuttgart, Berlin, Köln: Verlag W. Kohlhammer.
Otto, Eckart (1999), *Das Deuteronomium: Politische Theologie und Rechtsreform in Juda und Assyrien*. BZAW 284. Berlin and New York: Walter de Gruyter.
Otto, Eckart (2002), *Gottes Recht als Menschenrecht: Rechts- und literaturhistorische Studien zum Deuteronomium*. BZAR, 2; Wiesbaden: Harrassowitz.
Otto, Eckart (2007), *Das Gesetz Mose*. Darmstadt: Wissenschaftliche Buchgesellschaft.
Oudhoff, M. J., J. G. M. Bolscher, K. Nazmi, H. Kalay, W. van 't Hof, A. V. N. Amerongen, and E. C. I. Veerman (2008), "Histatins Are the Major Wound-Closure Stimulating Factors in Human Saliva as Identified in a Cell Culture Assay." *FASEB Journal* 22(11): 3805–12.
Pachis, Panayotis (2010), *Religion and Politics in the Graeco-Roman World: Redescribing the Isis-Sarapis Cult*. Thessaloniki, Greece: Barbounakis.
Painter, John (2002), *1, 2, and 3 John*. Sacra Pagina. Collegeville, MN: Liturgical Press.
Panagiotidou, Olympia and Roger L. Beck (2017), *The Roman Mithras Cult: A Cognitive Approach*. New York: Bloomsbury.
Pardee, Dennis (2002), *Ritual and Cult at Ugarit*. Writings from the Ancient World, 10. Atlanta, GA: Society of Biblical Literature.
Pedersen, Johannes (1926), *Israel: Its Life and Culture*. 4 vols. London: Oxford University Press.
Peterson, Gregory R. (2003), *Minding God: Theology and the Cognitive Sciences*. Theology and the Sciences. Minneapolis, MN: Fortress.
Piaget, Jean ([1931] 1948), *The Moral Judgment of the Child*. Glencoe, IL: Free Press.
Piaget, Jean (1932), *The Moral Judgement of the Child*. London: Kegan Paul.
Plummer, Alfred (1886), *The Epistles of St John*. Cambridge Greek Testament. Cambridge: Cambridge University Press.
Polaski, Donald C. (2001), *Authorizing an End: The Isaiah Apocalypse and Intertextuality*. Biblical Interpretation Series, 50. Leiden: Brill.
Porubanova, Michaela, Daniel J. Shaw, Ryan McKay, and Dimitris Xygalatas (2014), "Memory for Expectation-Violating Concepts: The Effects of Agents and Cultural Familiarity." *PloS One* 9(4): e90684. https://doi.org/10.1371/journal.pone.0090684.
Porubanova, Michaela, Daniel Shaw, and Dimitris Xygalatas (2013), "Minimal-Counterintuitiveness Revisited: Effects of Cultural and Ontological Violations on Concept Memorability." *Journal of the Cognitive Science of Religion* 1/2 (2013): 181–92.
Porubanova, Michaela, and John H. Shaver (2017), "Minimal Counterintuitiveness Revisited, Again: The Role of Emotional Valence in Memory for Conceptual Incongruity," in Luther H. Martin and Donald Wiebe (eds), *Religion Explained? The Cognitive Science of Religion after Twenty-Five Years*, 123–32. London and New York: Bloomsbury Academic.

Potterie, Ignace de la (1971), "The Impeccability of the Christian According to 1 Jn 3, 6-9," in I. de la Potterie and S. Lyonnet (eds), *Christian Lives by the Spirit*, 175-96. New York: Alba House (transl. of: *La vie selon l'Esprit, condition du chrétien*, Paris, 1965). The chapter originally appeared in "L'impeccabilité du chrétien d'après I Jn 3,6-9," in *L'Evangile de Jean. Etudes et problèmes*, ed. Marie-Émile Boismard (Paris: Desclée de Brouwer, 1958), 161-77.

Prell, Christina (2011), *Social Network Analysis: History, Theory and Methodology*. London: SAGE.

Preuß, H. D. (1995), "תועבה," in H.-J. Fabry and H. Ringgren (eds), *Theologisches Wörterbuch zum Alten Testament*. Band VIII, 580-92. Stuttgart, Berlin, Köln: Verlag W. Kohlhammer.

Propp, Vladimir (1968), *Morphology of the Folktale*. Translated by Laurence Scott. Austin: University of Texas Press.

Puech, Émile (1990), "Ben Sira 48:11 et la Résurrection," in Harold W. Attridge, John J. Collins, and Thomas H. Tobin (eds), *Of Scribes and Scrolls: Studies on the Hebrew Bible, Intertestamental Judaism, and Christian Origins, Presented to John Strugnell on the Occasion of His Sixtieth Birthday*, 81-90. College Theology Society Resources in Religion, 5. Lanham, MD: University Press of America.

Puech, Émile (1993), *La croyance des Esséniens en la vie future: immortalité, résurrection, vie éternelle? Histoire d'une croyance dans le judaïsme ancien*. Études bibliques, Nouvelle série, 21-22. Paris: Gabalda.

Pyysiäinen, Ilkka (2004), *Magic, Miracles and Religion: A Scientist's Perspective. Cognitive Science of Religion*. Walnut Creek, CA, Lanham, MD, and New York: Altamira Press.

Pyysiäinen, Ilkka (2009), *Supernatural Agents: Why We Believe in Souls, Gods, and Buddhas*. Oxford: Oxford University Press.

Quinn, Kimberly A. C., Neil Macrae, and Galen V. Bodenhausen (2003), "Social Cognition," in Lynn Nadel (ed.), *Encyclopedia of Cognitive Science*, vol. 4, 66-73. London: Nature Publishing Group.

Räisänen, Heikki (2010), *The Rise of Christian Beliefs: The Thought World of Early Christians*. Minneapolis, MN: Fortress Press.

Rawson, Elizabeth (1985), *Intellectual Life in the Late Roman Republic*. London: Duckworth.

Reiner, Erica (1958), *Šurpu: A Collection of Sumerian and Akkadian Incantations*. Archiv für Orientforschung, herausgeben von Ernst Weidner, 11. Graz: Im Selbstverlage des Herausgebers.

Rendtorff, Rolf (1983), *Das Alte Testament: Eine Einführung*. Neukirchen-Vluyn: Neukirchener Verlag.

Rendtorff, Rolf (1994), "Rezension, Brevard S. Childs, Biblical Theology of the Old and New Testaments: Theological Reflections on the Christian Bible," in Michael Beintker, Luis Alonso Schökel, and Ingo Baldermann (eds), *Sünde und Gericht*. Jahrbuch für Biblische Theologie 9, 359-69. Neukirchen-Vluyn: Neukirchener Verlag.

Repetti, Rena L. (1989), "Effects of Daily Workload on Subsequent Behavior During Marital Interaction: The Roles of Social Withdrawal and Spouse Support." *Journal of Personality and Social Psychology* 57(4): 651-59.

Richerson, Peter J., and Robert Boyd (2004), *Not by Genes Alone: How Culture Transformed Human Evolution*. Chicago, IL: University of Chicago Press.

Richerson, Peter J., and Robert Boyd (2005), *Not by Genes Alone: How Culture Transformed Human Evolution*. Chicago, IL: University of Chicago Press.

Ringgren, Karl Vilhelm Helmer (1985), "לבן‎," in G. Johannes Botterweck, Helmer Ringgren, and Heinz-Josef Fabry (eds), *Theological Dictionary of the Old Testament*, vol. 7, 438–41. Stuttgart: Verlag W. Kohlhammer GmbH. (English translation).

Robbins, Vernon K. (2007), "Conceptual Blending and Early Christian Imagination," in Petri Luomanen, Ilkka Pyysiäinen, and Risto Uro (eds), *Explaining Christian Origins and Early Judaism: Contributions from Cognitive and Social Science*, 161–95. Leiden and Boston, MA: Brill.

Robinson, Theodor H., and Friedrich Horst (1964), *Die zwölf kleine Propheten*, 3rd edn. HAT 14. Tübingen: J. C. B. Mohr.

Robinson, William E. W. (2016), *Metaphor, Morality, and the Spirit in Romans 8:1–17*. Early Christianity and Its Literature 20. Atlanta, GA: SBL Press.

Roitto, Rikard (2011), *Behaving as a Christ-Believer: A Cognitive Perspective on Identity and Behavior Norms in Ephesians*. ConNTS 46. Winona Lake, IN: Eisenbrauns.

Rosch, Eleanor (1973), "On the Internal Structure of Perceptual and Semantic Categories," in Timothy E. Moore (ed.), *Cognitive Development and the Acquisition of Language*, 111–44. Cambridge, MA: Academic Press.

Rosch, Eleanor (1978), "Principles of Categorization," in Eleanor Rosch and Barbara B. Lloyd (eds), *Cognition and Categorization*, 27–48. Hillsdale, NJ: Erlbaum.

Ross, Brian H., and Tom Spalding (1994), "Concepts and Categories," in Robert J. Sternberg (ed.), *Handbook of Perception and Cognition*, vol. 2 *Thinking and Problem Solving*, 119–48. San Diego, CA: Academic Press.

Rottschaefer, William A. (1998), *The Biology and Psychology of Moral Agency*. Cambridge: Cambridge University Press.

Rubin, David C. (1995), *Memory in Oral Traditions: The Cognitive Psychology of Epic, Ballads, and Counting-out Rhymes*. New York and Oxford: Oxford University Press.

Rumelhart, David E. (1975), "Notes on a Schema for Stories," in Daniel G. Bobrow and Allan M. Collins (eds), *Representation and Understanding: Studies in Cognitive Science*, 211–36. New York: Academic Press.

Sanders, E. P. (1969), *The Tendencies of the Synoptic Tradition*. Cambridge: Cambridge University Press.

Saunders, Barbara (2007), "Towards a New Typology of Color," in Robert E. MacLaury, Galina V. Paramei, and Don Dedrick (eds), *Anthropology of Color: Interdisciplinary Multilevel Modeling*, 467–79. Amsterdam: John Benjamins.

Sawyer, John F.A. (1973), "Hebrew Words for the Resurrection of the Dead." *Vetus Testamentum* 23: 218–34.

Schank, Roger C., and Robert P. Abelson (1977), *Scripts, Plans, Goals, and Understanding: An Inquiry into Human Knowledge Structures*. Hillsdale, NJ and New York: Laurence Erlbaum Associates.

Schank, Roger C., and Robert P. Abelson (1995), "Knowledge and Memory: The Real Story," in Robert S. Wyer, Roger C. Schank, and Robert P. Abelson (eds), *Knowledge and Memory: The Real Story*, 1–85. Advances in Social Cognition, V. 8. Hillsdale, NJ: Lawrence Erlbaum Associates.

Schjødt, Uffe, and Armin W. Geertz (2017), "The Beautiful Butterfly: On the History of and Prospects for the Cognitive Science of Religion," in Luther H. Martin and Donald Wiebe (eds), *Religion Explained?: The Cognitive Science of Religion after Twenty-Five Years*, 57–67. London and New York: Bloomsbury Academic.

Schnackenburg, Rudolf (1992), *The Johannine Epistles: Introduction and Commentary*. New York: Crossroad.

Schnelle, Udo (2010), *Die Johannesbriefe*. THKNT. Leipzig: Evangelische Verlagsanstalt.

Scholer, David M. (1975), "Sins Within and Sins Without: An Interpretation of 1 John 5.16–17," in G.F. Hawthorne (ed.), *Current Issues in Biblical and Patristic Interpretation*, 230–46. Grand Rapids, MI: Eerdmans.

Schreiner, J. (1974), "אָמַץ," in G. Johannes Botterweck, Helmer Ringgren, and Heinz-Josef Fabry (eds), *Theological Dictionary of the Old Testament*, vol. 1, 323–27. Stuttgart: Verlag W. Kohlhammer GmbH.

Schwartz, Baruch J. (1991), "Prohibitions Concerning the 'Eating' of Blood in Leviticus 17," in Gary A. Anderson and Saul M. Olyan (eds), *Priesthood and Cult in Ancient Israel*, 34–66. JSOTSup 125. Sheffield: Sheffield Academic Press.

Scurlock, JoAnn (2002), "Translating Transfers in Ancient Mesopotamia," in Paul Mirecki and Marvil Mayer (eds), *Magic and Ritual in the Ancient World*. Religions in the Graeco-Roman World, 141, 209–23. Leiden: Brill.

Segal, Alan (2004), *Life after Death: A History of the Afterlife in Western Religion*. New York: Doubleday.

Seitz, Christopher R. (2002), "The Book of Isaiah, Chapters 40–66," in Leander E. Keck (ed.), *The New Interpreter's Bible*, vol. 12, 6, 307–552. Nashville: Abingdon, 1994–2002.

Shantz, Colleen (2009), *Paul in Ecstasy: The Neurobiology of the Apostle's Life and Thought*. Cambridge and New York: Cambridge University Press.

Shennan, Stephen J. (2002), *Genes, Memes and Human History: Darwinian Archaeology and Cultural Evolution*. London: Thames & Hudson.

Sheppard, G.T. (1999), "Canonical Criticism," in John H. Hayes (ed.), *Dictionary of Biblical Interpretation*, 164–67. Nashville: Abingdon Press.

Slingerland, Edward (2004), "Conceptual Metaphor Theory as Methodology for Comparative Religion." *Journal of the American Academy of Religion* 72: 1–31.

Slingerland, Edward (2008a), *What Science Offers the Humanities: Integrating Body and Culture*. New York: Cambridge University Press.

Slingerland, Edward (2008b), "Who's Afraid of Reductionism?: The Study of Religion in the Age of Cognitive Science." *Journal of the American Academy of Religion* 76: 375–411.

Slingerland, Edward, and Brenton Sullivan (2017), "Durkheim with Data: The Database of Religious History (DRH)." *Journal of the American Academy of Religion* 85(2): 312–47.

Slone, D. Jason, Lauren Gonce, M. Afzal Upal, Kristin Edwards, and Ryan D. Tweney (2007), "Imagery Effects on Recall of Minimally Counterintuitive Concepts." *Journal of Cognition & Culture*, 7(3): 355–67.

Smalley, Stephen S. (1984), *1, 2, 3 John*. WBC 51. Waco, TX: Word Books.

Smart, John Jamieson Carswell (2014), "The Mind/Brain Identity Theory," in Edward N. Zalta (ed.), *The Stanford Encyclopedia of Philosophy*. Stanford, CA: The Metaphysics Research Lab.

Sørensen, Jesper (2007), *A Cognitive Theory of Magic*. Cognitive Science of Religion Series. Lanham, MD: AltaMira.

Sørensen, Jesper, and Kristoffer L. Nielbo (2014), "The Experimental Study of Religion: or There and Back Again." *Journal for the Cognitive Science of Religion* 1(2): 215–32.

Sparks, Kenton L.(1998), *Ethnicity and Identity in Ancient Israel: Prolegomena to the Study of Ethnic Sentiments and Their Expression in the Hebrew Bible*. Winona Lake, IN: Eisenbrauns.

Sperber, Dan (1996), *Explaining Culture: A Naturalistic Approach*. Oxford and Cambridge, MA: Blackwell.

Sperber, Dan (2000), "An Objection to the Memetic Approach to Culture," in Robert Aunger (ed.), *Darwinizing Culture: The Status of Memetics as a Science*, 163–73. New York: Oxford University Press.

Staal, Frits (1979), "The Meaningless of Ritual." *Numen* 26(1): 2–22.
Stacey, David (1956), *The Pauline View of Man in Relation to Its Judaic and Hellenistic Background*. London: Macmillan.
Stackert, Jeffrey (2007), *Rewriting the Torah: Literary Revision in Deuteronomy and the Holiness Legislation*. Forschungen zum Alten Testament, 52. Tübingen: Mohr Siebeck.
Stark, Rodney (1996), *The Rise of Christianity: A Sociologist Reconsiders History*. Princeton, NJ: Princeton University Press.
Stark, Rodney (2004), *Cities of God: the Real Story of How Christianity Became an Urban Movement and Conquered Rome*. Princeton, NJ: Princeton University Press.
Starr, Raymond J. (1987), "The Circulation of Literary Texts in the Roman World." *The Classical Quarterly* 37(1): 213–23.
Stearns, Stephen C., and Rolf F. Hoekstra (2005), *Evolution: An Introduction*. 2nd edn. Oxford: Oxford University Press.
Steenstra, K. (2005), *A Cognitive Approach to Religion: The Retention of Counterintuitive Concepts*. M.A. Dissertation. Radboud Universiteit Nijmegen, Nijmegen, 2005.
Stone, Linda, Paul F. Lurquin, and L. Luca Cavalli-Sforza (2006), *Genes, Culture, and Human Evolution: A Synthesis*. Malden, MA: Wiley-Blackwell.
Stovell, Beth M. (2012), *Mapping Metaphorical Discourse in the Fourth Gospel: John's Eternal King*. Linguistic Biblical Studies 5. Leiden: Brill.
Stowers, Stanley K. (1995), "Greeks Who Sacrifice and Those Who Do Not: Toward an Anthropology of Greek Religion," in L. Michael White and O. Larry Yarbrough (eds), *The Social World of the First Christians: Essays in Honor of Wayne A. Meeks*, 293–333. Minneapolis, MN: Fortress Press.
Stowers, Stanley K. (1998), "On the Comparison of Blood in Greek and Israelite Ritual," in Jodi Magness and Seymour Gitin (eds), *Hesed Ve-Emet: Studies in Honor of Ernest S. Frerichs*, 179–94. Brown Judaic Studies 320. Atlanta, GA: Scholars Press.
Strecker, Georg (1996 [1989]), *The Johannine Letters: A Commentary on 1, 2, and 3 John*. Hermeneia; Minneapolis, MN: Fortress Press. (Originally published as *Die Johannesbriefe* [KEK 14. Göttingen: Vandenhoeck & Ruprecht]).
Stuckenbruck, Loren T. (2007), *1 Enoch 91–108*. Commentaries on Early Jewish Literature. Berlin: Walter de Gruyter.
Swadling, Harry C. (1982), "Sin and Sinlessness in I John." *Scottish Journal of Theology* 35: 206–09.
Szell, Michael, and Stefan Thurner (2013), "How Women Organize Social Networks Different from Men." *Scientific Reports* 3(1214). doi: 10.1038/srep01214.
Tajfel, Henri (1982), *Social Identity and Intergroup Relations*. Cambridge: Cambridge University Press.
Tajfel, Henri, and John C. Turner (1979), "An Integrative Theory of Intergroup Conflict," in William G. Austin and Stephen Worchel (eds), *The Social Psychology of Intergroup Conflict*, 33–47. Monterey, CA: Brooks/Cole.
Tajfel, Henri, and John C. Turner (2001), "Intergroup Conflict," in Dominic Abrams and Michael A. Hogg (eds), *Intergroup Relations: Essential Readings*, 94–109. Philadelphia, PA and Hove: Psychology Press.
Tappenden, Frederick S. (2012), "Luke and Paul in Dialogue: Ritual Meals and Risen Bodies as Instances of Embodied Cognition," in Geert Van Oyen and Tom Shepherd (eds), *Resurrection of the Dead: Biblical Traditions in Dialogue*, 203–28. Bibliotheca Ephemeridum Theologicarum Lovaniensium, 249. Louven: Peeters.
Tappenden, Frederick S. (2016), *Resurrection in Paul: Cognition, Metaphor, and Transformation*. Early Christianity and Its Literature 19. Atlanta, GA: SBL Press.

Taves, Ann (2009), *Religious Experience Reconsidered: A Building Block Approach to the Study of Religion and Other Special Things*. Princeton, NJ: Princeton University Press.
Taylor, Shelley E., Laura Cousino Klein, Brian P. Lewis, Tara L. Gruenewald, Regan A. R. Gurung, and John A. Updegraff (2000), "Biobehavioral Responses to Stress in Females: Tend-and-Befriend, Not Fight-or-Flight." *Psychological Review* 107(3): 411–29.
Teehan, John (2003), "Kantian Ethics: After Darwin." *Zygon* 38: 49–60.
Thaden, Robert H van (2012), *Sex, Christ, and Embodied Cognition: Paul's Wisdom for Corinth*. Blandford Forum, Dorset: Deo Publishing.
Theißen, Gerd (1988), "Autoritätskonflikte in den johanneischen Gemeinden Zum 'Sitz im Leben' des Johannesevangeliums," in V. P. Stogiannos (ed.), *Diakonia: aphieroma ste mneme Vasileiou Stogiannou*, 243–58. Thessalonike: Aristoteleio Panepistemio Thessalonikes, Epistemonike Epetrida Theologikes Scholes.
Theißen, Gerd (1998 [1974]), *Urchristliche Wundergeschichten: Ein Beitrag zur Formgeschichtlichen Erforschung der Synoptischen Evangelien*. 7th edn. Studien zum Neuen Testament, Bd. 8. Gütersloh: Mohn.
Theißen, Gerd (2007), "Jesusüberlieferungen und Christuskerygma bei Paulus: Ein Beitrag zur Kognitiven Analyse Urchristlicher Theologie," in Michael Welker, Günter Thomas, and Andreas Schüle (eds), *Gegenwart des Lebendigen Christus*, 119–38. Leipzig: Evangelische Verlagsanstalt.
Theißen, Gerd (2008), *Die Religion der Ersten Christen: Eine Theorie des Urchristentums*. 3rd edn. Gütersloh: Kaiser.
Theißen, Gerd, Lungpun Common Chan, and István Czachesz (2017), *Kontraintuivität und Paradoxie: Zur kognitiven Analyse des urchristlichen Glaubens*. Münster: LIT Verlag.
Thelwall, Mike (2008), "Social Networks, Gender, and Friending: An Analysis of MySpace Member Profiles." *Journal of the Association for Information Science and Technology* 59(8): 1321–30.
Thrall, Margaret E. (2000), *A Critical and Exegetical Commentary on the Second Epistle to the Corinthians*. Edinburgh: T. & T. Clark.
Tigay, Jeffrey H. (1996), *Deuteronomy*. The JPS Torah Commentary. Philadelphia, PA and Jerusalem: The Jewish Publication Society.
Tomasello, Michael (1999), *The Cultural Origins of Human Cognition*. Cambridge, MA: Harvard University Press.
Tomasello, Michael (2009), *The Cultural Origins of Human Cognition*. Cambridge, MA: Harvard University Press.
Tomasello, Michael, Ann Cale Kruger, and Hilary Horn Ratner (1993), "Cultural Learning." *Behavioral and Brain Sciences* 16(3): 495–552.
Tooby, John, and Leda Cosmides (2000), "Toward Mapping the Evolved Functional Organization of Mind and Brain," in Michael Gazzaniga (ed.), *The New Cognitive Neurosciences*. 2nd edn. Cambridge, MA: MIT Press.
Turner, John C., Michael A. Hogg, Penelope J. Oakes, Stephen D. Reicherand, and Margaret S. Wetherell (1987), *Rediscovering the Social Group: A Self-Categorization Theory*. Oxford: Blackwell.
Ungerer, Friedrich, and Hans-Jörg Schmid (1996), *An Introduction to Cognitive Linguistics*. 1st edn. London: Longman.
Upal, M. Afzal, Lauren O. Gonce, Ryan D. Tweney, and D. Jason Slone (2007), "Contextualizing Counterintuitiveness: How Context Affects Comprehension and Memorability of Counterintuitive Concepts." *Cognitive Science: A Multidisciplinary Journal* 31(3): 415–39.

Uro, Risto (1998), "Thomas and Oral Tradition," in Risto Uro (ed.), *Thomas at the Crossroads*, 8–32. Edinburgh and Ithaca, NY: Snow Lion Publications and T & T Clark.
Uro, Risto (2003), *Thomas: Seeking the Historical Context of the Gospel of Thomas*. London and New York: Continuum and T & T Clark.
Uro, Risto (2010), "Ritual and Christian Origins," in Dietmar Neufeld and Richard E. DeMaris (eds), *Understanding the Social World of the New Testament*, 223–35. London and New York: Routledge.
Uro, Risto (2013a), "From Corpse Impurity to Relic Veneration: New Light from Cognitive and Psychological Studies," in István Czachesz and Risto Uro (eds), *Mind, Morality and Magic: Cognitive Science Approaches in Biblical Studies*, 180–96. Durham: Acumen.
Uro, Risto (2013b), "The Interface of Ritual and Writing in the Transmission of Early Christian Traditions," in István Czachesz and Risto Uro (eds), *Mind, Morality, and Magic: Cognitive Science Approaches in Biblical Studies*, 62–76. Durham: Acumen.
Uro, Risto (2016), *Ritual and Christian Beginnings: A Socio-Cognitive Analysis*. Oxford: Oxford University Press.
Van der Dennen, Johan M.G. (1987), "Ethnocentrism and In-group/Out-group Differentiation: A Review and Interpretation of the Literature," in Vernon Reynolds, Vincent S.E. Falger, and Ian Vine (eds), *The Sociobiology of Ethnocentrism*, 1–47. London: Croom Helm.
Van Hecke, Pierre J. P. van (2003), "Searching for and Exploring Wisdom: A Cognitive Semantic Approach to the Hebrew Verb 'haqar' in Job 28," in Ellen van Wolde (ed.), *Job 28: Cognition in Context*. Biblical Interpretation Series 64, 139–62. Leiden: Brill.
Van Seters, John (2003), *A Law Book for the Diaspora: Revision in the Study of the Covenant Code*. Oxford and New York: Oxford University Press.
Varela, Francisco J., Evan Thompson, and Eleanor Rosch (1991), *The Embodied Mind: Cognitive Science and Human Experience*. Cambridge, MA: MIT Press.
Vernant, Jean-Pierre (1989), "At Man's Table: Hesiod's Foundation Myth of Sacrifice," in Marcel Detienne and Jean-Pierre Vernant (eds), *The Cuisine of Sacrifice among the Greeks*, 21–86. Chicago, IL: The University of Chicago Press.
Vervenne, Marc (1993), "'The Blood Is the Life and the Life Is the Blood': Blood as Symbol of Life and Death in Biblical Tradition (Gen 9,4)," in J. Quaegebeur (ed.), *Ritual and Sacrifice in the Ancient Near East*, 452–70. Orientalia Lovaniensia analecta 55. Leuven: Uitgeverij Peeters en Departement Oriëntalistiek.
Viberg, Åke (1992), *Symbols of Law: A Contextual Analysis of Legal Symbolic Acts in the Old Testament*. Coniectanea Biblica Old Testament Series, 34. Stockholm: Almqvist & Wiksell International.
Weiher, Egbert von (1998), *Uruk: Spätbabylonische Texte aus dem Planquadrat U 18*, Teil V. Ausgrabungen in Uruk-Warka, Endberichte, Band 13. Mainz am Rhein: Verlag Philipp von Zabern.
Weinrich, Harald (1967), "Semantik der Metapher." *Folia Linguistica* 1(1/2): 3–17.
Westbrook, Raymond, and Bruce Wells (2009), *Everyday Law in Biblical Israel: An Introduction*. Louisville, KY: Westminster John Knox.
Westcott, Brooke F. (1886), *The Epistles of St John: The Greek Text with Notes and Essays*. Cambridge: Macmillan.
Whitehouse, Harvey (1995), *Inside the Cult: Religious Innovation and Transmission in Papua New Guinea*. Oxford Studies in Social and Cultural Anthropology. Oxford and New York: Clarendon Press and Oxford University Press.
Whitehouse, Harvey (2000), *Arguments and Icons: Divergent Modes of Religiosity*. Oxford: Oxford University Press.

Whitehouse, Harvey (2004), *Modes of Religiosity: A Cognitive Theory of Religious Transmission*. New York, Walnut Creek, CA, and Lanham, MD: Altamira Press.

Williams, Ronald J. (1976), *Hebrew Syntax: An Outline*. 2nd edn. Toronto: University of Toronto Press.

Williamson, Hugh G. M. (1999), "'From One Degree of Glory to Another': Themes and Theology in Isaiah," in Edward Ball (ed.), *In Search of True Wisdom: Essays in Old Testament Interpretation in Honour of Ronald E. Clements*, 174–95. Journal for the Study of the Old Testament: Supplement Series 300. Sheffield: Sheffield Academic Press.

Willis, Timothy M. (2001), *The Elders of the City: A Study of the Elders-Laws in Deuteronomy*. SBL Monograph Series, 55. Atlanta, GA: Society of Biblical Literature.

Wilson, David Sloan (2002), *Darwin's Cathedral: Evolution, Religion, and the Nature of Society*. Chicago, IL: University of Chicago Press.

Wilson, David Sloan (2003), *Darwin's Cathedral: Evolution, Religion, and the Nature of Society*. Chicago, IL: University of Chicago Press.

Wilson, David Sloan, and Edward Osborne Wilson (2007), "Rethinking the Theoretical Foundation of Sociobiology." *The Quarterly Review of Biology*, 82(4): 327–48.

Wilson, David Sloan, and Edward Osborne Wilson (2008), "Evolution 'for the Good of the Group.'" *American Scientist* 96(5): 378–89.

Wilson, Robert A., and Lucia Foglia (2011), "Embodied Cognition," in Edward N. Zalta (ed.), *The Stanford Encyclopedia of Philosophy*. Stanford, CA: The Metaphysics Research Lab, http://plato.stanford.edu/archives/fall2011/entries/embodied-cognition/.

Wolde, Ellen van (2008), "Sentiments as Culturally Constructed Emotions: Anger and Love in the Hebrew Bible." *Biblical Interpretation* 16: 1–24.

Woody, Sheila R., and Bethany A. Teachman (2000), "Intersection of Disgust and Fear: Normative and Pathological Views." *Clinical Psychology: Science and Practice* 7: 291–311.

Wright, David P. (1987a), *The Disposal of Impurity: Elimination Rites in the Bible and in Hittite and Mesopotamian Literature*. SBL Dissertation Series, 101. Atlanta, GA: Scholars Press.

Wright, David P. (1987b), "Deuteronomy 21: 1–9 as a Rite of Elimination," *Catholic Biblical Quarterly* 49: 387–403.

Wright, David P. (2003), "The Laws of Hammurabi as a Source for the Covenant Collection (Exodus 20:23–23:19)," *Maarav* 10: 11–87.

Wright, David P. (2009), *Inventing God's Law: How the Covenant Code of the Bible Used and Revised the Laws of Hammurabi*. Oxford: Oxford University Press.

Wright, N. T. (2003), *The Resurrection of the Son of God*. Minneapolis, MN: Fortress Press.

Xygalatas, Dimitris (2013), "Přenos Laboratoře Do Terénu: Využití Smíšených Metod Během Terénního Studia Náboženství." *Social Studies* 10(2): 15–25.

Yarbrough, Robert W. (2008), *1–3 John*. BECNT. Grand Rapids, MI: Baker Academic.

Zajonc, Robert B. (1980), "Feeling and Thinking: Preferences Need no Inferences." *American Psychologist* 35: 151–75.

Zakovitch, Yair (1975), "Between the Song of Songs and the Stories of Samson." *Beit Mikra: Journal for the Study of the Bible and Its World* 20(2): 292–94.

Zakovitch, Yair (1992), *Song of Songs: Introduction and Commentary*. Jerusalem: Am-Oved and Magnes.

Zimmermann, Ruben (2007), "Die Gleichnisse Jesu: Eine Leseanleitung zum Kompendium," in Ruben Zimmermann and Detlev Dormeyer (eds), *Kompendium der Gleichnisse Jesu*, 3–46. Gütersloh: Gütersloher Verlagshaus.

Index of Ancient Sources

Old Testament / Hebrew Bible

Genesis
1:11 64
1:12 64
2 68, 185 n.16
2:7 66, 68
3:19 65, 117, 192 n.20
4:10–11 63
9 63
9:4 63
22 21
24:67 78, 79
27 78, 79
29 78, 79
30:2 67
34 78
37–44 78, 79
37:35 117
43:32 182 n.22
46:34 182 n.22
47:30 193 n.29

Exodus 96, 181 n.9
4:14 67
8:26 182 n.22
12:19 182 n.33
13–14 93
16:7 189 n.19
16:10 189 n.19
19:2–24:15 181 n.9, 186 n.17
20:1 181 n.9
20:5 52
20:6 187 n.19
20:18–20 52
20:22–23:33 181 n.9
20:24-6 46
21–23 44
21:2–11 44
21:2 44
21:5 83, 187 n.19
21:12–14 184 n.55

22:6–14 53
22:10–11 50
22:19 52
22:20 181 n.19
22:20–26 44
22:20–23:33 186 n.17
22:20 45
22:21–23 53
22:21 46
22:23 46
22:24 45, 46, 53
22:25–6 45, 46
22:24–26 53
23 61, 182 n.29
23:9 45, 181 n.19
23:10–11 45
23:12 45
23:20–1 53
23:20–33 46, 53
23:27 46
23:31 46, 53
23:32–3 46
23:33 46
23:27 53, 183 n.42
23:32–3 53
24:3a 181 n.9
24:6, 10–15 181 n.20
29:43 94
33:18 189 n.19
40:34–35 94
40:35 93
48–49 182 n.33
60:1–2 93
62:2 93

Leviticus 61
1–16 49, 186 n.17
3 64, 65
3:2 64
3:8 64
3:18 64
3:3–5.9–11.14–16 64

3:16-17 64
4:13–14 153
9:6 94, 189 n.19
10 182 n.33
10:1–3 54
11 48, 51, 182 n.28
11:23 51
11:24–5 51
11:44 51
12 182 n.33
13 182 n.33
13:45–6 60
14 57
14:1–7 56
14–18 56
15 182 n.33
15:31 54
16 57
16:2 54
17 49, 182 n.33
17:8 182 n.33
17:10 182 n.33, 183 n.39
17-22 182 n.31
17–26 49, 186 n.17
17–27 54
18 50, 51, 183 n.40
18:3 51
18:1–5, 24–30 183 n.40
18:6-23 183 n.40
18:10 183 n.36
18:12 48
18:22 51, 183 n.40
18:24–30 50, 54, 55, 200 n.8
18:25–28 55
18:26 51, 182 n.33
18:27 51
18:28 51
18:29 51, 183 n.39
18:30 51
18–20 55
19 49, 55
19:2 183 n.38
19:5–8 55
19:9–10 50
19:18 83, 187 n.19
19:31 200 n.8
19:33–4 183 n.36, 187 n.19
19:34 83
19:37 183 n.38

20 48, 50
20:1–3 200 n.8
20:1–6 55
20:2 182 n.33, 183 n.39
20:7–8, 22-6 183 n.38
20:10-14 48
20:13 51
20:15–18 48
20:22 51, 183 n.44
20:22–24 55
20:22–26 50, 55
20:22–30 50
20:23 55
20:26 51
22:1–3 55
22:18 182 n.33
22:31–3 183 n.38
23 49, 94, 189 n.19
23:22 50
23–25 55
24:10–23 183 n.41
24:16, 22 182 n.33, 183 n.39
24:22 182 n.33
25:6 183 n.36
25-9 56
25:45 183 n.34
26 55, 62
26:1–2 183 n.45
26:32–5 55
26:14–39 50
26:33b–35 183 n.45
26:43–44 183 n.45
27:47–54 50
28 55
28:11 55
28:15 55
28:30 55
28:43, 44 55
35 183 n.36
49–53 56

Numbers 61
9:14 182 n.33
12:1 183 n.41
14:10 94, 189 n.19
14:22 189 n.19
15:14–16 182 n.33
15:27–31 153

15:30 183 n.39
15:37–41 138, 145
16:19 94, 189 n.19
16:29–33 192 n.22
17:7 94, 189 n.19
19:9 58
19:10 182 n.33
19:17 58
20:6 94, 189 n.19
25 183 n.41
26 183 n.33
29–30 182 n.33
35 184 n.55
35:9–34 59, 184 n.55
35:15 182 n.33
35:33–4 59, 200 n.8

Deuteronomy 37, 61, 62, 127
1:21 49
2:23 182 n.21
2:24 47
2:25 53
3:2 47, 49
3:6 182 n.21
4:2 180 n.19
4:37 82, 87, 186 n.18
5:10 187 n.19
5:22 180 n.19
5:24 189 n.19
6:4–9 47, 138, 145
6:5 187 n.19, 187 n.21
6:7 138
7 53
7:1 53
7:1–3 48
7:2 47, 48
7:8, 13 87, 186 n.18
7:9 187 n.19
7:10 54
7:12–13 82, 186 n.18
7:16, 25 54
7:18–19 49
7:23 54
7:25–6 48, 182 n.23
7:26 54, 182 n.21
8:19–20 54
10:10 83
10:12 187 n.19, 187 n.21
10:12–11:1 54

10:12–11:30 47
10:15 48, 82, 87, 186 n.18
10:17–19 47
10:18 82, 87, 186 n.18
10:19 47, 54, 187 n.21
10:20 54
11:1 187 n.19, 187 n.21
11:12 83
11:13 132, 145, 187 n.19, 187 n.21
11:13–21 138, 145
11:22 187 n.19, 187 n.21
12 63, 182 n.23
12:16 64
12:23–24 64
12:2 47
12:2–27 47
12:26 46, 186 n.17
12–30 48
12:31 182 n.23
13 54
13:1 180 n.19
13:4 187 n.19
13:15 182 n.21
14:3 182 n.23
14:3–19 182 n.28
14:21 183 n.34
14:29 48
15:16 83, 187 n.19
16:14 48
17 182 n.21
17:1 182 n.23
18 47
18:9 182 n.23
19:1–13 59, 184 n.55
19:9 187 n.19, 187 n.21
19:10 59
19:13 50, 59
19:14 50
19:15–18 50
19:18 50
19:33–4 50
19:34 50
20 47, 53
20:1 49
20:3 49
20:8 49
20:17 182 n.21
20:18 182 n.23
21 59

21:1–9 59
21:5 59
21:8, 9 59
21:10–14 49, 51, 53
21:15–16 83, 187 n.19
22 49
22:5 182 n.23, 187 n.21
22:6–7 65
22:7 65
23:3–4 182 n.25
23:6 82, 87, 186 n.18
23:8 182 n.23
23:8–9 182 n.25
23:11 187 n.21
23:19 182 n.23
24:4 182 n.23
24:6–22 54
24:13 54
24:14 48
24:15 54
24:17–22 48
24:19–22 50
25:16 182 n.23
26:2 194 n.36
26:9–11 194 n.36
26:16–18, and 20–1 194 n.36
26:12–13 48
27:15 182 n.23, 194 n.36
26:16–18 194 n.36
26:20–1 194 n.36
27:18 182 n.32
28 55, 62, 182 n.29
28:15–68 54
29 49
29:11 183 n.33
29:16–28 183 n.43
30:6 187 n.19
30:11–20 119
30:16 187 n.19, 187 n.21, 194 n.34
30:17–18
30:20 187 n.19, 187 n.21
31 47
31:6, 8 49
31:12 183 n.33
31:16 193 n.29
32:15–25 183 n.43
37:12 194 n.35

Joshua
22:5 186 n.17, 187 n.19
23:11 186 n.17, 187 n.19

Judges
14-16 78–9
16:4 79
16:7, 13 79
16:15 79

1 Samuel
1 78
1:1–10 78
1:4 78
4:21 94
16 78
16:21 79
18 78
18:1 79
18:3 79
18:16 80
18:22 79
18:28 79
20 78
20:17 79

2 Samuel
1 78
1:23 79
1:26 79
7:12 193 n.29
13 78
14:14 117

1 Kings
1:48 146
2:10 193 n.29
3:3 80
10:9 87
11:1, 2 80
11:43 193 n.29

2 Kings
22:3 47

Isaiah 10, 94
2:10 98, 190 n.27
2:10, 19, 21 190 n.27
3:18 94, 97

4:2 95, 98, 190 n.27
5:13 188 n.14
5:14 190 n.27
10:12 97
13:9 96
13:19 97, 98, 190 n.27
14 195 n.40
14:1 195 n.40
14:1–20 195 n.40
14:2 195 n.40
14:9 193 n.24
14:11–12, 15 195 n.40
14:15 117
16:6 95
16:14 188 n.15
17:3 188 n.14
17:4 188 n.14
20:5 97
21:16 188 n.15
23:9 190 n.27
24 195 n.38
24:16 190 n.27
26 113
26:14, 19 193 n.24
26:19 119, 196 n.51
28:1, 4, 5 97, 190 n.27
30:30 92, 97
35:2 93, 188 n.15, 189 n.19, 190 n.27
40:5 189 n.19
44:13 97
46 97
52:1 97
52:2 94
53:2 190 n.27
56–66 88, 91, 92, 93, 97, 188 n.7, 188 n.12
56 91
57 91
58 91, 97
58:8 93, 187 n.7
58:8–10 97
59 91
59:9–10 97
59:19 93, 187 n.7
60 91
60:1 93, 187 n.7, 189 n.23
60:1–5, 19–20 97
60:2 93, 94, 187 n.7, 189 n.19
60:7 94, 188 n.7

60:13 92, 188 n.7, 188 n.14, 188 n.15
60:15 95, 96, 188 n.7
60:19 95, 97, 188 n.7
60–64 94
60–66 92, 94, 189 n.17
61:6 92, 187 n.7, 188 n.14, 188 n.15
62:1 97
62:2 92, 187 n.7, 188 n.14, 189 n.19
62:3 94, 97, 188 n.7
63:12, 14, 15 188 n.7
63:15 94
64:10 94, 188 n.7
64:40 94
66:11 92, 188 n.7, 188 n.14
66:12 92, 188 n.7, 188 n.14
66:11, 12, 18, 19 188 n.7, 189 n.19
66:24 196 n.51

Jeremiah
2:11 188 n.14, 188 n.16
3:19 98
7:6 182 n.20
13:18 94
22:3 182 n.20
48:17 94
48:18 188 n.15
48:29 95
51:39, 57 193 n.28

Ezekiel
3:23 93, 189 n.19
4:10 189 n.23
7:16–22 94
9:6 95
10 94
10:11 95
11:3 95
16:12 94
16:17 94
16:39 94
16:49 189 n.24
20:6 98
22:7 182 n.20
22:29 182 n.20
23:26 94
23:42 94
24:21 94, 95
25:9 98
30:6 95

30:18 95
31:18 188 n.15
32:12 95
32:21, 27, 30 193 n.28
33:28 95
37 113
37:1–14 119
37:10 119
37:12 119
43:2 189 n.23
43–4 94
44:4 93

Hoseah
9:11 188 n.14

Amos
9:2 117

Jonah
2:4 94

Micah
1:2 94
1:15 188 n.14

Habakuk
2:20 94

Haggai
2 94
2:3–9 94

Zechariah
1 105, 108
1:8 10, 100, 105–7, 109, 190 n.6
1.8-17 190 n.6
1:8-11 105
2:13 94
6 105, 108
6:1–8 10, 100, 105–6, 107
6:2 107
6:2–3 107
6:3 107–9
6:5 106
6:6 107
6:6–7 107

6:7 108
7:10 182 n.20

Malachi
3:5 182 n.20

Psalms
5:8 94
8:6 98
11:4 94
20:10 138
21:6 98
22:30 117
26:8 94
30:4 117
30:10 117
40:3 193 n.23
43:3 94
45:4–5 98
45:7 96
55:16 117
63:3 94, 189 n.19
65:5 94
73:17 and 23–6 192 n.16
73:27–8 192 n.16
78:38 138
79:1 94
84:1 189 n.22
88:10 193 n.24
92 138
93 138
93:5 94
96:6 94
97:6 189 n.19
102:16 93
104:1 98
106:20 188 n.16
138:2 94
139:8 117
145 138

Proverbs
2:18 193 n.24
9:18 117, 193 n.24
15:9 187 n.18
21:16 193 n.24
31:25 98

Job
3:21 117
11:8 117
14:1–2 192 n.20
14:10–12 117
14:12 193 n.28
19:25–7 192 n.19
26:5 193 n.24
34:15 117
38:7 123
40:10 97

Song of Songs 10, 34, 75, 83, 85–6
1:3–4 77
1:7 77
2:3 77
2:5 77
2:7 77
3:1–4 76–7
4:9 76, 85
6:5 76, 85

Ecclesiastes
3:21 185 n.16

Daniel
8:9 98
10–12 195 n.41
11:40 122
12 113, 114, 123
12:1–3 112, 120, 122, 127, 195 n.40
12:2 127, 191 n.6, 196 n.51, 197 n.51
12:3 119, 123, 125, 195 n.43, 197 n.51

Nehemiah
2:3 95

1 Chronicles
22:5 189 n.21
29:10 146

2 Chronicles
3:6 189 n.21
5:14 94
7:1–3 94
7:2 93
7:3 93, 189 n.19
9:31 193 n.29

Dead Sea Scrolls

1QHa
13:32 95
18:11 93
20:3 94
20:15 189 n.23
20:18 95
24:11 94

1QS
4:8 98
10:3 94
III.13–IV.26 201 n.16
IV.20–23 158
IV.23–4 201 n.16
VIII.21–24 153

2Q20
f1:3 189 n.17

4Q268
8 ii, 6 183 n.51

4Q271
ii, 13 183 n.51

4Q276 183 n.51

4Q277 183 n.51
1 ii, 7 183 n.51

4Q369
f1ii:3 189 n.19

4Q377
f2ii:9 93

4Q400
f1i:4 94

4Q405
f14_15i:6 94
f19 94
f20ii_22:9 95

4Q457b
2:6 189 n.19

4Q504
f1_2riv:8 189 n.19
f1_2riv:12 94

4Q510
f1:3 98

4Q511
f1:7 189 n.23
f1:7-8 93

4Q525
f11_12:2 98

11Q5
22:4 94
22:5 94
26:9 98

11Q17
7:4 94
10:8 94

11QT
26:13 183 n.48

New Testament

Gospel of Matthew 23, 24, 25, 175, 176, 190 n.4
5:45 30
10:22 173
12:22-32 31
18:21-35 29
20:1-16 29

Gospel of Mark 24, 25, 35, 175
1:10 35
1:21-43 170
1:23-26 29
2:1-12 170
4:1-20 29
4:26-29 29
4:30-32 29
5:1-13 30
5:1-24 31
5:3-5 31
5:11-13 31
5:12 31
6:35-44 31
6:45-53 31
7:33 30
12:40 167
13:13 173
15:38 35
16:8 25
16:9-20 25

Gospel of Luke 25, 169
2:36-38 167
4:26 167
7:1-10 30
10:25-37 29
12:9 26
12:13-21 29
18:1-8 167
18:9-14 29
24:31 33

Gospel of John 25, 169
2:6-10 31
3:18 158
5:24 158
6 32
8:51 158
10:14 175
11 32
11:38-44 31
15:9 25
15:21 173
20:19 33
20:26 33

Acts of the Apostles 25, 26
4:30 173
6 167
9:2 173
10:43 173
16:16 31
19:9.23 173
21:10 31
22:4 173
24:14 173

Epistle to the Romans
5:1 26
6:1-14 174

7:20 156
16 166
16:23 169

First Epistle to the Corinthians
1:10 173
1–2 33
6:15 174
9:5 166
11 11, 19, 166
12 174
15:3–8 33
16 166
16:1 166

Second Epistle to the Corinthians 201 n.3
3:1 166
8:16–24 166
9 166
11 166

Epistle to the Ephesians
4:15–16 174
5:31–32 174

Epistle to the Phillipians
2:5–8 22

Epistle to the Galatians
1:6 166
1–2 166
2 166
2:4 166
2:6–10 166
2:10 166
3:1 166
3:28 173
5:25 157

First Epistle to Timothy
5 167
5:3–16 168

Second Epistle to Peter 37
2:13 26
3:16 37

First Epistle of John 11, 149, 150, 152, 153, 158, 160, 161, 200 n.11
1:4 25
1:7 150, 160
1:8 151
1:8–10 200 n.2, 201 n.15
1:8–2:2 149, 152, 153, 159–60
1:8–9 149
1:8–10 149, 155, 159
1:9 200 n.5, 201 n.14
2:1 151, 157
2:3 156
2:4 155
2:5 155
2:8, 17–18 201 n.20
2:9 155
2:10 155
2:11 155, 157
2:19 150, 155
2:22–23 154
3 157
3:1–10 159
3:4 154
3:6 149, 151, 153, 155, 157, 159, 200 n.4, 201 n.15
3:6–9 200 n.2, 201 n.15, 201 n.21
3:6–10 149, 155–6
3:8 149, 154, 156, 157
3:9 149–150, 151, 153, 155–6, 157, 159, 200 n.4
3:10 155, 156
3:11–18 154
3:11 155
3:14 150, 154–5, 158
3:16 155
3:16–18 151
3:17 154
3:23 155
4:7 155, 201 n.13
4:8 155
4:11 155
4:12 155
4:14 155
4:16 25
4:17–18 155
4:18 156
4:19 155
4:20 155

4:21 155
5:1 155
5:2–3 155
5:14–17 156, 160
5:15–17 159
5:16 151, 152
5:16–17 149, 150, 153, 159, 200 n.5, 201 n.15
5:16–18 156
5:18 149, 153, 155, 159, 201 n.15

Old Testament Apocrypha and Pseudepigrapha

Sirach
26:17 95
42:16 189 n.23
42:17 93
43:9 95
49:5 189 n.17
49:12 94

Wisdom of Solomon
5 123, 195 n.42

Jubilees
5.12 158
5:13–16 191 n.1
10:7 191 n.1
23:11 191 n.1
23:29–31 112, 190 n.1
23:22–32 190 n.1
46:2 189 n.17

1 Enoch
5:8 158
10:4–5 183 n.48
22:13 191 n.2
39:7 119
51 122
51:1 128
58:2–6 119
62 122
62: 14, 16 197 n.53
62:15–16 119
86:1, 3 123
90:20–7 122
90:21 123
90:33 120, 197 n.53
92:3 118
93:2 193 n.31
99:11–102:3 122
100:5–6 118, 194 n.31
103:7–8 122
104 123
104:2 119, 122, 123, 125
104:6 125
104:4, 6 123

Book of Watchers 112, 191 n.2, 192 n.10

Epistle of Enoch 114, 118, 122, 126, 192 n.11, 194 n.32

Similitudes of Enoch 114, 122

Enoch's Dream Visions 114, 120, 122

Testament of Moses (T. Mos.)
10 114, 122, 123
10:7–10 120
10:9 119, 123
10:9–10 123, 125
10:10 123

Testaments of the 12 Patriarchs
191 n.10

Testament of Levi
18.9 158

Psalms of Solomon
3 114, 194 n.31
3:1–2 118
3:5–8 151
3:11–12 122
3:12 119
9:5–7 151
13:7–10 151
16:11 151
17.32–33 158
63:3 189 n.19
106:20 188 n.14, 188 n.16

4 Ezra
9:31 158

2 Maccabees 120, 126, 195 n.41
7 114, 122
7:9 122
7:10–11 119
7:23 122
7:29 197 n.53
7:33 197 n.53
12:44–45 118, 193 n.31
14:43–6 119

4 Maccabees
3.2–5 156

Greek authors and Christian Apocrypha
(in alphabetical order)

Acts of John 33
30–36 167
100 175

Acts of Paul and Thecla 167

Acts of Peter
8, 21 167

Aristides
Apology 15 167

Aristotle
Rhet. II.3 153

Barnabas
8:1 59

Cicero
Inv. II.5 153

Didache (The Teaching of the Twelve Apostles) 25, 26, 177
11 166

Epictetus
Diatr. II.9 157

Gospel of Mary 167

Gospel of Philip 167

Hermas
Similitudes 5.3 167
Shepherd I.50.8 167

Iliad 184 n.7
XIV, 516–519 65
XIV, 518 185 n.8

Irenaeus
Against Heresies 3.11.8 38

Lucian of Samosata 171
Life of Peregrinus Proteus 12 167

Odyssey
XI 65, 184 n.6
XI, 95–96 65
XI, 152–154 65

Origen
Against Celsus
3 168
3.55 168

Philo
Decal. 142–153 156

Tertullian
De monogamia 11.1 167
De praescriptione 3.5 167
Pud. 19 153

Thucydides
On the Peloponnesian War
1.22 171

Rabbinic Sources

Mishnah
mBerakhot 1:2 143
mBerakhot 1:4 138
mKeritot 1:2 153
mParah 3:2–4 59

Talmud Bavli
Ta'anit 2a 199 n.23

Talmud Yerushalmi
Berakhot 29ab 199 n.23

Mekhilta de rabbi Simeon b. Yohai
23:25 199 n.23

Pesiqta de Rab Kahana
4:7 58

Maimonides
Mishne Torah, Hilkhot Tefilla
1:1 199 n.23
1:5–6 145, 199

Other sources

Vendidād
3.8–9 184 n.57
3.14 184 n.56
5.27–38 184 n.56
6.44–51 184 n.57
7.1–9 184 n.56
8.4–13 184 n.57
8.40–71 57
8.14–19 184 n.56
12–15 184 n.57
36–9 184 n.57

Shurpu
i 9–23 (Reiner 1958, 11) 57
vii 53–70 (Reiner 1958) 183 n.50

Atrahasis 66
Tablet I, iv 66

Enuma Elish 66
Tablet VI, 5–8 66
Tablet VI, 33–35 66

Laws of Hammurabi
47:61–62 181 n.18

Aqhat
KTU 1.18 IV: 24–25 185 n.14

Index of Modern Authors

Abelson, Robert P. 27
Ackerman, Susan 70, 84–6
Alden, Robert L. 107
Alford, Henry 158
Arrindell, Willem A. 43
Ashdown, Shelley 10
Atran, Scott 22, 24, 32, 170–1
Augoustinos, Martha 153
Aune, David E. 156
Axelrod, Robert 151
Azari, Nina P. 174

Bainbridge, William Sims 5
Balch, David L. 168
Bandura, Albert 44
Barrett, Justin L. 5, 20, 22, 32, 170
Barsalou, Lawrence W. 6, 101
Bartle, Philip F. W. 101–2
Bartlett, Frederic 20–2
Bauckham, Richard 128
Baumgarten, Joseph M. 183
Bechtel, William 3
Beck, Roger L. 2, 168–9
Becker, Howard S. 171
Bering, Jesse M. 30
Bernburg, Jón Gunnar 171
Beuken, Willem A. M. 91
Biale, David 65
Birnbacher, Dieter 174
Biró, Tamás 11, 129
Borg, Alexander 108
Bowden, Hugh 2
Bowling, A. 106
Boyd, Robert 14, 163, 172
Boyer, Pascal 4–5, 7–9, 20, 22, 32, 170
Bremmer, Jan N. 65, 167
Brenner, Athalya 70, 85–6, 107
Brevard S. Childs 35
Brown, Raymond E. 150, 153
Bulbulia, Joseph A. 5

Bultmann, Rudolf Karl 175
Burton, Marilyn E. 2, 10, 88–9, 91

Centola, Damon 155
Chalmers, David J. 5
Chalupa, Aleš 5
Charlesworth, James H. 114, 128
Chmiel, Jerzy 113
Choksy, Jamsheed 59–60
Cholewiński, Alfred 49
Chomsky, Noam 129
Clark, Andy 5–6
Clauss, Manfred 169
Cohen, Henry 99
Collins, John Jean 112, 127
Cosmides, Leda 4
Croft, William 118
Crossan, John Dominic 166
Cruse, D. Alan 118
Cushman, Fiery 158
Czachesz, István 1, 2, 5, 8–9, 11, 13, 17–19, 21, 23, 25, 28, 30, 32–4, 155, 162–3, 165, 167, 170, 174

Dalley, Stephanie 66
Damasio, Antonio 1, 40–1
D'Andrade, Roy 101
d'Aquili, Eugene G. 152
Darwin, Charles 7, 162
Davies, Stevan L. 167
Dawkins, Richard 8, 162–3
Deacon, Terence 14
de Blois, Reinier 99
Delling, Gerhard 171
de Vaux, Roland 58
de Waal, Frans B.M. 44
Dickson, Kwesi A. 110
Dodd, Charles H. 150–1, 159
Donald, Merlin 5, 10, 70–5, 84
Doojse, Bertjan 159
Downing, F. Gerald 18

Duhm, Bernhard 91
Duling, Dennis C. 171
Dunbar, Robin I. M. 44, 173

Ebeling, Gerhard 17
Eberhart, Christian A. 64
Ebrard, Johannes Heinrich August 151–2
Eidinow, Esther 2
Eve, Eric 23–4, 171
Es, Eelco van 75
Eysenck, Michael W. 3

Fauconnier, Gilles 6
Faulkner, Jason 44
Feldman Barrett, Lisa 70
Fessler, Daniel M.T. 44
Festinger, Leon 154
Fishbein, Harold D. 44, 52
Fodor, Jerry A. 3
Foglia, Lucia 6
Frend, William H. C. 162
Froehlich, Karlfried 17
Frye, Northrop 36

Gärdenfors, Peter 88
Geertz, Armin W. 5
Gibbons, Ann 8
Gibbs, Raymond W., Jr. 67, 128
Gilders, William K. 63–4
Gonce, Lauren O. 22
Granovetter, Mark S. 165
Green, Joel B. 2
Greimas, Algirdas Julien 19
Griffith, Terry 150, 154
Grimm, Jacob 13
Groom, Susan 89
Gross, James J. 156
Grünwaldt, Klaus 49
Gudme, Anne Katrine de Hemmer 10, 63
Guthrie, Stewart Elliott 4, 7

Haacker, Klaus 22
Haenchen, Ernst 35
Hagan, George P. 100
Haidle, Miriam N. 15
Haidt, Jonathan 41–2
Halpin, Harry 144
Harnack, Adolf von 162
Harnad, Stevan 99

Hartley, John E. 107
Haslam, Alexander S. 152, 154
Henrich, Joseph 8, 163
Hoekstra, Rolf F. 7
Hoffmann, Dirk L. 5
Hogg, Michael 152, 158–9
Holladay, William L. 91
Horrell, David G. 172
Horst, Friedrich 106
Houston, George W. 18
Houston, Walter 44
Houston McNeel, Jennifer 2
Howe, Bonnie 2
Hutchins, Edwin 5

Jablonka, Eva 8, 14, 19
Jackson, Bernard S. 45
Johnson, Mark 6, 40, 67, 113, 115–17, 120, 124
Johnson, Nancy S. 131, 144, 148
Johnson, William A. 18

Kammers, Marjolein P. M. 30
Kaufmann, Yehezkel 56, 58
Kazen, Thomas 2, 9, 40, 45, 56–7, 70, 84
Keane, Mark T. 3
Kedar-Kopfstein, Benjamin 107
Keil, Frank C. 22, 32
Kekes, John 41
Kelber, Werner H. 18, 23
Kelly, Michael H. 32
Kim, Uichol 99
Knuuttila, Simo 41
Kohlberg, Lawrence 41
Kolaczyk, Eric D. 164
Körtner, Ulrich H. J. 38
Köstenberger, Andreas J. 154
Kövecses, Zoltán 7, 115
Kratz, Reinhard G. 46–8, 62
Kruger, Ann Cale 17
Kruse, Colin G. 154
Kubo, Sakae 151, 158
Kundt, Radek 8, 163

La Barre, Weston 68
Lakoff, George 6, 28, 40, 67, 115–17, 120, 124, 128
Lamb, Marion J. 8, 14, 19
Lambert, Wilfred G. 66

Index of Modern Authors

Lancaster Patterson, Jane 2
Laney, Cara 22, 170
Larson, Jennifer 2
Law, Robert 150, 154
Lawson, E. Thomas 4, 11, 38, 130, 137, 145
Lefebvre, Claire 99
Leslie, Alan M. 153
Levine, Baruch 56, 58
Levinson, Bernard M. 45-7
Levy, Gabriel 2
Lewis, Ioan M. 31
Liénard, Pierre 5
Lieu, Judith 150, 159
Looy, Heather 41
Lundager Jensen, Hans Jørgen 64-5, 68
Lundhaug, Hugo 2
Luomanen, Petri 13, 175-7

Macy, Michael 155
Malley, Brian 17
Mandik, Pete 6
Mandler, Jean M. 105, 131, 144, 148
Markschies, Christoph 162
Marques, José M. 152, 159
Martin, Luther H. 2
Maul, Stefan M. 57-8
Mayr, Ernst 7, 162
Mazure, Carolyn M. 168
McCarthy, Dennis J. 65
McCauley, Robert N. 4, 11, 14, 16, 24, 38, 130, 137, 145, 170
McCullough, Michael 150-1, 159
McElreath, Richard 8, 163
McEvoy, Chad Joseph 43-4
McKnight, Edgar V. 36
Meyers, Carol L. 106
Meyers, Eric M. 106
Michèle, Girad 152-3
Milgrom, Jacob 48-9, 56-60, 64-5
Mirguet, Francoise 70, 85
Mithen, Steven 4
Moehring, Horst R. 171
Moll, Jorge 41
Moscovici, Serge 154
Mueller, Erik T. 144
Mullet, Étienne 152-3

Navarrete, Carlos David 44
Nichols and Knobe 158
Nickelsburg, George W. E. 120

Nielbo, Kristoffer L. 5
Nihan, Christophe 45, 49-50
Nikolsky, Ronit 10
Norenzayan, Ara 5, 22, 24, 170-1
Norin, Stig 46
Nyhof, Milanie A. 20, 22, 170

Oakes, Penelope J. 159
Oeming, Manfred 36
Öhman, Arne 43
Okasha, Samir 7
Ong, Walter J. 23
Osiek, Carolyn 168
Otto, Eckart 47, 49, 59
Oudhoff, M. J. 30

Pachis, Panayotis 2
Panagiotidou, Olympia 2
Pedersen, Johannes 66
Piaget, Jean 41, 153
Plummer, Alfred 150, 156-7
Porubanova, Michaela 20, 22, 170
Potterie, Ignace de la 158
Propp, Vladimir 144
Puech, Émile 112
Pyysiäinen, Ilkka 5, 32, 144

Quinn, Kimberly A. C. 99

Räisänen, Heikki 162
Ramble, Charles 20, 22, 170
Ratner, Hilary Horn 17
Rawson, Elizabeth 18
Reiner, Erica 57
Rendtorff, Rolf 35-6
Repetti, Rena L. 168
Richerson, Peter J. 14, 163, 172
Ringgren, Karl Vilhelm Helmer 106-7
Robbins, Vernon 2
Robinson, Theodor H. 106
Robinson, William E. W. 2
Roitto, Rikard 11, 149, 158
Rosch, Eleanor 99, 100, 104, 158
Ross, Brian H. 100
Rubin, David C. 18, 144
Rumelhart, David E. 144

Sanders, E. P. 23
Saunders, Barbara 111
Sawyer, John F.A. 113

Schank, Roger C. 27
Schmid, Hans-Jörg 99
Scholer, David M. 153–4
Schreiner, J. 108
Scurlock, JoAnn 57
Seitz, Christopher R. 91
Shantz, Colleen 2
Shaver, John H. 170
Shennan, Stephen J. 164
Slingerland, Edward 5, 67–8
Slone, D. Jason 22
Smalley, Stephen S. 156–7
Sørensen, Jesper 5
Sosis, Richard 5
Spalding, Tom 100
Sperber, Dan 8–9, 163–4, 170, 176–7
Staal, Frits 130, 137
Stacey, David 156
Stackert, Jeffrey 46
Stark, Rodney 162, 167, 169
Starr, Raymond J. 18
Stearns, Stephen C. 7
Steenstra, K. 20, 22
Stone, Linda 14, 163
Stovell, Beth M. 2
Stowers, Stanley K. 68
Strecker, Georg 157–8
Sullivan, Brenton 5
Swadling, Harry C. 150
Szell, Michael 168

Tajfel, Henri 152, 154, 171
Tappenden, Frederick S. 2, 10, 12, 112, 128
Taves, Ann 5
Taylor, Shelley E. 168
Teachman, Bethany A. 51
Teehan, John 41
Thaden, Robert H. von 2
Theißen, Gerd 2, 9, 30, 33, 37, 170, 175
Thelwall, Mike 168
Thurner, Stefan 168

Tigay, Jeffrey H. 59
Tomasello, Michael 8, 17
Tooby, John 4
Turner, John C. 152, 154, 158, 171
Turner, Mark 6, 115

Ungerer, Friedrich 99
Upal, M. Afzal 20
Uro, Risto 19, 23, 30, 70

Van Hecke, Pierre J. P. 88
Van Seters, John 45–6
Varela, Francisco J. 6
Vernant, Jean-Pierre 68
Vervenne, Marc 63, 65, 68
Viberg, Åke 45

Weiher, Egbert von 57
Weinrich, Harald 28
Wells, Bruce 53
Westbrook, Raymond 53
Westcott, Brooke F. 150–2
Whitehouse, Harvey 5, 19, 130
Wiemer-Hastings, Katja 6
Williamson, Hugh G. M. 91
Willis, Timothy M. 59
Wilson, David Sloan 152, 160, 163, 175–7
Wilson, Robert A. 6
Wolde, Ellen van 70, 84–5
Woody, Sheila R. 51
Wright, David P. 45–7, 57–8
Wright, N. T. 113

Xygalatas, Dimitris 5

Yarbrough, Robert W. 154

Zajonc, Robert B. 43
Zakovitch, Yair 75
Zimmermann, Ruben 30

General Index

adaptation 8, 14, 15, 21, 44, 58–60, 175
Akan 10, 100–5, 108–11
altruistic love 25

blending. *See* conceptual blending theory

canon 14, 34–9
categorization, categories 10, 27–9, 30, 42–3, 48, 63, 70, 73, 77, 80–7, 88–90, 99–100, 101, 104–5, 108, 110–11, 113–15, 123, 125–8, 132–6, 139, 141–3, 154–5, 157–9, 170. *See also* cognitive categories; color categories; ontological categories
cognigram 15–16, 23–7
cognition passim. *See* cognitive categories; cognitive exegesis; cognitive linguistics; cognitive science; cognitive science of religion; embodied cognition; texts and cognition
cognitive categories 9, 13, 27
cognitive exegesis 15, 20
cognitive linguistics 1–2, 6, 66, 88, 113, 115, 118, 128
cognitive science 1–3, 5–6, 9–10, 13, 16, 21, 36, 40, 90, 113
cognitive science of religion 2, 5, 11, 20–1, 129–30, 144, 146, 148. *See also* counterintuitive
color 6, 10, 99–111. *See also* color categories
color categories 10, 101–5, 107–11
conceptual blending theory 2, 6–7, 10, 12, 42, 56, 60, 74, 117, 119, 126, 137
conceptual metaphor theory 2, 6–7, 10, 66. *See also* metaphors
corpus–linguistics (corpus based analysis) 90, 96, 98
counterintuitive, minimally counterintuitive 4, 20–5, 28–34, 80, 130, 160, 170

cultural evolution 1–4, 7–9, 13, 14, 27, 56, 70, 73, 84, 86–7, 131, 148, 160, 162–4, 175–6
cultural group selection 163–4, 176–7
cultural narratives. *See* narratives

Darwin, Charles 7
divine love 47. *See also* emotions
docetism 33
domain, domain theory, conceptual domain 3–4, 10, 14, 28, 32, 88–98, 112–28, 147, 165

embodied cognition/mind 5–6, 11, 40, 113, 117, 119, 124
emotions 40–62. *See also* altruism; divine love; empathy; fear; love
empathy 10, 40, 42, 44–6, 48–9, 51–4, 61–2, 84, 170. *See also* emotions
eschatology 10, 93–4, 96–8, 120, 158
evolution (biological) 4, 7–9, 14, 16, 32, 40–1, 43–4, 60, 70, 73, 162–4, 168, 172, 175–6. *See also* cultural evolution; cultural group selection; evolution and cognition; evolutionary psychology; gene-culture co-evolution
evolution and cognition 1–12, 13, 15, 16, 40–1, 70
evolutionary psychology 3, 7, 15
exegesis 1, 9–10, 28, 39, 96, 98, 100, 105, 110, 131–2, 145

fat 64, 68–9
fear 9–10, 40–62, 71, 96, 156, 170
foreigners 9, 20, 29, 40, 43–58, 60–2, 80–3, 86–7, 92, 95, 120
forgiveness 11, 46, 59, 149–61
form criticism 21–3

gene-culture co-evolution 8, 172
generative linguistics 11, 130, 136–7, 144

generative syntax 11, 130, 144, 147
genes 7, 8, 14, 16, 19, 44, 162–3, 172, 176. See also evolution (biological)

hattat 57–9
Hume, David 41

immigrant 44–53, 60–2

Kant, Immanuel 41

love 10, 25–6, 47–8, 50–1, 54, 62, 70–87, 133–5, 141, 154–6, 160. See also emotions; empathy

maturationally natural 14, 16, 28, 170
Mesopotamia 10, 57–8, 63–9
metaphors 2, 6–7, 10–12, 28–9, 63, 66–9, 71, 75, 77–8, 87, 89, 113–20, 122–8. See also conceptual metaphor theory; primary metaphors; source domain
miracle stories 30–2
mythic cognition 77–82

narrative criticism. See narratives
narrative genres and forms. See narratives
narratives 10, 18, 21–2, 24–5, 27–8, 32–3, 45, 48, 52, 65, 70, 72, 74–5, 77–82, 84–7, 146, 154, 174, 177
neo-Darwinism 7, 162–3
networks. See social network analysis; weak links

ontological categories 4, 14, 20, 22, 28–9, 31–2
oral, orality 18–19, 21–4, 33, 45, 72, 77, 96, 99, 131

parables 22, 28–30, 33
primary metaphors 67. See also conceptual metaphor theory; metaphors
prototype 158
prototype theory 89
psyche 65–6

Q (sayings source) 175, 176

redaction criticism 23, 26
religious experience 174–5
resurrection 10–11, 23, 25, 32–3, 112–28, 170
ritual 1–2, 4–5, 9, 13, 16–17, 19, 34–5, 38, 40, 43, 48, 52, 56–61, 72, 103, 111, 130–2, 137–8, 143, 146, 148, 163, 174, 177

sacrifice 47–50, 54–9, 63–4, 68, 78–9, 114, 130, 132, 141, 145–6. See also shelamim; hattat
schema/schemata 11, 18–28, 39, 42, 60, 112–13, 115–28
script 18, 22, 25, 27–8
Septuagint (LXX) 107, 190 n.4, 193 n.30
shelamim 54, 64
social identity theory 152, 154, 158, 171
social network analysis 164–5
source domain/target domain 28–30, 112–28. See also conceptual metaphor theory
supernatural 9, 36, 40, 56, 103, 109–11
symbolic identity markers 171–4

texts and cognition 9, 13–39, 88–92
tit for tat 151–2
transmission 21

weak links (weak social ties) 165, 168–9